T0367884

I Believe:
A Fulfillment
of Promises

Lance Edwin Compton

WESTBOW°
PRESS
A DIVISION OF THOMAS NELSON
& ZONDERVAN

WestBow Press books may be ordered through booksellers or by contacting:

WestBow Press
A Division of Thomas Nelson & Zondervan
1663 Liberty Drive
Bloomington, IN 47403
www.westbowpress.com
1 (866) 928-1240

Because of the dynamic nature of the Internet, any web addresses or links contained in this book may have changed since publication and may no longer be valid. The views expressed in this work are solely those of the author and do not necessarily reflect the views of the publisher, and the publisher hereby disclaims any responsibility for them.

Any people depicted in stock imagery provided by Thinkstock are models, and such images are being used for illustrative purposes only. Certain stock imagery © Thinkstock.

ISBN: 978-1-4908-2927-2 (sc)
ISBN: 978-1-4908-2928-9 (hc)
ISBN: 978-1-4908-2926-5 (e)

Library of Congress Control Number: 2014904267

Printed in the United States of America.

WestBow Press rev. date: 6/26/2014

Contents

About the Cover Photographs

Front

As children, my brother Dustin and I frequently followed our parents' and grandparents' stories by exploring the countryside that comprised our and our neighbors' farms, hoping to find, from their instruction, some great forgotten or unknown treasure. Here, we are pictured outside our grandparents' home, having been equipped by them and our parents for one such treasure hunt.

Back

As an adult, I have followed the instruction of God the Father and, through His only begotten Son Jesus Christ, found the eternal treasures of His Truth in the Scriptures, though they are unknown to or forgotten by a dying world. Here, I am pictured standing atop Mount Nebo, looking out over the Promised Land in anticipation of the eternal Promised Land and my eternal reward.

Acknowledgments

I wish to express my profound gratitude to each individual who has prayed for and facilitated the distribution of this message. May you be greatly blessed at the Bema Seat of Christ.

Dedication

This book is dedicated in love to a generation who knoweth not the One True Living God.

This story has been bathed in prayer, that the Holy Spirit may accompany it, creating a thirst for the Word of God and drawing a lost generation to Christ.

> "If we receive the witness of men, the witness of God is greater: for this is the witness of God which he hath testified of his Son. He that believeth on the Son of God hath the witness in himself: he that believeth not God hath made him a liar; because he believeth not the record that God gave of his Son. And this is the record, that God hath given to us eternal life, and this life is in his Son. He that hath the Son hath life; and he that hath not the Son of God hath not life."

1 John 5:9-12 (KJV)

Epigraph

Thus by the Shepherds Secrets are reveal'd,
Which from all other men are kept conceal'd:
Come to the Shepherds then, if you would see
Things deep, Things hid, and that Mysterious be.

From The Pilgrim's Progress
By John Bunyan

CHAPTER 1

A Healed, Sealed Vessel

In my thirty-second year, I embarked upon a great journey to explore the physical evidences of timeless Truths. My travels through Israel, Jordan, and Egypt were like a journey through pages of great literature; for they yielded revelations comparable only to the most excellent production of a reader's vivid imagination. Though I believe such excursions are secretly hoped for in the recesses of every young man's heart, they were more than just the fulfillment of some yearning or sublime amusement for me and two of my closest friends.

The ruins of a deserted, ancient city somewhere outside Jerusalem, Israel was one of the first sites to which our archeologist tour guide and Christian brother, Tony, escorted us. Millennia had passed since the city's astonishing drama played out upon the world's stage yet it seemed to be awaiting our arrival as if our presence was a necessary prerequisite to its final exit from that stage. Unsure of what to expect or whom we might encounter, John, Christopher, and I exited Tony's van and hiked toward the ruins, entering the ancient city by way of a path almost thoroughly concealed by centuries gone by. We had the site to ourselves, with the exception of a young man who was sitting alone at the edge of a stone wall. As we got closer, it appeared he was deeply engaged in assembling some kind of puzzle. Curious, we approached him and saw that he was actually piecing together a breathtaking mosaic. When Tony inquired about his work, the young man, without so much as an upward glance, said he was assembling a masterpiece, the pieces of which he had taken from amongst the city's ruins. After we had all taken turns admiring the beautiful work of art,

Tony suggested that we scan the ground for artifacts, so we quickly spread out and started looking, busying ourselves for more than an hour and leaving no rock unturned.

"If I lived here and had the money," I replied, "I would unearth everything lost to time."

No sooner had the words left my lips than my roving fingers came across a few shards of pottery buried in the topsoil. I pulled them from the ground, carefully wiped away the crusted dirt, and marveled at their intricate detail.

"What's that you've got there?" Tony asked.

I passed the shards to him.

Examining them closely, he said, "These are from the thirteenth century, B.C.; they're over three thousand years old."

"…About half the age of Mankind," I thought. Ecstatic, I scoured the ground for more. Before long, we had amassed a small pile and each of us tried our hand at reassembling the pieces into a masterpiece. Turning the fragments over in my fingers… a handle here, a lip there, a fractured lid, and a few other pieces I could not even decipher…I realized that reassembling them was an impossible task for me. But, as I doubted the potential of these bits of ruin, I considered the young man we had encountered and the exquisite work he had so brilliantly constructed from these same broken and seemingly useless pieces of clay. I stood upright and looked in the direction where he had been sitting, but he was gone. Returning my attention to the shards in my hands, I marveled at the similarities between what we had just seen and the work of Jesus Christ and further appreciated the gem of Truth in Paul's words to the *Ephesians*:

> "For we are his workmanship, created in Christ Jesus
> unto good works, which God hath before ordained that
> we should walk in them."[1]

I was like this pottery before finding Jesus Christ – broken and in ruins. But, having accepted Him as my Lord and Savior, I have been grafted into His mosaic, and having devoted my life to the pursuit of His

---

[1]   Ephesians 2:10 (King James Version)

Truth and service to Him in the Great Commission, I have discovered the good works of service unto which He ordained me – bringing other broken shards of humanity to Him where they can be transformed from worthless ruin into His priceless mosaic, reflective of His transforming power, craftsmanship, and artistry and worthy to display His Truth to the entire world.

I first became cognizant of my brokenness in the seventh grade. At that time, I was the biggest and strongest kid in my class. I was not the best looking, the best dressed, or the skinniest but the biggest and strongest. (I have always thought that 'big and strong' rolls off the tongue far better than "fat!") During this blissful period of childhood, which I believed to be the prime of my life, my greatest worry was whether I had finished all of my homework or given the best excuse to the teacher if I had not. Other worries cropped up from time to time. Since I played football, wrestled as a heavyweight, and was the school's weightlifting champ, I was often concerned with games and matches, and the possibility of one of my buddies beating me in a weightlifting match was always in the back of my mind. But, the spectre of death was never a concern until early 1989.

In January, I was on a roll at the pinnacle of wrestling season. An agile two-hundred-twenty-five pounds, I possessed a keen advantage over every opponent because of my ability to combine lightweight and heavyweight maneuvers. I also had the advantage of having excellent hearing, which was always tuned to the voices of my coach, Jim Taylor, as he guided my every move, and my father, who made it a practice of shouting from the sidelines, "How bad do you want it?" Everything seemed to be going well when I suddenly developed a problem with my vision, and my left eye swelled shut. This is not an uncommon occurrence in sports. My teammates and I concluded that the swelling was caused either by a mat burn, some type of infection, or an allergic reaction; but after a few weeks of treating it with Benadryl accomplished nothing, I visited Dr. Ingram, and he prescribed a powerful round of antibiotics. Dr. Ingram was more than just a doctor. He was also my Sunday school teacher and a wise, Christian man. While a resident at an Oklahoma City hospital, he was on call when my grandfather, Papa Compton, had a section of his stomach removed, and they formed

3

a trusted friendship that never ended. As our town's only physician, he had doctored my entire family since 1954, garnering our deepest respect and trust in the process. When the antibiotics that Dr. Ingram prescribed did nothing to prevent my eyelid from protruding and pressing painfully against my eyeball, he was deeply concerned and recommended that I see a specialist immediately; but before I left his office, he prayed for my healing as he was accustomed to doing.

A few days later, I found myself in the office of Dr. Cynthia Bradford at *Dean A. McGee Eye Institute* – a facility that is world-renowned for its highly-qualified doctors and specialized care. Dr. Bradford was attractive, intelligent, and professional; she was gifted with a motherly demeanor and instantly made me feel at ease. I appreciated her kind, caring manner. Some physicians have no respect for their patients but not Dr. Bradford. I was not just a case study to her. Prepping me for an ultrasound, Dr. Bradford pried my eyelid open and filled it with a cold, clear gel, which caused my whole eye socket to go completely numb. She then took what looked like a writing pen and pressed it firmly against my eyeball. As my eyes crossed in an effort to see the object, hers carefully watched a television monitor on which was projected the orbit of my eye. From the exam chair in which I was sitting, I could sense the apprehension emanating from her body as she studied the images on the monitor. Finally, after about thirty minutes of continuous probing, she handed me some tissue and said I could wipe the gel off. I detected a distinct change in the tone of her voice, and her demeanor was almost apologetic as she instructed me to go wait in the lobby with my mother, saying she needed to study the film further.

"Well did ya find anything?" I asked.

"Let me show you something," she replied and led me around the corner to look at several small, x-ray films hanging on a light screen.

"Do you see this pear-shaped object?" she asked, pointing her pencil to the orbit of my eye on one of the films. "It's not supposed to be there. It's very suspicious."

"What is it, do ya think?"

"I want to talk to another doctor and get his opinion, and then I will call you and your parents to discuss it," she replied, almost in a whisper.

I made my way out to the lobby where Mom and my brother, Dustin, were waiting.

"What did they say?" Mom asked in a soothing, motherly voice but with a look that expressed a myriad of emotions.

"Is Dad here yet?" I inquired. "The doctor wants to talk to all of us at the same time."

"Is it bad?" Mom wanted to know.

I looked at her but could not find the words to express what I wanted to say. At thirteen years old, I wanted to be an adult, but news of this magnitude made me question whether I should pretend to be "grown up" or just collapse into her arms. Having spent much of my childhood around my grandparents, whose generation survived the Great Depression and two world wars, I had picked up a measure of their calm strength; and this moment became the first of many to come wherein I would draw upon it.

Shortly after Dad arrived, a nurse called my name, and we were all taken to an exam room. Dr. Bradford promptly entered, bringing another doctor with her.

"This is Dr. Robert Small," she said. "He is one of our top surgeons, and I have asked him to take over from here."

Dr. Bradford patted me on the arm and assured me that she was still my doctor.

Dr. Small was an older gentleman with snow white hair, nice but to-the-point. While Mom and Dad inundated him with questions that he calmly answered one by one, my mind wandered. I thought of my family, friends, and all the things I had not yet pursued or seen. I thought of death: it did not frighten me, but for some reason, the events that might precede it terrified me. Suddenly, I wanted to go home – back to the family farm my grandparents had owned since 1952. Set amidst the rolling hills of western Oklahoma and dotted with red cedar and blackjack trees, it was not only my home – it was my sanctuary. My brother and I had explored every square inch of that plot of ground. Guarded by a rusty, barbed wire fence, it was a place full of life – a place where my imagination soared – the place where my cousin, Michelle, taught me how to drive a pick-up truck and Papa showed me how to drive his old Ford tractor. It was where Papa and I showed my dog Hobo how to ride the three-wheeler with me. Time moved slowly there, if at all. It was my home and security blanket. The world could not find me there, and I was sure that nothing harmful could reach me there, either. My attention wandered back to Mom and Dad's conversation with Dr. Small just in time to hear him say he was scheduling a CT scan for the next day.

That evening, after the lights were turned out, I lay in bed with my thoughts. The great worry I had seen on my parents' and grandparents' faces troubled me deeply. I knew they were not ready to lose me. Even though I was not concerned with dying, I was worried about the effect my death would have on my family. I was confident that, if I died, I would immediately be with my Lord and Savior, Jesus Christ:

> "Therefore we are always confident, knowing that, whilst we are at home in the body, we are absent from the Lord: (For we walk by faith, not by sight:) We are confident, I say, and willing rather to be absent from the body, and to be present with the Lord."[2]

I had accepted Christ when I was eleven years old and trusted Him with all my heart. Even at that point in my life, I knew I could tell my Lord anything and that He would listen. In my long conversation with Him that night, I told Him I was okay with coming home if that was His will and He was ready for me, but I asked Him to help my family and friends get through my passing and care for them after I was gone. I then asked Him to walk with me and help me fight the evil which had come against me if it were His will that I live. Finally, I promised that, if He healed me and spared my life, I would tell others who He is and what He had done for me.

I awoke the following morning, February 27, 1989, the day before my birthday, a victim of cancer. As Mom and I pulled out of our driveway onto rural highway 152 and headed toward Oklahoma City, I was unsure of the day's outcome but mouthed, "I'll meet you there," to the Lord.

---

[2] 2 Corinthians 5:6–8 (KJV)

And so, we returned to Oklahoma City, where I was scheduled to undergo a CT scan to determine the severity of the cancer in my head. Upon arriving at Children's Hospital, Mom and I were escorted to the radiology department by a pleasant young woman who said the procedure would only take about thirty to forty-five minutes. While Mom waited in the waiting room, I was led to another room and greeted there by two young men who appeared to be in their late twenties. They showed me the CT machine, which I thought resembled a big donut. As I lay down on its narrow, platform-like cot, the young men explained in great detail how the test worked and what they would be looking for. After I was shoved inside the tube, I looked above me and saw a speaker and camera lenses staring back at me through a strip of plastic. Shortly, a voice came over the speaker, saying, "We're going to start now."

The apparatus began to move. The first pass scanned my entire head. The cameras stopped, started, then stopped, and started again. With each pass, a section of my head was captured on film. Half an hour later, a radiologist entered the room.

"You're not going to like me much," he said. "I've got to start an IV so we can put some dye into your veins."

The radioactive dye, he explained, would allow them to see everything better. After disclosing a list of warnings, he inserted the IV into my right arm. A sensation of warmth enveloped me as the dye traveled through my blood stream, first to my arms, then my heart. When it reached my mouth, I detected that same flavor that is in food which has been cooked in a cast-iron skillet.

The radiologist exited and the platform began moving again, its cameras clicking and spinning.

"Have you had any pain?" I heard one of the young men ask.

"No," I answered.

"What about headaches?"

"The pressure is very uncomfortable – and I look like something you'd pay a quarter to see at the fair!" I replied.

How odd, I thought when he laughed, that I wanted to reassure them and ease the tension that was building over my medical condition. I truly could not have done it without the Lord's presence.

The camera dragged on, clicking and spinning, but when the radiologist entered again and said they needed to do something difficult, a million thoughts raced through my mind.

"For this last set of pictures," he said, "You absolutely must hold your eye perfectly still. That means you cannot look in any direction but straight ahead. You cannot even blink. Try to lock your eye onto something and keep looking at it. This may take a while, but it's the most important part of the test!"

I scanned the tiny space for something to fix my gaze upon, but all I could see were solid white walls. I could not even find a stain on the ceiling.

"We're ready to begin," boomed the speaker. "Here we go."

I heard the camera begin to fire up again, but I was not ready. There was nothing to lock my eyes on, and all I could think of was my eyes spinning around in a circle.

Suddenly, without warning, there appeared directly in my line of sight a beautiful, majestic cross. Instantly, I locked my eyes onto the spotless image, focusing my very being upon it. The entire world, with all its evil and worry, fled from me. My consciousness of time seemed to end, and all thought escaped me. The cross was white, with a brilliant radiance, but was by no means ornate. It was plain and distinct. I knew it was more than just an image because it was accompanied by a palatable presence that surrounded and embraced me, warming the cold room. Its aura engulfed me with overwhelming peace that surpassed all my understanding. Waves of energy pulled yet held me in place. I felt like a piece of iron being drawn toward a powerful magnet – though I seemed disconnected from my body, my body felt like an aged casing that I longed to leave behind. My spirit was engaged in a conversation, and I was witness to the words that were spoken. Suddenly, a voice came over the speaker saying, "You're done!"

Just as quickly as the cross had appeared, it vanished. For more than ninety minutes, I had laid perfectly still, without blinking or moving. For over ninety minutes, I had focused on nothing but that pure and holy image. For over ninety minutes, I was conscious of nothing but the powerful presence of Christ, my Lord. I told nobody of this encounter for many years. As far as I was concerned, the wonderful way in which the Lord had revealed Himself to me was a private matter so I kept the encounter in my heart, secretly contemplating it every day for years to come.

After the radiologists removed the IV from my arm, I asked if they knew what was wrong with my eye.

"The doctor will let you know once he reads the test," one of them said.

"And yes, we found out that you do have a brain!" replied the other as he led me out to the waiting room where Mom had been waiting for three and a half hours.

The next day was my fourteenth birthday, which I observed under the shadow of the sobering reality that we are not promised another day. I do not remember the gifts I received or who they were from. I only remember being with my family. In the back of my mind, I feared my fourteenth would be my last birthday and initially resisted Mom's picture-taking efforts because I did not want to be remembered by my deformed, protruding eye. Finally, Grandma Compton, with whom I had a special bond, convinced me to take a few pictures. Grandma and I were often able to convince each other to do what nobody else could persuade us to do.

That evening, Dr. Small called and asked us to come to his office the following morning. Although his call sparked anxiety, God's promise was cemented in my heart. Nevertheless, the thought of surgery, the prospect of my appearance being permanently altered, and radiation and chemotherapy rattled my nerves. At such a young age, I did not have the worldly experience or knowledge that most people seem to draw upon in times of trouble. What I did have was an innocent, child-like faith that my God, who cared enough to die for me, would walk beside me regardless of how rocky or dangerous the path. In my short life, I had observed people on many occasions trying everything within their own power to solve a problem when hard times came upon them. Most, when they had finally given up all hope, would proclaim as an afterthought, "All we can do now is pray."

The first thing I had done was pray.

When we met with Dr. Small the next day to discuss the results of the CT scan, it was indeed one of the most dreaded moments of my life and one I desperately wanted to avoid. The x-rays were clipped to the light screen on the wall, and the light illuminated the enemy's aggressive invasion of my body. Dr. Small discussed the next step in what was fast becoming a battle to save my physical life. The decision was finally made to perform an exploratory operation to discover the type of tumor and extent of its damage. It sounded like someone else speaking as I heard myself ask if we could postpone the operation for a few days to give me some time to take care of a few things.

"He will tell us when he will perform the surgery," Mom urgently replied.

I looked at Dr. Small, who looked at my parents and then back at me.

"A few days will be fine," he replied. "That will give me enough time to make all the preparations."

Even at the age of fourteen, I knew he did not need additional time to make preparations. Emergency surgeries are performed every day without a second thought. He had simply overridden the objection of my parents to allow me the time I had so sheepishly requested, and I was grateful to him for it.

I spent the next few days as if they would be my last. Most of those priceless hours were spent with my grandparents, but I also raced three-wheelers with Dustin and spent as much time as I could with all my family and closest friends. Of course, I did eat as many of my favorite foods as I could stomach, all prepared by Mom, Grandma Compton, and Granny – my three favorite cooks. Even though I relished every moment, I considered it my gift to my family and friends. I wanted to impart cherished memories to them as well as some of the same peace of mind that I possessed.

I arrived at the *Bob Hope Surgery Center* at Presbyterian Hospital in Oklahoma City, where I was to have my surgery, only to hurry up and wait inside a preparation area that was nothing more than a room with several curtains extending from the wall. In my own partitioned space, there was a single bed and two chairs. It was a dreary scene. Some nurses came in and inserted IVs into my arm, and then the surgery team entered and introduced themselves one by one. My apprehension was comparable to the hair-raising moments before a parachute jump. I say confidently that anticipation must be one of the greatest agonies of surgery. Then, it was time. The surgery team began to wheel me to the operating room but stopped briefly so I could embrace my parents. We told each other that we loved one another. I took hold of Mom's hand, but as the surgical team pushed the gurney toward the operating room, our grasp was broken.

Once inside the frigid room, I was lifted onto the operating table and my arms strapped onto extensions.

"Count backwards to yourself," said the anesthesiologist as he began to administer the anesthesia.

I was not listening to his instructions because I was praying, but before I could finish, the anesthesia took effect and I slipped into unconsciousness. Guided by the x-ray pictures, the surgical team made an incision on my eyelid immediately above the left eye. Their intent was to biopsy the cancerous mass and its fingerlike tentacles that were stretching toward my brain. They hoped to determine the type of tumor and remove it—or, at least they hoped it could be removed. The procedure that was intended to last thirty to forty minutes turned into a time-consuming search. For several hours, the surgeons tediously examined the area. I later learned that they had completely removed my eyeball from its socket in a valiant effort to leave no area unexplored before carefully replacing it and stitching the incision.

While I lay in the recovery room, groggy from the effects of the anesthesia, the privacy curtain parted. Dr. Small entered, removed the surgical mask covering the lower half of his face, looked at my parents, and took a deep breath.

"Do you believe in miracles?" he asked.

The question was visibly disturbing to my parents. Unaware of my conversation with the Lord and vision of the cross, every conceivable horror seized them in that moment. Mom later confessed to me that Dr. Small's question convinced her that I was eaten up with cancer, that nothing could be done, and that they had just sown me up.

"In all my years of practicing medicine," Dr. Small continued, "I have never seen anything like this. All of the tests indicated the presence of a malignancy, and the CT scan showed a tumor with rapidly spreading, fingerlike projections. That being said, I want you to know that there is nothing there – absolutely nothing! There is no infection, no fluid pocket, and no tumor. We could not even find any abnormal tissue. Furthermore, we can't even tell there was ever any abnormal tissue in the area."

Dr. Small then advised my parents that he had consulted with an expert in internal medicine, Dr. Lodiver, who recommended that I remain in the hospital for an extended period so more tests could be performed. Dr. Lodiver was one of the greatest minds in the field of internal medicine. He later became world-renowned in the battle against AIDS. As Dr. Small walked out of the room, leaving my parents to absorb the news, he declared:

"Lance has a greater physician than me!"

Once I was fully awake, Mom and Dad gave me the news concerning the miracle which the Lord had performed, and I knew then that my encounter with Him was even more profound than I had first realized.

Later, Dr. Lodiver said, "At the rate that tumor was growing, it would've invaded your brain in less than two weeks."

It was upon hearing those words that the full weight of God's miraculous intervention settled upon my shoulders.

Though faith does not require miracles, my healing completely reassured me that God is real and humbled me before Him. It also showed me that He desired to accomplish a specific purpose with my life and created a great thirst for His Word, which I began to study daily. Like a blind child touching and feeling the face of his father, I examined every pore, wrinkle, and whisker on my Father's face as I read every sentence of God's Word and endeavored through prayer and study to learn and understand it in its full and complete context. As I journeyed through the Word of Truth, it became a living book in my hands; and as my understanding increased, I began to plead with the Lord in my daily prayers to further increase my knowledge, wisdom, and skills toward Him.

In the years that have passed since 1989, I have come to believe that my healing was God's method of sealing me for a predestined time wherein I would serve and fulfill His purpose. Though I had already been sealed by the Holy Spirit when I first believed in and accepted Jesus Christ as my Lord and Savior, my healing was a different kind of seal — it was something that was just between the Lord and me. In ancient times, when an animal was chosen as a sacrifice for the Lord, it was sealed, usually by placing a mark upon it. Similarly, contracts and letters were also marked with a seal, which was applied by melting hot wax over the document and imprinting a mark on it with a signet. Regardless of whether a seal was applied to a sacrificial animal or a document, it served three important purposes. Primarily, it was a proclamation that the sealed was set apart for a specific reason. Second, it was a means of protecting the sealed from any use other than that for which it had been set aside. And finally, it was an indicator that the sealed would be preserved until the time of its appointed use. For me, every time I look in the mirror and see the small scar above my left eye, I am reminded that the hand of Almighty God healed, sealed, and set me aside to serve His purpose.

CHAPTER 2

Politics, Pigs & the President

As the sun arose from behind the mountains of the Jordan River Valley and illuminated the landscape on my first morning in Israel, I watched the painted sky unfold from inside our car somewhere between Tel Aviv and Jerusalem. Looking out the window, I recalled the distant beginning of this journey – a promise I made to Grandma Compton to take a Bible class in college. That promise led me to *Introduction to Old Testament* at Oklahoma State University, and from the first day of that class, my interest in traveling to the Holy Land was stoked. Professor Robert L. Cate, gifted in bringing the characters and culture of the Old Testament to life, inspired my imagination to consider what it must have been like to be in the company of the Patriarchs, to stand beside Moses at the base of Mt. Sinai, to walk alongside King David, and to hear Samuel and the Prophets. As the semester progressed, my desire to visit the physical locations featured so prominently in the classroom grew even stronger, and by the semester's end, I was committed to visiting the Holy Land at some point in the future.

The purpose of my journey roughly ten years later was to see some of the physical evidences of Christ's Truth, but the Holy Land actually became somewhat of a meeting place where I met with a heightened understanding of the many Truths which Christ had been teaching and revealing to me since the day I accepted Him as Savior and Lord. In hindsight, I can truly say that the Lord has brought me to a greater understanding of all His Truths and in very unique ways, including the rather unorthodox method of politics. In my seventh year, Mom took my brother and me on the first of several tours of the Oklahoma State

Capitol. Introducing us to representatives, senators, and justices gave me a sense of appreciation for public service that eventually grew into a desire to change the world. During high school, following a football injury that robbed me of the ability to play sports, my desire to change the world evolved into a passion. Politics seemed like the perfect vehicle for that passion so, for the rest of my teenage years and well into my twenties, I fervently sought to become a political leader. As far as I was concerned, politics was the only way I could change the world and make a difference because it was how I believed I had been called to serve the Lord.

My first experience with politics came during my junior year in high school when Bruce Price, a local businessman and one of the greatest men I have ever known, ran for the Oklahoma Senate and asked Mom to chair his campaign. Bruce and his wife, Nikita, and his brother, Glenn, had been local farmers for many years. Together, they had amassed a fortune with their seedless watermelon business – the *Sugar Creek Seed Company*. Bruce's first campaign meeting was in the modest conference room of the *Sugar Creek Seed Company* office building, overlooking Red Rock Canyon State Park. Most of those who attended were his close friends and family. Bruce opened the meeting with the introduction of a man by the name of Ross Cummings, an expert in managing the public face of political campaigns. Ross' brilliant knack for creating instant name recognition had secured him respect and notoriety in the political world. After addressing the demographics of Oklahoma's twenty-third Senate district, Ross asked who would chair the campaign.

"There is only one person in this room who can be chairman!" replied one of the locals from the head of the table and pointed in Mom's direction.

"Well, we do want Bruce to win," Mom said, flattered but a little embarrassed. "I think someone else could do a better job!"

"We've already discussed it, and you're the only choice!" the man replied.

"Well, I'm glad we all agree on that," Bruce said and smiled at Mom.

Mom embodied all the qualities of a good campaign leader. Her accomplishments made her a household name in the education sector.

After earning two masters degrees, she began her career as a special education teacher for severely mentally retarded children and later became director of Oklahoma's Career Prep Program. In 1975, she addressed a joint session of the U.S. Congress and convinced lawmakers to fund the program. Thanks to her efforts, high school students can now receive college credit for vocational and technical classes.

Because Mom was chairing Bruce's campaign, I was in a position to get to know him. I quickly became his personal assistant and eventually formed a close bond with him and his brother, Glenn. Watching Bruce work as we traveled the district, I was drawn to his good character and impressed by the fact that he insisted on running a positive, amicable campaign and refused to speak negatively about his opponent. Because he was so respectful toward her, I was a little surprised when she broached the subject of Bruce's past financial trouble during a debate. Whether she or her advisors were responsible for that offensive move, I do not know, but it was one that yielded only a marginal lead for her in the primary and did not shield her from a runoff.

The runoff election was the turning point of the campaign. It was then that Dustin and I decided to go "grass roots" in the poorest neighborhoods, despite all of the conventional wisdom that suggested door-to-door campaigning was most useful in higher income neighborhoods. As it turned out, the people we visited seemed honored and pleased that two high school kids had thought of them and asked for their help. They invited us into their homes and listened to our testimony about Bruce and his family. Dustin and I, in turn, listened to their concerns and pledged to bring them to Bruce's attention. The majority of the people we visited said they would vote for Bruce and even agreed to place campaign signs in their front yards. Though we believed our efforts were miniscule, they produced a great harvest.

On the night of the runoff, Bruce's closest supporters gathered at the *Sugar Creek Seed Company.* I walked into the front office, where the core group was congregated, and picked up the telephone to dial the campaign office of Bruce's opponent. The phone rang twice.

"This is Lance Compton with the *Price for Senate* campaign," I said to the young lady who answered. "Get me your boss, will ya?!?!"

There was a brief pause on the other end of the line.

"Just a minute," she replied.

"I finally get to tell that woman what I think of her," I announced to a room full of stunned onlookers, each of whom was anxiously waiting to hear what I would say.

Linda Taylor, a longtime family friend, dashed over to the telephone and quickly pressed the receiver button.

"What did ya do that for?" I asked.

"Let that boy talk!" chimed Butch Courtney, the eldest member of the group.

"Butch, you know he was gonna say somethin' mean!" Linda replied.

"Yeah, and I was lookin' forward to hearing it, too!" he roared as he eased into a straight-back chair and sipped a cup of scalding coffee.

The room erupted in laughter.

"Words cannot convey the message like the reality of the tally," said Glenn as he walked into the room. "Remember, we won! In the end, victory silences the opponent and the critic."

Just as he finished speaking, the telephone rang. It was Bruce's opponent, calling to advise him that she would be demanding a recount. But, the recount only proved the truth of Glenn's words. Bruce won the primary by seventeen votes; and later, after winning the general election with ease, he went on to become one of Oklahoma's best statesmen.

After Bruce's victory, while I was still a junior in high school, he asked me to be a senate page at the State Capitol. Since our good family friends, Ron Langmacher and Jack Bonny, had also won seats in the House of Representatives that year, I had a first-class pass to observe the behind-the-scenes, inner workings of the Oklahoma Legislature and quickly learned that trust and hard work were the tickets into the inner circle. My boss and mentor was a wonderful lady by the name of Carol Haines – a long-time employee of the Senate. Carol became one of my most trusted friends. She taught me proper behavior and protocol and instilled in me a great deal of respect for the offices as well as the people who held them. I also made many friends among the Senatorial support staff; my favorites were Sam Jackson, the doorman; switchboard operators, Juanita Townsend and Dorothy Deming; and Carol Haines' assistant, Mike McEldery. Hearing them speak of their years of experience at the Capitol made me realize that I was just a naive country boy with much to learn.

One morning, Carol informed me that she was planning to introduce me to someone special.

"There's a lady I want you to meet; and after you've gotten acquainted, I want you to introduce her at tomorrow's lecture," she said. "It's Senator Helen Cole. If you'll go upstairs and tell this to her assistant, Estelle, she'll help you write the introduction to the Senator's lecture."

Senator Cole was a legend in her own right, and I was grateful for the opportunity to make her acquaintance. I soon discovered that we had many of the same values, and we formed an instant bond. During the course of time, she asked me to be involved in several of her projects. One of the most important to her was an inner city, Christian mission that assisted homeless and recovering drug addicts and alcoholics in finding temporary shelter, job training, and clothing for job interviews. The Senator and I visited the mission together many times and even ate lunch there occasionally. I got to know the workers as well as some of the people who had come there for help. My heart went out to them, and though I had a strong desire to do something, I did not know where to begin. At the time, I believed proper political leadership on this issue was the answer.

"When I'm a Senator," I mused, "I'll be able to do something for these people."

The following year was a rather hectic one at the State Capitol due to the scandal surrounding the sitting Governor so Carol asked Bruce to invite me back to be her personal assistant. It was during this second year at the Capitol, which was my senior year in high school, that I witnessed the dark side of politics. One of my responsibilities was couriering notes between the Speaker of the House and the President pro tempore of the Senate. In this role, I learned that the accusations against the disgraced Governor were far more sinister than what I had been hearing outside the Capitol building, but the Legislature seemed to have no intention of releasing details to the public. This was rather shocking to a young boy, and I wondered why. Nevertheless, I considered myself lucky to be in the presence of so many Oklahoma legends and fortunate to have some of the best political minds in Oklahoma taking an interest in me, mentoring me, and guiding me into what I believed and hoped was the career of my dreams. During my second year at the Capitol, I forged friendships with several influential people, among them being Representative Mary Fallin, Senator Brooks Douglass, Senator Ben Robinson, Linda Bostick, Peggy White, and Margaret Jolly.

My political aspirations continued beyond high school when, following my graduation in 1994, Dustin and I approached the Keating gubernatorial campaign, hoping to get involved with his race. To my surprise, he agreed to meet us, and Dustin and I visited with him for over two hours at his campaign headquarters.

"You guys are more thorough than the media," he said as we quizzed him on his past and every relevant issue we could think of.

"We've been taught to know a candidate well before giving our endorsement," Dustin replied.

"Oh, I see," he said and steered the questioning toward our future plans.

Mine were to work for the Keating campaign, and I followed through with that goal. In the fall of 1994, as a freshman at Oklahoma State University, I assisted the campaign in Stillwater, Hinton, and Binger. Upon meeting Frank's wife, Kathy, and getting to know the family more intimately through our developing friendship, my involvement took a giant step forward. From offering suggestions on agricultural policy to giving my opinions on fundraising and "grass roots" canvassing, I was allowed to be involved in just about everything. My hard work paid off, too, when the excitement surrounding the coming election gave way to the reality that Frank would be Oklahoma's next Governor and my friend, Mary Fallin, would be Lieutenant Governor.

After the election, I settled into college and fraternity life but harbored a continuous, burning desire for the political game that soon led me to contemplate running for the State House of Representatives myself. To my surprise, my friend, Senator Cole, encouraged me to run and told me, "You're not running against anyone – you're running for the position. I think you should run regardless of who the other candidates are if it's what you really want to do."

Initially, my opponent was incumbent Representative Calvin Anthony. Mr. Anthony was much older than I, more experienced, and very popular among the electorate. I began praying as to whether I should run and sought the Lord's advice daily, hoping in the back of my mind that He would work my aspirations into His will. A few weeks later, when Representative Anthony announced he was resigning to become a lobbyist for the pharmaceutical industry, I concluded that the Lord had given me His blessing. Since Mr. Anthony's retirement meant not having to fight the power of an incumbency, I made the decision to run and began assembling a group of supporters without giving it much more thought or prayer. Ross Cummings, whom I had met during Bruce's campaign, agreed to be my political advisor and strategist. Mace Patterson, my roommate and fraternity brother, agreed to be my treasurer, chairman, ethics officer, speech and article editor, and anything else I needed. His fiancée, Vanessa Hill, struggled to keep us both in line and used her connections to garner much-needed support, which came from various sources, including a local minister's wife, Sandy McIlnay, who was running for the State Senate, and Carmen Elaine Garland, a well-known political activist.

One of my biggest supporters though was Brenda Tiger, my fraternity's house mom.

"I believe you are the oddest brother who has ever come through here, Lance Compton!" she remarked after learning that I planned to toss my hat into the race. "Most of these young men can't wait to turn twenty-one so they can drink legally! But you—you want to turn twenty-one so you can run for office!"

Mom Tiger had a way of telling it like it was. I first met the sassy dame in the summer of 1994, at the residence of Mr. and Mrs. Turner, after becoming pledge number 1424 to the Pi Chapter of Alpha Gamma Rho, the men's agricultural social fraternity at Oklahoma State University.

"Hello!" she said, "I am Mom Tiger. I don't do laundry, cook, clean, or sew on buttons! But, my door is always open to help you."

"Okay," I replied, unable to refrain from laughing. "It's really nice to meet ya!"

"It's nice to meet you, too," she said and then embarrassed herself with the proclamation that we would all be sleeping together for a few years.

I thought she was the strangest woman I had ever met, but we became fast friends and shared many laughs during the good times but wept together through the tragic deaths of several brothers.

In July of 1996, I paid my filing fee to the state election board and officially embarked upon a race for the Oklahoma House of Representatives. Mom, Dustin, Mace and Vanessa, and Senator Cole were all present when the television cameras captured me making my political candidacy official. I had chosen to run as a Republican because I believed the Republican Party stood for values and morals; but my first party lesson, gleaned from the many policy seminars I was required to attend, revealed that I had been duped. These seminars, I concluded, were designed to indoctrinate the ideology of discouraging individualism, promoting unity, and ostracizing anyone who refused to conform. As I listened to this message, I wondered how many good ideas and voices had been silenced in the name of the Party. My skepticism must have been apparent because the local party made two attempts to derail my campaign.

The first took place at the Payne County Republican Convention in Stillwater, to which I was invited, along with the other candidates, to speak on the issues. After taking my place at the podium, I had no sooner announced who I was than the hostess marched up to where I was standing and slapped a note down in front of me.

"Wrap it up!" it read.

The hostess was a prominent member of the local party and highly opinionated. After rudely interrupting me, she retreated to the back of the room and glared at me until I was done. Just as I finished, a baby near the front row began to fidget in its mother's arms. Its movement created a loud clapping sound; and the crowd, mistaking the noise for an isolated pocket of applause, broke forth in approval. Within a few seconds, the audience was on its feet, and I stepped down from the podium and began to work the crowd. As I kissed the baby who started it all, I remembered Glenn Price's words and nodded at my adversary.

Just before the candidate's debate, another attempt was made to derail my campaign when I was advised by certain members of the debate commission that I could invite no more than two guests to the debate and that they would be prohibited from wearing t-shirts, buttons, or anything else in support of my candidacy. On the day of the debate, however, I entered the lecture hall to find it packed full of supporters for the local party's choice; and of course, they were all wearing t-shirts and caps that donned his name. It was a cheap shot, but I remained a gentleman. While helping Bernice Mitchell, the female candidate, onto the stage and to her chair, one of our democratic opponents elbowed his way past us, giving occasion for the crowd to contrast his behavior with my manners. The audience did not overlook this simple act of kindness, and it was also the beginning of a wonderful friendship with Mrs. Mitchell and her husband.

For the next nine months, I poured my heart and soul into the race. On the day of the primary, after I had voted, I retreated to *Kaw Lake* just north of Stillwater to spend the remainder of the day praying and reading my Bible. I thanked the Lord for the freedom and privilege to run for public office, especially at such a young age, and asked Him to intervene and direct every aspect of my life even if it meant losing. Late that afternoon, I returned to Stillwater and immediately headed to the AGR house for my watch party. More than a hundred people, including my family, campaign volunteers, fraternity brothers, and a few locals showed up to support me. Early returns revealed an unusually low voter turnout, and within an hour it was apparent that I had lost. I thanked my supporters for coming and then placed a painful, congratulatory telephone call to my opponent. As I wrestled with a hodgepodge of emotions, Ross quietly asked if I was ready to make a public announcement.

"Let's get it over with," I said.

With a great sense of dread hanging over me, I walked out of the fraternity house with Ross, and we headed for the local radio station, which was just across the street near the *Wormy Dog Saloon.*

"Lance!" I heard someone say. "Where are you going?"

I turned around to see one of my pledge brothers running toward us. He almost ran into me as he pulled me aside to prevent Ross from hearing what he had to say.

"You're not going to the *Wormy Dog* are you?" he asked.

"No," I replied.

"I don't want you going there!" he continued. "You've never taken a drink in your life so don't start tonight!"

Known around campus as a party animal, this particular brother spent the majority of his time in the bar. Most of our friends did not even know that he was fighting alcoholism's death grip on his soul. Having heard of my defeat, he was concerned that I was on my way to drown my sorrows in the bottle. I will never forget the look on his face as he firmly planted his hands on my shoulders and begged me to stay away from alcohol. I admired his courage, recognized that his motivation was love, and accepted his concern as a testament to our brotherhood and friendship.

"I'm not going to drink," I responded, "We're just going to the radio station so I can concede the race." I put my arm around his neck.

"Come and help me do this," I said.

"Yessir!"

At the station, I sat down behind the microphone and, while looking at Ross, my pledge brother, and Brian Woods (another brother and good friend who had dropped by to show his support), I announced my concession. It was very difficult to accept defeat after being the center of attention for so many months, but the experience reminded me that my life and future were built upon the strong foundation of Christ. Considering those who build their lives, careers, and hopes upon the things of this world rather than Him, I shivered and wondered how they survive in times of defeat.

A few days later, as I was putting away my campaign materials and pondering the inscription on a magnet that Mom had given me, which read, "Politics may not be the oldest profession, but the results are often the same," I came across and re-read a letter of support I had received during the campaign from an elderly couple in Hinton who had been following my accomplishments and failures since I was a child. It read:

"Dear Lance,

Received your most surprising letter today. I know it was a decision of finishing your college education—or POLITICS.

*We are all for you if this is your decision and know you will
do well.*

Charles and Wilma Tarrant

P.S. The best thing to happen to you would be for you to lose."

Though it was difficult to come to terms with my defeat, the Truth
of God's Word constantly reminded me that men cannot harm me:

> "The LORD is on my side; I will not fear: what can man
> do unto me? The LORD taketh my part with them that
> help me: therefore shall I see my desire upon them that
> hate me. It is better to trust in the LORD than to put
> confidence in man. It is better to trust in the LORD than
> to put confidence in princes."[3]

The next year, my attention was momentarily diverted from politics
to the brewing "hawg battle" in western Oklahoma, and I began to
develop an interest in big business. "Hawg battle" was actually a local
term of art for the economic firestorm sparked by environmental and
public health concerns related to corporate hog farms' waste disposal
practices. Their utilization of lagoons and the practice of spraying fields
to fertilize and irrigate crops created no small controversy in my neck
of the woods. There is nothing like the stench of hundreds of acres that
have been soaked with pig urine and kissed by the hot, August sun.
Despite the putrefying aroma, however, the smell of money prevailed.

Since I was dissatisfied with college life and still disillusioned by
my first political failure, I called Bruce and told him I wanted to get
involved in the pig business. He responded by introducing me to his
good friend, Senator Gene Stipe. The day Bruce walked me down the
long corridor to Gene's office on the fourth floor of the State Capitol,
I felt much like the cowardly lion who was about to meet the Wizard.
At that time, Gene Stipe was the most powerful man in Oklahoma and
a living legend.

---

[3] Psalms 118:6-9 (KJV)

"Go on in, Senator. He's expecting both of you," said his longtime assistant, Ginger Barns, as we entered his outer office.

Thick cigar smoke emanated from his private sanctuary as Bruce glanced at me with a raised eyebrow. We entered, and there sat the seventy-one year old Senator, fully reclined in a worn, leather chair, amidst a cloud of smoke. He looked like he had come straight out of the 1960s. His right leg rested on the corner of a solid wood desk. The lower leg of his trousers was hiked up, exposing pale, white skin and a thin, black sock that protruded through a thick-soled shoe. A pair of narrow, horn-rimmed glasses rested in the middle of his forehead. He was on the telephone.

"Why can't them rascals just do as they're told!" he hollered.

Without opening his eyes, he pointed to the two chairs in front of his desk, and we each took a seat.

I could hear a gravel-like voice coming from the telephone receiver as the Senator listened patiently. I chuckled nervously and noticed a lump had formed in the back of my throat. Suddenly, he jerked his foot off the desk, sat upright, and slammed down the telephone.

"This is the boy I was telling you about," Bruce said almost immediately.

"Ah, yes...Lance Edwin Compton," he replied, emphasizing my middle name.

He removed the horn-rimmed glasses from his forehead, tossed them on the desk, and studied me for a moment.

"Well son, there's a problem..."

Before I could ask what it was, he continued.

"But, I guess I'll forgive you for being a Republican!" he said getting up from his chair.

"Well, I'll leave the two of you to talk," Bruce said and made his way toward the door.

I wanted to get up and run after him, but I was glued to my chair. Sweat poured from my palms, and I felt my hand slip from the armrest.

"Can ya run a hawg bidness, boy?" the Senator asked.

"Uh, yessir," I proudly stated and straightened in my chair.

He began to examine the end of his tie.

"Well...I got half my dinner on my tie," he mumbled. "Why didn't you say something?"

He scraped it vigorously with his index finger. The intercom buzzed.

"Just a minute," he said. "I've been waiting on this call."

"Do I need to step outside?" I inquired.

"No, you're part of the group now. Keep y'er seat."

"Yeah, well is there an opening over there?" he asked the caller. "I have a lady...I'd really like for her to have a position. Tell me what openings we can make."

There was a pause, and I could hear fast talking coming from the telephone receiver.

"What about him?" the Senator asked. He's older than Methuselah! Why don't we just put him out to pasture. That'd make a nice job for her. When can this happen? I'd really like to call her this afternoon and let her know she's got the job. Okay, I appreciate it...let me know if I can help."

He finished the conversation and hung up.

"I understand you're from Binger?" he asked. "Did you know Lloyd Edwin Rader? He was a good friend of mine."

I proceeded to tell him that my grandparents had purchased their farm and house from Mr. Rader and said, "In the summer of '81, Mr. Rader's lawyer called Papa after they struck oil on the place with Compton No. 1 and told him there'd been a mistake with the mineral rights. He told Papa that if he'd send the deed to his office, he'd 'fix it right away.' Papa replied, 'I may have been born at night, but it wasn't last night,' and hung up on him. We never heard from Mr. Rader's camp again."

"That was Lloyd, alright," he said nodding his head. "He helped a lot of people, but you had to keep an eye on your pocket book."

After a few more minutes of conversation, we finally came to the reason Bruce had introduced us.

"If we're goin' into this 'hawg bidness,' I want it to be substantial," he said. "I'm willin' to put in seven million. My brother and I just sold a chain of stores, and we need somewhere to park the profits..."

He gave me the names of some individuals whom he thought would be willing to help with our venture, suggested that I contact them, and asked me to report back to him in two weeks. I spent that time accumulating as much information as I could about the swine industry and contacted Cal Coffin, a builder from Nebraska, and Keith Harbor, an executive at DeKalb, both of whom brought me up to speed on the industry. Dustin and I even shot some footage of a few active hog farms, which, with the help of Bruce's son, Wade, we compiled into a video. Dad helped me write a business plan and put together a financial portfolio; and when the deadline arrived, I strode into the Capitol, towing my presentation materials, which included an aged TV and VCR, in my Radio Flyer wagon.

"Who are you looking for?" the security guard asked.

"I'm here to see Senator Stipe."

"Go on up," he said.

"Looks like you've come up with quite a plan here," the Senator said, looking over the materials. "We might just have the potential for something profitable here." As he continued to comb through the information, he stopped abruptly.

"Well thank God you included the feed bill," he said and began to tell me the story of how, several years earlier, he had partnered with three friends to purchase a bankrupt turkey farm that was stocked to the tune of seven million turkeys. Coincidentally, it accounted for twenty percent of the nation's turkey population at the time. Having paid somewhere in the neighborhood of $15,000.00 apiece, the Senator and his friends were elated to find what they thought was a bargain.

"We just *knew* we'd discovered a gold mine," he said. "The next morning at about four o'clock, one of the partners called me and said, 'Gene, it's about these turkeys...how in the Sam Hill we gonna feed 'em?' Well...the only thing we could do was borrow the money, which was just shy of seventy million dollars..."

He reached into his desk and pulled out a cigar, trimmed it, and lit up.

"...We broke even just after Thanksgiving and made a decent profit after Christmas," he said as puffs of smoke escaped from his mouth.

"I was a nervous wreck the whole time we had 'em though," he continued. "Every time a thunder storm would start to brewin,' I'd have to get a drink! Them crazy turkeys nearly drowned themselves every time it rained. One drop would hit 'em, and they'd just look up toward the sky with their darned mouths open," he said, mimicking a floundering turkey.

Being around the Senator was entertaining. I felt like I had known him all my life, but there was one thing that bothered me. He had a vast vocabulary of curse words and frequently used them to express himself. I had also used such words in the past. Like a lot of young boys, I started cursing to "fit in" and appear "grown up." Before long, I was cursing without even thinking about it. But, that all came to an end one day when Grandma and Papa sat me down at the kitchen table and told me they were disappointed in my language.

"People who use words like that aren't smart enough to think of anything else to say," Papa said. Knowing that they were disappointed probably shamed me more than anything. I have been mindful of my words since then and limit my exposure to those who habitually use foul language. To this day, if my tongue ever slips, I am immediately convicted by the Holy Spirit. When someone takes God's name in vain or uses His name together with some curse word, it is physically painful for me to hear. In ancient times, some did not even speak or write the name of God because they feared and revered Him. This is quite a contrast to modern society, in which it is impossible to find a movie or television show that does not blaspheme or degrade the Lord's name in some way.

During the time I had spent with the Senator, I had witnessed his power and knew what he was capable of doing to anyone who crossed him. I never thought I would be the one to give the most powerful man in Oklahoma a lesson in cursing, but the time came when I had to do just that. The day he blasphemed the Lord's name, my respect for the Lord triumphed over risk and fear, and I spoke out.

"Senator," I began, "I mean you no disrespect, but can I say something that could end our friendship?"

"What have you done now?" he thundered.

I suddenly felt weak, but the Holy Spirit urged me to continue.

"I don't exactly know how to say this," I stammered.

"I like for people to get straight to the point," he snapped.

"Okay. I admire you and value our friendship, but I just cannot stand to hear anyone take the Lord's name in vain or use it as a curse word. Will you please not do that again in my presence?"

The Senator stared back at me with a look that sliced right through me. I sat there, looking at him, expecting the worst, but his stern stare slowly faded, and he suddenly took on the demeanor of a small child who had just been scolded. After a few quiet moments, he sat down in his chair and, to my surprise, began to share intimate details about his life. He told me about his battle with alcohol and some of the other temptations that had plagued him through the years and became very emotional when telling me that his prostate cancer had returned.

"You're trotting along, feeling good, and all of a sudden there's this monster looking to get you!" he said, and raised his hands in a claw-like stance. He later asked me to pray with him, and I never heard him take the Lord's name in vain again.

For the next several weeks, the Senator and I worked tirelessly on getting our hog business off the ground. After learning that DeKalb planned to liquidate its seed stock farms, we decided that Liberal, Kansas was the perfect location for our venture. While touring their facilities, I received a telephone call from fraternity brother, John Kelle. The timing of his call was just right because I had recently decided to drop out of college so I could focus entirely on my business venture with the Senator.

"I've decided to move out of the AGR house," he said. "I was wonderin' if you'd wanna room together next year."

"Well," I replied, "I've decided to leave school. I think I need to focus on this pig business right now. It's going to be tough for the first few months."

"Lance," he said, "I do believe that's the stupidest thing I've ever heard you say! I can't believe you'd even consider it. I know you've been unhappy with school, but dropping out is not the answer. I know you wanna make money…we all do…but dropping out when you're so close to finishing is crazy and just not in your character."

John's words hit me like a ton of bricks. He was my little brother in AGR, and it was usually I who was giving him the advice. I was a little surprised but knew in my heart he was absolutely right. I decided to listen to him just as a curious fate befell the swine industry.

Hog farms had been springing up all across the country. Since most of the produce of these farms was sold to corporate processors, the market was at an all-time high; but the stage had been set for big-time corporate players to seize control of the market. When all purchasing suddenly came to a halt in a single day, the market had been running in the mid-forty dollar range per one hundred pounds but was quickly driven down to eight cents. Needless to say, a panic ensued; but not long after the chaos, corporate processors announced they would offer long-term contracts to the small-time producers. The producers who contracted with them were essentially reduced to share croppers but many embraced the arrangement because it was the only alternative to losing their farms. In the long run, the corporate processors reaped enormous profits. Their executives received lavish bonuses, and their stockholders pocketed big dividends while industry regulators looked the other way.

As for my first trial run in big business, it was over; I was thankful that we did not lose one cent of Senator Stipe's money, but the "hawg bidness" was not my only attempt at breaking into big business with the Senator. On another occasion, Dustin and I decided we wanted to get into the "cheese bidness" when we found a cheese factory and retail facility for sale in Wisconsin. We secured a commitment from a venture capital group for a portion of the purchase price, which we had already agreed to "sight unseen" over the telephone, and then asked the Senator if he would fund the rest.

"I ain't ever been in the 'cheese bidness' before," he replied. "Let's try 'er out! After all, money is the name of the game!"

With the funding commitments in hand, Dustin and I piled into his Honda Civic and headed to Wisconsin — an arduous trip to say the least — but were greeted on arrival by disappointing news. The owners had sold the factory a day earlier to a higher bidder. Once again, I was thankful for having not lost a single penny of Senator Stipe's money.

Having decided not to drop out of college after talking with John, I decided to take him up on his offer to room together the following year. We ended up having to settle for a second story apartment in a complex just north of the football stadium which was notoriously known as the slums. Among its amenities were cracks in the walls big enough to drive a bus through, a front door that had to be locked with a screwdriver, and tattered, stained carpet. The place was not what we were accustomed to, but we filled it with electronics and furniture and made it cozy. My cousin, Michelle, donated two recliners and her husband Jimmy's deprivation became our comfort. As John's roommate, I learned that he was a ladies' man – a modern-day *Don Juan*. His dating schedule alone was more crowded than our class schedules combined but with apparent good reason: he was fond of telling his women that he was impoverished, and this somehow induced them to charitably donate a television here, a stereo there, a VCR, and countless other electronics. I doubt any of his girlfriends ever discovered he was heir to the Kelle Oil Empire, but his romantic enterprise became my motivation for many pranks. One day, when he called and asked me to locate a phone number for one of his women, I did what any good friend would have done – I gave him the wrong number. Within minutes, he called back to tell me that he had telephoned Beth instead of Amber and was caught off guard when Beth promptly chastised him for whispering sweet nothings into the wrong ear. Unfortunately, his vow of revenge left me with no choice but to preemptively strike when two Mormons appeared on our doorstep.

"If you guys will come back on Friday morning," I told them, "My roommate John will be glad to talk with you." That evening, I asked John, "Can you be home on Friday? I'm expecting a package and won't be here to sign for it."

He obviously suspected I was up to something because he was nowhere to be found when the Mormons reappeared on Friday. Unfortunately, I had forgotten about asking them to come back and felt obligated to invite them inside, which was a mistake:

> "Whosoever transgresseth, and abideth not in the doctrine of Christ, hath not God. He that abideth in the doctrine of Christ, he hath both the Father and the Son. If there come any unto you, and bring not this doctrine, receive him not into your house, neither bid him God speed: For he that biddeth him God speed is partaker of his evil deeds."[4]

---

[4] 2 John 1:9-11 (KJV)

My grandparents had warned me on several occasions not to invite either Mormons or Jehovah's Witnesses into my home because they are false teachers who do not abide in the doctrine of Jesus Christ. Individuals from each group had visited our farm frequently when I was growing up – and always during dinner or supper – but Grandma Compton forbad us to answer the door, though they persistently beat upon it, or to even look at them as they strained to see through the windows. I realized I should have followed Grandma's example after listening to them for less than a minute.

The fact that Mormonism is false teaching, inconsistent with the doctrine of Jesus Christ, is easily verified by the proclamations of its leading disciples and its many erroneous teachings. In the *Journal of Discourses*, a multi-volume collection of "discourses" given by early leaders of the Mormon Church, the so-called Mormon prophet, Brigham Young, denied the full and final atoning sacrifice of Christ's blood:

> "There is not a man or woman, who violates the covenants made with their God, that will not be required to pay the debt. The blood of Christ will never wipe that out, your own blood must atone for it. . ."[5]

He also denied the supernatural conception and birth of the Lord Jesus Christ:

> "The birth of the Saviour was as natural as are the births of our children; it was the result of natural action. He partook of flesh and blood--was begotten of his Father, as we were of our fathers."[6]

And, he denied Christ's conception by the Holy Spirit:

---

[5] Journal of Discourses, *Instructions to the Bishops – Men Judged According to Their Knowledge – Organization of the Spirit and Body – Thought and Labor to be Blended Together,* vol. 3, p. 247.
[6] Journal of Discourses, *Character of God and Christ – Providences of God – Self-government, etc.,* vol. 8, p. 115.

"Now, remember from this time forth, and forever, that Jesus Christ was not begotten by the Holy Ghost."[7]

Jesus was not conceived through a natural act of sexual intercourse. Rather, as the Scriptures clearly proclaim, He was conceived by the Holy Spirit and born of a virgin, which was nothing short of supernatural:

> "Now the birth of Jesus Christ was on this wise: When as his mother Mary was espoused to Joseph, before they came together, she was found with child of the Holy Ghost. Then Joseph her husband, being a just man, and not willing to make her a public example, was minded to put her away privily. But while he thought on these things, behold, the angel of the LORD appeared unto him in a dream, saying, Joseph, thou son of David, fear not to take unto thee Mary thy wife: for that which is conceived in her is of the Holy Ghost."[8]

Moreover, concerning his own discourses, Brigham Young stated:

> "I say now, when they are copied and approved by me they are as good Scripture as is couched in this Bible . . ."[9]

One false teaching of Mormonism is that the Word of God is not infallible or inerrant,[10] but this teaching is contrary to *2 Timothy 3:16-17 (KJV)*, which declares that, "All scripture is given by inspiration of God, and is profitable for doctrine, for reproof, for correction, for instruction in righteousness: That the man of God may be perfect, thoroughly furnished unto all good works." If the Word of God contained error, it could not be said that it was given by the inspiration of God because God

---

[7] Journal of Discourses, *Self-Government—Mysteries—Recreation and Amusements, Not in Themselves Sinful—Tithing—Adam, Our Father and Our God,* vol. 1, p. 51.

[8] Matthew 1:18-20 (KJV)

[9] Journal of Discourses, *Texts for Preaching Upon at Conference – Revelations – Deceit – Fulness of Riches – One-man Power – Spiritualism,* vol. 13, p. 264.

[10] Richard Abanes, *One Nation Under Gods: A History of the Mormon Church* (New York, New York: Basic Books, 2003), 383.

is perfect[11] and His ways are perfect.[12] Furthermore, if the Scriptures contained error, they would be incapable of delivering on the promises made by *2 Timothy 3:16-17 (KJV).*

A second false teaching of Mormonism is that the *Book of Mormon* is the Word of God[13] and superior to the Bible.[14] This cannot be true because the *Book of Mormon* violates God's commandment that, "Ye shall not add unto the word which I command you, neither shall ye diminish ought from it, that ye may keep the commandments of the LORD your God which I command you."[15] Concerning those who add to or diminish from His Word, God has declared, "For I testify unto every man that heareth the words of the prophecy of this book, If any man shall add unto these things, God shall add unto him the plagues that are written in this book: And if any man shall take away from the words of the book of this prophecy, God shall take away his part out of the book of life, and out of the holy city, and from the things which are written in this book."[16]

A third false teaching of Mormonism is wrapped up in its view of salvation which, according to Mormonism, is contingent upon participation in temple ceremony. However, only full tithe paying members can receive a recommend to enter the temple.[17] Therefore, it follows that one must be a full tithe paying member to be saved. This teaching is contrary to the Word of Truth, which makes it clear that salvation is a gift that cannot be obtained by any work:

---

[11] Matthew 5:48 (KJV)

[12] Psalm 18:30 (KJV)

[13] "Beliefs; The Book of Mormon," *The Church of Jesus Christ of Latter-day Saints (Mormon.org)*, accessed December 14, 2013, http://mormon.org/beliefs/book-of-mormon, stating, *"The Book of Mormon is the word of God, like the Bible. It is Holy Scripture, with form and content similar to that of the Bible."*

[14] Joseph Smith, *Book of Mormon* (Salt Lake City, Utah: Church of Jesus Christ of Latter-day Saints, 1981), Introduction Page, stating, *"I told the brethren that the Book of Mormon was the most correct of any book on earth, and the keystone of our religion, and a man would get nearer to God by abiding by its precepts, than by any other book."*

[15] Deuteronomy 4:2 (KJV)

[16] Revelation 22:18-19 (KJV)

[17] Douglas J. Davies, *An Introduction to Mormonism* (Cambridge, United Kingdom: Cambridge University Press, 2003), 182.

"For by grace are ye saved through faith; and that not of yourselves: it is the gift of God: Not of works, lest any man should boast."[18]

A fourth false teaching of Mormonism is that men can become gods (doctrine of eternal progression)."[19] This doctrine espouses the same lie that Satan told Eve in the Garden of Eden:

"And the serpent said unto the woman, Ye shall not surely die: For God doth know that in the day ye eat thereof, then your eyes shall be opened, and ye shall be as gods, knowing good and evil."[20]

It is impossible for men to become gods because the Word of Truth declares that there is only one:

"For there is one God, and one mediator between God and men, the man Christ Jesus; Who gave himself a ransom for all, to be testified in due time."[21] *(emphasis added)*

Related to the doctrine of eternal progression is the Mormon tenet that God the Father is just one among hundreds, thousands, or even millions of other gods in an ancestral-like line throughout the ages who achieved "godhood" by following the Mormon principle of "eternal advancement."[22] The Word of Truth debunks this teaching in the *Book of Isaiah*, declaring again that there is only *one* God:

"Thus saith the LORD the King of Israel, and his redeemer the LORD of hosts; I am the first, and I am the last; and beside me there is no God. And who, as I,

---

[18] Ephesians 2:8-9 (KJV)
[19] Douglas J. Davies, *An Introduction to Mormonism* (Cambridge, United Kingdom: Cambridge University Press, 2003), 79.
[20] Genesis 3:4-5 (KJV)
[21] 1 Timothy 2:5-6 (KJV)
[22] Richard Abanes, *One Nation Under Gods: A History of the Mormon Church* (New York, New York: Basic Books, 2003), 286.

shall call, and shall declare it, and set it in order for me, since I appointed the ancient people? and the things that are coming, and shall come, let them shew unto them. Fear ye not, neither be afraid: have not I told thee from that time, and have declared it? ye are even my witnesses. Is there a God beside me? yea, there is no God; I know not any."[23]

A fifth false teaching of Mormonism is that Satan is the brother of Jesus Christ;[24] but, in *Isaiah*, the Word of Truth proclaims Satan to be a fallen angel:

"How art thou fallen from heaven, O Lucifer, son of the morning! how art thou cut down to the ground, which didst weaken the nations! For thou hast said in thine heart, I will ascend into heaven, I will exalt my throne above the stars of God: I will sit also upon the mount of the congregation, in the sides of the north: I will ascend above the heights of the clouds; I will be like the most High. Yet thou shalt be brought down to hell, to the sides of the pit. They that see thee shall narrowly look upon thee, and consider thee, saying, Is this the man that made the earth to tremble, that did shake kingdoms; That made the world as a wilderness, and destroyed the cities thereof; that opened not the house of his prisoners?"[25]

And, in *Ezekiel*, the Word declares:

"Son of man, take up a lamentation upon the king of Tyrus, and say unto him, Thus saith the Lord GOD; Thou sealest up the sum, full of wisdom, and perfect in beauty. Thou hast been in Eden the garden of God;

---

[23] Isaiah 44:6–8 (KJV)
[24] Journal of Discourses, *Happy Prospects of the Saints – Persecution – Union, Etc.*, vol. 6, p. 207.
[25] Isaiah 14:12–17 (KJV)

every precious stone was thy covering, the sardius, topaz, and the diamond, the beryl, the onyx, and the jasper, the sapphire, the emerald, and the carbuncle, and gold: the workmanship of thy tabrets and of thy pipes was prepared in thee in the day that thou wast created. Thou art the anointed cherub that covereth; and I have set thee so: thou wast upon the holy mountain of God; thou hast walked up and down in the midst of the stones of fire. Thou wast perfect in thy ways from the day that thou wast created, till iniquity was found in thee. By the multitude of thy merchandise they have filled the midst of thee with violence, and thou hast sinned: therefore I will cast thee as profane out of the mountain of God: and I will destroy thee, O covering cherub, from the midst of the stones of fire. Thine heart was lifted up because of thy beauty, thou hast corrupted thy wisdom by reason of thy brightness: I will cast thee to the ground, I will lay thee before kings, that they may behold thee. Thou hast defiled thy sanctuaries by the multitude of thine iniquities, by the iniquity of thy traffick; therefore will I bring forth a fire from the midst of thee, it shall devour thee, and I will bring thee to ashes upon the earth in the sight of all them that behold thee. All they that know thee among the people shall be astonished at thee: thou shalt be a terror, and never shalt thou be any more."[26]

Fallen angels are created beings. They were created by Jesus Christ because the Word of God declares that all things were made by Him.[27] Because Christ created Satan, it is impossible for Him to be Satan's brother or equal.

Yet another false teaching of Mormonism is that one can personally assume the sins of the dead and pray them into heaven. This teaching denies mankind's need for the broken body and shed blood of Jesus

---

[26] Ezekiel 28:12-19 (KJV)
[27] John 1:3 (KJV)

Christ and cannot be reconciled with Jesus' account of the rich man and Lazarus, which reveals that one's position in eternity cannot be altered:

> "There was a certain rich man, which was clothed in purple and fine linen, and fared sumptuously every day: And there was a certain beggar named Lazarus, which was laid at his gate, full of sores, And desiring to be fed with the crumbs which fell from the rich man's table: moreover the dogs came and licked his sores. And it came to pass, that the beggar died, and was carried by the angels into Abraham's bosom: the rich man also died, and was buried; And in hell he lift up his eyes, being in torments, and seeth Abraham afar off, and Lazarus in his bosom. And he cried and said, Father Abraham, have mercy on me, and send Lazarus, that he may dip the tip of his finger in water, and cool my tongue; for I am tormented in this flame. But Abraham said, Son, remember that thou in thy lifetime receivedst thy good things, and likewise Lazarus evil things: but now he is comforted, and thou art tormented. And beside all this, between us and you there is a great gulf fixed: so that they which would pass from hence to you cannot; neither can they pass to us, that would come from thence. Then he said, I pray thee therefore, father, that thou wouldest send him to my father's house: For I have five brethren; that he may testify unto them, lest they also come into this place of torment. Abraham saith unto him, They have Moses and the prophets; let them hear them. And he said, Nay, father Abraham: but if one went unto them from the dead, they will repent. And he said unto him, If they hear not Moses and the prophets, neither will they be persuaded, though one rose from the dead."[28]

---

[28] Luke 16:19-31 (KJV)

The foregoing are but a few examples of the deceptive teachings of Mormonism, but it should be emphasized that Mormonism is not the only source of false teaching in the world:

> "And Jesus answered and said unto them, Take heed that no man deceive you. For many shall come in my name, saying, I am Christ; and shall deceive many."[29]

Another source is the religious organization known as the Jehovah's Witnesses. In their version of the Bible, for instance, the Jehovah's Witnesses deny the very deity of Jesus Christ:

> "In [the] beginning the Word was, and the Word was with God, and the Word was a god."[30]

Jesus Christ is not **_A god_**; He is **_THE_** **God** – the **ONLY** begotten Son of God.[31] The King James Bible declares it like this:

> "In the beginning was the Word, and the Word was with God, and the Word was God."[32]

Besides denying Christ's deity, the Jehovah's Witnesses promulgate other false teachings, such as this one:

> "As we have seen, Satan is 'the ruler of this world,' not Jehovah."[33]

God's Word expressly contradicts this teaching with several revelations that God is the absolute ruler of this world. For instance, when the Prophet Daniel was brought before King Belshazzar of Babylon to read the writing of God's hand and make known the interpretation thereof, Daniel declared:

---

[29]   Matthew 24:4–5 (KJV)
[30]   John 1:1 (New World Translation of the Holy Scriptures)
[31]   John 3:16 (KJV)
[32]   John 1:1 (KJV)
[33]   "Will You Trust God?" *The Watchtower*, May 1, 2013, 7.

"O thou king, the most high God gave Nebuchadnezzar thy father a kingdom, and majesty, and glory, and honour: And for the majesty that he gave him, all people, nations, and languages, trembled and feared before him: whom he would he slew; and whom he would he kept alive; and whom he would he set up; and whom he would he put down. But when his heart was lifted up, and his mind hardened in pride, he was deposed from his kingly throne, and they took his glory from him: And he was driven from the sons of men; and his heart was made like the beasts, and his dwelling was with the wild asses: they fed him with grass like oxen, and his body was wet with the dew of heaven; <u>till he knew that the most high God ruled in the kingdom of men, and that he appointeth over it whomsoever he will</u>."[34] *(emphasis added)*

Furthermore, if Satan were the ruler of this world rather than God, it would not have been necessary for him to obtain God's permission to launch an attack upon Job:

"Now there was a day when the sons of God came to present themselves before the LORD, and Satan came also among them. And the LORD said unto Satan, Whence comest thou? Then Satan answered the LORD, and said, From going to and fro in the earth, and from walking up and down in it. And the LORD said unto Satan, Hast thou considered my servant Job, that there is none like him in the earth, a perfect and an upright man, one that feareth God, and escheweth evil? Then Satan answered the LORD, and said, Doth Job fear God for nought? Hast not thou made an hedge about him, and about his house, and about all that he hath on every side? thou hast blessed the work of his hands, and his substance is increased in the land. But put forth thine hand now,

---

[34] Daniel 5:18–21 (KJV)

and touch all that he hath, and he will curse thee to thy face. And the LORD said unto Satan, Behold, all that he hath is in thy power; only upon himself put not forth thine hand. So Satan went forth from the presence of the LORD."[35]

In the second chapter of *Job*, Satan was required to obtain God's permission a second time to continue his attack upon Job. It should be noted that, each time, Satan was commanded by God to spare Job's life, and he complied:

"Again there was a day when the sons of God came to present themselves before the LORD, and Satan came also among them to present himself before the LORD. And the LORD said unto Satan, From whence comest thou? And Satan answered the LORD, and said, From going to and fro in the earth, and from walking up and down in it. And the LORD said unto Satan, Hast thou considered my servant Job, that there is none like him in the earth, a perfect and an upright man, one that feareth God, and escheweth evil? and still he holdeth fast his integrity, although thou movedst me against him, to destroy him without cause. And Satan answered the LORD, and said, Skin for skin, yea, all that a man hath will he give for his life. But put forth thine hand now, and touch his bone and his flesh, and he will curse thee to thy face. And the LORD said unto Satan, Behold, he is in thine hand; but save his life. So went Satan forth from the presence of the LORD, and smote Job with sore boils from the sole of his foot unto his crown."[36]

The doctrines of Mormonism and the Jehovah's Witnesses are just two examples of false teaching that is inconsistent with the doctrine of Jesus Christ. There are many others, but all of them have one thing

---

[35] Job 1:6-12 (KJV)
[36] Job 2:1-7 (KJV)

41

in common: they are all contrary to and oppose the Truth of God's Word.

Sometime after my first major run-in with false teaching, one of my best friends, Rick Vernon, suggested that I apply to Oklahoma City University's School of Law since he was planning to attend himself. After thinking and praying about the suggestion, I scheduled a meeting with my guidance counselor. Though it was October of 1997, I had only met with a counselor one other time in my entire college career. Unfortunately, during that second meeting, we uncovered a disturbing fact – in four years, I had managed to squeeze in less than half the credits required for a bachelor's degree and needed another fifty-four hours to graduate. Apart from the counselor, I conceived a plan that would allow me to finish in the summer of 1998 and enroll in law school that fall. First, I would take an interim class during Christmas break. Then, I would suffer through twenty-five hours in the spring and eight in the summer, all while taking correspondence courses. My plan seemed perfect, but when I attempted to implement it at the registrar's office, I ran into one roadblock after another. The registrar told me no student could take that many hours in such a short period of time so I decided to visit the dean of my college; but when I saw that he was without authority, I turned to the University Provost.

The pleasantries exchanged at the outset of my encounter with the Provost quickly turned into un-pleasantries when he saw that he could not persuade me to abandon my objective simply by voicing some silly anecdote about carrying a bucket of potatoes. Prompting the mood to deteriorate, he told me, "Your grades and performance are, shall we say, undesirable for such a request. You're just setting yourself up for failure!"

Though my GPA was better than a 3.25, I remained cool and asked him, "Who has the final say?" When he would not answer, I said, "I believe I'll just talk to the University President about this."

With that, his face turned reddish purple, presumably from anger because he then retorted very sarcastically that the President could not grant my request without petitioning the Board of Regents and claimed, "The President only has a few silver bullets to use with the Regents, and this is not something he'd want to waste a bullet on!"

"We'll see about that," I replied and left him standing alone in his office.

A few days later, my parents and I visited the President. Inside his office, the three of us took a seat on two luxurious leather sofas in front of a large, ornate fireplace while the President seated himself in a sumptuous wingback chair beside the hearth.

"Mr. Compton," he began, as he crossed his legs and clasped his hands together, "I have reviewed your transcript and spoken with your college dean and the University Provost…May I ask why this request is so important to you?"

"Well," I replied in a rather shaky voice, "The first and most important reason is my Grandma's health. She had open heart surgery two years ago and has been steadily declining since then. She is currently on dialysis, and her goal is to live long enough to see me graduate from college. I desperately want to give her that gift. The second reason is because I want to start law school next fall."

Looking inquisitively at my parents, he asked them, "Do either of you have an opinion about this?"

Their expressions of support displeased him, and he replied, "I'm not going to approve your request, Mr. Compton. We have your best interests in mind here at Oklahoma State University, and I believe you need to slow down and spend a little more time on your education."

With that, I decided to relay what the Provost had said about his limited number of silver bullets.

"I have never asked for a political favor from the Board of Regents!" he responded rather defensively.

"I didn't say that you did. I'm just telling you what the Provost told me. I also want you to know that I don't believe it's in my best interest to prevent me from graduating and moving on to the next phase of my life. I've humbly asked for your help, but if you refuse it, I'll personally speak to each one of the regents."

"Okay, Mr. Compton," he finally relented. "If you'll finish this semester with straight A's, get an A in your interim course and an acceptable LSAT score, and get accepted to a law school, I'll grant your request."

When I finished the fall semester with straight A's per my bargain with the University President, it was time for the interim course, which was an intensive, two-week political science class that required me to spend one week in the classroom and the second, as Professor Nixon put it, "schmoozing around Washington, D.C." I did not know anyone in the class but quickly became friends with Bart Garbutt, who was also planning to attend law school at Oklahoma City University, and a foreign exchange student from Japan named Kei. After an anxious first week, I departed to Washington, D.C. from Will Rogers World Airport on what was to be my very first airplane ride. Prior to the descent into D.C., two of the flight attendants, who were overjoyed to learn that I had never flown before, presented me with a bottle of champagne to commemorate my first flight.

Who are you anyway?" asked an elderly lady who was seated beside me as she carefully studied my face. Apparently, the crew's attention had aroused her suspicions that I was someone of notoriety.

"Just an ole hillbilly from western Oklahoma," I replied, affectionately caressing my bottle of champagne.

Later that afternoon, I arrived at George Washington University and met up with the rest of the class. After giving us our schedule for the week, Professor Nixon said, "This is a chance for all of you to see the face of our national government. I want you to get acquainted with its background and the culture that drives it."

According to the schedule, we had appointments with lobbyists, reporters, legislators, and just about everyone who was anybody in Washington, D.C. One of the first was with Oklahoma Congressman Wes Watkins and his staff. Though I knew Congressman Watkins, I chose not to divulge that fact to the class. As we were filing into his office, Angie Kraus, one of the Congressman's senior staff members, greeted me with a hug and proceeded to introduce me to everyone in the office. When Wes entered a few minutes later, he too greeted me with a hug and asked, "You mean they let you in here?"

All of this unexpected attention toward the country bumpkin in the group piqued the interest of our foreign exchange student, Kei, and brought him out of his shell. Though he spoke broken English, his interaction with me and my thick, country drawl from that day forth soon became the focus of everyone's attention.

Kei was clearly a fish out of water and demonstrated such one evening when, as the group was waiting to cross a street, he stepped off the curb and near to the path of a speeding car.

"Heeeeerrrrrrreeeee!" I hollered. "Watch out for that car!"

I pulled him back onto the curb just as it whizzed by, but I doubt he ever saw it.

Everyone in the group immediately scolded him, to which he replied, "I not understand slang. What is difference between watch out and look out?"

"They both mean move it, fast!" I said. And so, for the next week, Kei made it a practice of randomly declaring, "Move it, fast!" His declarations were always shortly followed by fits of laughter.

Kei confided to Bart and me that he wanted to "live it up" while we were in D.C. and insisted that we rent a limousine to tour the sites in style. Bart and I were hesitant because of the expense, but Kei persisted, and so we ended up traveling the streets in luxury at his expense. When we drove into the *Iwo Jima Memorial*, I noticed a large group of tourists and school children milling about and was moved to do a little acting.

"Watch this!" I said and asked the driver to circle the memorial slowly. I then cracked one of the darkly tinted windows just enough to extend my arm through the opening and proceeded to wave to the masses. Immediately, the crowd screamed and began chasing the limo. Pretty soon, the entire mob was seized with mad frenzy, and our driver was laughing so hard that he was having trouble steering. The mob eventually caught up with and surrounded the limo and took turns touching my hand and straining to see through the tinted windows. I wanted to drive away and leave them all in suspense but was overruled by Kei and Bart, both of whom wanted to get out and surprise everyone. When Kei and I opened the back door and stepped out, revealing that we were not celebrities, disappointment fell upon the crowd, and they all turned and walked away, many of them expressing anger.

Later, at Ruth's Chris Steakhouse, when someone mentioned that Kei had rented a limousine, the majority of our classmates were suddenly intrigued with the question of whether or not he was wealthy. Since he had already told me about his family's great wealth, I was not surprised when he responded to our classmates' curiosity with a pointed comment: "In Japan, millionaire mean nothing...billionaire control!"

The remark provoked a simmering of jealousy, which subsided only when Kei pointed to everyone and excitedly proclaimed, "I buy!"

Almost everyone at the table was elated and greedily agreed to his suggestion; but I, not wanting to see him taken advantage of, replied, "I'll get mine."

The euphemism of "getting mine" was apparently lost in translation because he just looked at me with a big grin and nodded vigorously; but when Bart said, "Kei, you don't need to buy mine, either. I can pay for it," he emphatically replied, "In Japan, it rude to refuse offer!"

"But," I said in return, looking at him with a big grin and hoping to diffuse his quick temper, "We're not in Japan...and you're not the Emperor!"

He again laughed uncontrollably and relented with, "Okay! Okay! I not buy!"

It goes without saying that Bart and I endured a barrage of dirty looks when most everyone at the table realized that they would be buying their own steaks.

When I had time to reflect on my classmates' sudden interest in Kei's financial status, I was saddened to think that he was probably accustomed to being judged according to his wealth and reminded that those who judge as the world judges are known as such:

> "Judge not, that ye be not judged. For with what judgment ye judge, ye shall be judged: and with what measure ye mete, it shall be measured to you again."[37]

After supper, Kei asked me to accompany him to an ATM machine before returning to the GWU dorm, asserting that, "No one crazy enough to bother with you size! You protect me!"

"Well," I replied, "If a group of thugs come around that corner, you're on your own 'cause I'm outta here!"

"But how quick you remember my family in mafia..." he said, laughing diabolically.

---

[37] Matthew 7:1-2 (KJV)

"I guess I'll fight then," I replied, slumping under the prospect of forced duty.

As we walked back to the dorm, Kei opened up about his family and their arrangement for him to marry a girl that he did not know.

"In Japan, you not know who you marry...everything arrange..."

I listened to him as he expressed fear that he would never find true love and tried to cheer him up with a little humor.

"Well, for someone with my looks, an arranged marriage would be a dream come true," I replied, to which he burst into laughter and nodded vigorously yet again.

What began as a matter of humor between a country bumpkin from Oklahoma with a thick, country drawl and a foreign exchange student from Japan who spoke in broken English had evolved into an unlikely friendship in just a matter of days, probably because we made quite a pair, a truth that was exemplified on our final day in D.C.

When everyone but Kei and I had departed for the airport, and since we were scheduled on a later flight, I figured we had enough time for a quick tour of the White House so I telephoned Angie in Congressman Watkins' office and asked if she could get us VIP passes. She was able to get the passes, and from the moment Kei and I stepped onto the White House grounds, we were so enthralled with everything from the "whispering white" paint on the building's exterior to the halls and corridors of history that we almost lost track of time. Though the tour was one of the highlights of my life, we had to truck it back to the dorm with very little time to gather up our luggage and find a taxicab.

"There taxi!" Kei shouted, after we had toted our suitcases for two blocks in search of a cab, and pointed to a car that was parked several yards away adjacent to a construction site. Hoping that nobody would beat us to it, we sprinted for the car, flung both rear doors open at once, tossed our luggage inside, and jumped in.

"Take us to airport!" I hollered, to which the driver responded by flailing his arms wildly and shouting over his shoulder in a tongue that sounded like Chinese. I looked at Kei over the top of the suitcases between us and asked, "Do you know what he's saying?"

"He no Japanese...I not know," Kei replied.

I then attempted to find out whether the driver spoke English, but he just shouted ever the louder and more persistently.

"QUIET!" I hollered. "My friend here is Japanese mafia! Get us to the airport!"

With that, the tires squealed as the driver slammed his foot onto the accelerator. The violent acceleration forced me down into my seat. Suddenly, rather than following the detour around a construction zone, the driver hopped onto the curb and sped down the sidewalk. I cracked my window to let some air inside; but just as I did, we passed alongside some type of construction equipment that sprayed me with black oil. Murmuring unintelligibly, the driver flipped on the windshield wipers just as we plowed into a row of plastic dumpsters, hurling pieces of plastic high above us and scattering trash all over the oil-streaked windshield. After a hair-raising fifteen minutes, during which I caught more than one glimpse of Kei gritting his teeth, we arrived at the airport terminal, and I asked the driver how much we owed him.

"I'm NOT a taxi!" he shouted in perfect English and pointed to the writing on the side of the car door, which I had not previously seen.

"Well, why didn't you say something?" I asked.

After we had exited but before I could pass him a twenty dollar bill, the driver peeled out, slamming both rear doors shut as he fled the scene.

Kei and I were still laughing about it when we boarded the plane.

During the flight home, he asked me, "Who is this Christ and what He about? I listen and learn, but I not believe."

Unsure of how to respond, I just replied, "You need to come to church with me sometime." Kei's inquiry caught me off guard, and I was unprepared to give him an answer as we have been commanded to do:

> "But sanctify the Lord God in your hearts: and be ready always to give an answer to every man that asketh you a reason of the hope that is in you with meekness and fear..."[38]

---

[38] 1 Peter 3:15 (KJV)

Having observed me for two weeks, Kei obviously detected something different about me; and since he knew I was a Christian, he wanted to know more about Christ and whether He was the reason that I was different. The fact that I did not give him an answer is one of the greatest regrets of my life. Hindsight has given me the ability to see that my decision to continue college, my determination to graduate early, and the interim political class had all transpired to bring me into contact with Kei, who obviously felt as if he could inquire of me concerning Christ. Yet, despite God's mighty act of bringing us together, I neglected my duty to testify of my personal relationship with Christ. Thus, I cheated Kei out of an opportunity to accept Him and find the true love he longed for. How easy it would have been to point to the scar above my left eye and say, "This is what Jesus has done for me." But, despite my failure, my Lord and Savior is the God of second chances, and he immediately began preparing me for other opportunities.

Once back in Stillwater, I passed my interim class with an A+ and later received an acceptable score on the LSAT and was accepted to Oklahoma City University School of Law. I had accomplished the impossible and kept my end of the bargain with the University's President, but I soon learned that he had no intention of keeping his word. When my repeated telephone calls were unreturned and my unannounced visits yielded no results save a letter informing me that nothing could be done, I told Senator Price, and he spoke with one of the University's lobbyists. A few weeks later, while OSU was seeking legislative approval to acquire a small college, the University's President found himself face to face with a procedural stall and apparently concluded that it had something to do with Bruce and me because shortly thereafter, a very unhappy lobbyist visited Bruce's executive assistant, Yvonne Phelps, my self-described "caretaker," with a personal message, the gist of which was that I could take any class I wanted to take, whenever I wanted to take it. A few months later, I was a college graduate.

CHAPTER 3

The Comforter

It was around 9:00 A.M. when John, Christopher, and I arrived at the Crowne Plaza Hotel in Jerusalem on our first day in Israel. After flying for two nights in a row and spending the intermediate day sightseeing in London, I was running on adrenaline and anxious to see the revelations God had in store for me. Upon settling into the hotel room, John and Christopher decided to sleep off their jet lag while I went down to the lobby to meet up with Tony, our tour guide. Two weeks earlier, after we had all spent several days praying for a Christian guide, John contacted our travel agent who was able to make arrangements with Tony through our hotel's concierge service. Educated in the United States, Tony was Palestinian and had previously been in the service of a British Ambassador as his driver and bodyguard. He now operated a small tourism business in the Holy Land and was also a part-time Biblical archeologist. A last minute change in his schedule made it possible for him to be our guide for the entirety of our ten-day stay in Israel. I recognized him the moment I stepped off the elevator into the hotel lobby.

"You must be Tony," I said holding out my hand.

"And you must be Lance," he replied.

We shook hands and sat down to visit. I was convinced after just a few minutes that God had answered our prayers and knew He would reward our request for a Christian guide by allowing us to see the Holy Land from the proper perspective.

The first place Tony took me was the Mount of Olives. Due east of Jerusalem, directly across from the ruins of the Temple, the Mount of Olives forms the eastern slope of the Kidron Valley. From the observation deck at the summit of the Mount, Tony pointed to the graveyard on the mountain's side below us and said, "This is a Jewish cemetery…Jewish families rent these plots, which can go for as much as $125,000 for a five year term."

"Why do they pay that much for a temporary plot?" I asked.

Tony then explained that most of the Jews buried there probably did not believe Jesus Christ is the Messiah because burial in that particular cemetery was indicative of their desire to be near the Temple's Eastern Gate when the messiah comes.

"If they had been believers in Christ, they would've recognized that it doesn't matter where you're buried," he said.

I gazed at the thousands of stone burial boxes dotting the hillside where Jesus had once walked, wondering why the first scene the Lord wanted to show me was one of death and separation. I was surprised to see a massive cemetery near the place where Jesus ascended into Heaven and will set His feet at His second coming; but the field of stone, which Tony told me housed the remains of many of Israel's illustrious dead, brought a familiar scripture to mind:

> "My sheep hear my voice, and I know them, and they
> follow me: And I give unto them eternal life; and they
> shall never perish, neither shall any man pluck them out
> of my hand. My Father, which gave them me, is greater
> than all; and no man is able to pluck them out of my
> Father's hand. I and my Father are one."[39]

Those who believe in Him shall never perish, but those who do not believe in Him are forever separated from Him regardless of where they are buried. As I beheld the scene, I recalled my first experience with the painful separation of death and the Holy Spirit's gentle reminder that it was only temporary.

I was in my first semester of law school at Oklahoma City University. The first round of final exams was just a few weeks away. Life outside of school and the people who mattered most had been relegated to the

---

[39] John 10:27-30 (KJV)

proverbial back burner. Grandma Compton's health was fading fast and inching me closer to the moment I had long dreaded. My stress level was at an all-time high, and fear and anticipation of the unknown had caused me to retreat into a meaningless existence. Grandma had always maintained that I had a sixth sense, but what she attributed to enhanced awareness was, in fact, the Holy Spirit. I know this because He has spoken to me on numerous occasions since I became a Christian – whether it be warning me, recalling scriptures from the archives of my memory, or calling me to prayer. On the night of November 2, 1998, when I began experiencing tormenting nightmares which lasted for several days, I did not immediately recognize them as warnings from the Holy Spirit but later realized they were. The dreams were not ordinary dreams. They were so convincing that I awoke after each one, convinced that I had lived them.

The first came on the night of my grandparents' sixty-third wedding anniversary. In this dream, our farm's pastures caught fire. As the flames lapped their way toward the house, I saw that Grandma was trapped inside the old chicken coop behind the house. Three of my friends looked on as I feverishly attempted to save her but did not even offer to help. I awoke and sat straight up in the bed, wringing wet with sweat. I could not go back to sleep nor could I forget the dream. The following day, I tried to think about anything but the dream. Since it was Election Day, I decided to skip class and go home to vote. After leaving the polls, I drove out to my grandparents' house and spent the next five hours with them. We talked about everything from politics to old family stories. Our visit was a good one. When I kissed them goodbye, I noticed how much Grandma looked like her mother, Ethel Alexander.

"I love you," I said as I walked out the door.

"And I love you, too…more than you know," she replied.

That night, I dreamed I was suspended on the ceiling of my grandparents' bedroom. I watched in terror as Grandma collapsed across the bed and noted the time on the clock, which was 6:10 P.M. I awoke, sweating and gasping for breath, and went into the living room to watch television. Rick Vernon, who was now my roommate, came out of his room and asked why I was up so late. I told him about both dreams, and we stayed up for the rest of the night, talking about how blessed we were to have a God-fearing family. I awoke the next morning shrouded in uneasiness. I was unable to do anything that day; and when I finally went to sleep that night, I found myself hovering above the ground in yet another dream as Grandma was carried out of her house on a stretcher and loaded into the back of an ambulance. Before I could register what was happening, I was inside the ambulance, hovering against the ceiling. After noting that we were headed south, I saw an oxygen mask covering Grandma's nose and mouth and paramedics attempting to revive her. I woke up, terrified, and picked up a textbook to read for class but could not focus. I turned on the television, but the mindless chatter just exacerbated my state of mind. Finally, I went back to bed. The next morning, I went for a walk then called Dustin and his wife, Carrie, and invited them to eat pizza that night. As I was walking out the door to meet them later that evening, I suddenly had an overwhelming urge to call my grandparents but did not do it. To this day, I wish I had called.

As I drove back into town after Dustin, Carrie, and I had eaten dinner, I saw the blue neon lights that outlined the top of Saint Anthony's Hospital in downtown Oklahoma City and breathed a sigh of relief because I did not have any loved ones there. When I opened the door to my apartment, Rick was waiting on me.

"You need to call Michelle," he said solemnly.

"What's the matter?" I asked.

"You just need to call her," he answered.

"I'll call her in a minute," I replied, knowing something was wrong but hoping to convince myself that everything would be alright.

"I think you need to call her *now!*" Rick responded in a tone that raised the hair on the back of my neck.

I picked up the telephone and dialed Michelle's number. She answered on the first ring.

"I tried to catch you while you were with Dustin, but you had just left…," she said. There was a pause. "It's your Grandma," she continued. "She had a heart attack."

"Where is she?" I asked.

"I'm sorry—she didn't make it."

I handed the phone to Dustin, who had just walked through the front door with Carrie.

"The dreams...," I said and looked at Rick. "I should've realized..."

He nodded his head, but I walked to my bedroom, closed the door behind me, grabbed Grandma's picture from the wall, and clutched it tightly against my chest. Numbed by the harsh realization that I would not see Grandma again in this lifetime, I just sat on the edge of the bed for several minutes before mustering the strength to pack an overnight bag and return to the living room.

"We must go to Papa," I said; and, without a word, Dustin and Carrie got up and followed me to the pickup truck, and we drove to Binger. The minutes crept by like days – it was one of the longest rides of my life. We turned into the dirt driveway of my grandparents' farm, and as we passed beneath the imposing elm and pecan trees, I could see Papa standing in the window, holding back the curtains just as he always did when someone came up the driveway. As the pickup came to a stop, I looked toward the house and saw him coming outside to meet me. Unable to hold back the tears, I got out and ran to him. We stood on the porch for what seemed like hours, weeping together and holding onto each other. Later that night, after he had gone to bed, I laid down on the old sofa in the living room. Memories, like the delicate shadows creeping across the room in the pale light given by the solitary lamp in the front yard, flickered before my eyes. I stared at the front door and its aged wood, antique doorknob, and skeleton keyhole. The tarnished, brass knob testified to the many guests whose hands had graced it throughout the years. The knotty pine paneling on the walls, with its ambered finish, and the fatigued furniture sparked feelings of warmth and security. The old house creaked and groaned as if conversing with me in a language that charmed and magnified my senses. A fusion of odors resounded in my nostrils and enveloped me in comfort as I eased into the soft cushions and pulled a handmade, antique afghan over me.

Alone with thoughts and memories, I grappled with the void that had suddenly settled over my life. Grandma was one of a kind, and time had proven our relationship to be rare. There was nothing I could not ask of her and nothing we could not discuss. Whether trying to understand myself or others or learning from her how to discern the

Holy Spirit's conviction, I could always depend on being able to pour out my soul to her without fear of ridicule, judgment, or rejection. The experience and wisdom she had received from several decades of walking with the Lord gave her the ability to offer me guidance, and she never allowed her own passions or opinions to stand in the way of God's Word. As the night wore on, my sorrow grew, but I awoke the next morning to the soft light of dawn – the rays of which peered through the windows over the front door and outlined the cross in the door's rustic wood paneling. Tears welled up in my eyes, and I prayed to God for the strength to get through the difficult day ahead.

"I've decided to take some time off from law school," I said as I met Papa in the kitchen and began to prepare his breakfast.

He did not respond but was visibly relieved. He and Grandma had been sweethearts since the second grade and were married for over six decades. I could not take her place, but I wanted to be there for him during the grieving process. Years earlier, I had promised each of my grandparents that I would take care of them if something happened; and only a few months before her passing, I had reassured Grandma once again that I intended to keep my promise.

Later that day, our family gathered at the *Turner Funeral Home* in Hinton, Oklahoma to plan Grandma's funeral. My childhood friend, Andee Turner, his wife, Kori, and parents, David and Nancy, were all there, as brothers and sisters in Christ, to guide us through the difficult process. Their ministry was a great comfort for me. Still, seeing the casket showroom was not easy. Only Mom seemed able to handle the sight with poise so we deferred to her decision while we waited in the chamber of repose. The smell of freshly cut flowers penetrated the dimly lit room, and the faint sound of gospel hymns could be heard from somewhere overhead. When Andee finally wheeled Grandma into the room in her casket, I wept openly. For the next two days, Dustin and I spent most of our time at the funeral home, trying to ease our pain by visiting with friends and family. We placed a beautiful bouquet of flowers in Grandma's hands – our way of expressing that she had not entered Heaven "empty-handed." Fortunately, Grandma had been saved by the grace of Jesus Christ in the *Oney Baptist Church* in Albert, Oklahoma at a very young age, affirming to us the promise of *2 Corinthians 5:8*: "We are confident, I say, and willing rather to be absent from the body, and to be present with the Lord."

The night before the funeral, I was sitting alone in Papa's chair in the bedroom sitting area when Mom came in and asked if I was okay. With tears running down my face, I replied, "I loved her so much."

"And she loved you too," Mom said, leaning down to hug me. "That's why it hurts so much. The pain of a loved one's death is the price of love."

I later wrote Mom's words in the back of my Bible as a permanent reminder of how precious love is and have never forgotten them. From where I was sitting, I could hear Papa, Dad, and the others talking in the dining room. As they retold the tragic details of Grandma's death, I was stunned to hear that my dream had followed the actual events of her death like a script. Remarkably, every detail of my dream matched the things which had actually transpired – from the way she had fallen across the bed to the time on the clock and the southerly route taken by the ambulance. I knew then that the dreams I had experienced in the days before Grandma's death were the work of the Holy Spirit, carefully preparing my spirit for Grandma's departure and cushioning my heart before it was even broken.

The following morning, I stood on the front porch and watched in dread as Andee drove down the driveway in his signature blue, Buick limousine. After he had deposited us at the church parking lot, I led the procession into the sanctuary. The sound of creaking wood resonated in my ears as the congregation stood. David and Nancy guided us to the second pew in the middle section, and we took our seats – I, on the outside of the pew beside the aisle, and Papa on my right side with Dustin next to him. I looked to my left to see the pallbearers – Dustin Tackett, my close friend; Larry Mills, one of Dad's closest friends; Keith Gardner, the son of one of Grandma and Papa's closest friends; and Uncle Rick, Andee, and Jimmy. Seated directly behind them were the honorary bearers – Papa's domino buddies, Troy Lovell, Ted Jackson, J.C. DeVaughn, Orval Dorsey, and his fishing buddy, Kermit Gardner. I also saw Elmer and Howard Jones – two of Grandma's students – sitting together. It was a great comfort to see that God had placed so many good people in our lives, each of whom had come to support and show us that we need not travel this rocky path alone. Sippy Scott began the service with a piano prelude and Kathy Daugherty, my high school Sunday school teacher, sang *Soon and Very Soon* as Papa grabbed ahold of and held tightly to mine and Dustin's knees. After the beautiful strains of *In the Garden* and *Amazing Grace* had filled the nave with the Holy Spirit's presence, Brother Marty Ingram delivered the message.

When the service concluded, Andee and David rolled the casket toward the rear exit for the final viewing. As the metal box passed my pew, I reached out and ran my fingers along its cold trim, which filled the church with an eerie squeaking sound. Amidst faint sobbing, the guests arose and slowly trickled out of the church. When the auditorium had finally emptied, Andee retrieved from Grandma's body the 1935 Silver Peace Dollar necklace that commemorated the year of my grandparents' marriage and the diamond ring that Papa had given to Grandma on their fiftieth wedding anniversary. Then, the clicking sound of the casket being sealed resounded like gunshots in the stillness.

Facing south in Murray Cemetery, beneath a green canopy, I fixed my eyes upon the red roses, white daisies, and thick fern that adorned the top and hung over the side of the grayish blue casket and listened closely to Brother Marty read the twenty-third Psalm. Afterward, a palpable silence descended over the gravesite, interrupted only by the cold wind and periodic clanking of the tent. Carolyn Stover, my cousin, stood behind me with her arms wrapped around my neck as I listened to the dreadful hand crank lower the casket into the ground. Several minutes passed, and then I was alone. I peered into the cold grave, thanked the Lord for the wonderful lady who had played such an important role in my life, tossed a single red rose into the gaping hole, and walked away.

The coming days and weeks went almost unnoticed as I passed through the five stages of grief and learned that it affects each of us differently. Papa's grief prompted him to suggest selling all of Grandma's personal belongings and household furnishings. Claiming he needed to recover the money spent on her funeral, he pressured me daily to sell off her personal effects. Of these, Grandma's clothing seemed to bother Papa the most and he hounded me continually to get rid of it. He also resorted to rolling Grandma's coin collection, hoping to deposit it in the bank. Pennies that had belonged to my great, great grandparents — some worth a lot more than their face value — were rolled and stacked in a shoebox. Initially, I was perturbed by Papa's behavior and did not understand that it was just a manifestation of his grief. My grief surfaced in other ways. One of the most unexpected was that, for no apparent reason, I began to harbor uncontrollable anger toward Mom which only seemed to get worse as the days progressed. Concerned, I prayed in earnest about my feelings, and the Holy Spirit eventually showed me that my anger was actually a defense mechanism, sparked by the subconscious fear of losing her too.

Papa eventually abandoned his efforts to sell Grandma's belongings but took up, as an alternative, the notion of remarriage. It was a painful subject for the entire family, especially for Dad; and since Papa had always been highly respected in the community, I was embarrassed for him. In time, however, I saw that this too was just another expression of his grief.

Mine and Papa's daily visits to the cemetery were just about the only common expression of our grief even though we did not usually go together. I preferred going alone because keeping the grave perfectly sculpted — flat on top with sloping sides — had become an obsession for me. Since I was a mere child, I had been responsible for doing whatever my grandparents could not do for themselves, and I just could not let go of that duty as it pertained to Grandma. Every so often, I could see the faint imprint of two knees and grip marks in the carefully manicured soil, which bore witness to the heart-wrenching scene of Papa on his knees, grasping the red dirt that separated him from the love of his life.

Death gave way to renewed life as the long slumber of winter came to an end at last. When spring appeared, Papa and I lost ourselves in tending to our locally famous garden and launched the old fishing boat, hoping to catch that big bass that always seemed to elude us. When we were not in the garden or at the lake, we sat at the domino table reliving the past, enjoying the present, and pondering our futures. Time passed, and Papa returned to socializing in town and playing dominoes with his buddies. He and Mom insisted that I return to law school, but I was reluctant to leave him alone even though Mom promised to check on him and prepare his supper daily; and our life-long friend and neighbor,

Allen Findley, had assured me that he would drive him to the senior citizens' center for lunch each day. As things began to change, it seemed like we were leaving Grandma behind, which left me feeling guilty. I continued to visit the cemetery regularly. The soil I had nursed for so long was now covered with a thick, protective layer of bermudagrass. Like tightly-clasped fingers, the fibrous runners had spread over the grave, replacing Papa's mournful grip and weaving a perfect substitute for my diligent husbandry. During a visit to the grave in late spring, a Word from the Lord came to me as I gazed intently at the emerald-colored grass:

> "My sheep hear my voice, and I know them, and they follow me: And I give unto them eternal life; and they shall never perish, neither shall any man pluck them out of my hand. My Father, which gave them me, is greater than all; and no man is able to pluck them out of my Father's hand. I and my Father are one."[40]

By this Word, the Holy Spirit ministered two crucial Truths to my spirit at just the right time. First, the memorization of Scripture is essential in providing the Holy Spirit with a means by which to penetrate the believer's mind and heart to communicate the Word of God and impart comfort, conviction, and reassurance. Second, it was time for me to let Grandma go and follow my Lord.

"Lance?"

Tony's voice jolted me from my thoughts.

"Are you ready to go?"

"Yes," I replied.

I looked out across the graveyard one more time, understanding now why the Lord wanted the Mount of Olives' cemetery to be my first impression of the Holy Land — it was a sobering reminder that those who have not believed in Jesus Christ do not have the believer's blessed assurance that death is only a temporary separation. For them, it is eternal.

---

[40] John 10:27-30 (KJV)

CHAPTER 4

Irreparable Loss

One of the first sites Tony took all of us to see was Herodium, a manmade mountain that was built by Herod the Great in 40 B.C.[41] on the location of his victory over Antigonus II Mattathias,[42] the last Hasmonean king of Judea.[43] While John, Christopher, and I stood marveling at almost forty acres of ruins, including what was left of the fortress' enormous swimming pool and the remains of the pool's columned pavilion and promenades, Tony made an interesting statement: "When Jesus spoke of having faith as a grain of mustard seed and said to His disciples, '... ye shall say unto this mountain, Remove hence to yonder place...,'[44] he was likely calling this mountain to their remembrance and using it as an example of what faith can accomplish."

"What do you mean?" I asked.

"Well," he replied and pointed to a smaller hill, contiguous to Herodium, which looked as if it had been sliced in half, "Do you see that mound over there that looks like the bottom of a mountain?"

"Yeah..."

"Herod ordered his builders to dismantle that mountain and remove and stack its earth on top of Herodium. So, the original mountain was literally moved from one place to another. This would have been

---

[41] "Herodium," *Bible Places*, accessed October 22, 2013, http://www.bibleplaces.com/herodium.htm.

[42] Ibid.

[43] "Antigonus II Mattathias," *Wikipedia*, accessed October 22, 2013, http://en.wikipedia.org/wiki/Antigonus_II_Mattathias.

[44] Matthew 17:20 (KJV)

considered a remarkable feat of engineering in Jesus' day and was probably used by our Lord to drive home His point concerning faith."

As Tony spoke, Jesus' words entered into my ears:

> "And Jesus said unto them...for verily I say unto you,
> If ye have faith as a grain of mustard seed, ye shall say
> unto this mountain, Remove hence to yonder place;
> and it shall remove; and nothing shall be impossible
> unto you."[45]

Even if Jesus was not making a point of reference to Herodium when He spoke these words to His disciples, I certainly saw a bigger picture after hearing Tony's theory. Faith in Christ, even if equal in measure to a grain of mustard seed, can achieve the impossible. This was the lesson I took away from Tony's theory, and this visual demonstration of Christ's Truth served as a reminder to me that the Lord has accomplished a number of impossible feats in my life through nothing more than my faith.

In the fall of 1999, I succumbed to the nagging of Mom and Papa to return to law school. I did not really want to but concluded that going through the motions would satisfy everyone. My new home was a bottom-floor, two-bedroom suite in Cokesbury Court, the campus apartment complex. During my first night there, I heard gunfire and someone told me the next day there had been a drive-by shooting right across the street from my apartment. The semester had not even started, but I was already contemplating how I could return to the peace and quiet of the farm. On the second day of classes, I had the pleasure of meeting George Collins, a self-described ladies' man, who had come all the way from Malvern, Arkansas.

"Excuse me," I watched him say to the arrogant woman who had stolen his seat between classes, "I think you're in my seat."

"...and your point is?" she replied, without an upward glance, as she casually ran a nail file along the tips of her two-inch golden fingernails. I was unable to restrain myself from laughing as he just stared back at her in disbelief with his mouth agape.

---

[45] Matthew 17:20 (KJV)

"Well," he said, looking at me, "Is there anyone sitting next to you?"

"No sir," I replied. "Have a seat and rest your troubles."

Being the genuine "country boys" that we were, George and I became fast friends and did our best to avoid law school's pervasive intellectualism and cut-throat competitiveness; and being so labeled by most of our classmates, we were not very highly esteemed. Nevertheless, our easygoing personalities did attract some kindred spirits, one being Nick Hadzellis, a funny-talking Greek from Long Island, New York. There was also Wendy Cornett, the quintessential southern belle; Carrie Christie, the girl from behind the pine curtain of East Texas; everyone's favorite Hawaiian, Renee Gish; and slap-stick humorist, Carol Nagel. Of course, there were also my buddies from OSU, Bart Garbutt and Joe Carson, the latter of whom is perhaps more country than I am.

Two interesting latecomers to the group were John Chaffin and Carrie Burnsed, both of whom I met during class elections. I met John first, on the stairs outside the front door of my apartment, when he solicited my vote for class president like a typical politician.

"Can I can count on your vote for President?" he asked.

"I'll see what I can do," I replied and retreated into my apartment. Hoping to secure support from the class' elite, he had taken to marketing himself by wearing a black Hugo Boss suit every day.

Later that night, Cokesbury Court experienced an electrical blackout; and less than two minutes after the lights went out, every looter within a ten block radius could be seen scavenging on the opposite side of the perimeter fence. I watched the commotion through the blinds while maintaining a close look out over the new Chevy pickup truck that Mom and Papa had recently bought for me. While peering into the darkness, my concentration was suddenly shattered by voices, and the racket liked to have scared the wits out of me. Then, there was a knock at the door. I picked up my shotgun, looked through the peephole, and breathed a sigh of relief when I saw that it was John, accompanied by his inseparable companion – Carrie Burnsed of Florida, whose acquaintance I had not yet made. She, too, was running for class office, and the word had gone forth that her prior employment by two Florida governors qualified her for the position. Deciding to entertain myself, I flung the door open.

"Get in here, quick!!" I shouted.

Before they could even respond, I grabbed Carrie by the arm and pulled her inside.

"They're lootin' like crazy out there! Ya'll are gonna get yourselves shot!"

"What in the world are you doing with a shotgun in this apartment?" Carrie asked pointedly as if we had known each other for a coon's age.

"Well, this *is* Oklahoma," I replied. "Here, we don't leave home without a rifle."

"Why don't you get some clothes on and run to IHOP with us," John said, glaring disapprovingly at my pajamas.

Sharing many interests, not the least of which was traveling, John, Carrie, and I quickly became great friends and found ourselves in the sky lanes almost as often as we were in class, traveling to ports of call throughout the country. Two of the most memorable trips for me were to New York City. One of these excursions was prompted when Carrie went for a student bar association function. When John and I decided it would be unfair for her to have all the bragging rights, we headed there ourselves and ended up staying at the *Waldorf Astoria,* where I was oft seen wandering around the lobby in amazement. While we were checking in at the front desk, I saw a familiar face and hollered, "Hey! It's the Nanny!" Determined to get her autograph, I left my suitcases unattended and followed the big-haired spruce through the lobby and around the corner, where I stumbled into a gift shop only to find that she was not Fran Drescher but the gift shop clerk. Disappointed, but hoping to appear inconspicuous, I browsed through the shop for a few minutes until I spied a hand-painted, moon dial watch beckoning to me from inside a glass cage.

"How much for that watch?" I asked.

"One-forty-five," she replied.

"Dollars?"

"Thousand...," she said.

"Uh..." I stammered, at a loss for words, "...I could buy three farms for that back home..."

"Pardon?"

Having removed the precious watch from its cage during our short exchange, but now perceiving that I lacked the funds to consummate the transaction, she promptly withdrew it from my sight in a crushing scene.

I rallied from the blow by strolling through the streets and talking freely to the street vendors and merchants, most of whom were so intrigued by my country accent and inner hillbilly that they gave me free merchandise. For the most part, everyone seemed to love me in New York City, but I soon encountered some more disapproval in the prohibition-era speakeasy known as the *21 Club*. Having previously seen the *21 Club* featured on television, I was so intrigued by its lacquered-looking façade and the colorful, ornamental jockeys on the balcony above its entrance that I insisted upon taking at least one meal there. We made a dinner reservation, but being unaware of the dress code, we arrived in casual attire. After scanning the menu that was posted outside the entrance, we prepared to enter, but the doorman stopped us and said, "Excuse me…Are you aware that we have a dress code?"

"No," I said. "We did not know. May we go in and change our reservation to this evening?"

"Where are you guys from?" he asked, grinning slyly, to which we replied in unison, "Oklahoma!"

"Ahhhhhh…I see…"

He pulled a door open for us, and we stepped through the brass-plated doors but were quickly encircled by the fashion police. I took my eyes off the barricade long enough to see a podium-like, mahogany desk upon which sat a dimly lit reading lamp which cast an eerie glow on the hostess' frowning face as she forcefully declared, "A jacket and tie are required!"

"Ma'am," I responded, "We had a dinner reservation, but we didn't know there was a dress code so we'd like to change the reservation to supper this evening."

"Just *leave* and call us!" she replied, stepping around from behind the desk to shove a business card into my hand.

"Can't we just change our reservation now?" I inquired, but we were quickly herded out the doors and onto the sidewalk.

"*Supper!*" the hostess smirked as the doors closed behind us.

"You know," the doorman said, looking at us rather inquisitively, "Our manager is from Oklahoma. You should come back later and tell him what happened this afternoon."

"We should've known better than to wear street clothes into a place like this," John said as we walked away in disappointment. "I can't believe we didn't bring any dress clothes."

Suddenly, I had an idea and heralded a taxi and asked the driver to take us to *Macy's* on West 34th Street. When we finally found the men's section, John browsed through the suits and searched for matching cuff links while I looked for a golden tie and recalled Granny giving me a one-hundred dollar bill and telling me to "buy something nice." After a diligent search, I found the perfect tie and carried it to the clerk. As I handed him the crisp one-hundred dollar bill, I wondered how long Granny had been saving it and what she went without by giving it to me.

I also remembered Grandma Compton telling me about her and Papa living in Los Angeles during World War II while Papa was working as a construction superintendent in the Navy. One evening, as they strolled through the city's downtown area, Papa spied a famous restaurant and insisted on eating there, but Grandma refused, telling him that, "Poor country folk like us don't have any business in a place with white tablecloths and crystal." Though Papa had grown accustomed to lavishing Grandma with fine gifts, mostly because he feared being killed in the line of duty, he reluctantly gave in, settled for admiring the sea of white tablecloths through the restaurant's large windows, and ate at a "cheap burger joint" instead. Like Grandma, I knew I had no business eating at the *21 Club*, but I could not justify coming all the way to New York City just to settle for a burger. I silently thanked Granny for the gift as the clerk handed me the receipt.

Later that night, our stretched, black limousine pulled alongside the curb outside the *21 Club*. The same doorman we had seen earlier hollered out, as we exited the car in immaculate dress, "Hey! It's my good friends from Oklahoma!"

"Don't we clean up nice?" I asked as he led us to the entrance and pulled a door open.

"I hope you guys have a great evening," he said. "Remember what I told you earlier."

To my surprise, we were treated like royalty, and even more surprising was the fact that nobody seemed to remember us at all.

Supper was superb, but I asked our waiter if we could have a word with the manager following the dessert course.

"Is everything alright, Sir?"

"Everything was perfect," I replied. "But, I'd like to meet your manager; I hear he's from Oklahoma."

The waiter excused himself, and our check was delivered moments later amidst a few stares. After parting with a few hundred dollars, we arose from the table and headed for the hostess' desk.

"May I please have a word with your manager?" I asked.

"Of course," she replied and pointed to the lounge area. "He's right over there. Just go on over and introduce yourself. I have already informed him that a party from Oklahoma is dining with us this evening."

Per the hostess' command, I walked over to him, held out my hand, and said, "Hi, I'm Lance Compton from Oklahoma..."

The manager's face immediately lit up as if he had just encountered a long-lost friend, and he asked, "Do you know where Covington is?"

"I certainly do," I replied.

"Well, that is where I'm from..."

We visited for a few minutes, and he disclosed to us that his mother would be undergoing open-heart surgery the following day and that he was planning to fly back to Oklahoma to be with her. It was so exciting to find that the man in charge was from our neck of the woods, but I also learned that he was a fellow graduate of Oklahoma State University and a member of one of the fraternities next door to the AGR house. When our discussion turned to the restaurant, I said, "I must apologize for our behavior earlier this afternoon."

"This afternoon?" he asked curiously.

"Yes, we were so eager to try this place that we never even thought about a dress code. We just waltzed in here in our street clothes, and they threw us out. We didn't mean any disrespect..."

"They threw you out?" he interrupted.

"...we should have known better...it's okay," I said.

"No, it's not okay, and it will not happen again! You have a seat right here; I'll be right back..."

We sat down in two red, leather wingback chairs and waited while he walked outside and exchanged a few words with the doorman.

After a few moments, he stepped back inside, motioned us to the door, formally introduced us to the doorman with whom we had already become acquainted, and said, "He will take good care of you."

He reached into his jacket, removed a card, and said, "Here, take my card. I know everyone in this town. If you ever visit New York City again, please let me know, and whatever you need will be yours. As friends of mine, I can assure you that you'll be taken care of."

We thanked him, and he bid us farewell. Then, as if it were perfectly timed, the doorman raised a gloved hand and motioned us toward him. Smiling, he said, "Your car is ready, Sir," and opened the door to a beautiful Rolls Royce sedan. "I hope you enjoy it. It's on the house! By the way, did everything turn out as you expected?"

"Much better than I expected...thanks to you," I said and handed him a tip. Pushing my hand aside, he replied, "I've been treated like you guys were treated earlier today. It's not a good feeling so I do my best to see that it doesn't happen to others. You guys have made my whole year worthwhile. Your 'thank you' is good enough!"

As we drove away in luxury, I realized that we had just witnessed the Golden Rule in living color.

Back in Oklahoma, I had to come to terms with the fact that neither my long list of interesting, law school friends nor my spontaneous travels with them could mask the realities that I just did not enjoy law school and did not really care whether I became a lawyer or not. Moreover, the stress that accompanied every aspect of graduate school led to a mass exodus of what remained of my hair and forced me to come to terms with that, too. Throughout my youth, my identity had always been synonymous with my size, distinct voice, and fire red hair. Unfortunately, after being prescribed certain medications for premature ventricular contractions (PVCs), a severe heart arrhythmia, I began to lose my hair, but even the loss caused by the medications could not compete with the havoc that law school reaped upon my scalp.

"Why don't you just buy some hair?" Papa asked one day when I was complaining about it. "I'll pay for it if it means that much to you."

I took him up on the offer and within a few days, I was the newest member of an exclusive group – *Hair Club for Men.*

"Oh my! You're two-toned!" Michelle hollered when she dropped by to see my first piece, expressing one of the many shock-ridden reactions to my new look. Despite the laughter from family and friends, I believed my hair finally looked normal again, thanks to my good friend, Joy Bly, now of *Executive Hair Designs,* and five hundred dollars a month. The "hair system," as the wig is discreetly referred to by cosmetologists, is made of real human hair and secured by a combination of glue and tape. I did not get to choose who donated the strands, though – a misfortune that occasionally resulted in unforeseen embarrassment. Once, after scuba diving off the coast of California, a group of Chinese tourists clamored to have their photographs taken with me when I emerged from the water. At first, I thought their attention had been captured by the pink flippers and mask I had gotten on sale at a shop on the beach but learned after developing my own pictures that they just wanted some photos of my hairpiece, which the saltwater had transformed into a ball of frizz.

There were other embarrassing moments, too. Once, while a high school buddy was introducing me to his new bride in the Wal-Mart parking lot, an Oklahoma thunderstorm announced its arrival with a gust of wind that swept across my scalp and laid the hairpiece flat against the top of my head, hanging in the back by a thin piece of tape. Even as my friend and his wife pretended not to notice, I brushed it back into place, keeping a lid on my humiliation.

Even more embarrassing was the fact that my sister-in-law developed the habit of announcing to dinner guests, "Oh, did I mention that Lance is wearing a wig?" Though many found humor and entertainment through my baldness, coping with and disguising it was difficult for me. To make matters worse, when people who were not "in-the-know" complimented me on my red hair, I felt like an imposter.

Soon after resolving the issue of my baldness, I received my final, second semester grades. Though I had earned one of the highest grades in Property, I fell short of passing some of the other classes. Because of my low GPA and the fact that I had previously taken a leave of absence when Grandma died, I was found unfit to continue my legal education, and my permanent departure from law school was hastened by the dean himself. I secretly breathed a sigh of relief, but Mom, being disappointed and angry, wearied me to appeal the school's decision to terminate me. Reluctantly, I agreed to go through the process but was thankful when the appeal was denied and all other avenues that may have led me back to law school were closed.

Thinking I would be relieved to have graduate school behind me, I was unprepared for what happened next. My premature departure, coupled with my hair loss, political defeat, and unrealized business ventures with Senator Stipe bothered me greatly and contributed to feelings of insecurity, which, of course, exacerbated my greatest insecurity of all, my weight problem. Now, I have always been fat. When I was about six years old, Mom and Dad were so concerned with my weight that they took me to a pediatric specialist, but there was not much he could do. You see, I am a compulsive eater. I eat when I am worried, stressed out, happy, upset, or trying to suppress my emotions and have spent the better part of my life being tormented physically, mentally, and spiritually by my addiction to food. Throughout the years, my emotions have been stretched right along with my skin. The judgmental looks and remarks I have endured have always isolated and reminded me that I am different. My endless struggle with food, the emotional fallout of having to leave law school, and my refusal to evaluate my temptations to eat from a spiritual standpoint eventually led to my morbid obesity. The world's solution to the predicament in which I found myself was so appealing that I made a decision to undergo vertical gastro banding and stomach stapling. The operation only offered a fifty percent chance of long-term survival; and ironically, it could make no promises concerning my spiritual health.

Following the surgery, I lost over one-hundred fifty pounds but was greatly burdened by the Lord to focus on my spiritual condition. Meanwhile, Papa's memory began to fail, and I found myself facing one of the greatest mountains of my life. I was blessed by the Lord to be in a position to be Papa's caretaker. Furthermore, upon realizing that his needs were greater than my problems and insecurities, I promptly diverted my attention away from them and onto Papa. Mine and his journey into what eventually became Alzheimer's was one of faith – one that required me to be totally dependent upon the Lord. In hindsight,

I know I could never have gotten through that horrible period in my life without my faith in Christ.

Papa and I arose and ate the same breakfast every morning – eggs that I had scrambled in the cast-iron skillet, toast with butter and jelly, and coffee, which he usually sipped from his favorite brown mug. Some mornings he was himself, but sometimes he wanted me to teach him how to cook. As his disease progressed, the mornings involved my telling him what day of the week it was and showing him how to read the calendar on the kitchen wall. He usually wanted to review the bank and investment account statements following breakfast, and I found it amusing and interesting that money never ceased to concern him. Home health came to the house each day, and our favorite nurse, Anita Woods, had a special way of imparting a sense of security to both of us. One of Papa's favorite pastimes was eating, and Alzheimer's could not rob him of that joy. I tried my best to simulate Grandma's cooking; but, when I failed, Mom was always standing by to pick up the slack, and Allen Findly helped us a great deal by bringing Papa a meal from the senior citizens' center every day.

We usually spent the afternoons working in the yard, doing some kind of chore in the barn, or playing dominoes at his and Grandma's old Burlington game table in the sun room. Papa was an expert domino player and had been a world champion in the 1970s. Each time we sat down for a game, I learned something new. Every Tuesday and Thursday evening, some of the local farmers stopped by the house for a few rounds; but our private, afternoon games were my favorite. I made time for dominoes because, even though there was always something that required my attention, I knew the time was fast approaching when we would no longer be able to play.

One afternoon, as we sat down for a game, Papa's mind was particularly clear, and he was concerned about a friend who had no faith in Christ.

"What does he believe?" I asked.

"He believes that when you're dead, you're dead," he replied. "Let's invite him over here for a game tomorrow."

Papa had a strong desire to witness to his friend and said he needed me there to "pick up the conversation" in case he faltered. I agreed and telephoned his friend, Tom, and handed the receiver to Papa.

The following afternoon, we sat on the porch and watched as the elderly but stout Tom slowly worked his way out of the driver's seat of his sedan and braced himself for a moment against the car door. He began to roll a cigarette and tried to hide the fact that he was having trouble keeping his balance. He mumbled something under his breath and shuffled up the sidewalk. Small talk was the first order of business as we greeted him and went inside – the drought and the hot weather – these were popular topics during the summer months in our neck of the woods. But, as the three of us played our first hand of dominoes, Papa signaled me to initiate the conversation. All domino partners have a system of secret signals whereby information about the next move and so forth is passed between partners, and Papa and I had earlier agreed upon the signals we would use as we witnessed to Tom. I took a long swig of iced tea and proceeded to question Papa about Jesus. His answers led us into a long discussion, and we pulled Tom into the debate and consulted the Bible so he could read the scriptures for himself. We ended up talking for several hours, focusing on the death, burial, and resurrection of Jesus Christ. Tom listened closely but never wavered in his unbelief.

Some days after Tom's visit, an uncle of mine, who was battling terminal cancer, was admitted to the local nursing home. An unrepentant sinner, he, too, had no faith in Jesus Christ. Granny, his mother-in-law, had attempted to witness to him for many years, and the two of us discussed his unbelief extensively following his admission to the nursing home. Knowing he would not live much longer, Granny intensified her efforts, and I met with Pastor Marty Ingram because I wanted to witness to him too but felt like I needed some guidance since my efforts to win Tom to Christ had been unsuccessful. After talking with Brother Marty, I accompanied Granny to the nursing home. When we entered my uncle's room, all the visitors made a hasty exit – I think they knew why we were there. Once we were alone with him, Granny and I proceeded to have a long discussion with my uncle concerning the death, burial, and resurrection of Jesus Christ and why sinners need a Savior. When the conversation finally turned to Heaven and Hell, it was Granny and I who were doing all of the talking.

Less than a month later, the entire family was summoned to the nursing home late one evening to be there as my uncle passed away. As we stood around his bed and watched him draw his final breath, we all breathed a sigh of relief because, just a few days earlier, he had sent word to Granny that he had placed his faith in Christ, made peace with God, and regretted having waited until the end of his life to do it. These were the words of a converted believer, but I only had a few moments to cherish them. As the drama of my uncle's death played out in that small, dreary room, I heard a sudden commotion as several nurses ran down the hall. We soon learned that someone else was dying that evening. It was Papa's friend, Tom. Not long after our game of dominoes, Tom had a massive stroke and was also admitted to the nursing home. That evening, as my uncle entered the presence of his Savior, Tom passed into eternity an unsaved man.

Two men – one who had lived a so-called "good life" and one whose life was characterized by unimaginable sin – had died in different directions. It was a powerful reminder that it is a man's relationship to and faith in Christ, and not his life, which determines his eternity. Not everyone will enter the Kingdom of Heaven. Just because someone lives a "good life" and is known for kindness does not mean they are saved. The Bible declares that all have sinned and fallen short of the glory of God, that the wages of sin is death, and that there is but one mediator between God and men – the man Christ Jesus. One of the best passages of scripture in this regard comes from the Gospel according to John:

> "He that believeth on Him is not condemned: but he that believeth not is condemned already, because he hath not believed in the name of the only begotten Son of God."[46]

Though time had compromised Papa's physical health, and Granny's for that matter, their faith in Christ and concern for the lost did not waver. I know the Lord allowed me to be witness to these events for my own benefit because they have come to symbolize how the smallest kernel of faith can move mountains.

To keep Papa's mind and memory functioning, I occasionally took him on short, day trips, during which we often found ourselves

---

[46] John 3:18 (KJV)

fishing at *Fort Cobb Lake*. Fishing was another of his favorite pastimes, but loading and unloading the old Chrysler bass boat was sometimes more than the two of us could handle so our maritime excursions were limited. One mid-summer afternoon, when Dustin was able to accompany us, we launched the old boat into *Fort Cobb Lake* one more time and glided lazily through the water, taking in the scenery and trolling for a catch, until the propeller suddenly lodged in a sandbar. As Dustin and I struggled to free the boat, Papa got a bite on his lure, and we abandoned our efforts to free the propeller from the sand. Dustin dropped his hook back into the water, and I helped Papa free the fish from the line. For the next twenty minutes, we caught a fish with every lure that was cast and could hardly reel the lines in fast enough. We were having so much fun that we forgot about the propeller shaft. Then, just as quickly as the fish had started biting, they stopped. When Dustin and I revisited our efforts to free the disabled boat, the sand offered no resistance, and we glided back to the dock with plenty of fish to clean, laughing and reliving the moment. Then, it occurred to me: there had been four fishermen on that sandbar. The Lord had stopped and held our little boat amongst the school of fish, giving Dustin and me a pure moment with Papa – one completely free of the cares of the future.

As time claimed more and more of his memory and personality, he became a stranger but realized in lucid moments that he was "lost in a fog." One afternoon, as we played a game of dominoes, he attempted to count the ivory pieces, and then looked up at me with fear, frustration, and uncertainty in his eyes and asked, "What's going to happen when I wake up one morning and don't know who you are?"

"Well," I began, trying not to reveal that his question had struck me like a blow to the head, "We'll cross that bridge if we ever come to it just like we've done with everything else. I'll be here by your side whether you know me or not so just try not to worry about it."

Our conversation then turned to the reality of his death, which seemed more imminent than we cared to admit, and hoping to lighten the mood, I told him, "When you get up there, send me a red flower so I'll know you made the trip all right."

Tears welled up in his eyes as we continued the game.

Like autumn leaves, the fun times we shared began to wither and blow away as Papa sank deeper into the winter of his life. The journey was lonely and uncertain. His calm, patient demeanor was replaced by sudden fits of anger and rage. Reality was skewed, and he resorted to child-like behavior. Our roles were reversed as he became the child, and I assumed the role of parent. Mom was my greatest help during this time. She tried stimulating his mind by talking to him about the past and making her famous blackberry cobbler, but he sometimes did not even acknowledge her presence. Before long, he was telling the home health nurses that I was starving and locking him in the bedroom, but they kindly and patiently pointed to the large amounts of food in the kitchen and told him the door must be catching since it had no lock.

We frequently visited a number of physicians in Oklahoma City. In the past, as we had driven along rural highway 152, Papa had always reminisced over the many funny stories from his days as a highline construction worker. He knew some bit of historical information about every house along the route, and I never grew tired of hearing his stories. Yet, the day came when, as we passed the houses and landmarks, he was silent.

"I don't believe I've ever been this way before," he said one day.

How right he was. Everything we had held so dear was fading quickly as the old, familiar things slipped through our fingers. Although his physicians tried every remedy they knew of, nothing seemed to help. All the money, love, and medicine in the world could not stop the thief from robbing Papa of his former self.

One evening in August of 2001, I came in from working in the yard and sat down to rest. Something was severely wrong with Papa, and he finally told me there was a man watching him from the corner of the room. The fear of his mind taking another detour was overshadowed by the dreadful spiritual aspect of what he had just said. I convinced him to go to the hospital, and following hours of testing, Dr. Ahmad reported having discovered a small to moderate sized but inoperable brain bleed. My greatest fear was suddenly a reality; and for the next several days, we sat in the hospital, hoping and praying his mind would heal. I felt like I was in a vast wilderness – completely disconnected from the rest of the world. As our nation reeled from the September

11, 2001 attacks, I held Papa's hand and watched him slip further and further into an abyss.

One day, I went to visit him and found him sitting alone in the patient lounge. It took him forever to recognize me; but suddenly, in a tone of desperation, he asked, "Where have you been?" My heart sank. I had only been gone for a few hours, and he did not remember me being there earlier. His hand shook as he tugged at the plastic table cloth on the dining table and asked me, "Did I make this?"

"No," I said patiently. "This is something they bought..."

"When did I make it?"

When my attempts to convince him that he had not made the tablecloth yielded no progress, I finally just agreed with him.

"Fifteen...sixteen...four...," he muttered as he counted the tiny squares then stared blankly into space. For a moment, it seemed like I was wandering aimlessly and hopelessly though some twilight zone. When I finally came to my senses and began looking for a doctor, I saw that we were all alone. The hospital wing was unusually quiet. Papa needed help, but I knew in my soul there was no help. A horrifying feeling took over as I ran aimlessly through the corridors. I eventually found a nurse, who called for Dr. Ahmad. Following another battery of tests, I learned that Papa had suffered a stroke. I remained at his bedside and watched the painful scene of him fighting the nurses and removing his feeding tube and IVs. Dr. Ahmad suggested a nursing home, but when I refused to consider it, he calmly said he would not discharge Papa until I came to my senses.

After much prayer, I reluctantly visited the Binger Nursing Home to discuss whether they could provide the care he needed and the attention I demanded. The decision to place Papa in the nursing home was the most difficult, agonizing one of my life. It was a cool, October afternoon when Dr. Ahmad discharged him from the hospital. Mom and I picked him up and noticed his mind was unusually clear that day, which made the entire ordeal all the more terrible. Drowning in guilt, I could hardly speak as we drove him back to Binger. He had literally trusted me with everything and had been totally dependent upon me. This man, who had shared his wisdom with me since I was a child, could no longer advise me what to do. For the first time in my life, I had made a life-altering decision and wondered whether it was right. I felt like I was committing the ultimate act of betrayal against my best friend and hero. As the grey suburban pulled in front of the nursing home, my heart raced. Unable to witness the heart-wrenching scene that was sure to follow, Mom rushed inside, leaving me to relay the news to Papa.

"No! No! No! No!" he pleaded as I helped him out of the car, "Not this!"

My jaw tightened as I desperately fought the worst moment of my life and held back a flood of tears. The agony in my soul was so deep that my body quivered. I quietly begged the Lord to provide an alternative, but the Holy Spirit spoke these words to my heart:

"I can do all things through Christ which strengtheneth me."[47]

The next morning, I returned to the nursing home and found Papa sitting alone near the lobby. I approached him with mixed emotions of hope and apprehension. When he saw me coming around the corner, he lit up and smiled.

"Sit down," he said anxiously. "I have to talk to you."

Miraculously, his mind was clear.

"I just want you to know that it's okay," he said, reaching across the table and taking my hand in his. "We've fought this thing with all we had. You have kept your promise and have been with me the entire way. From now on, we'll take it one day at a time. This is where I need to be for now."

I sincerely believe that God lifted the veil clouding Papa's mind and allowed us to talk freely that day. It was our last real conversation and remains a treasure in the archives of my memory.

I felt sure that having a loved one in the nursing home was worse than their death. Nursing homes, with their depressing smells, sights, and sounds, are for those whose lives have exceeded the expiration date. Though Mom and I hung pictures on the walls of Papa's room, brought furniture from home, and set up bird feeders outside his window, every ounce of my soul was in turmoil. Depression and nightmares haunted me. Though he was still alive, it seemed that he was already gone. I wanted to mourn his death, but his body was still there. There were

[47] Philippians 4:13 (KJV)

occasional moments when he was clear-minded, and even when he appeared not to know me, I always saw a flicker of recognition in his eyes when he heard my voice, but his long-term memory was a thing of the past.

The worst and saddest moment came on my twenty-seventh birthday – February 28, 2002. I arrived in the morning and began the routine. The best present I could receive was just being there with Papa. I got out the card table and set a place for us to play a few hands of dominoes. I shuffled and set the dominoes up as he sat slumped in his chair, placed the double six in the center of the table, and waited for him to make the next move.

A few moments passed, and then he feebly stacked a randomly selected domino upright onto the double six and asked, "Is this how you play this game?"

I continued to play, hoping the pain of that scene would subside. For two hours, we stacked the dominoes in different formations. Bittersweet memories of the past came and went as I realized this final game was played out of love rather than competition and was a gift from the Lord.

Before spring arrived, Papa contracted pneumonia following an episode of aspiration and had to be hospitalized in the intensive care unit. He was unresponsive and his breathing shallow. Over the following three days, Mom, Dustin, and I never left his side. Brother Marty came by and lead us in prayer, John stopped by and sang a couple of hymns, and a few close friends showed up to offer their support. At 9:00 P.M. on April 11, 2002, I was alone by his side after Mom and Dustin had stepped out of the room. Papa moved a little, and I quickly stood up and attempted to talk to him. I felt a faint squeeze from his hand as two nurses rushed in. With their hands on my shoulders, I said my final goodbye and could almost feel the warmth of Heaven as the gates opened to receive my Papa. His battle was over at last. Tears filled my eyes as his spirit flew.

On Sunday, April 14, 2002, I sat beside Dustin on the front-row pew of the Binger Church of God. My cousin, Carolyn, accompanied John on the piano as he sang *I Know Who Holds Tomorrow*. "I don't know about tomorrow…it may bring me poverty…" As the strains rang in my ears, I somehow knew poverty would find me. A sobering reality settled over me, and I realized my battle was just beginning, but my faith comforted me when I heard how it would carry me through:

> "But the one who feeds the sparrow, is the one who stands by me. And the path that is my portion may be through the flame or flood; But His presence goes before me and I'm covered with His blood."

I watched as the pallbearers carried the flag-draped, hand-carved, oak casket to its final resting place. *Taps* was played, and Dustin and I were each presented with an American flag as the naval officer who knelt at our feet said, "On behalf of the President and a grateful Nation, I present to you this flag in honor of your Grandfather's service during World War II." From a nearby hilltop, John's brother, David, played *Amazing Grace* on the bagpipes as the casket was lowered into the ground. I alone remained behind until the grave was closed. As I walked up the sidewalk upon returning to the farm, I stopped in my tracks when I saw a single, red tulip standing tall in the flowerbed near the front of the house.

The hollow emptiness of Papa's passing waited until friends and family had returned to their lives to make its visitation. There was nothing to keep me company but the sounds of the old, creaking house and silence as I sat alone at the old domino table. I studied the scratches on the surface of the wood as voices from the past echoed in my head. Running my fingers along the indentions, I considered Papa's permanent imprint on my life and wondered whether the indentions that my life made on others ran as deep. I felt the brush of a half-opened card quietly touch the side of my hand. I removed the card from its envelope and read aloud:

"April 19, 2002

Dear Lance,

Please accept our condolences on your Guy's demise. Guy was a wonderful person who will be missed. May God give you and your family the courage to bear this irreparable loss. Please convey our heart-felt sympathies to the family.

Sincerely,
Iftikhar Ahmad, M.D."

I took a deep breath and laid my head upon the cool table as the Holy Spirit reminded me not to forget Him in whom my faith rested and comforted me with these words:

"I can do all things through Christ which strengtheneth me."[48]

---

[48] Philippians 4:13 (KJV)

CHAPTER 5

The Virtuous Woman

While strolling through an ancient olive grove during a second visit to the Mount of Olives, I caught a glimpse of a tiny vineyard, and the Holy Spirit brought this scripture to my mind:

> "I am the true vine, and my Father is the husbandman. Every branch in me that beareth not fruit he taketh away: and every branch that beareth fruit, he purgeth it, that it may bring forth more fruit. Now ye are clean through the word which I have spoken unto you. Abide in me, and I in you. As the branch cannot bear fruit of itself, except it abide in the vine; no more can ye, except ye abide in me. I am the vine, ye are the branches: He that abideth in me, and I in him, the same bringeth forth much fruit: for without me ye can do nothing. If a man abide not in me, he is cast forth as a branch, and is withered; and men gather them, and cast them into the fire, and they are burned. If ye abide in me, and my words abide in you, ye shall ask what ye will, and it shall be done unto you. Herein is my Father glorified, that ye bear much fruit; so shall ye be my disciples."[49]

The word *abide,* which appears seven times in this scripture, comes from the transliterated Greek verb, *meno,* which means, in reference

---

[49] John 15:1–8 (KJV)

to place, to sojourn, not to depart, or to continue to be present; in reference to time, to continue or endure; and in reference to state, to remain as one and not to become different. In the context of this scripture, *abide* literally refers to a state of *oneness* with Christ, just as a vine and its branches are one, and plainly reveals that *oneness with Him* is a condition precedent to fruitfulness; to being in a position to ask Christ for anything, knowing that He will provide it; and to remaining clean from sin. My maternal grandmother, whom we called Granny, exhibited perhaps one of the best examples of this manner of oneness with the Lord Jesus Christ and was, in my opinion, a personification of the virtuous woman depicted in the *Book of Proverbs*:

> "Who can find a virtuous woman? for her price is far above rubies. The heart of her husband doth safely trust in her, so that he shall have no need of spoil. She will do him good and not evil all the days of her life. She seeketh wool, and flax, and worketh willingly with her hands. She is like the merchants' ships; she bringeth her food from afar. She riseth also while it is yet night, and giveth meat to her household, and a portion to her maidens. She considereth a field, and buyeth it: with the fruit of her hands she planteth a vineyard. She girdeth her loins with strength, and strengtheneth her arms. She perceiveth that her merchandise is good: her candle goeth not out by night. She layeth her hands to the spindle, and her hands hold the distaff. She stretcheth out her hand to the poor; yea, she reacheth forth her hands to the needy. She is not afraid of the snow for her household: for all her household are clothed with scarlet. She maketh herself coverings of tapestry; her clothing is silk and purple. Her husband is known in the gates, when he sitteth among the elders of the land. She maketh fine linen, and selleth it; and delivereth girdles unto the merchant. Strength and honour are her clothing; and she shall rejoice in time to come. She openeth her mouth with wisdom; and

in her tongue is the law of kindness. She looketh well
to the ways of her household, and eateth not the bread
of idleness. Her children arise up, and call her blessed;
her husband also, and he praiseth her. Many daughters
have done virtuously, but thou excellest them all.
Favour is deceitful, and beauty is vain: but a woman
that feareth the LORD, she shall be praised. Give her
of the fruit of her hands; and let her own works praise
her in the gates."[50]

Granny was born in rural, eastern Oklahoma in February 1914. Her
father died shortly after she was born, and her mother soon remarried
an evil man who, among other things, threw Granny into a wall when
she was a toddler and raped her sister. I have always maintained that she
could have used her abusive childhood, as so many others have done,
as an excuse to lead a sinful life but chose instead to pursue an intimate
walk with the Lord. On Christmas Eve of 1930, Granny married
Lawrence "Elvis" McKee at the tender age of fifteen and moved to
Alden, a small farming community in western Oklahoma, where she
and her new husband farmed and raised cattle. Before they could have
children of their own, the wife and infant son of their close friend,
Charles Dietrich, died during childbirth. At the prompting of the
Holy Spirit, Granny and Elvis took and raised Charles' three children,
Kenneth, Joyce, and Ross, making a lifelong commitment which they
were not bound to make but one which reaped many rewards for years
to come. Later, Granny and Elvis had their own children, Joy Nell,
Lynda, and Rick. Though the burden of raising and providing for a
large family in the post-depression era was great, Granny did not cease
to practice Jesus' commandment to love:

"A new commandment I give unto you, That ye love
one another; as I have loved you, that ye also love one
another. By this shall all men know that ye are my
disciples, if ye have love one to another."[51]

---

[50] Proverbs 31:10-31 (KJV)
[51] John 13:34-35 (KJV)

In 1971, Elvis suffered a massive heart attack at the wheel of his pickup truck while he was working the wheat harvest in Laurence, Kansas and had a fatal wreck. Without batting an eyelid, Granny, with Mom's help, transitioned into the role of matriarch, assumed management of the family's farming operation, and kept it alive for many years thereafter so she could provide for her entire family.

For as long as I can remember, the family traditionally assembled at Granny's little white house in Carnegie, Oklahoma every Sunday afternoon for a meal and fellowship. Everyone was always welcome and forgiven in Granny's house, and she was the one who led the other believers in the family to extend love and forgiveness whenever there was any trouble. The dedication she exhibited toward those whom she loved, the manner in which she held her family together, and the way in which she interceded on our behalf in so many situations provided all of us with a glimpse of Christ.

Though she did not have a formal education, Granny was wise – one of the wisest women I have ever known – and she obtained that wisdom through her intimate walk with the Lord. She frequently drew upon the wisdom she had gained from Him to teach me and the rest of the family the Truths of God's Word and often referred to current events, family history, and politics as a springboard to the lesson. Practically all of her lessons were accompanied by the warning that, "Anybody can make an argument for just about anything they want by twisting the Scriptures, but one must have the Holy Spirit before they can understand the Word of God, and you must depend on Him to teach and interpret it for you." Granny's lessons on denominational doctrines, which she always imparted in accordance with specific scriptures, were invaluable to me in helping to shape my spiritual discernment, a skill that all Christians must have if they are to avoid being ensnared by the false teaching that is continuously working to lure the spiritually ignorant and undiscerning. Granny also had a way of teaching me how to listen for the wooing and leading of the Holy Spirit and how to distinguish it from other influences. I will never forget the day I told her I felt like the Lord was calling me into politics and disclosed my desire to run for the Oklahoma State House. Her reply was, "Are you sure it's the Lord talking to you and not the devil?"

Though my initial reaction was a defensive one, I pondered her question for many years and ultimately concluded that it had been posed by the Holy Spirit, working through Granny's words, and learned from that precious experience that the first response to the Truth is often anger.

On the Memorial Day following Papa's death, Granny and I took our annual trip to the *Old Settler's Cemetery* in Alden, which is surrounded, as far as the eye can see, by prairie and velvety green fields and yields a picturesque view of the Wichita Mountains rising toward the sky on the southwestern horizon. Meadow larks sang praises to the Creator from amid the prairie's blanket of dainty, yellow wild flowers that rustled quietly in the gentle breeze as Granny and I walked to the family plot. The flowers were of particular interest to her that day, and she reminisced about how Elvis used to pick them for her.

"He used to say, 'here are some roses for you,' and hand me a bouquet of something he had picked, but he didn't know a rose from a weed," she said.

Granny was especially fond of flowers and roses in particular. When I was a child, I used to roll my spare change and take it to her good friend, James Hemming, who owned a local nursery. Mr. Hemming would then help me find a special rose bush for her and deliver and plant it, too. Whenever the blooms wilted and fell to the ground, her sadness was evident, but she would say, "They'll bloom again." I always thought this saying exemplified her faith in Christ's words that, "Verily, verily, I say unto you, Except a corn of wheat fall into the ground and die, it abideth alone: but if it die, it bringeth forth much fruit."[52]

When we reached the family plot, I positioned an old metal folding chair and helped Granny into it. As I weeded around the headstones and anchored flowers into the soil, she relived the past for a few minutes and then was silent for a long while.

"There's a storm coming," she finally said, breaking the peaceful serenity of the beautiful spring day.

I turned to look at the sky, expecting to see storm clouds in the distance.

"Well, Granny, there's not a cloud in sight," I replied.

[52] John 12:24 (KJV)

"I'm not talking about that kind of storm," she said and pointed to the empty plot beside her husband's grave. "There is where my body will be placed."

"Don't talk like that," I protested.

"Lance, listen to me..." she interrupted. "I haven't got long. My heart is failing...your mother gets mad when I talk about death and won't listen to me. She's my strongest child, but I fear my death is going to be hardest on her because she refuses to face it. You're the only one who can see to it that my wishes are carried out. It's something I'm asking you to bear."

Just a few short weeks after we shared that day together, I found myself at St. Anthony's Hospital in Oklahoma City yet again as Granny was being prepped for emergency surgery. She had been admitted to the hospital during Papa's final days, but the Lord was merciful to us then. Now, a blood clot had sloughed off her heart and traveled to her small intestine where it lodged and killed approximately two feet of it.

While at Granny's side, I received more devastating news when Mom Tiger called to tell me that my good friend and fraternity brother, Kyle Aebi, was dead. Strangely, he had lost control of a truck that was loaded with wheat and had a fatal accident while working a summer job in the wheat harvest. The similarities between his and grandfather McKee's deaths were striking. Twenty-two years old, and a junior at Oklahoma State University, Kyle was in the prime of his life. He was a Christian and had a reputation for greeting everyone with a handshake and smile. We shared a common bond in that Mom Tiger had drafted both of us to be her assistants. I wondered why God had allowed such a tragedy to befall him while the drug addict, the thief, and the wicked seemed to prosper. I had no idea that the Lord would someday use the work of my ministry to answer this very question in a personal way.

As we were laying Kyle's body to rest, Granny's condition began to deteriorate rapidly. Although she came through surgery without incident and improved somewhat thereafter, her recovery stalled. One afternoon, while Mom and I were visiting her in the hospital, Mom left the room for a few minutes, leaving us alone to talk. When I began to discuss my political aspirations once again and outlined my plans for the future, she abruptly interrupted me and said, "Lance, while we're alone, I need to tell you something that I've never shared with a living soul."

The anticipation of her coming revelation made me uneasy.

"When your parents got married, we had our concerns; and our fears were realized when it looked as if your mother would never be able to have children. This fear continued for several years. Your mother confided in me many times, and I begged the Lord, day after day, to allow her to have children. Finally, He spoke to me one afternoon and let me know that He had heard my prayers and that your mother would have children. He also told me that her children would seek Him and that her firstborn would proclaim His name. Less than a year later, you were born. Regardless of whether you ever serve in public office, always remember that politics is a small part of our lives. 'Whereas ye know not what shall be on the morrow: for what is your life? It is even a vapour, that appeareth for a little time, and then vanisheth away.'[53] Life goes by quickly, and the hope and the life that we have in Jesus Christ is ALL we have at the end of the day."

I listened intently as she quoted scripture from memory and finally knew the reason why, from the day I had spoken my first word, she had told everyone that I would someday be a pastor. I used to get so aggravated with her for saying that! A few days later, in the presence of several family members, Granny asked Mom to fetch her purse. With weak hands, she slowly pulled it open and retrieved a tightly folded piece of paper, handed it to Mom, and instructed her to give it to me.

"He'll know what to do with it," she said.

"What is it?" I asked.

Tears filled my eyes when I unfolded the piece of paper and saw that it was her endorsed pension check – in the amount of thirty-three dollars. For the second time in my life, one of my grandparents had given me everything. I felt embarrassment, sadness, humility, shame, honor, and pride all at the same time.

"Granny, I can't...," I attempted to speak as I choked back tears but could not find the right words.

"You'll know what to do with it," she replied, looking at me as if we were the only two people in the room.

---

[53] James 4:14 (KJV)

At noon on June 27, 2002, with Mom holding her right hand, I tightly to her left, and the rest of the family surrounding her bed, we told her we loved her, she nodded slightly, and then peacefully went to be with the Lord.

The dreadful, terrible sound of metal pulleys rang in my ears as Granny's casket was lowered into the ground, but the wonderful words of *His Eye is on the Sparrow* and *Roses Will Bloom Again* lifted my spirit as I fastened my eyes on the yellow wildflowers which had blossomed into a thick carpet since Granny and I last visited the cemetery. After the grave had been closed, I drove away from the peaceful prairie and back to Granny's house where I discovered something so sorrowful that it rivaled the grief of her passing.

When I walked into the guest bedroom to retrieve extra chairs for the guests, I noticed someone had tampered with the antique door leading to the basement. Since I was the only one Granny allowed down there, I decided to investigate. After making my way down the rickety, narrow staircase, I pulled the low hanging cord attached to the light switch and scanned the room. Suspicion raced through my mind since some of my cousins had been "too grief-stricken to attend the graveside service." Just as I was beginning to feel guilty for suspecting them of something, the light revealed fresh handprints in the dust that had been collecting for years. Before Granny had even been laid to rest, someone had combed her house, looking for something to steal. Overwhelmed by the scene, I just sat down on the arm of a ragged sofa and glared in disbelief at the overturned mason jars and smudged handprints. Tears began to roll down my cheeks for the first time since Granny's passing. In the cool, musty silence, I struggled with the realization that my cousins seemed to have missed the point of Granny's role in our lives and all of the great Truths which the Lord desired for the family to learn from her presence. How tragic it was that they had overlooked the real treasure.

There was a marked contrast between my two visits to the Mount of Olives. During the first, I was given a sobering reminder that, for those who have not believed in Jesus Christ, death is an eternal separation. During the second, I learned that, for the believer, death is one of the methods used of the Lord to prepare him for the richest fruitfulness because the Word of God declares that, "…but we glory in tribulations also: knowing that tribulation worketh patience; And patience, experience; and experience, hope: And hope maketh not ashamed; because the love of God is shed abroad in our hearts by the Holy Ghost which is given unto us."[54] Furthermore, of patience, God's Word testifies that it produces godliness, brotherly kindness, and love,[55] and declares that, "…if these things be in you, and abound, they make you that ye shall neither be barren nor unfruitful in the knowledge of our Lord Jesus Christ."[56]

One of the statements Jesus made concerning the believer's fruitfulness was, "…every branch that beareth fruit, he purgeth it, that it may bring forth more fruit."[57] The word *purgeth* comes from the transliterated Greek verb, *kathairo*. One of the meanings of *kathairo* is to prune, which is the act of trimming a vine in the interests of promoting its growth and fruitfulness. Though I could never have fully understood the rapid succession of Grandma, Papa, Kyle, and Granny's deaths at the time of their occurrence, the Lord has since revealed to me that their passing effectually promoted my oneness with Christ and pruned me a little closer to reaching my full potential in Him.

---

[54] Romans 5:3–5 (KJV)
[55] 2 Peter 1:6–7 (KJV)
[56] 2 Peter 1:8 (KJV)
[57] John 15:2 (KJV)

CHAPTER 6

The Family

George, a friend and associate of Tony's, and one of the most highly respected and sought-after experts on the city of Jerusalem, took John, Christopher, and me to see many of the sites in and around the Old City, including the Temple Mount, the Church of the Holy Sepulchre, and the Last Supper Room, which is located on Mount Zion just outside the walls of the Old City. Also known as the Cenacle, the Last Supper Room is traditionally believed to stand on or near the actual site of the Last Supper. According to George, one of the reasons for this belief is a marble column in the room, upon which is sculpted a peculiar scene. Chiseled into the capital of this column is a group of three pelicans – a mother bird with one young bird standing on each side of her. The young birds are eating their mother's flesh and drinking her blood. Because pelicans are known to sacrifice themselves for their young by tearing flesh from their own bodies and feeding it to them, this carving is symbolic of Jesus' sacrifice and thus material to the belief that the Last Supper Room stands on or near the actual site of the Last Supper. As I stood at the foot of the marble column, considering the mother pelican's sacrifice, I remembered Jesus' words at Capernaum:

> "Then Jesus said unto them, Verily, verily, I say unto you, Except ye eat the flesh of the Son of man, and drink his blood, ye have no life in you. Whoso eateth my flesh, and drinketh my blood, hath eternal life; and I will raise him up at the last day. For my flesh is meat indeed, and my blood is drink indeed. He that eateth

my flesh, and drinketh my blood, dwelleth in me, and
I in him."[58]

When a man partakes of the flesh and blood of Jesus Christ, that
is, accepts Jesus' sacrifice for the remission of his sins, he attains eternal
life, oneness with Christ, and becomes a royal member of the family
of God – a truth that is woven throughout the Scriptures but concisely
stated in the Gospel according to John:

> "But as many as received him, to them gave he power
> to become the sons of God, even to them that believe
> on his name: Which were born, not of blood, nor of the
> will of the flesh, nor of the will of man, but of God."[59]

They who have partaken of and received Christ have been
commanded to remember the breaking of Jesus' body through the
taking and eating of bread and the shedding of His blood through the
taking and drinking of the cup – a commandment given by Christ
Himself at the Last Supper. There, the Lord took bread, blessed and
brake it, and said to His disciples, "...Take, eat; this is my body."[60] He
then took the cup, gave thanks, and passed it to His disciples, saying,
"...Drink ye all of it; For this is my blood of the new testament, which
is shed for many for the remission of sins."[61] By these words, Christ
affirmed that He is the sacrificial Lamb of God, that His body and blood
are the New Covenant, and that His death, burial, and resurrection are
the most important events in the history of creation.

The practice of remembering Jesus' sacrifice for those who have
accepted it is commonly referred to as communion. The purpose of
communion is to allow the child of God to privately reflect on Christ's
sacrifice and commune with Him while publicly proclaiming His death
until He returns:

---

[58] John 6:53–56 (KJV)
[59] John 1:12–13 (KJV)
[60] Matthew 26:26 (KJV)
[61] Matthew 26:27–28 (KJV)

"For I have received of the Lord that which also I delivered unto you, that the Lord Jesus the same night in which he was betrayed took bread: And when he had given thanks, he brake it, and said, Take, eat: this is my body, which is broken for you: this do in remembrance of me. After the same manner also he took the cup, when he had supped, saying, this cup is the new testament in my blood: this do ye, as oft as ye drink it, in remembrance of me. For as often as ye eat this bread, and drink this cup, ye do shew the Lord's death till he come."[62]

Being privy to this purpose, it is imperative that the child of God participate in communion with a right heart and keep it free of error. If error enters the equation, the result will be similar to the spectacle of that early communion at the Corinthian Church, wherein drunkenness, division, and contention conspired to defeat its entire purpose by making a mockery of Christ's sacrifice rather than showing it forth to the world in splendor.

Most of the error associated with communion is the result of widespread ignorance of the Word of God, which has made it possible for Satan to inject misunderstanding and confusion, primarily through tradition and erroneous denominational doctrines, to the intent of making the remembrance of Christ's sacrifice empty and meaningless to the believer and a repugnant spectacle to the world.

As touching that misunderstanding and confusion which has gone forth through tradition, here are a few examples: some church congregations prohibit anyone other than their own members from participating in communion; some allow believers who are living in open, unrepentant sin and even non-believers to partake in it; and others indulge in prohibiting their own members from participating for various, inappropriate reasons.

As touching that misunderstanding and confusion which has spread abroad through erroneous denominational doctrines, here are three such doctrines. First is the doctrine of transubstantiation, a

---

[62] 1 Corinthians 11:23-26 (KJV)

Roman Catholic belief that the bread and wine of communion are transformed into the literal body and blood of Christ by certain words and gestures of a priest.[63] The practice of this doctrine was aptly characterized by Anglican priest, John Tillotson, who wrote in 1694, "In all probability those common juggling words of 'hocus pocus' are nothing else but a corruption of the 'hoc est corpus' by way of ridiculous imitation of the priests of the Church of Rome in their trick of transubstantiation."[64]

Another is the doctrine is consubstantiation, the quasi-magical belief in the actual, substantial presence and combination of the body and blood of Christ with the bread and wine of communion. A third is the teaching that salvation is contingent upon communion – a philosophy that substitutes works for the sacrifice of Christ and denies Him altogether.

To be effective for the believer in Christ and before the world, communion must be observed in Truth, in the manner prescribed by the Word of God, and with a pure, reverent heart. Therefore, prior to dining at the Lord's Table, we must allow the Holy Spirit to remove the bacteria of sin, misunderstanding, confusion, tradition, and error from our minds and hearts by the spiritual washing of God's Word, just as we would physically wash our hands prior to eating. After we have been thoroughly cleansed by the Word of Truth, we are in a position to show forth the Lord's death to the world while reflecting on His sacrifice through the complete, five-dimensional experience that was intended by the Holy Spirit and described by the Apostle Paul in the eleventh chapter of *1 Corinthians*:

> "Now in this that I declare unto you I praise you not, that ye come together not for the better, but for the worse. For first of all, when ye come together in the church, I hear that there be divisions among you; and I partly believe it. For there must be also heresies

---

[63] Steven Otfinoski, *Roman Catholicism* (Tarrytown, New York: Marshall Cavendish Benchmark, 2007), 62-63.

[64] John Tillotson, *A Discourse Against Transubstantiation,* New Edition (London: Gilbert & Rivington, 1833), 35.

among you, that they which are approved may be made manifest among you. When ye come together therefore into one place, this is not to eat the Lord's supper. For in eating every one taketh before other his own supper: and one is hungry, and another is drunken. What? have ye not houses to eat and to drink in? or despise ye the church of God, and shame them that have not? what shall I say to you? shall I praise you in this? I praise you not. For I have received of the Lord that which also I delivered unto you, that the Lord Jesus the same night in which he was betrayed took bread: And when he had given thanks, he brake it, and said, Take, eat: this is my body, which is broken for you: this do in remembrance of me. After the same manner also he took the cup, when he had supped, saying, this cup is the new testament in my blood: this do ye, as oft as ye drink it, in remembrance of me. For as often as ye eat this bread, and drink this cup, ye do shew the Lord's death till he come. Wherefore whosoever shall eat this bread, and drink this cup of the Lord, unworthily, shall be guilty of the body and blood of the Lord. But let a man examine himself, and so let him eat of that bread, and drink of that cup. For he that eateth and drinketh unworthily, eateth and drinketh damnation to himself, not discerning the Lord's body. For this cause many are weak and sickly among you, and many sleep. For if we would judge ourselves, we should not be judged. But when we are judged, we are chastened of the Lord, that we should not be condemned with the world. Wherefore, my brethren, when ye come together to eat, tarry one for another. And if any man hunger, let him eat at home; that ye come not together unto condemnation. And the rest will I set in order when I come."[65]

---

[65] 1 Corinthians 11:17-34 (KJV)

1 Corinthians 11:17-34 (KJV) emphasizes the five-dimensional communion experience in this regard:

- <u>First</u>, we are directed to look back in <u>verse 23</u>. By doing this, we can <u>hear</u> the hammer driving the nails into the sacrifice of grace. (*"For I have received of the Lord that which also I delivered unto you, that the Lord Jesus the same night in which he was betrayed took bread..."*)

- <u>Second</u>, in <u>verse 25</u>, Paul directs us to the present day, which allows us to <u>smell</u> the fragrance of Jesus as our High Priest and Lord of our lives since Jesus is presently at the Father's right hand, interceding on our behalf. (*"After the same manner also he took the cup, when he had supped, saying, this cup is the new testament in my blood: this do ye, as oft as ye drink it, in remembrance of me."*)

- <u>Third</u>, in <u>verse 26</u>, Paul directs us to the future. By being obedient to this this command, we eagerly anticipate the <u>sight</u> of God unveiled in all of His glory. (*"For as often as ye eat this bread, and drink this cup, ye do shew the Lord's death till he come."*)

- <u>Fourth</u>, in <u>verse 27</u>, we are instructed to look inwardly and consider our spiritual condition. Doing so will allow us to <u>feel</u> God's love through a conscious awareness of our personal relationship with the Lord. (*"Wherefore whosoever shall eat this bread, and drink this cup of the Lord, unworthily, shall be guilty of the body and blood of the Lord."*)

- <u>Finally</u>, in <u>verse 33</u>, Paul tells us to look around at others. This enables us to <u>taste</u> the sweetness of life by sharing, as a family, the Mercy and Grace of our Savior. (*"Wherefore, my brethren, when ye come together to eat, tarry one for another."*)

Shortly after the Holy Spirit grafted me into the family of God at the age of eleven, my local church prohibited me from partaking in communion because certain elders within the congregation adhered to the traditional belief that I should join that particular church prior to being allowed to participate. The misguided opinions of these well-meaning neophytes and their attempts to transform me into who they thought I should be, rather than allowing the Holy Spirit to mold me in

Christ's image, caused me a great deal of spiritual pain and even led me to despise, for a time, events like the Lord's Supper because I was made to feel like an outsider. It was not until the Holy Spirit gave me greater understanding of the Word of God that I understood I was worthy to participate in communion from the very moment that I spiritually partook of the flesh and blood of Jesus Christ and became one with Him.

I made the eternal decision to accept Him on a humid, summer evening in 1986 at *Cedar Hills Youth Camp* in western Oklahoma. *Cedar Hills*, as its name implies, is nestled among a thicket of red cedar trees and neatly tucked away in the rolling hills of Caddo County. Worship services were held at the camp each evening inside the open tabernacle atop the highest hill at the center of the campground. Situated to harness the wind as a natural air-conditioner, the tabernacle always reminded me of David's threshing floor at the summit of Mount Moriah. On the evening of June 22, 1986, the sermon was delivered by Brother Phil Ratliff, a man whom I did not know at the time but who would later play a major role in my life. Sandwiched in between friends in the middle of a pew at the rear of the tabernacle, and surrounded by distracting chatter, I focused, with great interest, on the topic of Brother Phil's sermon, listening closely as he expounded upon Jesus' conversation with Nicodemus in the third chapter of the Gospel according to John. A great burden stirred within me as the Word of Truth fell upon my ears. After hearing Jesus' words to Nicodemus, I knew that I must be born again, as Jesus said, to find peace with God and avoid the flames of Hell. Thus, when the invitation went forth to come forward and accept Christ as Savior, as it did each evening, I was suddenly prompted by the Holy Spirit to make a life-altering decision. Amid the strains of *Ye Must Be Born Again*, the hot, humid air faded into a cool, refreshing breeze; and I, while picturing myself seated in the company of Jesus and Nicodemus, listening to the Lord compare the Spirit to the wind, was quietly separated by the Spirit's breeze as it wooed and convicted me to go forward. When I started to stand, a battle began to rage in my mind as fears of what my friends may think of me crafted a number of reasons to remain seated.

"They'll laugh at you…," I thought, "…and think you're a sissy… and, they won't treat you the same anymore…you're just going to make a fool of yourself when everyone sees that you believe in a fairytale!"

The pestering thoughts, however, were no match for Jesus' words; and so I stood to my feet and stared at the friends who were seated to my right – unable to speak and waiting for them to just get out of my way.

"I'll knock the whole row down if I have to," I thought, "But, I'm going to Jesus..."

Upon seeing my determination when I made eye contact with them, they promptly moved aside; and I quickly made my way to the front, along with several others, and gathered with them at the foot of the stage. As the final verse of *Ye Must Be Born Again* drew to a close, Brother Phil stepped down from the pulpit, and silence fell upon the tabernacle. For some reason, he placed his hand upon my shoulder and proceeded to lead the group in prayer before asking the counselors to come forward.

Bobby Pain, a high school student who was serving as a sponsor for my church's group, immediately left his seat and walked down the aisle toward me. I do not recall whether Bobby was a star athlete or whether he was popular among the student body. What I remember about him is that he led me to the east side of the tabernacle and knelt with me in prayer under a blackjack oak tree. As the wind rustled its leaves, Bobby told me to tell Jesus Christ through prayer and faith that I realized and believed I was a sinner who needed Him, that He was God's one and only Son who came to Earth, was born of a virgin, died on the Cross for my sins, and rose again on the third day according to the Scriptures. He then held my hand and prayed alongside me as I silently admitted those things through prayer and asked Jesus to forgive me of my sins and be my Lord and Savior. To this day, I have not forgotten the words I sent to Heaven.

The Holy Spirit clearly used Jesus' discourse with Nicodemus to convict me of my need for a Savior; and, in the many years that have passed since that humid June evening in 1986, I have concluded that Jesus' words to Nicodemus are some of the most important words in the Scriptures:

> "Now when he was in Jerusalem at the passover, in the feast day, many believed in his name, when they saw the miracles which he did. But Jesus did not commit himself unto them, because he knew all men, And

needed not that any should testify of man: for he knew what was in man. There was a man of the Pharisees, named Nicodemus, a ruler of the Jews: The same came to Jesus by night, and said unto him, Rabbi, we know that thou art a teacher come from God: for no man can do these miracles that thou doest, except God be with him. Jesus answered and said unto him, Verily, verily, I say unto thee, Except a man be born again, he cannot see the kingdom of God. Nicodemus saith unto him, How can a man be born when he is old? can he enter the second time into his mother's womb, and be born? Jesus answered, Verily, verily, I say unto thee, Except a man be born of water and of the Spirit, he cannot enter into the kingdom of God. That which is born of the flesh is flesh; and that which is born of the Spirit is spirit. Marvel not that I said unto thee, Ye must be born again. The wind bloweth where it listeth, and thou hearest the sound thereof, but canst not tell whence it cometh, and whither it goeth: so is every one that is born of the Spirit. Nicodemus answered and said unto him, How can these things be? Jesus answered and said unto him, Art thou a master of Israel, and knowest not these things? Verily, verily, I say unto thee, We speak that we do know, and testify that we have seen; and ye receive not our witness. If I have told you earthly things, and ye believe not, how shall ye believe, if I tell you of heavenly things? And no man hath ascended up to heaven, but he that came down from heaven, even the Son of man which is in heaven. And as Moses lifted up the serpent in the wilderness, even so must the Son of man be lifted up: That whosoever believeth in him should not perish, but have eternal life. For God so loved the world, that he gave his only begotten Son, that whosoever believeth in him should not perish, but have everlasting life. For God sent not his Son into the world to condemn the world; but that the world through him might be saved. He that believeth on him is not condemned: but he that believeth not is condemned already, because he hath not believed in the name of the only begotten Son of God. And this is the condemnation, that light is come into the world, and men loved darkness rather than light, because their deeds were evil. For every one that doeth evil hateth the light, neither cometh to the light, lest his deeds should be reproved. But he that doeth truth cometh to the light, that his deeds may be made manifest, that they are wrought in God."[66]

For reasons I did not fully understand back then, Nicodemus' quest for the Truth and determination to meet Jesus personally fascinated me, especially in light of his background and who he was. At the time of his personal encounter with Christ, Nicodemus was, religiously and spiritually, a Pharisee. The Pharisees were the most influential of Judaism's societies at the time of Christ[67] and known for defending the Jewish way of life against foreign influences.[68] The origin of this strict, legalistic sect is unclear but is believed to have grown out of the Maccabean Revolt, even though a group of Jews resembling the Pharisees can be traced back to the Babylonian captivity.[69] Politically, Nicodemus was a ruler of the Jews and a member of the *Sanhedrin*, the ruling council that probably originated with Moses' father-in-law's (Jethro) suggestion to Moses that he appoint "able men"[70] from among all the people to assume the responsibility of judging certain matters.[71] Professionally, Nicodemus was a teacher, as indicated by Jesus' reference to him as a "master of Israel."[72] The word *master* comes

---

[66] John 2:23 – 3:21 (KJV)

[67] T. Alton Bryant, *Zondervan's Compact Bible Dictionary* (Grand Rapids, Michigan: Zondervan, 1999), 453.

[68] J. Vernon McGee, *Notes & Outlines: Matthew* (Pasadena, California: Thru the Bible Radio Network, 2010), 7.

[69] T. Alton Bryant, *Zondervan's Compact Bible Dictionary* (Grand Rapids, Michigan: Zondervan, 1999), 453.

[70] Exodus 18:21 (KJV)

[71] Exodus 18:22 (KJV)

[72] John 3:10 (KJV)

from the Greek noun, *didaskalos*, which means teacher. As a teacher, Nicodemus was probably one of the most educated men of his time concerning the Mosaic Law; and, as a scholar of the Old Testament, he likely remembered Malachi's prophecy when he saw or heard that Jesus had cleansed the Temple:

> "Behold, I will send my messenger, and he shall prepare the way before me: and the LORD, whom ye seek, shall suddenly come to his temple, even the messenger of the covenant, whom ye delight in: behold, he shall come, saith the LORD of hosts. But who may abide the day of his coming? and who shall stand when he appeareth? for he is like a refiner's fire, and like fullers' soap: And he shall sit as a refiner and purifier of silver: and he shall purify the sons of Levi, and purge them as gold and silver, that they may offer unto the LORD an offering in righteousness. Then shall the offering of Judah and Jerusalem be pleasant unto the LORD, as in the days of old, and as in former years."[73]

At the time of Nicodemus' personal meeting with Christ, John the Baptist had been proclaiming throughout the land that Jesus was the Promised One, and Nicodemus obviously had questions. I believe he sought an audience with Jesus at night, not because he feared being seen with Him, but because he wanted a private, one-on-one meeting wherein he could learn the Truth. Though the Gospel according to John reveals that he knew Jesus had come from God, it also shows us that he did not immediately recognize Jesus as the Son of God. This is evidenced by his statement that, "...Rabbi, we know that thou art a teacher come from God: for no man can do these miracles that thou doest, except God be with him."[74] Without flattery, political correctness, or human reasoning, Jesus immediately addressed the heart of Nicodemus' reason for wanting to meet Him personally and disclosed the Truth which Nicodemus sought when He pointedly declared, "...

---

[73] Malachi 3:1-4 (KJV)
[74] John 3:2 (KJV)

Verily, verily, I say unto thee, Except a man be born of water and of the Spirit, he cannot enter into the kingdom of God."[75]

These words implicated the Lord's proclamation through the Prophet, *Ezekiel,* that His people would be restored by water:

> "Then will I sprinkle clean water upon you, and ye shall be clean: from all your filthiness, and from all your idols, will I cleanse you. A new heart also will I give you, and a new spirit will I put within you: and I will take away the stony heart out of your flesh, and I will give you an heart of flesh. And I will put my spirit within you, and cause you to walk in my statutes, and ye shall keep my judgments, and do them."[76]

Water is representative of the Word of God and symbolic of its cleansing power, a Truth recorded in the Gospel according to John:

> "Now ye are clean through the word which I have spoken unto you."[77]

And, in Paul's epistle to the Ephesians:

> "Husbands, love your wives, even as Christ also loved the church, and gave himself for it; That he might sanctify and cleanse it with the washing of water by the word, That he might present it to himself a glorious church, not having spot, or wrinkle, or any such thing; but that it should be holy and without blemish."[78]

The Word of God is essential to being born again:

> "Seeing ye have purified your souls in obeying the truth through the Spirit unto unfeigned love of the

---

[75] John 3:5 (KJV)
[76] Ezekiel 36:25-27 (KJV)
[77] John 15:3 (KJV)
[78] Ephesians 5:25-27 (KJV)

brethren, see that ye love one another with a pure heart fervently: Being born again, not of corruptible seed, but of incorruptible, by the word of God, which liveth and abideth for ever."[79]

And, the Word of God is Jesus Christ:

"In the beginning was the Word, and the Word was with God, and the Word was God. The same was in the beginning with God. All things were made by him; and without him was not any thing made that was made. In him was life; and the life was the light of men."[80]

When Adam and Eve transgressed in the Garden of Eden, sin and death entered and passed upon the entire human race and separated humanity from God. Since man is both a physical and spiritual being, both his physical body and spirit are under a death sentence from the time of his birth. When the body finally wears out or is compromised by illness or injury, physical death occurs. The spirit, however, which was created to be eternal, lives on. After the body dies, the spirit leaves and either returns to God or is cast into Hell for all eternity, depending upon whether the individual accepted or rejected Christ during his physical life. From cover to cover, the Word of God reveals in no uncertain terms that the sacrifice of Jesus Christ's body and blood is the only atonement for the sins of mankind and the only way one's spirit can be saved from eternal damnation.

"Verily, verily, I say unto thee, Except a man be born of water and of the Spirit, he cannot enter into the kingdom of God." This, Jesus' declaration to Nicodemus, is THE message for the ages and to anyone who has not accepted the Lord Jesus Christ. If you have not accepted Him, know this: He wants to reconcile you to God; to graft you into His royal family; to have a personal relationship with you; and to dine, commune, and fellowship with you at His table. Christianity is not a religion, an ideology, or a philosophy. It is a personal relationship with

---

[79] 1 Peter 1:22-23 (KJV)
[80] John 1:1-4 (KJV)

Jesus Christ. Being born again is not a ceremony or ritual. It is a real transaction by which the sinner is released from the death sentence upon his spirit and placed into the body of Christ. If you will accept, for the remission of your sins, the sacrifice of Jesus' body and blood, which He made upon the cross, He will cleanse you from your sins and remember them no more, just as He cleansed Nicodemus and me. The invitation to be born again is open to everyone:

> "And as Moses lifted up the serpent in the wilderness, even so must the Son of man be lifted up: That whosoever believeth in him should not perish, but have eternal life. For God so loved the world, that he gave his only begotten Son, that whosoever believeth in him should not perish, but have everlasting life. For God sent not his Son into the world to condemn the world; but that the world through him might be saved. He that believeth on him is not condemned: but he that believeth not is condemned already, because he hath not believed in the name of the only begotten Son of God."[81]

This is what you must do to be born again and receive God's free gift of salvation. First, you must believe in your heart that Jesus Christ is the one and only begotten Son of God, who died on the cross for your sins, was buried, and rose again on the third day according to the Scriptures. Second, you must pray a sincere, trusting prayer to Christ in faith, admitting that you are a sinner, confessing and asking Him to forgive you of your sins, and asking Him to come into your heart and be Lord of your life. You do not need the permission or vote of any man or organization to be saved, and nobody can exercise any power over whether you enter the Kingdom of Heaven except you. The gift of eternal life is yours for the taking. Jesus Christ has already paid the price of your sin and desires to welcome you into His family. God has given you the free will to accept or reject His Son. Will you accept Christ? Nobody can accept Him for you. You must do it yourself.

---

[81] John 3:14–18 (KJV)

CHAPTER 7

The Prodigal Son

Prior to leaving for Israel, I repeatedly asked the Holy Spirit to guide me to the sites that He wanted me to see; and, after giving Tony a map on which I had marked several of these, he asked, "Why these places?"

"Because I'm curious," I replied.

"Only someone who has studied the Scriptures would even know they exist," he said.

"Well," I replied again, "I *have* studied the Scriptures, and the Holy Spirit has laid these locations on my heart…"

Willing to accommodate my prayers and the Lord's answer to them, Tony patiently escorted us to all the accessible sites I had asked to see and more, including a small orphanage on the outskirts of Jerusalem, which he and some other Christians were subsidizing. It was here that the Holy Spirit gave me a glimpse into one of the many dimensions of God the Father's unconditional love.

With adulation fit for celebrities, a mass of orphaned children overwhelmed John, Christopher, and me with affection as we exited the van in the orphanage parking lot. Greetings, followed by questions in Arabic and English, filled the air as they eagerly strained their tiny bodies to hug us and competed with each other to shake our hands. On the heels of Tony's grand introduction, as Christopher and I followed the house dad up a flight of stairs for a guided tour, I suddenly heard a crescendo of voices and, turning back toward the courtyard, saw John standing at the bottom of the stairs, towering above the thronging children, all of whom were excitedly reaching for him and shouting.

"Hello little children," he said and waved his hand over the heads of his new fan club, which had mistaken the large man for an ex–football player from the United States.

"Should we rescue Mr. John?" the house dad inquired. "He has not been around children much, no?"

"No," I replied. "But, he's an attorney and likes the attention. He'll be fine."

We continued up the stairs to the second floor, where the house dad commenced with the tour, beginning with a very modest laundry and dining room. We then proceeded down the hall to the living quarters, where posters of American athletes adorned the walls of the dorm-like bedrooms. From NFL and college football players to basketball pros and golfing legends, just about every famous player known to sports was represented. The most cherished possessions and behavior of these young orphans attested to their dreams of someday meeting a celebrity athlete. As we meandered through the second level and into one of the bedrooms, I casually walked to an open window and peered into the courtyard below.

"Hey!" I hollered, "There's a redhead!"

John and Christopher followed me to the window and looked out.

"He is like you," the house dad said, as we looked down upon the redheaded kid who was sweeping the courtyard. The young boy, who appeared to be about twelve years old and looked somewhat out of place among his dark-haired peers, looked up when he heard our voices.

"Who is he?" I asked.

"His name is Saif," the house dad replied. "He came from a Muslim home; after his brother was stricken with a bad disease when they were young, his father left…his mother was not able to raise two children on her own, so she sent him here."

I looked down upon the redheaded boy from the second story window with a strong desire to shelter him from the awful realities of the world and wondered whether he would ever find Christ. While considering all of the ways in which I might be able to help him, I even wondered whether it would be possible to adopt him. Enabled by the Holy Spirit, I recognized that, as a child of God, my desire to protect this young boy whom I did not even know was a reflection of God the

Father's desire toward anyone who is not His child to find protection in His perfect, unconditional love through Christ. The Holy Spirit also used my compulsion to shelter Saif from the world to give me a glimpse of how the Lord had desired to shelter me when my political aspirations roared back to life in 2002.

After my law school career ended, I found myself gazing into the far country, first contemplating, and then deciding to run for the United States Congress. Having previously seen the nature of the Republican Party while running for the State House, I figured I would just switch parties and run as a Democrat. After suggesting to Dustin, John, and my cousin, Josh Kohen, that we might just find a pot of gold in the process, they all agreed to help me get my campaign off the ground so we rented an office and got to work. Before long, we had compiled a list of names for just about every need and assembled some exceptionally-well-networked advisors, not the least of which was my cousin, Kenneth McKee.

Every family has at least one colorful character, and Kenneth played that role well within our family. After a stint in the Army and Navy, he joined the police department in Fayetteville, Arkansas and then became an Arkansas state trooper under Francis Cherry's governorship. Later, he provided personal security for Governor Orval Faubus' and was appointed director of the Arkansas Highway Patrol by Governor Winthrop Rockefeller. He also served as Rockefeller's personal aide, a position in which he negotiated halts to violent civil rights disputes and helped bring an end to widespread illegal gambling. Having spent years in influential circles, Kenneth was a friend to a whole lot of important people, including, as he was fond of telling us, every president from J.F.K. to Bill Clinton, and he often regaled us with the tales of his fantastic experiences with these friends, including how he came to know President Clinton, how he had introduced President Clinton to Alice Walton, the daughter of Sam Walton, and his interrogation of Jack Ruby for the Rockefeller family. When I told Kenneth that I needed his help with my bid for Congress, he said he would be glad to help me; and one of the ways in which he attempted to was by introducing me to some of his important friends, two of whom were Betsey Wright and Tommy Cornwell.

I met Betsey and Tommy for the first time at the famous *Inn at the Mill* restaurant in Fayetteville, Arkansas, after Kenneth had asked me to drive out there for that specific purpose, and knew immediately that we would hit it off because I no sooner had exited my car in the *Inn at the Mill* parking lot when Betsey approached me, carrying two huge orchids, and said, "Here, help me take these inside!"

"This is how we're gonna pay for the meal," she said and began to detail the conversion of her basement into a greenhouse for the sake of growing orchids. With Dustin and Josh in tow, I followed her into the restaurant, where she passed the orchids to the hostess, and then cupped her hand over her mouth while looking back at us over her shoulder and confiding that the restaurant supplied the "perfect environment" for her meetings but she supplied the orchids. It was evident that Betsey knew her way around politics and no surprise that she had been Governor Bill Clinton's chief of staff, the deputy chair of his 1992 presidential campaign, and a past director of the Arkansas Democratic Party. As the meeting progressed, she cozied up to me with her charming wit and dry sense of humor as if we had been friends for many years.

After we were seated and Kenneth had applied a liberal dusting of salt to his tap water and designated our dining room an official smoking area, Betsey retrieved a notebook from her oversized handbag and tore out a few sheets. With a pencil, she drew two stick men with outstretched arms and touching hands, placed the drawing in front of me, and said I needed to meet the voters in my district at least three times – preferably at rallies or other public forums or through radio announcements and television ads.

"Connecting with your voters is as simple as telling them why the race is important to you and articulating why you want the job, but it must be done," she said, emphasizing that personal connections were always preferable to standing behind a podium.

"Another thing," she said, "is that you always need to present yourself as if you're running for the Presidency."

"Most people want to see their congressman in a suit," Tommy chimed in, backing her up, and hinting that a few tailored suits would do the trick. Tommy, a successful businessman and influential player in the national political scene whom Kenneth said was Hillary Clinton's cousin, advised me that he had passed my campaign materials along to the Clintons and suggested that they might be willing to host fundraisers for me if I could win the primary.

"You'll need a solid platform," Betsey continued. "Tell us some of your ideas…"

I began with what I believed to be the collective death of western Oklahoma's small towns and the decay of rural life. After giving a brief refresher on "Hoovervilles," President Hoover's shanty towns of the Great Depression, I unveiled a clever term for western Oklahoma's dying towns – "Lucasvilles." Everyone agreed that the term by which I hoped to convey what I believed to be sub-standard leadership by incumbent Congressman Frank Lucas, and my soon-to-be opponent, would stick.

I then segued into the subject of economic reform and argued, among other things, for the implementation of a commodity formula, which had been developed by my friend, Glenn Price, to curtail government meddling in the food supply chain. After impressing the table with Glenn's ideas, I turned my attention to educational reform, one of my cornerstone policies.

"Everyone who runs for public office…" I started, "…says that children and public education are near and dear to their hearts…but related government programs are typically the first to see budget cuts in hard times and the last to be funded in times of prosperity. Having grown up in a family of educators, I'm convinced that merit pay, tenure-based competition, and sacrificing regional learning to standardized testing are fruits of the poisonous tree…"

There was silence at the table. Whether it was due to my ignorance or the fact that I had been interrupted by the food's delivery, I guess I will never know.

"Those are some very good ideas," Betsey finally said, after consuming her first bite and dabbing her lips with a napkin. "I'm pleased to see that you've got a tight grasp on policy. Those ideas will definitely secure you some pockets of support. But, you need something that resonates with the entire electorate. Remember, the voters are hiring you to do a job; they want you to say what they'd like to say. What are some of the biggest issues in your district right now?"

Fearful of looking foolish, I retreated to the same old regurgitated nonsense that politicians are known for, but Betsey caught on fast and interrupted me.

"That's not what I'm talking about. What you need to do is marry yourself to an emotional issue. Let's see...doesn't I-40 run through your district?"

"Yes," I replied.

"Well, I'm sure that everyone in your district is concerned about what is being transported over that interstate," she said.

"I don't know, ignorance is bliss...," someone mused, which elicited a round or two of laughter but also brought us to the most enlightening moment of the evening, at least for me: I was told that I would need to campaign behind the scenes in Washington, D.C. and prove myself worthy of a seat in the U.S. Congress to various important folk, including certain legislators, lobbyists, and members of the media. Upon hearing that this secondary campaign would be just as important as my public candidacy back home, I realized that getting elected was one thing but being accepted in Washington was a whole other ball game.

Later, before heading to D.C. with my entourage, Kenneth personally scheduled several appointments for me and even volunteered to contact some influential, local unions and law enforcement leaders with whom he was acquainted. Upon arriving in D.C. with Dustin and Josh, one of my first meetings was with a prospective fundraiser at *The Caucus Room.*

"You guys are sitting in one of the most exclusive clubs in the District of Columbia – one that has witnessed a great deal of political wrangling," the fundraiser said with simmering pride as he made a special point to address all the bartenders and waiters by name and they, in return, showered him with compliments. After asking for his down payment, as it were in passing, he eased forward in his chair, tapped his index finger on the table and said with a cock-eyed grin, "If you're elected, you'll have to join this club..."

Though most of my meetings in D.C. seemed productive and everything appeared to be going well on the surface, I was fighting an inward, nagging feeling that I was headed down the wrong path. The afternoon before we were to travel back to Oklahoma, as we were cleaning up in our hotel room and preparing to go out for supper that evening, Carrie telephoned to tell Dustin that the bank was threatening to repossess their car. While he got in touch with his bank and Josh watched television from his bed, I stared out the window at the city of power, with my conscience pricking me, afraid to admit how ridiculous it was that I, a twenty-seven-year-old hillbilly from western Oklahoma, actually thought I had a chance of becoming a United States Congressman. I was practically broke and could not even afford to give my cousin gas money or save my brother from losing his car. Guilt chastised me for having led them down this path with promises of prosperity when I had just been taken by *The Caucus Room* shyster. Even my own silhouette, which I beheld in the glass window, seemed ashamed of me as my mind called up an old sixteenth century rhyme:

"A foole and his monie be soone at debate,which after
with sorrow repents him too late."[82]

Suddenly, my thoughts were shattered by Dustin shouting, "Just kiss it lady!" I immediately ran over to him and took the telephone from his hand, and after spending the better part of thirty minutes trying to smooth things over with his irate creditor, I agreed to mail a payment.

"And just where are you gonna get the money?" Dustin asked when I ended the call.

"I may have some stashed away at the house," I replied. "You've been helping me so I'll try to help you get caught up."

The following day, as we began the long journey back to Oklahoma, my conscience continued to prick me as the Holy Spirit reminded me of Granny's words when I told her of my aspirations: "Are you sure it is God who is talking to you and not the devil?"

When I got home, John came by the house to inquire about the trip. At first, I pretended to be excited and shared what I thought we had accomplished, but my countenance soon fell, and I was moved to unload my concern. John suggested that we take the situation to the Lord in prayer so I moved the antique coffee table away from the sofa,

---

[82] Thomas Tusser (1573, 1577, 1580), *Five Hundred Pointes of Good Husbandrie*, ed. W. Payne and Sydney J. Herrtage (London: Trübner & Co., 1878), 19.

and we both got on our knees and prayed. Our prayer was essentially that the Holy Spirit would make it clear to me whether He wanted me to continue the campaign or abandon it. In the coming weeks, the Lord answered our prayers loud and clear – so loudly, in fact, that it was almost audible. Unfortunately, I did not listen since I had just received the endorsement of Congressman Brad Carson and a few other public officials. Nevertheless, the cracks in my disobedience were beginning to spread.

My campaign's perpetual lack of money was one of its greatest maladies, and it only worsened when I discovered that my fundraiser had no intention of raising any funds whatsoever. So critical was this ailment that I decided to pay a visit to Senator Stipe. When I arrived at his law office in McAlester, his longtime secretary, Charlene, escorted me into his private office where he was barricaded behind a large desk in the far corner of the room.

"Boy, whatta ya up to now?" he boomed.

As soon as Charlene had closed the door behind her, I launched into my well-rehearsed plea for help, knowing even as I spoke the words that I had sunk to the depths. Fortunately, I was in the wrong place at the right time.

"I'm *not* giving you *any* money!" he replied sternly. "I'd like to see you win because you want it so badly, and I remember how I felt when I was in your shoes, but I'm not convinced that politics is your destiny…"

"If I get elected," I stammered, "I'll help you with whatever…"

"And I have no doubt you would, either!" he roared, raising the hairs on the back of my neck. When his furrowed brow finally softened, he leaned back in his chair, clasping his hands across his stomach and studying me over the rim of his glasses.

"I've got a pack of wolves after me," he divulged. "They've tasted blood, and they're gonna try to break me. They've been after me for a long time, and it don't matter whether they lie or get someone else to lie for 'em – they're gonna make something stick. They've been investigating my family, my friends, and anyone I might've talked to on the street, trying to find something. If I were to give you so much as a hundred dollar bill, they'd be on you before you could get outta town."

"But…I don't think…"

"That don't mean a darn thing!" he interrupted. I want you to understand my reasoning here. These sorts of people make names and fortunes for themselves by destroying somebody else. Politics is overrun with their kind. I've been in this game a long time, made a lot of enemies, and ought to know. I've also watched you around the capital and in our business trials, and there's something different about you. You have a rare presence, and I don't want to see it destroyed. These people would destroy you in a heartbeat, and I can't give them an opportunity."

I thanked the Senator for his time and turned to walk toward the door.

"Lance?"

I turned around and looked at him.

"I know you didn't get what you came here for, and I told you what you didn't want to hear, but you remember what I said."

"How bout goin' into the turkey bidness?" I asked.

He laughed.

"You find something that's beneficial for you, and I'll back you all the way."

It was one of the greatest gestures of friendship I have ever received, but I closed the door behind me and did not give it a second thought.

Around that time, the Oklahoma Legislature was preoccupied with its attempt to redraw the state's congressional districts. With so much power hinging on the outcome, the Legislature did not disappoint when the various factions within it proposed one redistricting plan that appeared to benefit the Democratic Party, another that appeared to promote the outgoing Speaker's chances of winning a Congressional seat, and one that appeared to give the son of a former U.S. Senator a hefty advantage. Predictably, the legislative session ended in a deadlock, setting the stage for the congressional districts to be redrawn judicially. After the media had stoked emotions to the breaking point, a special judicial hearing was docketed to announce which plan would be implemented. At the appointed hour, the courtroom was packed to capacity. Representatives of all the major players in the state and U.S. House and Senate, the Governor's office, and the media were present. In the midst of that crowd sat Dustin and me, hoping for the best.

"All rise! The District Court of Oklahoma County is now in session."

The Judge, clutching a bundle of papers against her bosom, briskly and with determination made her way to the bench, her black robe swirling in the wake behind her.

"Be seated," she said and proceeded to declare the Governor's proposed plan to be in the best interests of the State of Oklahoma.

The courtroom erupted in chaos as everyone in attendance realized the redrawn congressional districts would likely favor the Governor's political party and one prominent player in particular, and a great mass of people bolted for the courtroom doors as the gavel fell. Amid the hand-shaking and back-slapping that followed among those who remained in the courtroom, Dustin and I just stared at each other in disbelief.

Seeing that I had arguably witnessed a coup by the Republicans, my emotions were stoked to the boiling point; and my determination to be elected began to consume me. Hoping to improve my chances of winning, I changed course in mid-stream and decided to run against the Republican incumbent in my neighboring district. There appeared to be more fuel for a journey in that direction rather than through the "Lucasvilles" of my own district since the incumbent was rumored to have amassed a number of "enemies," all of whom were said to be more than glad to help someone defeat him. And so, ignoring the great warning of Truth in *James 1:8 (KJV)* (*"A double minded man is unstable in all his ways."*), I, like ancient Israel, whom the Holy Spirit called a silly dove[83] as they fluttered from one country to another in search of help during times of trouble, also fluttered to and fro, searching for help in the most unlikely of places and exhibiting the symptoms of my disobedience.

Fluttering about in the world, however, did afford me at least three insightful observations of its folly and the emptiness of perceptions. The first of these has become known among my friends and family as the "sign war." Sometime in July 2002, Dustin, John, Uncle Rick, and I set about to stencil my campaign slogan, "Compton for Congress," on four hundred sheets of plywood in the sweltering heat. Afterward, we posted as many of these homemade signs as possible. Josh secured a

---

[83] Hosea 7:11–13 (KJV)

prime location for one of them in the town of Lindsay, which Dustin and I posted there early one morning during one of our many journeys throughout the district. Later that evening, we decided to drive back through Lindsey to see if we could get a glimpse of my sign from the road. As we passed, I was utterly dejected to see that fifty others were blocking mine from view. I careened into an abandoned gas station parking lot, whereupon Dustin and I jumped out, intending to take the other signs down. Not more than ten seconds later, I heard sirens popping and turned around to see two police cruisers approaching us. I could just see the next day's newspaper headlines – "Congressional contender and brother arrested in Lindsay..."

The officers exited their cruisers and walked over to Dustin and me and asked to see our drivers' licenses. One of them shined a flashlight in Dustin's face as he retrieved his, revealing his disheveled hair and dirt-smeared chin. I noted, too, that Dustin's clothes were stained with sweat and covered in dirt. Sensing his impatience with the situation, the officer who was holding the flashlight shined it back and forth in Dustin's face while trying to provoke him. I knew it would not take much for Dustin to lose it, so I chimed in and said, "Now let's just calm down; if ya'll will put your flashlights down, we'll answer your questions..."

"Have you got a problem with authority, boy?" the other officer shouted at Dustin, to which he responded with a few choice words.

"Hey! Relax!" I hollered.

"Who do you work for?" one of them asked me. Though I was standing directly in front of my own sign that was emblazoned with my campaign slogan, "Compton for Congress," and the officer was looking at my driver's license, he never made the connection that I was running for public office.

"Who owns this property?" the other officer asked.

"The bank," I replied.

"Are you gettin' smart with me, boy?"

"No," I said, pointing to a foreclosure sign.

After no less than thirty minutes of interrogation, the officers finally released us. Dustin was silent for a long time afterward as we continued toward home but finally said, "These signs aren't working!"

"What do you mean?" I asked.

"Well, we were standing right there in front of your sign with the flags flappin' in the wind and that idiot was looking right at it and at your driver's license and still didn't make the connection!"

I made my second observation into the world's folly and the emptiness of perceptions while riding in the military parade in Lawton, Oklahoma. As I tossed candy from my open window and waved to the crowd, I overheard a young woman on the curb ask the guy with her, "Who's that?"

When I glanced in her direction, I saw that she was pointing to the "Compton for Congress" sign on my door.

"He's the Congressman!" the young man replied with an air of confidence, to which they both clapped and followed my vehicle with astonied eyes.

I made my third and most memorable observation at the Grady County Fairgrounds in Chickasha, Oklahoma, to which I was invited to speak on my candidacy during a Democratic rally. Having heard beforehand that the crowd would probably consist of a hyper-critical bunch of both Blue and Yellow Dog Democrats, I decided to put on a show. I prepared a great speech, hired a professional trumpet player to accompany me to the podium, dressed like a presidential candidate just as Betsey and Tommy had advised me to do, and arrived with a large entourage.

The eyes of the crowd were fixed on me throughout the evening, and since not many people knew me, the crowd's anticipation to find out grew hotter by the minute until I finally took the podium to deliver my speech.

"I have a confession to make..." I began. Immediately, the atmosphere was gripped with tension as every itching ear in the room became mine; and the mob salivated for the revelation of some deep, dark secret.

"As you're all aware, I'm the youngest candidate in this race... some of my opponents and critics have tried to capitalize on that fact, claiming I don't have any experience, but they've all neglected to tell you an important detail!"

I paused to achieve the maximum effect and then said, "I'm the only candidate in this race who doesn't have an active prescription for Viagra!"

Gasp upon gasp permeated the tense atmosphere but could not hold a light to the thunder clap of laughter that followed. I turned to my left and saw that two of my opponents were doubled over, feigning a humorous fit; then I laughed aloud, albeit for my own benefit, and waited for everyone to regain their composure before starting in on my speech like a Mississippi preacher. Without a hitch, I shared a very personal story, hit the highlights of my policies, and articulated why I wanted to be their Congressman. I quashed the question of my experience with the introduction of my advisory team and finished strong by asking for the crowd's vote and support. Then, without any hesitation whatsoever, my hired trumpet player, who had been raising eyebrows all evening, leapt to his feet and broke into the familiar strains of *Oklahoma!* The crowd went haywire and was soon on its feet, clapping and singing, as I stepped down from the platform and went to shaking hands.

My friend, Hewie Long, a longtime political activist, characterized the evening perfectly when he said, "It was a political show to end all shows!"

In hindsight, I believe the Holy Spirit was working through these incidents to show me the foolishness of the world's deceptive practices and great wisdom of His commandment to, "Forsake the foolish, and live; and go in the way of understanding.[84]

In the final week before the primary, my family and close friends, including John and his family and Rick Vernon and his family, never wavered in supporting and helping me, traveling the district daily, distributing candy, fruit baskets, and trinkets to schools, clubs, and various gatherings. Then, on the evening of August 27, 2002, the day of the primary, it all came to an anti-climactic end. I had a modest watch party at Mom's house with family and a few close friends, but the party was about the only fun part of the evening because the results quickly showed that I had come in third place, with ten percent of the vote. Everyone reminded me that the percentages proved just how many people believed in me, thought I was the best candidate, and trusted me with their precious vote; but I felt like a complete failure.

---

[84] Proverbs 9:6 (KJV)

The day after the primary, I went outside to move the car out of the oppressive, August heat. When I put it in gear and started toward the barn, I felt a slight bump and got out to find that I had run over Papa's little dog, Joe, who had taken refuge from the midday sun under the car, unbeknownst to me. I knelt down beside him, but it was too late. Little Joe was gasping for his last breath – just like all of my grandparents had done before they died. I looked up toward Heaven and then back at my precious dog, so broken hearted that I was unable to speak. I held him as he died, then cried like a baby right there on the hot pavement. I finally managed to fetch Papa's old shovel and buried him beneath the boughs of the old pecan tree in front of my house. When I finished, I leaned against the shovel and cried my eyes out as the hot, arid wind blew in the first consequences of my disobedience. Alone and hobbled with grief, I dropped the shovel and walked back to the house, went inside, drew the curtains, and mourned.

I soon fell into a deep depression and was a recluse by September. Completely poverty-stricken and barely able to face each new day, I was in no shape to deal with the grievous onslaught of creditors whose telephone calls, at all hours of the day and night, became my constant companion and almost drove me to a nervous breakdown. Each time the telephone rang, I was consumed with embarrassment; and since I had no clue how or where to begin in the way of making even one payment, I stopped answering the telephone altogether, but the chorus of threatening voicemail messages continued to shake the dungeon of my depression, sinking me even deeper into my complex of unsound thought. Shame gnawed at my soul the day I watched two men repossess my suburban from behind the kitchen curtains. Later, as the fear of losing my home crept into the recesses of my mind, my depression worsened; and I found myself toying with something Senator Stipe had told me in the planning stage of our hog venture.

"We're going into this pretty deep!"

"What happens if we get in too deep?" I asked.

"We'll just take bankruptcy and move on," he said.

Well, I found out when I finally did file for Chapter 7 – total liquidation – that moving on was easier said than done. I will never forget the paralysis of failure I felt when I admitted to Mom how much

I owed and that I had poured just about everything into my campaign. Though my creditors' incessant telephone calls finally ended, I lost both my cell phone and land line, and the entire house went silent when the cable television was disconnected, too. Caddo Electric, the local electric cooperative, was merciful to me and continued to provide me with electricity out of respect for Papa's position as their first lineman. Mom came by the house every day and did her best to get me active, but I refused to leave Papa's old chair. Dustin and Carrie stopped by occasionally and took care of various chores around the house. He even rigged up an old television antenna so I could get the local news; he was very understanding most of the time, but it was not easy for him to see me in that condition.

"You've got that Compton depression," he finally said one day. "You just need to snap out of it!"

Part of me wished I could snap out of it, but another part of me just wanted to wallow in self-pity. Brother Marty Ingram stopped by, too, and actually got me out of bed several times. Sometimes he took me to lunch. Other times, we just talked. Not once did he lecture me but consistently lived the Scriptures by listening, letting me know that he was there for me, and being a true friend. By example, he showed me one of the greatest principles of being a pastor. Allen Findly also came to see me regularly. On October 29, 2002, he came by and woke me out of a deep sleep.

"I'll wait 'til you get dressed," he said after I had stumbled to the kitchen door to let him inside. "Everyone at the senior citizens' center wants you to come eat lunch with us today."

It was all I could do to dress myself and follow him to the car.

"Today is Papa's birthday," I said as we drove into town.

"I know," he replied. "That's why we wanted you to eat with us today."

I felt somewhat better after being around people again so when Dustin and Carrie, who were both in college and struggling to make ends meet, said they wanted to move in with me — dogs and cat in tow — I agreed. For the first time in months, the window shades and curtains were opened, allowing sunlight to penetrate the sixty-year-old windows once again. But, even with the light shining into the old house once more and Dustin and Carrie there to keep me company, my depression persisted. Feeling obligated to help with groceries and supplies, I was forced to face the reality that I needed a job, but all I could focus on was what people might say about me if I applied for one.

"Who would want to hire a bankrupt failure?" I thought, envisioning people referring to me as an example of what not to become. Satan was talking to my emotions, and I was listening. Without a job or prospects, I finally broke down and applied for food stamps because I could not bear the thought of going hungry, too. In the welfare line, I turned around to see if anyone had recognized me and saw someone from back home. We embraced and talked about the hard times that had befallen us. One day, I would see our conversation in its grandeur; but on that day, I felt like a thief. There I was, an able-bodied man in the prime of his life, taking food stamps ahead of widows and children. It was one of the lowest points of my life; but just when I thought the coals on top of my head could not get any hotter, I wanted to crawl under the carpet when I saw that the man processing my paperwork was the father of one of my best friends.

A few days later, as I was drowning my sorrows in the comfort and protection of Papa's old chair, Mom and Dustin came in the front door and relayed the news that they had found me a job. Actually, after they had visited with a family friend, Cameron Stephenson, about my circumstances, he got me the job of security guard at a nearby casino. I did not really want it but did not want to disappoint Mom and Dustin, either so I agreed to take it and was assigned the graveyard shift, with minimal responsibilities.

My duties included guarding the shift and floor managers as they collected and counted money, escorting old ladies to their cars, deterring undesired behavior, and walking the perimeter once every hour. I spent the remainder of my time eavesdropping on the patrons and staff while pretending to read the newspaper. One evening, I decided, just for the fun of it, to test the managers' honesty. As they counted the money from the machines, I silently counted it to myself while watching them. It was not long before I observed inaccurate recording practices. Though I immediately reported my findings to management, my allegations were not taken seriously since I am not a Native American. But, shortly thereafter, management announced that the casino was in dire financial straits, and the hours of operation were cut in half. Under the new schedule, the casino was closed for most of the graveyard shift, but management wanted me to remain on the premises so my post was moved from the double-wide trailer that housed the casino to a one-room, A-frame shack.

Just before dawn, after one of my first nights alone in that pitiful hutch, the spiritual burden I had been carrying as a result of my most recent political aspirations finally became so heavy that I could not take another step. Seeing that my circumstances closely paralleled those of certain Biblical characters, the thought entered my mind that perhaps my suffering was due to my willful sin and disobedience to God. Granny's question, "Are you sure it is God who is talking to you and not the devil?" entered my mind yet again, and I had to admit that, rather than remaining in God's will, I had forsaken my Master's voice and chased after the world's instead. In that moment, as I allowed the Holy Spirit to convict my heart of my sins, the Lord showed me that straying from Him had produced absolute failure – I had gotten away from Him, squandered my savings, wasted precious time, fallen into a deep depression, filed for bankruptcy, applied for food stamps, and was ultimately reduced to working in an establishment devoted to sin.

Harkening to the Holy Spirit's conviction, I knew there was only one thing I could do so I fell prostrate upon the dirty floor of that dismal shack and begged my Heavenly Father to allow His prodigal son to come home:

> "And he said, A certain man had two sons: And the younger of them said to his father, Father, give me the portion of goods that falleth to me. And he divided unto them his living. And not many days after the younger son gathered all together, and took his journey into a far country, and there wasted his substance with riotous living. And when he had spent all, there arose a mighty famine in that land; and he began to be in want. And he went and joined himself to a citizen of that country; and he sent him into his fields to feed swine. And he would fain have filled his belly with the husks that the

swine did eat: and no man gave unto him. And when he came to himself, he said, How many hired servants of my father's have bread enough and to spare, and I perish with hunger! I will arise and go to my father, and will say unto him, Father, I have sinned against heaven, and before thee, And am no more worthy to be called thy son: make me as one of thy hired servants. And he arose, and came to his father. But when he was yet a great way off, his father saw him, and had compassion, and ran, and fell on his neck, and kissed him. And the son said unto him, Father, I have sinned against heaven, and in thy sight, and am no more worthy to be called thy son. But the father said to his servants, Bring forth the best robe, and put it on him; and put a ring on his hand, and shoes on his feet: And bring hither the fatted calf, and kill it; and let us eat, and be merry: For this my son was dead, and is alive again; he was lost, and is found. And they began to be merry. Now his elder son was in the field: and as he came and drew nigh to the house, he heard musick and dancing. And he called one of the servants, and asked what these things meant. And he said unto him, Thy brother is come; and thy father hath killed the fatted calf, because he hath received him safe and sound. And he was angry, and would not go in: therefore came his father out, and intreated him. And he answering said to his father, Lo, these many years do I serve thee, neither transgressed I at any time thy commandment: and yet thou never gavest me a kid, that I might make merry with my friends: But as soon as this thy son was come, which hath devoured thy living with harlots, thou hast killed for him the fatted calf. And he said unto him, Son, thou art ever with me, and all that I have is thine. It was meet that we should make merry, and be glad: for this thy brother was dead, and is alive again; and was lost, and is found."[85]

---

[85] Luke 15:11-32 (KJV)

The parable of the Prodigal Son is a wonderful picture of God the Father's unconditional love, His grace, and His forgiveness; but it is also one of the most misunderstood Scriptures in the Word of God. Recorded only in the Gospel according to Luke, the story of the prodigal son is actually the third portion of a three-part parable. The first part is the parable of the lost sheep, which represents the work of God the Son in restoring a sinning son. The second is the parable of the lost coin, which represents the work of God the Holy Spirit in restoring a sinning son. Finally, the parable of the lost or prodigal son represents the work of God the Father in restoring a sinning son. The greatest Truth of this parable is that the "certain man" in it represents God the Father, and the two sons represent believers in Jesus Christ.

The father and his sons lived together in the father's home, and the sons enjoyed all of its luxurious amenities – comfort, security, nourishment, and fellowship. While the father expected his sons to be disciplined in their work and behavior, the youngest began to lust after the world. He asked for his inheritance; and his father, desiring that his unconditional love and affection be reciprocated, granted his son's request and gave him free will to follow his desires. Jesus tells us that this young man then departed on a journey into a far country – the world – where he wasted his substance on riotous living and joined himself to its citizens – non-believers. The parable is a picture of all Christians who forsake God's Word to live a sinful lifestyle. Regardless of whether it is one of drugs or alcohol, premarital or adulterous sex, homosexuality, the pursuit of compromising business ventures, or political power, they are all variations on the theme of riotous living. Sin always removes believers from Godly fellowship and eventually leaves us alone with the pigs. Yet, it is essential to note that the son was a foreigner in the far country. He was not accepted by the world and never lost the underlying sense that he did not belong there. When he finally came to his senses, he longed for the sanctity and security of his father's home. He humbled himself, overcame his pride and fear of rejection, and set his heart upon confessing to his father that he had sinned against him and was no longer worthy to be called his son.

The father gave his sons everything, which is a picture of the gift of Jesus Christ; and though the younger son departed into the far country, his father was watching diligently for him to return, and when he saw him afar off, he had mercy on him, ran to him, and kissed his neck. The father forgave the son, clothed him, placed a ring upon his finger, and celebrated. It should be noted that the audience to which Jesus first spoke this parable was Jewish, and it was considered undignified in Jewish culture for a Jewish man to run, especially to embrace someone who had trespassed against him. But, the father did run and did more than that. He clothed his son in the finest robe, which not only meant that his basic needs were provided for, but also that his sin had been covered and he had been cleansed. He placed a ring upon the son's finger, which was an outward indication that he was an heir. Shoes were placed upon the son's feet, which signified the immediate restoration of his dignity; and the son was restored, without works, a probationary period, or a lecture, simply because he returned to his father and humbly and sincerely confessed his sin.

To celebrate the joyous occasion, the father hosted a glorious feast to proclaim his son's restoration. Despite the joyous occasion, however, the parable ends on a sad note, revealing that the eldest son is in disobedience to his father and out of fellowship with him. Much can be deduced from Jesus' description of this son. He was in the field, indicating his devotion to works. Though faithful in his works, he lacked understanding, as evidenced by the fact that he addressed a servant rather than his father when inquiring about the celebration. Upon learning of his brother's return and restoration, this son was so angry that he complained to his father and rejected the wisdom of his decision. The eldest son is a picture of believers whose hearts are out of fellowship with the Lord. Rather than going directly to God, they seek Him through men. They place unattainable standards upon the brethren and demand punishment for their sins while desiring mercy for their own.

As I lay prostrate on the dirty floor of a dirty environment during the filthiest period of my life, with the scene of the Prodigal Son in my mind, my Heavenly Father rushed to embrace and welcome me home as I acknowledged my sins at the feet of Christ and plead from the depths of my soul for Him to forgive me for departing from His presence. And, I was forgiven...clothed...shod...and restored.

CHAPTER 8

Equipping a Sower

Even after visiting the orphanage in Jerusalem, I was still deeply burdened with the young, redheaded boy I had seen there but did not fully understand why until we visited *Caesarea Philippi*. Known during the Hellenistic period as *Panyas*, and later as *"Banyas"* in Arabic, *Caesarea Philippi* was named by the Greek, Ptolemaic kings of Egypt in tribute to Pan, the pagan god of herds and shepherds, and was a major center of cult and pagan worship. Near the end of the first century before Christ, Rome annexed *Banyas* to Herod the Great's empire. To show his appreciation, Herod built a temple near the *Banyas* springs and renamed the city *Caesarea* after the Roman Emperor, Augustus. Upon Herod's death, his son, Philippus, established the seat of his rule in *Caesarea* and renamed it *Caesarea Philippi* in honor of himself. The *Banyas Cave*, from whence the headwaters of the Jordan River emerge into three separate streams, was once part of the Sanctuary of Pan, a pagan temple where ceremonial child sacrifices were offered to Pan. There, children were thrown into the base of the spring that emerged from the cave while priests waited for their blood to surface downstream, the appearance of which signified Pan's acceptance of and pleasure with the sacrifices. According to local tradition, ancient pagans believed that the mouth of the *Banyas Cave* was the literal gate to the underworld, and the massive, flat-topped rock upon which thousands of children were slaughtered in the name of false religion could still be seen when we visited.

It was against this terrible backdrop that Jesus asked His disciples, "Whom do men say that I the Son of man am?"[86] In response to His

---

[86] Matthew 16:13 (KJV)

question, the disciples reported that some said He was John the Baptist while others said that He was Elijah, Jeremiah, or one of the other prophets. Jesus replied, "But whom say ye that I am?"[87] Simon Peter answered for all of the disciples, saying, "Thou art the Christ, the Son of the living God."[88] And, Jesus responded: "...Blessed art thou, Simon Barjona: for flesh and blood hath not revealed it unto thee, but my Father which is in heaven. And I say also unto thee, That thou art Peter, and upon this rock I will build my church; and the gates of hell shall not prevail against it."[89]

Though Catholicism has interpreted "...thou art Peter, and upon this rock I will build my church..." to mean that Peter was the rock upon which Christ has built His Church, this interpretation cannot be reconciled with the wording of the scripture. In the original text, the Greek word for Peter is *Petros*, which means a smaller stone or pebble; the Greek word for rock is *Petra,* which means a larger rock or boulder; and the Greek word for church is *ekklesia,* which means a called-out assembly of people. When the meanings of these words are considered along with Peter's declaration in his first epistle ("Ye also, as lively stones, are built up a spiritual house, an holy priesthood, to offer up spiritual sacrifices, acceptable to God by Jesus Christ"[90]), wherein the Greek word for *are built up* in the original text is *oikodomeo,* which means to build up from the foundation in the same manner as a house is built, it is clear that the literal meaning of Jesus' statement ("...thou art Peter, and upon this rock I will build my church...") is this: the called-out assembly, which is Christ's Church, is composed of individual, smaller stones, of which Peter *(Petros)* was one, and they are built upon the *Petra,* which is the foundation.

This foundation (*"Petra"*) upon which Christ's Church is built is Christ Himself – a Truth that was confirmed by the Apostle Paul in the third chapter of *1 Corinthians*: "For other foundation can no man lay than that is laid, which is Jesus Christ."[91] And, in the tenth chapter of *1 Corinthians*: "Moreover, brethren, I would not that ye should be ignorant,

---

[87] Matthew 16:15 (KJV)
[88] Matthew 16:16 (KJV)
[89] Matthew 16:17-18 (KJV)
[90] 1 Peter 2:5 (KJV)
[91] 1 Corinthians 3:11 (KJV)

how that all our fathers were under the cloud, and all passed through the sea; And were all baptized unto Moses in the cloud and in the sea; And did all eat the same spiritual meat; And did all drink the same spiritual drink: for they drank of that spiritual Rock that followed them: and that Rock was Christ."[92] Here it should be noted that the Greek word for *Rock* in the phrase, "...and that Rock was Christ," is *Petra*.

By asking His disciples who men said that He was at this particular location, Jesus was doing more than revealing Himself as the Rock and foundation upon which those who believe Him to be the Son of God are built. He was also utilizing the mountain from whence the life-sustaining waters of the Jordan River emerged as a reminder that He is the source of living water, just as He told the Samaritan woman at the well ("But whosoever drinketh of the water that I shall give him shall never thirst; but the water that I shall give him shall be in him a well of water springing up into everlasting life."[93]) and that He is the Rock from whence it flows, just as He was the One who sent forth the water from the rock that Moses struck in the wilderness. Further, He was demonstrating how one receives that living water, which is, as Simon Peter declared, by believing that He is the Son of the living God, and revealing that the gates of Hell cannot prevail against those who believe in Him. And, when He said, "And I will give unto thee the keys of the kingdom of heaven: and whatsoever thou shalt bind on earth shall be bound in heaven: and whatsoever thou shalt loose on earth shall be loosed in heaven,"[94] He was declaring that the keys to the Kingdom of Heaven are the Gospel of Jesus Christ – the Truth that He is the Son of God – and that He was giving them, together with the authority to use them, to those who believe He is the Son of God to open the Kingdom to the lost by the sowing that very Truth.

As I pondered these things at the mouth of the *Banyas Cave*, the Holy Spirit revealed to me why I had been burdened with Saif and what it was that the Lord wanted me to do for him; and that was to pray for his salvation, which I continue to do to this day. Because prayer is a Kingdom principle to be used in opening the Kingdom of Heaven

---

[92] 1 Corinthians 10:1-4 (KJV)
[93] John 4:14 (KJV)
[94] Matthew 16:19 (KJV)

to sinners and because I believe that Jesus Christ is the Son of God, I am but one who has been entrusted with the keys. Therefore, I have a duty to petition God for Saif's salvation, especially since the Holy Spirit burdened me to do so; and I am unable to directly minister to or teach him about Christ. When I had finished offering up my first prayer that Saif would come to know Christ, I marveled that the Lord had brought me to the point of praying for sinners in foreign lands and reflected upon how far I had come in learning to use the keys that have been entrusted to me.

Immediately following my repentance as a prodigal son on the floor of that dismal, A-frame shack beside the casino where I was working, I finished my shift and headed home. When I got to the house, I made myself comfortable and turned on the television to watch the early morning news. The local network was interviewing a man named Ron Shea, who announced that Billy Graham would be hosting a crusade in Oklahoma City during the coming summer, which was the summer of 2003. My interest piqued when Mr. Shea reported that the Crusade would be hiring a local staff, and I was instantly compelled by the Holy Spirit to submit a resume. The following day, I drove to Oklahoma City and personally delivered a copy to Scott Lenning and Sam Hardy, both of whom looked at me a little strangely, probably because I had over-dressed for the occasion, but promised to review my resume and get in touch with me soon. Two weeks passed without any word, as I paced by the telephone, praying fervently to God to give me an excuse to leave the casino. Just as I was beginning to doubt whether He would answer my prayers, Sam telephoned and asked me to come in for an interview.

On the day of the interview, two of the first people I met were Ron Shea's wife, Kathy, who pleasantly asked me, "Are you going to be working with us?" and Chris Mechsner, who looked at me askance, as if he were sizing me up for some sort of competition, but said nothing.

"I would sure like to," I replied.

"You've gotta get past me first!" I heard Sam say and turned around to see him coming out of his office. It did not take long for me to feel at ease around Sam, and since we had many things in common and he had also been very close to his grandparents, we developed a special rapport.

126

"Why don't you come on back to my office, and we'll talk about your resume," he said. "I've contacted your references, and they've told me some very interesting stories about you!"

"Well, I guess I should've been more careful," I replied, knowing that my references – Bruce and Brother Marty Ingram – were both praying for my interview at that very moment. Sam laughed. "I don't want to insult you," he continued, "But, I was thinking that you'd make a good office assistant…"

"No job for the Lord would be an insult…I'm willing to do whatever you need me to do or go wherever you need me to go!"

"If you're our office assistant," he said, "You'll get to see all aspects of the Crusade and be involved in everything. Of course, we could use a big man like you to help us with all the lifting and moving."

"Sounds good to me…," I replied.

"Well then, let me show you around," he said and then walked me down the hall to the volunteer room, where he introduced me to a short lady with an infectious smile, saying, "This is Mary Joyce Triplet; she's our volunteer coordinator and pretty much came with the building…"

What he meant was that M. J., as I came to know her, had been a long-time employee of Jack Humphreys. Jack's son, Oklahoma City Mayor Kirk Humphreys, who was serving as the local Crusade chairman, had generously converted his father's old building into office space for the Crusade, and donated M.J. too, as a way of showing his appreciation for the fact that his father had surrendered his life to Christ at a Billy Graham crusade in the 1940s.

"Are you going to be working with us?" M.J. asked, but before I could respond, Sam answered the question for me: "Yes, I believe he is."

With that, I was hired and immediately quit my job at the casino. But, though the Lord had answered both short-term and longstanding prayers by giving me a job with the Billy Graham Crusade, it was not long before those old desires for a career and life in politics began to rekindle, and I was once again tempted and pulled toward the world. In hindsight, I believe my political aspirations returned because, rather than keeping my eyes on Christ and moving forward, I continued to look back on my two political defeats with an unhealthy anger and desire for revenge. Satan exploited this weakness by enticing me with the possibility of victory and the chance to right all wrongs by running for yet another political office. This time it was Chairman of the Oklahoma Democratic Party, and my decision to toss my hat in the race initially seemed like a good one. My family and closest friends all agreed to attend their own precinct meetings so they could qualify to vote at the party's convention, and I received some important endorsements. But, when the convention finally rolled around, I quickly realized that I had made another serious mistake.

The convention was held in the spring of 2003 over a single weekend at the Westin Hotel in downtown Oklahoma City, with caucus and special interest gatherings and other social functions on Friday night and the election on Saturday. When Dustin, John, Carrie Burnsed, and I showed up on Friday evening, hoping to fish for votes and drum up support, I was surprised to see that hard-core partying was the special interest of the hour. As we mingled from one hotel room to another, I saw underage patrons being served alcohol from a bar that had been set up in one of the rooms and cocaine lines on a coffee table for the first and only time in my life. My behind-the-scenes tour confirmed to me that, "Politics may not be the oldest profession but the results are often the same."

As we were leaving the hotel, I ran into Josh, who had gone to work for the President Pro-tem of the Senate after my Congressional campaign was over. Even though the President Pro-tem had previously pledged to support my candidacy as Chairman of the Democratic Party, Josh reported that he had just ordered him to vote against me the next day. Since I did not want Josh to lose his job, I assured him that I was okay with it. Nevertheless, Josh's news brought me down and when he had departed, I told my friends, "Let's get outta here; I don't belong here," to which Dustin responded, "We've all been working very hard on this campaign! We've helped you up to this point and you're not gonna quit now!"

On Saturday morning, my delegation of supporters – which consisted of Dustin, John, Carrie, Aunt Rita, and Rick Vernon – passed out my materials and worked the crowd while I wrestled with the Holy Spirit's conviction of my soul. My desire for a career in politics was driving me forward, but the wooing of the Holy Spirit was convicting me to separate myself from the iniquity that was manifesting itself all around me. Even as the battle in my spirit continued to rage, the convention started and my small delegation and I took our seats on the front row of the arena near the stage. Having earlier secured some support from Tulsa County, I was contemplating how many votes their delegation would yield when the Vice-chairman approached the microphone and announced that the Tulsa County delegation would not be eligible to vote because the credentials committee had uncovered a technical error. Outraged, I jumped up and walked to a microphone and very loudly replied, "Point of Order!" but the microphone was dead.

"Point of Order!" I repeated, much louder this time, as the Vice-chairman, who had heard me the first time, attempted to ignore me again but stammered at the seriousness of my tone and looked to the Chairman for direction.

"Point of Order!" I hollered out a third time. This time, I was acknowledged, and a brief, unilateral discussion of *Robert's Rules of Order* followed. To my surprise, I was the only one who seemed to be familiar with them. Since the crowd sat in clueless apathy, I finally just gave up and stood there – overwhelmed by the spectacle.

During the nominating and candidate speeches, my only opponent, the incumbent Chairman, spoke briefly then yielded his final minutes to a former Governor who had pleaded guilty to a misdemeanor to avoid a multi-felony indictment. Though the former Governor was welcomed to the stage with great applause, the crowd was not as accepting of John and Carrie, whose nominating speeches were interrupted multiple times by a jeering crowd that disapproved of their suggestions that moral values should be a priority. As they were shouted down, I remembered and wished that I had heeded the warnings of Bruce and Representatives Langmacher and Bonny, all of whom had warned me that I was making a big mistake. When John and Carrie finished their speeches, it was my turn to speak; but sadly, I delivered one of the worst speeches of my life, making the final vote all the more painful.

The next Monday morning, I regurgitated the weekend's sickening details to just about everyone at the Crusade office, telling my ministry colleagues that I was hated without a cause for speaking out against the status quo; but, as I ruminated over the debacle, I recognized that

I was standing at a fork in the road and had to make a choice. On one hand, I could choose the path of my own will. Or, I could choose to be obedient to the Lord. When I compared the fruit of my past, fleshly endeavors to the potential to bear fruit within a ministry committed to sowing the Gospel of Jesus Christ, I was led to contemplate the true meaning of leadership and concluded that anything God had planned for my life was far greater than the best the world could offer me. It was then that I chose to be obedient to the Lord and finally surrendered my political aspirations, memorializing the decision in the back of my Bible with this inscription: "Unless God leads me otherwise, I give up my life's passion of pursuing a career in politics for His sake." Afterward, I shared the intimate experience with Scott Lenning, who offered up a prayer that marked a turning point in my life.

"Lord," he prayed, "Thank you for giving Lance a mountain top view of life. We are also thankful to you for allowing him to share it with us, and we further ask that you bless and equip him to share your wisdom with others."

Scott's prayer that I be equipped to share the Lord's wisdom was quickly answered in a number of ways. First, since one of my duties was running errands, I spent a great amount of time in one of the ministry's many vehicles and noticed the radios were always tuned to that syndicated, Christian radio station known as K-LOVE. I was not much of a fan of the station's contemporary praise music, but the absence of dirty jokes, sexual innuendo, and mindless chatter which characterizes so many other stations was so refreshing that I soon became a routine listener. Over time, however, I noticed that continuously listening to Christian music had a significant, positive effect on me, which led me to appreciate the importance of keeping Christ, His words, and His grace ever present and near, a principle that is expounded upon in the *Book of James*:

> "From whence come wars and fightings among you? come they not hence, even of your lusts that war in your members? Ye lust, and have not: ye kill, and desire to have, and cannot obtain: ye fight and war, yet ye have not, because ye ask not. Ye ask, and receive not, because ye ask amiss, that ye may consume it upon

your lusts. Ye adulterers and adulteresses, know ye not that the friendship of the world is enmity with God? whosoever therefore will be a friend of the world is the enemy of God. Do ye think that the scripture saith in vain, The spirit that dwelleth in us lusteth to envy? But he giveth more grace. Wherefore he saith, God resisteth the proud, but giveth grace unto the humble. Submit yourselves therefore to God. Resist the devil, and he will flee from you. Draw nigh to God, and he will draw nigh to you. Cleanse your hands, ye sinners; and purify your hearts, ye double minded."[95]

Second, through various Crusade programs, the Holy Spirit equipped me with valuable ministerial skills that would prove useful to spreading the Truth of Christ in the future. One of these programs, *Operation Andrew,* was started by Rev. Graham in 1955 to motivate crusade-participating church congregations to reach out to their friends and acquaintances, tell them about Christ, and bring them to crusade events. From it, I learned how to mobilize ordinary people toward bringing their friends, neighbors, and family members to Christ, just as Andrew did with his brother, Simon Peter:

> "One of the two which heard John speak, and followed him, was Andrew, Simon Peter's brother. He first findeth his own brother Simon, and saith unto him, We have found the Messias, which is, being interpreted, the Christ. And he brought him to Jesus. And when Jesus beheld him, he said, Thou art Simon the son of Jona: thou shalt be called Cephas, which is by interpretation, A stone."[96]

Other programs included the prison ministry program, *Love in Action,* and the language accommodation program. Ron Shea, who oversaw the prison ministry and *Love in Action,* taught me the importance of sowing the Gospel seed to prisoners and those bound for prison.

---

[95] James 4:1-8 (KJV)
[96] John 1:40-42 (KJV)

Because opportunities for these individuals to accept Christ are fewer and since prisons are typically overrun with lay, inmate "preachers" who can easily lead others astray, ministering to these people should never be discounted or neglected when an opportunity to do so presents itself.

Through *Love in Action*, which distributed school supplies to inner city, public schools throughout Oklahoma City, I learned how to use a person's physical needs to plant the seed of Christ's Truth.

Assisting Wanda McCurdy with the language accommodation program prepared me to interact with diverse cultural backgrounds and belief systems while penetrating those barriers with the Gospel of Jesus Christ and keeping His message consistent.

Another program, the children's ministry, which was managed by Tami Lenning and Ryan Free, created a ministry opportunity for my family and equipped me with a very personal testimony which I would use to share the Lord's wisdom many times in the future. When Tami and Ryan asked if I knew any kids who would be willing to participate in *Kidz Gig*, the Crusade's youth ministry event, the Holy Spirit laid my little cousin, Dalton, on my heart, and I recommended him. Though I did not know it at the time, the Lord was working through Tami and Ryan's request. Dalton agreed to participate, and since Mom and Michelle had to transport him to and from Oklahoma City twice a week for practice, they ended up making use of the spare time by volunteering for the Crusade.

Besides the skills I gleaned and great lessons I learned from the various crusade programs, I was also equipped to some extent by almost all of the people with whom I worked, especially the volunteers. I formed a special bond with the retired regulars, most of whom reminded me of my grandparents, and spent hours in the crusade office with them, doing whatever task was necessary to prepare for the Crusade and lighten the burdens of others.

M.J. was also a great influence and teacher, teaching me to believe and accept that my limitations cannot prohibit me from serving the Lord in the manner in which He intended.

"Every soul has been given a gift to serve our Lord," she was fond of telling me. "To serve Him is an inner need; and if you don't do it, you will serve the devil instead."

M.J. possessed a strong, Christian work ethic, and that ethic rubbed off on me. She was a tireless worker, frequently reminding me during the long hours that completing the Lord's work to His satisfaction produces wisdom. She also made it a habit of leaving Bible verses on my desk each morning and telling our colleagues that I was her "baby boy" who could do no wrong. The running joke in the office was that, while M.J. was around, Sam was limited to blaming Chris and Ryan for any problems that surfaced because I was off limits.

Other influences were Sam Hardy and Karen Woods. Sam, a meticulous perfectionist with a talent for management, succeeded in creating a work environment that one would expect of a Christian organization and was true to his word in placing me in critical positions that allowed me to experience every aspect of the crusade. Karen Woods, the attorney who coordinated the Oklahoma City office with headquarters in North Carolina, taught me the importance of seeking the Lord's guidance in every decision, regardless of how insignificant it may seem. Karen was also instrumental in facilitating my friendship with Cliff Barrows and his wife, Ann, both of whom were profound influences upon me. Cliff, together with George Beverly Shea, had served as Billy Graham's ministry partner for decades. He was a Christian servant of rare caliber, with whom the anointing of the Holy Spirit was very noticeable; and his knowledge of the Word of God and ability to quote and interpret it from memory and with ease inspired me to want the same abilities. I was amazed by the fact that he did not use books, one-liners, or clichés in his teaching – he just taught from the Word of God – and I found myself striving to be the kind of leader I saw in him.

Not everyone with whom I worked or came into contact set a good example, and though I cannot claim that these people influenced or equipped me in some direct fashion, they did help in fine-tuning my discernment. One of these individuals was one of the ministry's executives, a former used car salesman, whose habitual self-praise and numbers-driven, salesman-like approach to sowing the Gospel of Jesus Christ was offensive to me. Furthermore, I seriously questioned his sincerity when he strong-armed M.J. into overnighting his clothing and golf clubs to Kansas City with Crusade funds.

Another individual who comes to mind had some key position in the bank that was in charge of the money. My only encounter with this individual transpired just a few days after the Crusade ended when Waynetta, the finance manager, dispatched me to his office for the purpose of obtaining his signature on a bank draft so the surplus funds from Oklahoma City's Crusade could be transferred out of his bank to be used as "seed money" for the next Crusade. Though the money, which was a substantial amount, was earmarked for the Kansas City Crusade, that fact did not prevent this man from expressing a few choice words and asserting that, "They promised me that money would stay here for a while!" As far as I was concerned, his priorities discredited him.

Perhaps the most memorable, however, was a man who was invited to speak at one of the Crusade's youth events. After his black sedan, which resembled a Secret Service vehicle, suddenly wheeled into the restricted area with its lights flashing and the driver, who was an off-duty highway patrolman, jumped out and informed me who was in the car, I mistakenly thought he said, "John Ashcroft."

"Does somebody need to get the door for him?" I asked, leaning toward the sedan, trying to steal a glimpse of who I thought was the U.S. Attorney General.

"No, he'll only get out for Scott Lenning, the crusade director," reported the driver, rolling his eyes.

"Well, he might be sittin' there for a while," I replied. "Scott's in a meeting, but I'll see if I can find Sam Hardy for you."

As I searched for Sam, I wondered why John Ashcroft was gracing us with his presence. I could not remember seeing his name on the schedule or the guest list but figured it must have been kept quiet for security purposes. I finally found Sam and said, "Security is here with John Ashcroft, but he won't get out of the car unless you or Scott are there to meet him."

"The Attorney General?!?!" Sam gasped in disbelief, to which I nodded in the affirmative. He rushed off to meet our unexpected visitor but caught up with me roughly an hour later and, in between spurts of laughter, croaked the words, "Lance, you're crazy!"

"And, your point is?" I asked, sensing that I had gotten confused again.

"That was *not* General Ashcroft!" he replied, doubling over with laughter after seeing the expression on my face. "It was tonight's speaker!"

Later, as Sam and I walked past the stage during the sound check, I noticed the speaker's wife acting skittish and looking paranoid and frightened – sort of like a field mouse during a spring plow – as she urgently tugged at her husband's shirt and scanned the empty arena with fast-moving, wide eyes. After catching the attention of the security detail, she was finally escorted from the stage. As they were walking her off the stage, I turned to Sam and asked, "Who *are* those people? Is there something wrong with them?"

Though Sam did his best to advocate their need for security, alleging that they had received several death threats and one assassination attempt, all of which apparently stemmed from the man's messages, I wondered how he reconciled being so fearful with Paul's declaration to the Ephesians:

> "Finally, my brethren, be strong in the Lord, and in the power of his might. Put on the whole armour of God, that ye may be able to stand against the wiles of the devil. For we wrestle not against flesh and blood, but against principalities, against powers, against the rulers of the darkness of this world, against spiritual wickedness in high places. Wherefore take unto you the whole armour of God, that ye may be able to withstand in the evil day, and having done all, to stand. Stand therefore, having your loins girt about with truth, and having on the breastplate of righteousness; And your feet shod with the preparation of the gospel of peace; Above all, taking the shield of faith, wherewith ye shall be able to quench all the fiery darts of the wicked. And take the helmet of salvation, and the sword of the Spirit, which is the word of God: Praying always with all prayer and supplication in the Spirit, and watching thereunto with all perseverance and supplication for all saints; And for me, that utterance may be given

unto me, that I may open my mouth boldly, to make
known the mystery of the gospel, For which I am an
ambassador in bonds: that therein I may speak boldly,
as I ought to speak."[97]

Scott's prayer that I be equipped to share the Lord's wisdom with others was further answered when I, following the example of *Operation Andrew*, decided to invite Dusty Boling, one of my best friends since the fifth grade, to the Crusade so he could hear Rev. Graham's sermon. Dusty and I shared quite a history and a whole lot of memories – like the one of me falling on him while riding a three-wheeler just after his appendectomy, the one of our shoe polish fight on his mother's sofa, and those of us racing Papa's new pickup truck – but despite our long friendship, my frequent efforts to bring him to Christ were always met with some sort of objection such as, "You know I have a hard time believing that stuff!" or "How do we know the Bible is true?" One of his more common responses was, "How did we get the scriptures?" Further, any mention of Christ always found Dusty reminding me of the parade of hypocritical church members, whom we both knew, who feigned righteousness on Sunday but practiced wickedness during the week. For weeks, my ministry colleagues had been praying that Dusty would come to know Jesus Christ as his personal Lord and Savior. Unable to fathom an eternity without my friend or him being lost for eternity, I knew that my responsibility in the matter was inviting him to the Crusade.

At first, he was hesitant to commit but finally agreed to come if I would just "shut up about it," as he put it. When he arrived through the VIP entrance on the night that I had invited him to attend, I escorted him to a reserved seat then returned to my duties. Even though several people advised me that he would probably be more receptive to Christ if he could listen to the sermon without any distractions, I was torn about whether to leave him alone. Just before the service began, I felt an urgent need to check on him. When I did, I discovered that he was gone. I frantically dialed his cell phone number, and after several attempts, finally got ahold of him.

[97] Ephesians 6:10-20 (KJV)

"Where are you?"

Clearly upset, he retorted, "I left!" Before I could respond, he said, "I went to get a drink and someone stole my seat."

"Wait right where you are!" I said. "I'll come meet you and get you a parking space."

I hung up the phone before he had time to refuse and desperately began searching for someone who had the authority to give me permission to leave. I finally found Rick Marshall, Director of World Missions, preparing to enter the prayer room with Rev. Graham so I ran to him and advised him of my predicament. Placing his hand on my shoulder, he replied, "Go get your friends and sit with them. And, always remember that people don't come to hear the Word of God; they come because of who invites them or who is delivering the message."

With Rick's permission, I sprinted out the doors, praying the entire time that Dusty would not leave. I finally found him and his fiancée, Brandi, who had also been praying for his salvation. Together, we herded Dusty back to the arena, and the Lord blessed our diligence that evening with a private, bird's eye view of the Crusade from the press box. As I listened to Rev. Graham's sermon, I first sensed that the Holy Spirit was speaking to me through it and then realized He was laying a tremendous burden upon my heart which I could not ignore:

> "Lay not up for yourselves treasures upon earth, where moth and rust doth corrupt, and where thieves break through and steal: But lay up for yourselves treasures in heaven, where neither moth nor rust doth corrupt, and where thieves do not break through nor steal: For where your treasure is, there will your heart be also. The light of the body is the eye: if therefore thine eye be single, thy whole body shall be full of light. But if thine eye be evil, thy whole body shall be full of darkness. If therefore the light that is in thee be darkness, how great is that darkness! No man can serve two masters: for either he will hate the one, and love the other; or

else he will hold to the one, and despise the other. Ye cannot serve God and mammon."[98]

Recognizing the Holy Spirit's wooing to invest in my eternity, I finally and clearly understood that choosing politics or the path of my own will would have forever enslaved me. As Rev. Graham closed his sermon, I was overwhelmingly endowed with the awareness that the Lord was creating a clean heart within me, a process that continued until the following evening when, as the Rev. Graham concluded his sermon and extended the invitation that night, I was enveloped by an experience similar to the one I had at the hilltop tabernacle of *Cedar Hills Youth Camp* back in 1986; and just as I had done then, I stepped out and followed the Holy Spirit down to the crowded stage. There, I bowed my head and obediently answered the Lord's official call to service: "Also I heard the voice of the Lord, saying, Whom shall I send, and who will go for us? Then said I, Here am I; send me."[99]

Following my decision was a barrage of confirmation that only the Lord could have provided. The very next evening, I was asked to provide transportation for Michael Tait's band, *DC Talk*, as they wanted to tour Oklahoma City. Around midnight, after the youth concert, some of the band's members asked me to take them to the *Oklahoma City National Memorial* in downtown. While they toured the site, I examined The Survivor Tree. Its bark shimmered in the moonlight by reason of thousands of pennies which mourners and visitors had deposited in it. I then came to the Field of Empty Chairs, and the reality that they represented 168 lives that had been prematurely snuffed out, and 168 suffering families, broke my heart. Struggling to process the scene, I shuddered at the thought of losing my loved ones; but when I came to the Reflecting Pool and looked into its placid, glass-like surface, I noticed something different about my reflection. I saw a vessel which the Lord had promised to use. At the Holy Spirit's prompting, I bowed my head and asked Him to fulfill His purpose and promises for my life, unaware that powerful answers were already on the horizon.

---

[98] Matthew 6:19-24 (KJV)
[99] Isaiah 6:8 (KJV)

Shortly after the Crusade, John told Dustin and me about a conversation he had overheard between some attorneys concerning the need for drug and alcohol treatment facilities in Oklahoma and suggested that Dustin and I look into it. Following his advice, Dustin and I discussed the possibility of opening one and decided it would be a great ministry opportunity. Dustin drafted a business plan, and Mom agreed to put up her real estate as collateral for a Small Business Administration (SBA) loan. Uncle Rick, who had worked in various drug and alcohol treatment facilities, volunteered his expertise. After securing the SBA loan, we found and leased a building that was less than a mile from the Crusade office, hired a nurse, and began searching for our first counselor. Karen Woods spent hours praying with me for the Lord to bless our new business and make it a ministry above all else, Ron Shea obtained permission to donate all of the crusade's office equipment to us, Chris set up and programmed all of our phones and computers, Dustin and Aunt Rita recovered a cash register drawer from the side of the road, and Dustin and I found some old, used chairs for the waiting room for pennies on the dollar which, thanks to Mom's designer skills, soon looked brand new. Remarkably, everything just seemed to fall into place as if it had all been prearranged. When the phone number that had been used by the crusade office was transferred to our new business and M.J. and I locked the doors for the last time, I embarked upon my first solo assignment in Christ's service.

CHAPTER 9

New Beginnings

Besides touring Israel, John, Christopher, and I also journeyed into Jordan and later crossed the Red Sea into Taba, Egypt. There, by Tony's arrangement, we were met by a new tour guide, driver, and bodyguard who escorted us to Cairo, Egypt. As we sped through the Sinai desert, I pulled back the curtains that covered the bullet-proof window in our van beside my seat and watched in safety while the vast wasteland raced by like a movie reel and marveled that I was beholding the same wilderness through which Christ had brought the Israelites. The Sinai desert seemed an eerie metaphor for the wilderness of drug addiction, aptly suggesting at least one way of looking at an addict's trek through addiction. Indeed, the Apostle Paul wrote to the *Corinthians* that those things which befell the Israelites in the Sinai wilderness happened unto them for examples unto us:

> "But with many of them God was not well pleased: for they were overthrown in the wilderness. Now these things were our examples, to the intent we should not lust after evil things, as they also lusted. Neither be ye idolaters, as were some of them; as it is written, The people sat down to eat and drink, and rose up to play. Neither let us commit fornication, as some of them committed, and fell in one day three and twenty thousand. Neither let us tempt Christ, as some of them also tempted, and were destroyed of serpents. Neither murmur ye, as some of them also murmured, and

were destroyed of the destroyer. Now all these things happened unto them for examples: and they are written for our admonition, upon whom the ends of the world are come."[100]

Though foreign to me before we opened *New Beginnings Medical Center*, I quickly learned that drug addiction is a wilderness of sin. It is a springboard to every imaginable evil and a veritable wasteland of physical and spiritual destruction, littered with the bones of dead minds, bodies, and souls. To me, passing through the Sinai desert in safety symbolized how the Lord had allowed me, as His minister and servant, to observe the wilderness of drug addiction from a position of security, to the intent that I, by testifying that Jesus Christ is the Son of God, might help lead some out of that wilderness.

The vehicle from which I observed drug addiction was *New Beginnings Medical Center*. As an opioid treatment provider, *New Beginnings* provided pharmacotherapy and counseling for patients addicted to pain medications and alcohol but also offered counseling for other substance abuse addictions. Most of our patients, however, were addicted to opiates. Opiate addiction is physiologically complicated, especially for recreational users (those who take opiates in the absence of pain). For these users, addiction is rather a given – a consequence of their habitual consumption of more and more of the drug, which is taken in pursuit of the same physical effects they experienced as first-time users, even though that "initial high" can never be regained. The "pursuit" of that first high is known in the drug world as "chasing the dragon" and rightly so because, as I observed, it leads the addict deeper and deeper into the wilderness of sin – a dark underworld that is opposed to Truth and love and ruled by the powers and principalities of darkness.

Less than a week after *New Beginnings* opened, the Lord sent me my first assignment – a young man whom I will refer to as Dean, whose shaved head, baggy clothes, and dark-circled, raccoon eyes suggested gang affiliation and sinful living. Margie, with whom I had worked at the Billy Graham Crusade and later hired to be our receptionist, was working the check-in counter the day Dean came in, handed her one

---

[100] 1 Corinthians 10:5-11 (KJV)

of our flyers, and said through slurred speech, "I just got out of jail. My bondsman said ya'll could help me, and one of the conditions of my bond was to come right over here 'cus my lawyer fired me..."

"What kind of trouble are you in?" Margie asked.

Dean gave her his crumpled, four-page rap sheet.

"You do realize this is a methadone clinic, right?"

"I just need help!" he replied.

Margie took Dean to Ginger's office, where she and two other counselors, Tammy and Linda, explained to him that he did not meet the criteria for methadone pharmacotherapy. When he continued to plead for help, Ginger told him, "I'm going to let you visit with Lance. He's one of the owners and may be able to steer you in the right direction."

When I arrived later that day, Ginger relayed the whole story, showed me a copy of Dean's driver's license, and reported that she had asked him to come back the following Monday morning.

"Wow!" I exclaimed, looking at his license, "Is he a skin head?"

"I'm not sure," she said and then showed me his rap sheet. "He was scaring us so we just told him to come back and see you Monday morning."

It was Monday afternoon, however, before the troubled young man returned. Margie buzzed me to let me know he had arrived.

"I've messed up big time," he began as we took a seat in my office.

"I can see that you're in a sinful mess," I interrupted as I perused his rap sheet.

"But, I don't want to know about that. What I want to know about is the young man behind the gang clothing and dark-circled eyes. Tell me something about yourself, your family, and your dreams."

Somewhat hesitant, Dean started to tell me about his life. He was the oldest child of a broken home and lived with his father, a respected businessman in the community. At the age of thirteen, he began abusing alcohol and marijuana and embarked upon the life of crime that was reflected on his rap sheet. As he talked, he seemed to be more comfortable with sharing, and so before long, I knew much about his life's story.

"If you die today, where will you spend eternity?" I asked.

"Heaven, I believe," he replied, clearing his throat nervously.

"How do you know?"

"Because I'm a Christian—I believe in Jesus and have asked for His forgiveness."

I leaned forward in my chair and began to read the laundry list of criminal charges from his rap sheet: "Drug trafficking...robbery... driving while intoxicated...possession of a firearm after prior felony convictions...assault with a deadly weapon...resisting arrest..."

I stopped and looked at him earnestly.

"Are you willing to change your ways? Or, are you going to keep resisting the Holy Spirit's conviction and continue on your present course?" I paused and waited for a response, but he said nothing. "If you want to change your life and walk with Christ, I can help you do that; but if you think you're going to use me just to get you out of trouble, Beware! God protects His servants."

Dean's eyes widened and, stammering a bit, he replied, "Yes, I want to change and live a good life...I want what you have..."

As we had been talking, the Holy Spirit brought a passage from the sixth chapter of *Galatians* to my mind:

> "Brethren, if a man be overtaken in a fault, ye which are spiritual, restore such an one in the spirit of meekness; considering thyself, lest thou also be tempted. Bear ye one another's burdens, and so fulfil the law of Christ. For if a man think himself to be something, when he is nothing, he deceiveth himself. But let every man prove his own work, and then shall he have rejoicing in himself alone, and not in another. For every man shall bear his own burden."[101]

This scripture speaks to bearing, in addition to one's own burden, the burdens of others, while helping them restore, repair, and clean up their lives. The Greek word for *restore* in the original text is *katartizein*, which is a verb that has three meanings. Its first meaning is to set a broken bone. Since a broken bone is painful and useless, the idea presented by this meaning is to restore something that is painful and

---

[101] Galatians 6:1-5 (KJV)

useless. The second meaning of *katartizein* is to remove a tumor. A tumor, of course, is life-threatening so the idea here is to remove that which is life-threatening. The third meaning of *katartizein* is to repair or put back together something that is broken; therefore, the idea presented by this meaning is to repair something which has been broken. The Greek word for *burdens* in the phrase, "Bear ye one another's burdens..." is *baros*, which means heaviness, weight, or trouble and refers to burdens that can be shared by others. Such burdens include fault, ignorance, infirmity, weakness, stress, or grief. The Greek word for burden in the phrase, "For every man shall bear his own burden," is *phortion*, which means a burden or load, as of the freight of a ship or a child in its mother's womb and refers to burdens which can be borne only by one person. Such burdens include physical or mental suffering, death, and the Bema Seat Judgment of Christ.

Seeing that the Holy Spirit had led Dean to me and that Dean was asking for help, saying that he wanted to change, and confessing his belief in Jesus Christ, I believed the Holy Spirit wanted me to help restore him and bear his burdens, so I replied, "Very well, Dean... Here's the plan...For starters, you'll meet with Ginger and me each day. You'll see her for counseling concerning your addiction, and you'll see me for spiritual counseling. Since you've told me that your driver's license is suspended, I'll transport you to and from your appointments. You'll be required to submit to a drug test each week and test negative. You'll need to start attending a Bible-teaching church, and I'll help you find one. You also need to get a job and work on getting your drivers' license reinstated, and I'd like for you to call your attorney and permit him to speak freely with me concerning your case. I know you said earlier that he fired you, but perhaps he'll take you back as a client if he sees that you're serious and willing to pay your bill."

I rose to my feet, walked around the corner of my desk, and extended my hand to him.

"This is the offer that's on the table – you can either take it or leave it – the choice is yours."

"Okay, I'll do my best," he replied and grabbed me in a grateful embrace. His frail, emaciated frame, which was indicative of both physical and spiritual starvation, prompted me to tell him, "We need to get you a cheeseburger!"

Within a few days, I found myself sitting on a sofa next to Dean's lawyer in the district attorney's office, where the assistant district attorney who was prosecuting Dean's case sat before us, along with her supervisor. Following a brief introduction of everyone in attendance, I began to nervously articulate why Dean should not be sent to prison for forty years, but I had barely gotten two sentences out when the supervisor condescendingly replied, "I don't mean to sound flippant, but is a common criminal worth the extra time and effort it's going to take to make special arrangements? We have to think of the taxpayers and represent their wishes."

A cold silence fell upon the room and, for a moment, all seemed lost, but just as I was about to concede defeat, the Holy Spirit blanketed me with His authority and urged me to continue.

"I remember when Peter uttered a similar sentiment..."

"Now who is that?" asked the assistant district attorney, interrupting me. "Is there yet another party involved?"

As the others glared at her with bitter sternness, I continued.

"If memory serves me correctly...it was in the tenth chapter of the *Book of Acts* that God told Peter, '...What God hath cleansed, that call not thou common.'[102] Now, I would venture to say that you don't give audience to every ole country boy who comes in here wanting to help the accused. I suspect this is a rare meeting. The fact that God has arranged it is evidence of His regard for Dean. He doesn't view Dean as common, and neither do I. Moreover, I'd hate to be numbered among those who did. Further, I believe that, if you ladies had a loved one in Dean's predicament, you wouldn't want someone treating them as common but would prefer instead that God's will for their life be considered."

Once again, silence fell upon the room. Finally, after what seemed like hours, the supervisor looked up from Dean's rap sheet and said, "There has to be some kind of punishment. What did you have in mind?"

At that point, Dean's attorney took over and spent the next several minutes negotiating a plea agreement whereby Dean would spend the

---

[102] Acts 10:15 (KJV)

next few months in a boot camp for young offenders, which would be followed by two years of probation.

After the meeting concluded, I shook the supervisor's hand and said, "I can't make any promises as to Dean's behavior; but, I'll do my best, and if he doesn't abide by the terms of his plea agreement, I'll contact you myself because I do respect and appreciate your assistance."

"Mr. Compton?" she asked as we were almost to the door. I stopped and turned around.

"Yes?"

"I'm curious...Do you respond to all of your patients with the same determination?"

"Yes Ma'am. None of them is hopeless."

"If you keep that attitude, you and your people will affect many lives," she replied and retreated into her office.

Indeed, Dustin and I had determined from the moment we opened *New Beginnings'* doors that we would treat everyone who walked through them in accordance with the Golden Rule in *Matthew 7:12 (KJV)*: "Therefore all things whatsoever ye would that men should do to you, do ye even so to them: for this is the law and the prophets." I suspect that, having been on the receiving end of a unique application of it at the *21 Club* in New York City, the Holy Spirit had used the experience to inspire me to adopt a unique way of expressing it.

When word of the special attention Dean had received at *New Beginnings* began to travel and patients from other clinics started transferring to ours in droves, we entered a long era of competitive and regulatory woes, which began early one morning when Margie buzzed my office to let me know that I had a telephone call from the Advocate General's office, a sub-department within the Oklahoma Department of Mental Health and Substance Abuse Services (ODMHSAS) that was responsible for investigating patient complaints.

"Hello, this is Lance," I said, picking up the telephone.

"Mr. Compton, this is the Advocate General for the Department of Mental Health and Substance Abuse Services. I also have on the line with me one of our lead investigators."

"What can I do for you today?" I asked, remembering I had been told that the Advocate General was chummy with the owners of another clinic.

"Sir, it's about your patients, whom you've been using to pressure patients at other clinics to transfer to yours."

I paused, unsure of whether I had heard correctly.

"That's not true," I replied. "Who made this accusation?"

"Well, it may not be you, but some of your patients have been telling patients at other clinics how much better it is at your clinic and trying to convince them to transfer."

"With all due respect, I don't have any control over what our patients say," I replied. "But, this doesn't really sound like a patient complaint. Can you tell me who made this complaint?"

"That is confidential," she said. "Mr. Compton, all I can tell you is that you need to get control of your patients. If they keep trying to persuade patients at other clinics to transfer to yours, we'll be forced to contact them at their places of employment, and that could be very embarrassing for them, as you can imagine!"

"Are you saying that you're planning to violate our patients' privacy as well as your own regulations?" I asked.

"Yessir!"

"Well, you must have more money than I've got," I replied.

"Excuse me?!"

"If you do, you'll probably have some lawsuits filed against you!" I said and hung up the telephone. I then buzzed Dustin and Uncle Rick to tell them what had happened, and Dustin suggested that we eliminate the competition by reducing our prices. Since regulations did not set minimum pricing at the time, we started offering competitive, one-dollar-per-week pricing to all new patients for their first month of treatment and sliding-scale rates for long-term patients. The move brought us national attention and even provoked a few death threats but eventually led to revised treatment standards, which undoubtedly improved the quality of thousands of lives. Because we had no money for professional advertising in the beginning, we spread the word about our new rates on the flyers which we were already passing out in all places where drug addicts were known to congregate. As the word spread, we were literally swamped with new patients.

At approximately four o'clock one morning, Dustin and I were passing out flyers on the south side of Oklahoma City when two friends who were helping us, Jimmy and Michael, telephoned and informed Dustin that "Pat and Eugene," the owners of another clinic, had pinned them into a parking space and were assaulting them. Dustin and I rushed to the scene and got there just in time to overhear threats being made to Jimmy's family.

"What seems to be the trouble?" Dustin asked, as Pat pulled a camera from her jacket and began taking pictures of me and Eugene hollered, "Ya'll need to get out of here, NOW!"

It was a good idea to leave so I told Jimmy and Michael to meet us at the IHOP down the street; but as we were driving away, Eugene pulled in behind Jimmy and Michael in his Lincoln Town Car, and Pat wheeled in behind Dustin and me in her dually.

"Can you believe these people?" I asked. Suddenly, I saw Pat's fog lights in the rearview mirror, gaining on us at a high rate of speed, and concluded that she was attempting to ram my green Buick LeSabre.

"There's the mall!" I shouted. "I'll try to get her on the cameras!"

I headed for the empty, mall parking lot, hoping to catch the high speed chase on the mall's security cameras. After several laps around the parking lot, Pat continued to follow us around the south side of Oklahoma City for at least thirty more minutes before we finally lost her and headed for the IHOP.

"There they are again!" exclaimed Dustin as we turned into IHOP. Pretending not to notice that Pat and Eugene had perched themselves on either side of the parking lot, Dustin and I parked, went inside, found Jimmy and Michael, and sat down with them. Suddenly, there were Pat and Eugene – standing outside the window by our booth! Pat had retrieved her camera and was once again taking pictures. The repetitive flashing caught the attention of the manager, who came over to our table to investigate. While he watched the bizarre scene unfold, Eugene made a gun gesture with his hand and pointed it at each of us.

"Would you object if I called the police?" the manager asked.

"Please do!" we all replied in unison.

Within minutes, police officers surrounded the building and approached Pat and Eugene with hands on their firearms. Later, while taking our statements, the chief officer advised us that Pat and Eugene had accused us of breaking the law by passing out flyers and had been given the choice of leaving or being arrested. While the officer relayed the details, Jimmy looked out the window and hollered, "Looks like he's back!" I looked out the window and spied Eugene's Lincoln in the far corner of the dimly-lit parking lot.

"Just a moment," the officer replied. "I'm going to take care of this."

We watched as he approached Eugene and engaged him in a lengthy conversation. Finally, Eugene drove away, and the red-faced officer returned to our table to finish taking our statements.

Following the IHOP incident, more trouble surfaced concerning our medical director, whom we had hired because he had been Granny's primary care physician so we knew and trusted him. In addition to working for us, he maintained a private practice and was on staff at a hospital. Unfortunately, his supervisor at the hospital, who had a reputation for cursing Christ, was also the medical director at Pat and Eugene's clinic. Thus, we were not surprised when we learned that his supervisor was pressuring him to resign from *New Beginnings* and "making things difficult for him." On the day of his resignation, we received a telephone call from an ODMHSAS inspector who wanted to know if we were operating without a medical director. Curiously, we were also contacted on the same day by a representative of the Substance Abuse and Mental Health Services Administration (SAMHSA), our federal regulator, who asked the same question. The timing of these inquiries suggested that someone had informed our regulators of his resignation, but since he had given us advance notice, we had plenty of time to bring in a replacement before his departure.

Soon after the new medical director came aboard, I was sitting at the conference table in my office one morning with a young couple, preparing to answer their questions about the Word of God, when the peaceful atmosphere was shattered by sirens and screaming in the front lobby. Dustin, Rick, and I rushed to the front just as federal marshals, dressed in black raid gear, came flooding through the front doors and proceeded to line our employees up against the wall like criminals. I demanded to know what was going on but was silenced and told to "back away." The raiders identified themselves as United States Marshals following Dustin's request for identification and claimed to be following up on a "tip" that there was a "known fugitive" on our premises. Before I could even process the accusation, I glanced out the window and saw two Marshals handcuffing our new counselor. I then watched in amazement as the motorcade of unmarked cruisers drove away, carrying our counselor to God knows where. As my eyes followed the cruisers, I spotted a Lincoln Town Car, parked at the curb down the street with a shadowy figure sitting inside.

I immediately contacted the director of the U.S. Marshal's office for our district and opined that the show of force was damaging to our business and credibility and advised of my intention to complain to our U.S. Senator. Interestingly, the individual to whom I spoke admitted that the raid had been unusual and gave me some useful information. Interestingly, two inspectors from ODMHSAS showed up the following morning, asking to see the new counselor's files. As they examined them, the inspectors counted the number of times our new counselor had written "CADC" after his name and suggested that I contact the Oklahoma Drug and Alcohol Professional Counselor Association (ODAPCA) if I wanted to know what was going on. CADC is an acronym that stands for certified alcohol and drug counselor, and ODAPCA is an associational organization for such counselors. After the inspectors left, I telephoned ODAPCA's director and continued to call over the next several days but never received a response. This prompted Mom and me to make a personal visit to ODAPCA's office, which, to our surprise, was not in an office building at all but in a dilapidated house that reeked of mustiness and decay. Upon entering, we were greeted by a disorganized but pleasant secretary whose desk was smack-dab in the middle of what had once been a living room. Mom and I introduced ourselves and asked for an audience with the director, but the secretary's demeanor instantly changed and she replied sharply, "He's very busy!" even though I could see from where I was standing that he was just on the telephone. When he hung up, I walked to his converted bedroom of an office and knocked loudly on the door frame.

"I don't have time to talk to you!" he uttered. "I'm busy with state business!"

Mom came up behind me and responded, "I understand you're attempting to get a bill passed in the Senate."

"Yes! It's very important; but frankly, I don't have time to discuss it with you!"

"We haven't even told you why we're here," I calmly said as we entered his office and took a seat. Mom then asked what our new counselor was accused of doing and whether we could do anything to help him.

"That man has never been a certified alcohol and drug counselor and needs to be in jail!" he shouted in reply. "Now, I have to get some work done so please leave!"

"Not so fast," I said. "You say that he's never been certified? I have copies of his certificates. I also have a letter, signed by you, which states that he was in good standing on the date we hired him. If you knew there was a problem, why didn't you let us know?"

"I already told you I'm not going to discuss this any further," he replied while violently shuffling a handful of papers.

"Which senator is sponsoring the bill that you're working on?" Mom asked. "We have friends in the Legislature, and they may want to take a closer look at this bill."

"Look," he replied, softening his tone, "Your counselor's former employer reported to us that he illegally dispensed pharmaceuticals at their clinic. Like I said, the man deserves to be in prison."

Of course, the "former employer" of whom the director spoke was none other than Pat and Eugene's clinic. Mom scanned the director's degree, certificates, and other credentials which were prominently displayed on the walls of his office and asked, "What are the requirements for a CADC certificate? I have two masters' degrees in counseling. Am I qualified?"

With defeat in his voice, the director replied, "Yes, my secretary has all the information."

I smiled when I saw that the director had no degrees on the wall besides a bachelor's degree and realized Mom had put him in his place.

Not long after we uncovered the truth behind what had prompted the U.S. Marshal's raid, two auditors from SAMHSA, our federal regulator, appeared on our doorstep, unannounced of course, and claimed to be "visiting treatment facilities across the country to offer their expertise." I was immediately suspicious because, whenever the government claims to be there to help, it is, "Katy, bar the door!"

Over the next three days, the SAMHSA auditors examined every file in our building and interviewed our staff and a few patients before confessing to having been dispatched to Oklahoma for the sole purpose of investigating us. Though I was not surprised, I was a little shocked to hear that we had been under "surveillance" for an entire day before they made their presence known. At first, they reported their surprise visit to be related to ODMHSAS' concerns that *New Beginnings* was the fastest growing clinic of its kind in the United States. Oddly, the expression of this alleged concern was laced with the suggestion that, since *New Beginnings* was growing so rapidly, somebody must be doing something wrong or illegal. Later, the auditors revealed the true reason for their visit: concern that *New Beginnings* might be responsible for the death of a recently deceased patient. A tense silence penetrated the room as I rebutted the accusation with plenty of evidence and gave an unexpected testimony of how the deceased patient, who had transferred from Pat and Eugene's clinic, had accepted Jesus Christ as her Lord and Savior on the very day that she passed away.

"Soon after she transferred," I reported, "I was having a conversation with her about our Bible studies when she told me, 'Something is missing in my life.' As I was encouraging her to come to a Bible study, she picked up a couple of the *Steps to Peace with God* tracts that were left over from the Crusade and asked, 'Will you tell me about this in your Bible study?' Rather than waiting, I replied, 'I'll explain it to you now.' And so, with a Christian friend by her side, she listened while I detailed the plan of salvation and answered her questions. When I finished, she said, 'I need to think about it,' and smiled at me. The following week, her friend reported that she had been able to lead her to Christ before she died."

I could have heard a pin drop as the auditors and everyone else in the room listened with rapt attention.

"Interestingly," I continued, "One of this patient's family members, who had also been a patient at Pat and Eugene's clinic, later transferred to *New Beginnings*, whereupon she informed us that Pat and Eugene had been threatening to withhold her medication in what she believed was an attempt to strong-arm her into suing us for the death of her relative. She also reported that Pat and Eugene had contacted her family and promised to pay for an attorney if they would sue us."

I paused, looked directly at the two SAMHSA auditors, whose eyes were as wide as saucers, and said, "I can arrange for you to meet with her relative if you wish."

To my amazement, they declined. At last, the auditor who had said the least throughout the entire three-day ordeal finally spoke up.

"This is one of the top clinics I've visited in my career," he said and encouraged us not to lose sight of whom we really served.

Around the same time as the surprise SAMHSA audit, we experienced another bizarre incident, this time at the hands of auditors from the accrediting commission. Accreditation was a very pricey regulatory requirement, which necessitated periodic submission of our medical and administrative practices to the careful scrutiny of persons whom I found to be steeped in bureaucracy but generally unlearned in practical matters. When the two accrediting auditors arrived at the clinic on the morning of the survey, we learned that one of them owned a clinic and the other was some sort of career consultant in Washington, D.C. Following a short, introductory meeting with the staff, the auditors commenced a grueling, two-day survey. Everything seemed to be going smoothly until ODMHSAS dispatched the state methadone authority, whom I will refer to as Woody Holiday, to meet the auditors. Mr. Holiday arrived just in time to invite them to lunch, and when they returned, the proverbial writing was on the wall. The career consultant, whom I will refer to as Ms. Parnell, immediately tore into citing us for pretty much anything she could think of, including "no thermometer in the employee break room refrigerator" and the fact that we were using file folders as patient files rather than three-ring binders. It did not seem to matter to her that our folders were the exact same ones used by most hospitals, nor did it matter what the regulations dictated. What did matter was that she preferred binders. After communicating her petty citations to us, Ms. Parnell hastily took up the cause of completely removing Jesus Christ's name from the premises, even going so far as to say, "You need to remove all references to Christ in your motto and mission statement; I'm concerned that you're forcing Christ on your patients and employees, and someone might be offended."

Before I could say anything, Dustin spoke for me: "But, that's who we are! Christ is our mission. Our motto and mission statement reflect that mission. Isn't that supposed to be the purpose of a mission statement?"

"Well, Mr. Businessman!" she sassed. If you want to get points for it on your survey, you'll change it!"

"In that case, just deduct those points," Dustin replied.

Not surprisingly, the survey took a nosedive from that point on, leading us to conclude that, once the points were tallied, we would be...unaccredited.

While we waited for the official word, more trouble stirred: we received a notice that ODMHSAS was holding a public hearing on proposed amendments to its pricing regulations, which, of course, threatened to end our competitive prices. Dustin, Uncle Rick, and I decided to attend. On the day of the hearing, the tiny, designated hearing room was filled to capacity. Just as we were being seated, Pat and Eugene entered, accompanied by a small entourage. Pat, albeit hesitantly, took the only remaining seat in the room, which was just a few feet away from me. Woody Holiday then made a few announcements and informed everyone that we would "go around the room introducing ourselves" like school children. When it was my turn and I stood to recite my name and place of employment, I heard Pat say of my socks to somebody seated beside her, "Will you just look at those white socks! That is soooooooooo tacky!" That she had given herself to insulting my footwear in public seemed like a sign of desperation to me; and though I was a little embarrassed, I pitied the fact that her character, behavior, and priorities did not reflect the image of Christ.

Within a few weeks, we received the results of the survey, and the news was not good. The letter read, "ACCREDITATION DENIED." In keeping with consistency, an ODMHSAS inspector showed up almost before we could finish reading the letter, unannounced of course; and within a few days of his inspection, we received word that ODMHSAS was planning to revoke our license. Exasperated, I visited Senator Price and asked whether he could help us. He and another friend of ours, Senator Ben Robinson, the then chairman of the Senate appropriations committee, contacted the Senate liaison for ODMHSAS and demanded an explanation concerning the bizarre "goings on." The next morning, I happened to be standing near the front door and looked outside to see the same ODMHSAS inspector getting out of his car, accompanied by another inspector. Curiously, he wanted to re-review the files he had previously inspected. After perusing them a second time, he emerged from the file room and admitted to having made a "mistake;" informed us that we should have received a perfect score; and confirmed that all efforts by ODMHSAS to revoke our license would cease. On his way to the door, however, and outside the hearing of his companion, he told me, "I just do what I'm told so please know this is nothing personal, but I want you to know that they're coming after you when those two Senators leave office!"

"Who is coming after us?" I asked.

"Just be ready when they leave office," he replied.

As he was walking out the door, in came a letter from SAMHSA, the essence of which was that they had initiated proceedings to revoke our license due to the outcome of our accreditation survey. Since it was only two or three days before Christmas, we resolved to forget our problems, at least for the next few days, and focus completely on celebrating the birth of Jesus Christ. For me, the highlight of that Christmas was the fellowship that we had with our patients. Mom made each of them a personalized stocking, and we catered a family-style dinner for them and gave gifts to their children. The joy I saw in the eyes of some whom I had never seen smile was worth every ounce of trouble we had endured and reminded me of Jesus' words: "...and your joy no man taketh from you."[103] What is more, I was reminded that, "...This day is holy unto the LORD your God; mourn not, nor weep. For all the people wept, when they heard the words of the law. Then he said unto them, Go your way, eat the fat, and drink the sweet, and send portions unto them for whom nothing is prepared: for this day is holy unto our LORD: neither be ye sorry; for the joy of the LORD is your strength."[104]

Though surrounded by trouble on all sides, the joy of the Lord was our strength; and even in the midst of our woes, I faithfully tended to the Lord's service and addressed every assignment that He laid upon my heart. One of the most important was teaching a weekly Bible study.

---

[103] John 16:22 (KJV)
[104] Nehemiah 8:9-10 (KJV)

Daily Bible study had become a habit for me during the months leading up to the Billy Graham Crusade, and the Holy Spirit used the learning, guidance, and satisfaction I had received from this discipline, as well as encounters with three separate patients, to show me that our patients desperately needed to hear the Word of God and that a Bible study was the perfect vehicle by which to deliver it.

Two of these individuals, whom I will call Blake and Jessica, were a couple. Both were on the fast track to Hell, being so hopelessly addicted to Oxycontin that they had resorted to unconventional, end-stage methods of getting high, and both had come to *New Beginnings* in search of something more than just rehab. When Blake was just a pre-adolescent, his father was a first responder to the Oklahoma City bombing and witnessed many things which caused him to openly question why a Holy God would permit such evil. Consequently, Blake heard lots of false and damaging information about Christ and the Bible in his home. Though I was aware of this background, I was still stunned the day Blake asked me if Shakespeare had written the Bible. Jessica was no better off. Having been abandoned at a young age by a mother who chose a life of drugs and liquor over her own daughter, Jessica was raised by grandparents who had never darkened the door of a church, let alone prayed, and this raising was reflected in her life. The third individual, whom I will refer to as Eric, responded when I inquired of him whether he had a personal relationship with Jesus Christ, "I was raised Catholic," to which I replied, "That doesn't answer my question. If you died today, would you go to Heaven or Hell?"

He shrugged his shoulders and said he did not know.

After hearing and observing these things, I was convinced of just how ignorant the world is when it comes to Christ and His Word, and the Holy Spirit burdened my heart with this scripture: "How then shall they call on him in whom they have not believed? and how shall they believe in him of whom they have not heard? and how shall they hear without a preacher? And how shall they preach, except they be sent? as it is written, How beautiful are the feet of them that preach the gospel of peace, and bring glad tidings of good things!"[105]

---

[105] Romans 10:14-15 (KJV)

This was the impetus to begin a daily Bible study at the clinic, which was open to anyone who wanted to attend – even our employees and patients' family and friends. In the beginning, fewer than five patients showed up, but that number quickly grew to more than a dozen. In less than three months, interest in God's Word exploded, and I was soon teaching three Bible studies per week. I began with the fundamentals of salvation. Besides the fact that salvation is the all-important objective, it is a prerequisite to being indwelt by the Holy Spirit, the true teacher of God's Word, upon whom we must rely to learn the deep things of God: "But as it is written, Eye hath not seen, nor ear heard, neither have entered into the heart of man, the things which God hath prepared for them that love him. But God hath revealed them unto us by his Spirit: for the Spirit searcheth all things, yea, the deep things of God. For what man knoweth the things of a man, save the spirit of man which is in him? even so the things of God knoweth no man, but the Spirit of God. Now we have received, not the spirit of the world, but the spirit which is of God; that we might know the things that are freely given to us of God."[106]

Being a teacher who relied upon the Holy Spirit's leading, I emphasized the importance of submitting to Him for wisdom, guidance, and learning and taught my students how to apply God's Word in faith with the full expectation that it would sanctify, cleanse, produce obedience to God, and effect a supernatural mental, physical, and spiritual change within them and in their lives.

Further, I taught them that the sixty-six books of the Bible must be studied one line at a time: "For precept must be upon precept, precept upon precept; line upon line, line upon line; here a little, and there a little:"[107] I emphasized that Scripture *must* be interpreted by other Scripture: "Knowing this first, that no prophecy of the scripture is of any private interpretation."[108] And, I admonished them to be mindful of: 1) historical context, including the date and locale of each book's authorship; 2) economic and political settings; 3) the author of the book or epistle; 4) the author's life and relationship to the Lord; 5) the

---

[106] 1 Corinthians 2:9-12 (KJV)
[107] Isaiah 28:10 (KJV)
[108] 2 Peter 1:20 (KJV)

audience (group, nation, or race); 6) the culture, customs, and lifestyle of the audience; and 7) the reason the book or epistle was written.

Finally, I taught that every word in the Bible is the infallible, inerrant Word of God, given to human authors by the Holy Spirit as they consulted Him through prayer, and written by His supernatural sensitivity and guidance. The Bible's authorship itself testifies to the infallibility and inerrancy of God's Word; dually authored in three separate languages by more than forty authors in a span of approximately fifteen hundred years, God's Word intricately and beautifully reflects the character of Jesus Christ. Like Him, His Word is alive. And, like Him, it is fully God and fully man. It was written by hands of men as they were guided by the hand of God – a Truth that should come as no surprise since God has, from the dawn of time, used the crown of His creation, mankind, to reveal His nature and plans.

As the Bible studies progressed, the Holy Spirit began to convict me that Blake and Jessica were ready to accept Christ. Fearful of making a mistake by attempting to lead them to the Lord myself, I arranged to take them to the Billy Graham Crusade in Kansas City. Michelle and Jimmy agreed to let me take their vehicle, and my old buddies from the Crusade, Chris Mechsner and Ryan Free, agreed to go with us. I was thankful that they were able to go because I wanted Blake and Jessica to experience Godly fellowship and see that they could live better lives than what they were accustomed to living. Chris and Ryan exemplified patience as they witnessed to Blake and Jessica during the drive to Kansas City. When we reached Arrowhead Stadium in Kansas City, we were greeted with open arms by Karen, Ron, Cathy, Wanda, and Larry, all of whom I had informed beforehand of the significance of the visit. My old colleagues rolled out the red carpet for Blake and Jessica, granting them access to every aspect of the Crusade. They were given VIP passes to and privilege of sitting near the stage when *Mercyme* and Michael Tait of *DC Talk* performed. Larry Ross even gave Blake and Jessica front-row seats at a backstage set where the media interviewed these Christian artists, and they were allowed to ask questions of and spend a few minutes with *DC Talk*. Michael Tait shared his testimony with them, and they beamed as he shook their hands and wished them luck.

On the night of the service, we watched from a secure, reserved area on the field. Blake and Jessica were transfixed as Rev. Graham delivered the message of salvation. In the midst of the cool evening breeze, as Chris, Ryan, the crusade staff, and a host of family and friends back home prayed that Blake and Jessica would be receptive to the Gospel of Jesus Christ and led by the Holy Spirit to accept Him, I felt the Holy Spirit descend upon the stadium as He blanketed the cool breeze with warmth. During the invitation, the Holy Spirit's powerful call brought Jessica to the stage in a sprint. As Blake stood next to me, immobile and with his head down, I pleaded with the Lord to convict his heart and bring him to salvation; and in the middle of my prayer, he looked up at me and said, "I want to change and be saved! I don't want to live like this anymore." It was a joyous moment as I prayed with him to accept Christ and observed Larry Ross' sister-in-law, Beth Ellis, who was the appropriate person to witness to Jessica about Christ, counseling her.

That night, two great victories were won in a sports arena but neither had anything to do with sports. For me, knowing that two names had been added to the Lamb's Book of Life minimized the woes we had been experiencing at *New Beginnings*. And, seeing the fruit of my labor for Christ heightened my efforts in getting out the Word of God and ministering to our patients. I carried a great spiritual burden for all of them, though their experiences were foreign to me and I had trouble relating to them at times. Thanks to my Lord, family, and local community, I had lived a very sheltered life. As my friends and family were so fond of saying, I truly was "fresh off the farm." Even so, the Lord had set up *New Beginnings* as a lab of sorts wherein I could observe the depths of the sin nature and learn somewhat of the infinite length to which God's grace abounds. As I observed and learned, I encountered sins that I could never have imagined; and after concluding that society had discarded our patients, labeling them as druggies, criminals, juvenile delinquents, and proclaiming them to be beyond redemption, God allowed me to peer through the lens of His microscope and see their potential in Christ, to the intent that I would know the boundless Truth of these words: "But where sin abounded, grace did much more abound..."[109]

---

[109] Romans 5:20 (KJV)

Early one morning, sometime after we had returned from the Kansas City Crusade, Margie and Ginger came into my office to tell me that Mom was holding on the telephone line and needed to speak with me. I knew from their demeanors and tone of voice that something tragic had happened and so I picked up the telephone only to hear that one of the greatest advocates of my budding ministry, Brother Marty Ingram, had passed away unexpectedly. Brother Marty, my pastor, mentor, and friend, had suffered a fatal heart attack in his sleep at the age of forty-three. He was one of my greatest supporters, and one whom I had called upon for advice practically every week, sometimes just to double-check the scriptures I planned to teach from. After his passing, I initially felt as if a support beam had been taken away from me and my ministry, until I remembered the most important Truth that he ever taught me, which was to depend, in my ministry, upon the Lord rather than him. Thereafter, following much prayer and consideration, I made an important decision concerning my ministry: I decided to return to the study of law; but this time, rather than enrolling in law school, I enrolled as a seminary student at *Southwestern Baptist Theological Seminary* to study God's law.

CHAPTER 10

The Soil

From his perch atop a camel's back at the Giza Necropolis, Christopher hollered, "I can't understand what he's saying, but I think you might have to give him some money before he'll let me down."

When I looked and saw the withered Egyptian to whom he was referring, stretching forth his hand toward me in expectation of receiving another payment, I reminded Christopher of the many warnings we had received about camel scams in Egypt and said, "You should've listened!"

"Yeah, I remember," he grinned. "Just pay the man, and I'll listen to your lecture later!"

After John gave the Egyptian a twenty dollar bill, Christopher dismounted, and we continued our tour of the ancient monuments that dotted the landscape around the Great Pyramids. Before long, we came to the tomb of one of Egypt's ancient dynastic queens, which was open to anyone not opposed to descending some fifty yards into the earth through a narrow tunnel. Not surprisingly, John and Christopher decided this was the perfect time to go exploring. I watched with some amusement as they got down on their hands and knees and crawled onto a rickety, wooden ladder at the mouth of the entrance.

"Are you not going?" John asked as I peered down into the long shaft after them.

"Nosir! I'd better stay up here just in case another payment is needed to get ya'll out."

After they had descended out of sight, I continued to peer into the dark tomb, trying to envision what that experience must have been like for Peter and John as they looked into Jesus' empty tomb. John's account of the Gospel records it as follows:

> "The first day of the week cometh Mary Magdalene early, when it was yet dark, unto the sepulchre, and seeth the stone taken away from the sepulchre. Then she runneth, and cometh to Simon Peter, and to the other disciple, whom Jesus loved, and saith unto them, They have taken away the LORD out of the sepulchre, and we know not where they have laid him. Peter therefore went forth, and that other disciple, and came to the sepulchre. So they ran both together: and the other disciple did outrun Peter, and came first to the sepulchre. And he stooping down, and looking in, **saw** the linen clothes lying; yet went he not in. Then cometh Simon Peter following him, and went into the sepulchre, and **seeth** the linen clothes lie, And the napkin, that was about his head, not lying with the linen clothes, but wrapped together in a place by itself. Then went in also that other disciple, which came first to the sepulchre, and he **saw**, and believed. For as yet they knew not the scripture, that he must rise again from the dead."[110] *(emphasis added)*

What Peter and John experienced as they looked into Jesus' empty tomb was actually a transformation, as evidenced by the different meanings of the three Greek words for "saw" and "seeth" in the original text. In verse five, "saw" comes from the Greek word *blepo*, which means to gaze upon or examine. Thus, the first thing John did when he came to Jesus' empty tomb was to examine it. In verse six, "seeth" comes from the Greek word *theoreo*, meaning to view attentively or consider. Here, Peter considered Jesus' empty tomb; and undoubtedly, he did so in light of the scriptures and Jesus' own prediction of His resurrection. In verse eight, "saw" comes from the Greek word *eido,* which means to perceive, discern, or know and is a picture of John's belief.

---

[110] John 20: 1-9 (KJV)

While I waited for John and Christopher to return to the surface, I took a seat near the tomb's entrance and began to ponder the many patients to whom I had ministered at *New Beginnings*. Some of them, having truly been transformed by their belief in and acceptance of Jesus Christ, revealed themselves to be "good soil;" but others, having rejected Christ, were not transformed at all, and showed themselves to be "bad soil."

Early in *New Beginnings'* life, the Holy Spirit, through the loss of two very special people, revealed to me that the window of opportunity for sowing the seed of the Gospel of Jesus Christ would not be open for long. The first of these losses was M.J., my good friend and mentor with whom I had worked at the Billy Graham crusade. Her sudden death from a brain aneurysm became a daily reminder of something Granny had said to me shortly before she passed away: "Life goes by quickly, and the hope and the life that we have in Jesus Christ is ALL we have at the end of the day."

The day I received word that M.J. had been taken to the hospital, I rushed to her side. Soon after I arrived, the chief surgeon came to her room; and after drawing a brain diagram on the dry erase board and then pointing to the center of it, he said rather matter-of-factly, "The bleed is here, and it's inoperable. Even though her body is still strong, there's no brain activity. I can keep her shell alive for a while, but the person we all knew as M.J. is gone."

The surgeon's words plunged into my heart like a dull knife; it was a painful diagnosis. Later that night, after at least a hundred family members and friends had passed through the intensive care unit to say their goodbyes, I stood next to M.J.'s daughter, Carolyn, as the nurses removed the respirator tubes and life support. Nine and a half minutes later, M.J.'s spirit flew to be with her Lord.

While I was yet mourning her passing, one of our patients, whom I will call Todd, committed suicide. Todd had come to the clinic in a desperate attempt to turn his life around. His best friend, a brown boxer named Charlie, quickly became our mutual interest; and he often brought Charlie to my office for a doggie treat, which I kept hidden for those special occasions. Though Todd was intelligent and full of potential, he had wasted much of it on partying and abusing prescription drugs. His initial progress in treatment seemed promising, but it was short-lived. The emotional problems created by his drug use eventually conquered him after his fiancé broke off their long-term engagement; and he, rather than coming to the loving arms of Christ, turned to the cold, hard barrel of a shotgun instead.

The sudden deaths of M.J. and Todd resounded like an alarm clock within my spirit, waking me to the reality of how quickly death can come, especially to those who do not know Christ and have not believed in Him. Once my spirit was fully awakened to this reality, I asked the Holy Spirit to help me deliver the Gospel of Jesus Christ to as many patients as I could before the window of opportunity closed. He answered my prayers almost immediately when several of Todd's friends, who were also patients at the clinic, inquired of me whether suicide was an unpardonable sin.

Mark's account of the Gospel reveals but one unpardonable sin:

> "Verily I say unto you, All sins shall be forgiven unto the sons of men, and blasphemies wherewith soever they shall blaspheme: But he that shall blaspheme against the Holy Ghost hath never forgiveness, but is in danger of eternal damnation."[111]

Blasphemy against the Holy Spirit is the rejection of the Holy Spirit's testimony, which is that Jesus Christ is the Son of God and the only path to salvation. Therefore, since rejecting the Holy Spirit's testimony is an inherent rejection of Christ, we can see that it is actually the rejection of Christ which makes blasphemy against the Holy Spirit an unpardonable sin – a truth confirmed in the *Book of Acts*:

> "Neither is there salvation in any other: for there is none other name under heaven given among men, whereby we must be saved."[112]

Though suicide was promulgated as an unpardonable sin by the Catholic Church during the Bubonic Plague of the fourteenth

---

[111] Mark 3:28-29 (KJV)
[112] Acts 4:12 (KJV)

century, it is not an unpardonable sin for the believer in Christ because there is no sin which cannot be atoned for and forgiven by His blood. As the Apostle John wrote to fellow believers in *1 John 2:1-2 (KJV)*, "My little children, these things write I unto you, that ye sin not. And if any man sin, we have an advocate with the Father, Jesus Christ the righteous..." Additionally, the Apostle Paul wrote in his epistle to the *Romans* that there is nothing that can separate one who believes in Christ from God: "For I am persuaded, that neither death, nor life, nor angels, nor principalities, nor powers, nor things present, nor things to come, Nor height, nor depth, nor any other creature, shall be able to separate us from the love of God, which is in Christ Jesus our Lord."[113]

For these reasons, suicide is not an unpardonable sin for the Christian. For unbelievers, however, there is no remedy. Condemnation, according to Word of God, is the consequence of unbelief and unbelief only: "He that believeth on him is not condemned: but he that believeth not is condemned already, because he hath not believed in the name of the only begotten Son of God."[114] If one does not believe in God's only solution to sin, which is His Son, Jesus Christ, it is impossible for that person's sins to be forgiven. Therefore, if an unbeliever commits suicide, which is a sin, his act of killing himself, like all of his other sins, is on him rather than on Christ.

The overwhelming response to my teaching on suicide led me to implement *Operation Paul* – a program that was inspired by Billy Graham's *Operation Andrew*. I started *Operation Paul* for the purpose of teaching those who were attending my Bible studies how to better understand their addictions by considering them as spiritual struggles against the flesh. The message of *Operation Paul* was that believers in Jesus Christ can glory and take pleasure in such struggles because Christ's grace is all sufficient, and we are strengthened against our struggles by and through our dependence upon Him. This message was based on the Apostle Paul's declaration that, "And lest I should be exalted above measure through the abundance of the revelations, there was given to me a thorn in the flesh, the messenger of Satan to buffet

---

[113] Romans 8:38-39 (KJV)
[114] John 3:18 (KJV)

me, lest I should be exalted above measure. For this thing I besought the Lord thrice, that it might depart from me. And he said unto me, My grace is sufficient for thee: for my strength is made perfect in weakness. Most gladly therefore will I rather glory in my infirmities, that the power of Christ may rest upon me. Therefore I take pleasure in infirmities, in reproaches, in necessities, in persecutions, in distresses for Christ's sake: for when I am weak, then am I strong."[115]

In this passage of scripture, the Greek word for *infirmities* in the original text is *astheneia,* which, in addition to referring to the physical body's natural weakness and frailty, can also refer to the weakness or infirmity of the soul, including the want of strength or capacity requisite to restrain corrupt desires. Speculation has always abounded concerning Paul's thorn in the flesh; and Bible expositors, theologians, and preachers have offered many explanations as to what it was. Some have said it was poor eyesight, poor health, or even guilt. However, I personally believe that Paul's thorn in the flesh may have been related to his want of strength to restrain some fleshly desire. Regardless of what it was though, the important thing to remember is that we have all the strength necessary to overcome our own personal thorn by and through our dependence upon Jesus Christ; and His grace, which is the forgiveness made possible by His death, burial, and resurrection, is sufficient for every thorn in the flesh, irrespective of what it may be or whether it is a physical or spiritual struggle.

Operation Paul brought a number of newcomers to the Bible studies; and fortunately, we experienced a contemporaneous interlude of peace from the tumult surrounding us, which allowed me to concentrate on witnessing and teaching the Word of God. During this period of peace, we applied to be re-surveyed by our accrediting commission and received accreditation. We also received an apology from the Secretary of the Department of Health and Human Services together with confirmation that *New Beginnings* was in good standing with SAMHSA.

Meanwhile, as I was sitting in my office one morning, preparing for another Bible study, the Lord sent me another assignment with a knock at the door.

---

[115] 2 Corinthians 12:7-10 (KJV)

"Come in!" I hollered.

The door opened, and a tall, lanky kid, whom I will call Dale, strolled into my office.

"Whatsup, Hillbilly?" he said, greeting me with a hug.

Dale was a Christian, whose thorn in the flesh, like many of the patients with whom I was working, was his addiction to Oxycontin and marijuana. Dale's significant progress in treatment was due in large part to his participation in the Bible studies.

"I've got a favor to ask!" he said, sitting down in front of my desk.

"You and everybody else," I laughed. "What is it that you need?"

"I brought some guys with me today that are really bad off, and I was wondering if you can help them? I think they're ready to make a change, and I want you to help them like you've helped me."

"These are friends of yours?" I asked.

"Yes, they're my best friends. One of them is my twin brother."

"Alright, I'll see what I can do. Let's go outside, and you can introduce them to me."

I arose from my chair and walked to the private waiting room outside my office where Dale's friends and twin brother were waiting. The sight of them, sitting in a row on one of the sofas, in varying stages of withdrawal, gave me mixed emotions. Their pasty skin, skinny bodies, and sunken eyes – were a disgusting sight. With orphan-like visages, they stared almost straight ahead, suggesting that they were just as dazed spiritually as they were physically.

"I'm Lance," I said, extending my right hand to each one of them.

"I'm Lane—Dale's brother," replied the first.

"Christopher," said the one in the middle, his chin pressed tightly against his chest.

"Austin," said the third.

"Please come and have a seat in my office." I pointed to my open door. "I'll be right back."

I was walking to the file room to gather three new file folders for the admissions counselor when I suddenly remembered that Blake had brought Christopher to the clinic once before, intending to deceive the medical staff, and I had forbidden him to bring Christopher back on the premises. As I pulled three empty folders from the shelf, I began to have doubts and felt apprehensive for leaving them in my office unattended, but the Holy Spirit responded to my concerns:

> "A foolish woman is clamorous: she is simple, and knoweth nothing. For she sitteth at the door of her house, on a seat in the high places of the city, To call passengers who go right on their ways: Whoso is simple, let him turn in hither: and as for him that wanteth understanding, she saith to him, Stolen waters are sweet, and bread eaten in secret is pleasant. But he knoweth not that the dead are there; and that her guests are in the depths of hell."[116]

I immediately recognized that these young men had briefly turned aside from their folly and found their way to *New Beginnings* by the leading of the Holy Spirit; and I knew that, as an under-shepherd of Jesus Christ, I was responsible for sowing the message of Christ during their brief interlude from sin:

> "...For unto whomsoever much is given, of him shall be much required: and to whom men have committed much, of him they will ask the more."[117]

I shivered as I considered the judgment I would face in the future at the Bema Seat of Christ if I failed in this task:

> "Wherefore we labour, that, whether present or absent, we may be accepted of him. For we must all appear before the judgment seat of Christ; that every one may receive the things done in his body, according to that he hath done, whether it be good or bad."[118]

So, with the file folders clutched against my chest, I sat down at the desk in the middle of the file room and prayed.

---

[116] Proverbs 9:13–18 (KJV)
[117] Luke 12:48 (KJV)
[118] 2 Corinthians 5:9–10 (KJV)

Following Christopher's admission to the clinic, I wasted no time in counseling him about Christ, an exercise which led to my discovery of some interesting facts. He, along with some of the other patients, freely acknowledged their reasons for not attending church. One of the most shocking reasons I heard, concerning a church in Del City, was that its pastor was a drug dealer. Equally notable among the reasons I heard involved a prominent church in Moore, a deacon of which had sold Oxycontin to one of our patients. Upon hearing these and other equally shocking reasons for laying out of church, I felt led of the Holy Spirit to emphasize that those things which they had witnessed were the workings of Satan, not Christ, which brought forth a study of persecution and infiltration, two methods that Satan has used for centuries in his effort to destroy the testimony of Christ and the witness of His church.

The persecution of early Christians by the iron-fisted Roman Empire is perhaps the best historical example of persecution. Under Rome's rule, early Christians suffered many things, even death. With the exception of John, all of the New Testament writers were killed. Matthew died from wounds inflicted by a halberd, an ax-like weapon with a sharp spike at the end. Mark was dragged to death. Luke was hanged. Peter and Jude were both crucified. James was beaten to death. And, Paul was beheaded. Lesser known Christians were tortured for denouncing Rome's paganism, tried for treason because they protested the government's use of their tax money to support false religion, accused of atheism for refusing to worship idols, labeled cannibals because unbelieving Romans did not understand the Lord's Supper, ridiculed for their monogamous lifestyles, and demonized for refusing to assimilate into Rome's sexual culture. Persecution has changed little since Roman times; in some parts of the world, it is still just as violent. In "civilized" or religious-tolerant countries, where Christians may not be persecuted to the point of death, they are persecuted in other ways. In my own neck of the woods, I have seen that those who stand up for Jesus Christ and the Word of God or call out the false teachers among them are criticized, ostracized, and boycotted among other things. But, persecution still strengthens the True members of the body of Christ just as it did in Ancient Rome.

By contrast, infiltration by predatory, disguised unbelievers threatens to weaken the Church rather than strengthening it. Of infiltrators, the Gospel according to Matthew warns:

> "Beware of false prophets, which come to you in sheep's clothing, but inwardly they are ravening wolves. Ye shall know them by their fruits. Do men gather grapes of thorns, or figs of thistles?"[119]

Christians must continually be on guard against infiltration to avoid being taken captive:

> "Beware lest any man spoil you through philosophy and vain deceit, after the tradition of men, after the rudiments of the world, and not after Christ."[120]

In addition to being on guard, Christians must earnestly contend for their faith in Christ Jesus:

> "Beloved, when I gave all diligence to write unto you of the common salvation, it was needful for me to write unto you, and exhort you that ye should earnestly contend for the faith which was once delivered unto the saints. For there are certain men crept in unawares, who were before of old ordained to this condemnation, ungodly men, turning the grace of our God into lasciviousness, and denying the only Lord God, and our Lord Jesus Christ."[121]

Finally, Christians must always be prepared to correct and follow through with correcting errors propounded by infiltrators. They must also reprove and rebuke those who have embraced such error:

---

[119] Matthew 7:15–16 (KJV)
[120] Colossians 2:8 (KJV)
[121] Jude 1:3–4 (KJV)

"Preach the word; be instant in season, out of season; reprove, rebuke, exhort with all long suffering and doctrine. For the time will come when they will not endure sound doctrine; but after their own lusts shall they heap to themselves teachers, having itching ears; And they shall turn away their ears from the truth, and shall be turned unto fables. But watch thou in all things, endure afflictions, do the work of an evangelist, make full proof of thy ministry."[122]

After hearing about the drug peddling pastor and deacon and various other wolves in sheep's clothing, I sought the Holy Spirit's guidance; and He responded by leading me to take some of the patients who had reported these things to church with me in Binger and in sending others to churches whose pastors and leaders I knew and trusted. He also laid it upon my heart to teach the parable of the sower, using the same teaching method my grandparents had used to teach it to me when I was six years old.

To recount how I first learned about the parable of the sower, it happened one day when my grandparents were preparing to plant a new patch of Bermuda grass in their front yard. When Papa finished working the clay soil with his old *Sears & Roebuck* rototiller, we took rakes and evened out the soil until it was level with the sidewalk. After we had manicured and cleared the soil of debris, we filled some large, antique salt shakers with seed and sprinkled it on top of the freshly tilled soil. When we finished spreading the seed, we sat down in the metal chairs on the front porch, admiring the product of our toil.

"What are we gonna do with the rest of that seed?" I asked pointing to the crumpled, brown paper sack that was resting at the edge of the front porch.

"We might need it later on down the road," Papa replied.

"Let's just scatter it all around," I suggested. I heard whispering behind me and turned around to see my grandparents leaned in toward each other, trying to keep me from hearing what was being said.

---

[122] 2 Timothy 4:2-5 (KJV)

"We'll use the rest of the seed, and it'll be a fun lesson," Grandma said, getting out of her chair and going inside the house.

Papa instructed me to follow him. He reached inside the paper bag, pulled out some seed, and cast it upon the ground. The seed fell all around.

"Your turn," he said. "Do it just like that."

I eagerly grabbed a handful and tossed the seed in every direction. Some fell on the sidewalk, porch, in the flowerbed, among the weeds – but some fell into the inviting soil. Just then, Grandma came out of the house with a worn Bible.

"Come here," she called.

Papa and I sat down beside her as she thumbed through the Bible, searching for the parable of the sower. The sheepskin pages rustled in the wind as the Holy Spirit opened my ears to a memorable Truth. I listened with great anticipation as she read the parable and Jesus' interpretation.

"See," Papa remarked, pointing to where the seed had fallen. "It's just like Jesus said. Now, we'll watch and see what happens."

For weeks, I watched the seed and saw some of it get blown away by the wind, eaten by birds, and choked out by the weeds. Some of it, however, sprouted and turned into a carpet of beautiful, green grass.

Knowing I had to incorporate this lesson into the Bible studies, I retained Mom's assistance in purchasing flower pots, potting soil, and flower and grass seed. Then, with the help of Ginger and Margie, I labeled and placed each pot on the wooden deck outside the clinic. During the next Bible study, I asked the patients to help me pour the best soil into the pot labeled "good soil," and we planted flower seed in that pot. Next, we buried a flat rock approximately an inch deep in the pot that represented the stony places and planted flower seed in it. In the pot that represented the thorny places, we planted a generous amount of shade grass together with the flower seed. Finally, we tossed some of the flower seed along the sidewalk and on top of the deck to illustrate the wayside. After the seed had been sown and the soil watered, I arranged the pots in a row along the edge of the deck and sat down to read the parable from the Word of God. Just as I was about to read, the breeze began to rustle the pine tree branches overhead.

"The same day went Jesus out of the house, and sat by the sea side. And great multitudes were gathered together unto him, so that he went into a ship, and sat; and the whole multitude stood on the shore. And he spake many things unto them in parables, saying, Behold, a sower went forth to sow; And when he sowed, some seeds fell by the way side, and the fowls came and devoured them up: Some fell upon stony places, where they had not much earth: and forthwith they sprung up, because they had no deepness of earth: And when the sun was up, they were scorched; and because they had no root, they withered away. And some fell among thorns; and the thorns sprung up, and choked them: But other fell into good ground, and brought forth fruit, some an hundredfold, some sixtyfold, some thirtyfold. Who hath ears to hear, let him hear."[123]

In this parable, which is one of the parables of the Kingdom of Heaven, the soil represents the human heart, the seed represents the Word of God, and the birds that devoured the seed represent Satan. Jesus said he who received the seed by the way side is the individual who hears the Word but does not understand it, and Satan takes it away from his heart. The wayside hearer is a non-believer. There are generally two kinds of wayside hearers: those who have rejected Jesus Christ as the Son of God and the only way to Heaven and professing Christians who do not believe the Bible is entirely true, accurate, or relevant. Jesus said he who received the seed into stony places is the individual who hears the word and receives it with joy, but because he is not rooted in the Word, it endures only until tribulation or persecution arises, and then he is offended by it. Stony hearers are also non-believers. They profess to be Christians, but their profession of faith is usually nothing more than an emotional experience of the flesh and is not genuine. Many of these individuals live double lives, masquerading in public as moral and obedient but privately devoted to the flesh. Jesus said he who received the seed among thorns is the individual who hears

---

[123] Matthew 13:1-9 (KJV)

the Word but the cares of the world and deceitfulness of riches choke the Word, and he becomes unfruitful. These are also non-believers. Made in the image of the world, they exhibit a love for money and materialistic accoutrements but deny Christ when it is convenient to do so or when worldly opinion or pressure dictates. Circumstances such as careers, achievements, and illness often determine their degree of faith and obedience, and they sometimes fall back on childhood events as a means of justifying their sin rather than confessing it. Finally, the Lord said he who received the seed into good ground is the individual who both hears and understands the Word, becomes fruitful, and brings forth varying amounts of fruit. The good soil represents true believers in Christ who want to hear the Word and know what it means. These are the ones who are given understanding, as Jesus said in the parable: "Who hath ears to hear, let him hear."[124] The good soil hearers know the sound of their Master's voice:

> "My sheep hear my voice, and I know them, and they follow me: And I give unto them eternal life; and they shall never perish, neither shall any man pluck them out of my hand."[125]

As I sowed the seed of the Word through my ministry at *New Beginnings*, the Lord sent a number of patients to me whom I believe were "good soil." One of these I will refer to as Mark, an intelligent college student who had been brought up in a Christian home by affluent parents. Another I will refer to as Trevor, a champion high school weight lifter and baseball player. When Mark came to us for help, he was fighting to sever ties with his former drug dealers – a father and son team who lived respectable lives in public as an assistant fire chief and a full-time student at a private, religious school, respectively. Mark claimed that they were threatening and harassing him daily to continue buying drugs from them; but I advised him the only way to break free from his sinful past was to totally surrender every aspect of his life to Christ and depend on Him for protection, and I believe he did.

---

[124] Matthew 13:9 (KJV)
[125] John 10:27-28 (KJV)

Before coming to *New Beginnings*, Trevor had been arrested and charged with drug possession. The first time I discussed his criminal charges with him, he alleged that, because he was unable to afford his legal fees, his attorney had suggested that he provide him and a complicit judge with cocaine and marijuana as "payment." Deeply troubled by Trevor's allegations, I immediately telephoned his probation officer, who assured me that she would recommend in-patient treatment to the prosecutor assigned to Trevor's case. Fortunately, the prosecutor agreed with the recommendation, and we were able to get Trevor admitted to an out-of-state facility. Because he had previously attended in-patient treatment but failed to follow through, I decided to drive him to the facility myself. Before leaving him there, I cultivated his heart, sowing the Gospel seed with these parting words: "Trevor, for the most part, people don't need rehab. They need Christ. The only way you'll ever be free from the grip of evil is to accept Jesus Christ as your personal Lord and Savior and be obedient to Him." Trevor finished rehab, and I know the change I later witnessed in him demonstrated his surrender to Christ.

Sadly, for each "good soil" individual I encountered, I met a multitude from the other groups, one of whom was a high school, state wrestling champion whom I will refer to as Thomas. Thomas' parents were obsessively career-oriented and driven by the pursuit of money, but although they provided a good lifestyle for their son and lavished him with gifts, they did not seem to notice that his greatest desire was their attention. Because Thomas' parents harbored many misconceptions about Jesus Christ, it was no surprise that they had fallen for the lie that "all paths lead to Heaven." To their amazement, I agreed to counsel their son free of charge; but since we often met at their home because they feared being seen at the clinic, I counseled all of them, begging and pleading with them to turn to Christ and repeatedly advising them that, "For the love of money is the root of all evil: which while some coveted after, they have erred from the faith, and pierced themselves through with many sorrows."[126] Tragically, they had no capacity for Christ and dismissed my pleas.

---

[126] 1 Timothy 6:10 (KJV)

One day, Thomas' mother telephoned me in a panic, wanting me to help her find Thomas. When I arrived at her home, she was inconsolable. After pouring out her heart to me, we climbed into her pricey, luxury sedan and drove to a seedy part of town to look for Thomas. Since the age of thirteen, he had made that part of town his second home as he sold his body into sexual perversion for money and drugs. When we finally found him, he was unrecognizable and reeked from the stench of sin. After we brought him home, I read several passages of Scripture to all of them and did everything I could to convince them with the Word of God that submission to one sin opens the door for Satan to seize full control. Sadly, their refusal to heed the warnings which the Lord had so mercifully placed before them led to such complete blindness that they were no longer capable of seeing the one and only cure for sin. Neither could they see that their world would soon crumble with unspeakable tragedy.

Another of these individuals was a patient whom I will call Donna, a prostitute in her mid-forties who came to my attention when her pimp threatened another patient in the parking lot. Following that incident, I took an interest in Donna and learned she had been using drugs for twenty years and was totally imprisoned by her sinful lifestyle. She had two wonderful teenage children who lived with her ex-husband and his second wife. The children were very concerned for their mother's safety and desperately wanted her to forsake the drugs and prostitution. I repeatedly sounded the warning that her choices were leading her straight to Hell, pointed her to certain Scriptures, and implored her to accept Christ. Donna's counselor even set up a family intervention, during which her ex-husband and current wife invited her to live with them until she could get on her feet. They told her they had secured a job for her and even offered to pay her bills until she could pay them herself. Their offer was an unheard-of, once-in-a-lifetime opportunity; but she rejected it, choosing instead to remain in her sins.

One of the most memorable of these individuals was a young man whom I will call Bryan. I had known Bryan and his family for many years but had no idea he was addicted to cocaine or that he was manufacturing methamphetamines and selling prescription pharmaceuticals. Following a raving, drug-induced fit outside his home, he was arrested and charged with several drug-related offenses. With a host of prior convictions on his record, he was facing life in prison at a very young age. I did everything I could think of to help Bryan, from counseling him repeatedly about Christ to finding him an attorney. Ultimately, my efforts failed. Like so many others, Bryan also turned his back on the Word of God, refused to acknowledge that Christ was the only answer to his predicament, and became another spiritual casualty.

As one engaged in the sowing of the seed of God's Word, I have seen the Word of God fall by the way side, upon stony places, among thorns, and onto good soil. Like a natural seed, God's Word faces a host of obstacles after it has been sown. Just as the natural seed is opposed by the elements, birds, and other forces and must compete with other seed, so too is the Word of God faced with opposition and forced to compete with the seed of evil in taking root and developing to fruition. And, just as the natural seed requires good soil to develop to fruition, so too does the Word of God require good ground to produce a harvest. Only the "good soil" hearers of the Word of God will be transformed, but the bounty which God's Word brings forth once it has been sown is truly miraculous, just as Jesus said, "...So is the kingdom of God, as if a man should cast seed into the ground; And should sleep, and rise night and day, and the seed should spring and grow up, he knoweth not how."[127]

---

[127] Mark 4:26-27 (KJV)

CHAPTER 11

The Storm

Sailing across the *Sea of Galilee* was one of the most tranquil experiences of my visit to the Holy Land. So peaceful was the calm that one could have easily forgotten that the *Sea of Galilee* is susceptible to sudden and ferocious storms. The modern-day replica of the first-century fishing vessel in which we sailed glided across the smooth water with ease while our fellow passengers sang gospel hymns in their native languages, calling to my mind two great Truths I had learned while assisting Wanda McCurdy with the Crusade's language accommodation program – that the message of Jesus Christ does not change from one language to another and is not inhibited by cultural barriers. As I listened to the familiar tunes in a foreign tongue, I stood at the boat's railing, peering into the glassy, emerald-colored water, trying to imagine what it must have been like to see Jesus calm a great storm on the *Sea of Galilee*.

As lively stones, built upon the Rock of Jesus Christ, one of the greatest assurances a believer has in Him is protection from the storms of life, for He said, "…Whosoever heareth these sayings of mine, and doeth them, I will liken him unto a wise man, which built his house upon a rock: And the rain descended, and the floods came, and the winds blew, and beat upon that house; and it fell not: for it was founded upon a rock."[128] Moreover, we have the authority to ask Christ to rebuke whatever storms come against us, just as His disciples did on the *Sea of Galilee*: "And the same day, when the even was come, he saith unto them, Let us pass over unto the other side. And when they had sent away the multitude, they took him even as he was in the ship. And there

---

[128] Matthew 7:24-25 (KJV)

were also with him other little ships. And there arose a great storm of wind, and the waves beat into the ship, so that it was now full. And he was in the hinder part of the ship, asleep on a pillow: and they awake him, and say unto him, Master, carest thou not that we perish? And he arose, and rebuked the wind, and said unto the sea, *Peace, be still.* And the wind ceased, and there was a great calm."[129]

Though I could only imagine Jesus calming that first-century storm, I did observe Him calm another storm which blew into mine and my family's lives in 2005. That summer was a very difficult time for *New Beginnings.* Thanks to continuous government interference, attorney fees, a couple of sticky-fingered employees, patients who were either unable or unwilling to pay for their treatment, a staggering overhead, and various other factors, our financial condition tanked. What is more, the continuing competitive and regulatory woes were beginning to take a toll, and it was becoming increasingly difficult to focus on our purpose. Though Dustin managed to keep our precarious financial situation a secret for months, it finally came to light the day our pharmaceutical provider notified us that, unless our accumulating account balance was paid down, they would not continue to supply us with pharmaceuticals. Mine and Mom's efforts to find a solution to the problem epitomized the pitiful condition in which we found ourselves. Resolved to pay at least a significant chunk of the amount we owed to the pharmaceutical company, Mom, donning her favorite crocheted shawl, and I, dressed in tattered work clothes and worn-out shoes, visited our local bank to secure a cashier's check. Creaking loudly, the unstable floor of the converted double-wide trailer announced our entry.

"We need to get a cashier's check," I said.

While Vera, the teller, consulted a computer from the Commodore 64 era, Mom rummaged through an old soup can that someone had loosely wrapped in felt and converted to a Dum Dum receptacle. Helping herself to a free sucker, she then offered one to me, but I politely declined. When Vera finally found our account, she jotted the balance on a card and, almost apologetically, slid it across the counter with her left index finger. On the card, beneath a prominently displayed, yellow smiley face and pre-printed bold text that read, "Your current balance is…," was written

---

[129] Mark 4:35-39 (KJV)

"$10,873.56," preceded by a *minus* sign. Mom's hand went limp when she saw the negative balance, causing the Dum Dum to fall from her mouth; and I simply replied, "Uh...okay, thank you...we'll come back later."

The floor creaked again as we made our way to the exit, hoping to leave without being seen. Neither Mom nor I said a word as we climbed into my pickup truck and slammed the doors. But, as Mom adjusted her shawl and I started the ignition, I fell back into my seat, sighed heavily, and said, "Well, I think that went well!" to which we responded with a burst of laughter.

On the morning of Monday, August 29, 2005, on the campus of Oklahoma Baptist University, the satellite forum where I was taking seminary classes through Southwestern Baptist Theological Seminary, my professor, Dr. Clyde Cain, called upon me before class began to offer up a prayer to the Lord for the people of the Gulf Coast Region because *Hurricane Katrina* was making landfall in Louisiana at that very moment. As I led the class in prayer, we petitioned God to protect those in the storm's path, reassure them of His presence, send His people to help them recover from the destruction, and use the event to draw people to Christ. Even after class had ended, I continued to offer up those same petitions for the remainder of the day, unaware of just how powerful and personal the Lord's answer to my prayers would be.

A few days after the hurricane had passed, Chris Mechsner telephoned to tell me that a friend of his was organizing and taking a team of workers to the Gulf Coast region to assist with the reconstruction and cleanup. Knowing that Dustin and I were always on the lookout for employment opportunities for our patients, Chris informed us that there were hundreds of temporary jobs available in the devastated region, most of which consisted of blue-tarping damaged residential roofs, and said the average pay for just a few weeks of employment was somewhere in the neighborhood of ten thousand dollars per worker. Chris suggested that Dustin and I organize our own team so Dustin and I researched and prayed about the idea and concluded that the Lord could be opening the door to another ministry opportunity while, at the same time, making it possible for us to improve our patients' financial conditions as well as our own. After much consideration, Dustin and I finally decided that Uncle Rick and I would take a team of workers to the Gulf Coast region while he stayed behind to manage the operation. This decision required me to take a leave of absence from my seminary classes, which I did without so much as a hint that I was on the cusp of learning lessons far greater than anything I could ever learn in the classroom.

Since some fifty people, including twenty patients, had volunteered to go with us, I knew that I would need dependable help so I invited Brian Woods, one of my fraternity pledge brothers, and he, in turn, invited his friend, Russell. With our team assembled, we departed for the Gulf Coast; and almost two days later, in the dead of night, we reached our pre-assigned campground in Hattiesburg, Mississippi, which was nothing but a pine grove directly behind a truck stop. There, we parked, commenced to unloading supplies, and started setting up the camp. As Brian unloaded a trailer in the light from the headlights of my truck, he suddenly disappeared from my sight. When I jumped out to see what had happened, I discovered that he had stepped off into an open septic tank.

"That leg needs tending to!" I said after we had pulled him back to the surface.

"I'm fine!" he replied as I peeled his shredded pants away from the torn flesh on his leg. "Let's just get this stuff done."

"Not 'til something is done for that leg," I said. "There's no tellin' what kind of bacteria was on that metal...you could get the lock jaw... and then you wouldn't be able to gripe at me..."

With that, I took a bottle of rubbing alcohol from a first aid kit that someone had placed beside me and, in the dim glow of a flashlight, poured its contents over Brian's open wounds. The alcohol's ferocious sting was just about to bring him out of his skin when someone decided to move my truck and drove it off into the same septic tank.

Looking at the scene in disbelief, Brian asked me, "Compton, what are we doing here?"

The answer proved to be that, each evening, as we all recouped from the day's labor, everyone gathered around for my Bible study, which I held every night without fail in the glow of a kerosene lantern. These studies of the Word of God opened the door for me to privately share the Word of Truth with several of the young men who had made the trip with us. One of them, whom I will call Rodney, was not even a patient at the clinic. Having been intrigued with the Gospel of Jesus Christ from the moment I told the group to watch the leaders they encountered for the purpose of observing that Christians handle matters differently from non-believers, Rodney asked me many questions; and one morning, as I was preparing to leave the campsite, he said that he wanted to spend the day with me.

"Fine with me," I replied. "I could use your help."

While driving to the military base in Biloxi to pick up a load of drinking water for the crew, Rodney engaged me in a discussion of questions that he had concerning the Bible. Some of his questions were answerable in a sentence or two but others merited lengthy explanations. In the course of our conversation, it became apparent that Rodney's beliefs concerning Christ were based on what he had heard rather than his own learning, but his questions did reveal a great deal of thought pertaining to and interest in spiritual matters. They also proved that he was seeking the Truth and testing the depth and sincerity of the faith, knowledge, and belief which he had observed in me.

"How do you know the Scriptures are true?" he asked.

I said, "When I was saved, I, like everyone who is saved, received the gift of the Holy Spirit. He is the One who has taught and given me discernment to know that the Scriptures are the Truth. I have also been helped in reaching this conclusion by my Christian brothers, including my family, some of my friends, and the true pastors and ministers to whom I have listened over the years."

"I've heard that the term 'saved' was thought up by the Baptists and isn't even in the Bible," he replied.

"Where did you hear such a thing?" I asked. When he named a popular, secular television channel, I responded, "Well, it's a sad individual who gets his information about Christ from television programs that are produced by workers of iniquity and natural men who have no spiritual discernment."

I asked him to retrieve my Bible from the console as well as the Bible concordance which I had previously placed behind the seat. While he located them, I said a silent prayer, asking the Holy Spirit for His wisdom and guidance. He responded by directing me to ask Rodney to read *John 10:9 (KJV)* aloud:

"I am the door: by me if any man enter in, he shall be saved, and shall go in and out, and find pasture."[130]

I then explained the concept of Jesus as the Good Shepherd and only door to the sheep fold and directed Rodney to read *Romans 10:13 (KJV)*:

"For whosoever shall call upon the name of the Lord shall be saved."[131]

"Salvation belongs to anyone who will believe in Jesus Christ," I replied. "But, let's also look at the original Greek text." After I had showed him how to use the concordance, he found the scriptures that he had just read and the Greek word from which the phrase *shall be saved* was translated.

"*Sozo*," he said.

"Okay, good," I replied, "Now read the definition of *sozo*."

"To save, keep safe and sound, to rescue from danger or destruction, injury or peril...to save a suffering one from perishing from a disease, to make well, to cure...to preserve one who is in danger of destruction, to save or rescue...to save in the technical biblical sense...to deliver from the penalties of the messianic judgment...to save from the evils which obstruct the reception of the Messianic deliverance..."

He stopped reading aloud but continued silently for a few moments and then said, "Wow! This phrase *'shall be saved'* occurs several times in the New Testament. Here's a list of all the verses that contain it: Matthew 10:22 and 24:13; Mark 13:13 and 16:16; John 10:9; Acts 2:21, 11:14, and 15:11; Romans 5:9, 5:10, 9:27, 10:13, and 11:26; 1 Corinthians 3:15; and 1 Timothy 2:15. And, it's also in several Old Testament verses: Numbers 10:9; Psalm 80:3, 80:7, and 80:19; Proverbs 28:18; Isaiah 64:5; and Jeremiah 17:14, 23:6, and 30:7."

"Now," I replied, "What is the *Hebrew* word and definition from the Old Testament?" I smiled as he speedily thumbed through the

---

[130] John 10:9 (KJV)
[131] Romans 10:13 (KJV)

concordance with determination that was indicative of his thirst for the Truth.

"*Yasha*...To save, to be saved, to be delivered; to be liberated; to be saved as in battle; to be victorious; to save from moral troubles; to give victory to..."

He finished reading just as we arrived in Biloxi. After picking up our water and getting back into my truck to head to his group's worksite, we returned to our conversation. One of the things Rodney wanted to discuss was the widespread evil that had surfaced in *Katrina's* wake. The corruption that we had seen and heard about clearly bothered him. Governmental finger pointing, contracts for crony contractors, avoidance of liability by insurance companies...and that was just the tip of the iceberg. When we finally reached his worksite, he changed the subject back to the Bible, then looked at me and said, "I just can't believe that, for so long, I have not known the Truth and that 'saved' is an actual Biblical term. Why would people say it's made up?"

"Well," I replied, "I think the very definition of '*sozo*' is your answer because evil is always going to attempt to obstruct one's deliverance from it."

Pointing to the folder on the dashboard that held the pink Right of Entry forms, I added, "The owner of this house couldn't tarp his own roof. He needed our help, but before we could provide it, he had to sign one of these forms, which granted us the authority to help him. Similarly, we have all sinned, and there's nothing we can do to help ourselves where sin is concerned. God, on the other hand, *can* help us. He has provided a solution to our sin, which is Jesus Christ; but we must believe He is the Son of God before we can be saved from our sins. If and when we do that, we give Christ the 'right of entry' into our hearts – and that, my friend, is what it means to be saved or born again. So, why don't you think on these things while you're working today?"

Rodney looked at me as if a veil had been lifted and later believed upon and accepted Jesus Christ as his personal Lord and Savior.

Meanwhile, Brian disclosed to me that his physician back in Oklahoma had discovered a mass below his sinus cavity shortly before we had departed for Mississippi and advised him to have a CT scan immediately. When I inquired as to whether the mass was malignant, he replied, "Oh, the doctor isn't certain. I want to put the scan off until we get home, but he thinks it's a bad idea to wait."

"Well, what are you thinking?" I asked.

Staring at the carpet of pine needles beneath his work boots, Brian answered, "I don't know. I'm not sure what removing it will involve. And, I don't want to end up being deformed or something."

Hoping a little humor would help alleviate his fear and worry, I replied, "I guess we could travel around the country, charging a quarter apiece for school children to look at you. I bet we'd make a fortune!"

"Or at least a good living!" he said. For a minute or two, both of us were silent; and only the breeze that was rustling the tops of the pines could be heard in the empty campsite as the Holy Spirit brought a passage of scripture to my mind:

> "Therefore I say unto you, Take no thought for your life, what ye shall eat, or what ye shall drink; nor yet for your body, what ye shall put on. Is not the life more than meat, and the body than raiment? Behold the fowls of the air: for they sow not, neither do they reap, nor gather into barns; yet your heavenly Father feedeth them. Are ye not much better than they? Which of you by taking thought can add one cubit unto his stature? And why take ye thought for raiment? Consider the lilies of the field, how they grow; they toil not, neither do they spin: And yet I say unto you, That even Solomon in all his glory was not arrayed like one of these. Wherefore, if God so clothe the grass of the field, which to day is, and to morrow is cast into the oven, shall he not much more clothe you, O ye of little faith? Therefore take no thought, saying, What shall we eat? or, What shall we drink? or, Wherewithal shall we be clothed? (For after all these things do the Gentiles seek:) for your heavenly Father knoweth that ye have need of all these things. But seek ye first the kingdom of God, and his righteousness; and all these things shall be added unto you. Take therefore no thought for the morrow:

for the morrow shall take thought for the things of itself. Sufficient unto the day is the evil thereof."[132]

"We'll just turn this burden over to the Lord in prayer," I finally said, breaking the silence. "And, it'll be fine."

A day or two later, Brian telephoned his doctor and arranged to have a CT scan at one of the local hospitals, which we found to be staffed by a skeleton crew thanks to *Katrina's* displacement of the local population. The hospital's empty and dimly lit corridors looked much like how I would have envisioned an abandoned airport terminal as Brian and I made our way down a long, silent hallway to the radiology department. When we found it, I took a seat in the waiting area and listened as he spoke with a woman in a small office around the corner.

"How much!?!?" I heard him exclaim loudly and chuckled. Having to part with money had always been difficult for Brian so I knew we might be there for a while. I must say that he bargained valiantly with the woman in the office until she summoned a supervisor; but the supervisor relented rather easily, and Brian soon returned to the waiting area wearing a Texas-sized grin.

"I got 'em down fifty percent!" he boasted.

"I heard. How'd you manage that?"

"Well, I put it to 'em like this...I could either get the test done here or back home...and since they're not raking in the money right now, it'd benefit both of us to cut a deal."

"I believe you're the only person I know who'd haggle over something as important as a medical test!" I replied.

"You bet I would," he said proudly, hoping the two onlookers seated on the other side of the waiting room were listening to us.

"Brian Woods!" a nurse hollered in a loud voice.

"This should only take a few hours," he said, heading toward the swinging doors.

"I'm parked in a tow-away zone so hurry up!" I hollered back.

As he disappeared behind the door, I took a deep breath and began to think. When Brian and I first met in 1994 as pledges to the AGR Fraternity at OSU, I found him to be a man whose belief in Jesus Christ

---

[132] Matthew 6:25-34 (KJV)

governed his entire life; and we quickly developed a close friendship that continues to exemplify Christian brotherhood. Brian is one of the few individuals whom I trust with my life and the lives of my family, and I can only make this claim because he is a trusted brother in Christ.

Besides the assurance of protection from the storms of life, another great assurance that we have as stones built upon the Rock of Jesus Christ is the assurance of brotherhood. Every believer in Christ is a stone that makes up that spiritual house ("Ye also, as lively stones, are built up a spiritual house...".[133]), of which Christ is the head ("...he is the head of the body, the church...".[134]). Indeed, believers in Christ are of one body: "For as the body is one, and hath many members, and all the members of that one body, being many, are one body: so also is Christ. For by one Spirit are we all baptized into one body, whether we be Jews or Gentiles, whether we be bond or free; and have been all made to drink into one Spirit. For the body is not one member, but many."[135] And, in this brotherhood, we are bound together: "That there should be no schism in the body; but that the members should have the same care one for another. And whether one member suffer, all the members suffer with it; or one member be honoured, all the members rejoice with it."[136]

While Brian faced the trial of a CT scan and an uncertain future, I, in accordance with the Word of God, begged and pleaded with my Father to heal my brother: "...pray one for another, that ye may be healed."[137] When I had finished lifting Brian up to the Lord in prayer, my thoughts turned to the friendships I had observed in the lives of our patients. Sadly, many of them did not know nor had they ever experienced the pinnacle of friendship and brotherhood that is available to those who are joined to Christ; but I was endeavoring to change that by being the friend whom they could one day say had brought them to Christ: "And they come unto him, bringing one sick of the palsy, which was borne of four. And when they could not come nigh unto him for the press, they uncovered the roof where he was: and when they had broken it up, they let down the bed wherein the sick of the palsy lay.

---

[133] 1 Peter 2:5 (KJV)
[134] Colossians 1:18 (KJV)
[135] 1 Corinthians 12:12-14 (KJV)
[136] 1 Corinthians 12:25-26 (KJV)
[137] James 5:16 (KJV)

When Jesus saw their faith, he said unto the sick of the palsy, Son, thy sins be forgiven thee."[138]

Of course, the statement I had recently made to Rodney – that evil is always going to attempt to obstruct one's deliverance from it – soon proved to be true as I capitalized upon our presence in Mississippi to bring the lost before Christ.

Shortly after Brian's hospital visit, Dustin arrived in Hattiesburg to evaluate our progress. I was refreshed by his presence but had no idea the Lord had sent him to me at that particular time to help strengthen me for a particular purpose. A day or two after his arrival, while we were buying supplies in town, I received a telephone call from one of the patients who had come to the Gulf Coast with us.

"Lance," he said with a bit of a stammer. "You and your family have tried so hard to help all of us…and I don't want anyone to get us into trouble or cause problems for you."

Fearing that something terrible had happened, I replied, "Tell me what's going on, and I'll look into it without using your name."

To my horror, he proceeded to inform me that another one of our patients was in possession of illegal drugs and selling them at one of the local schools. My face burned with red hot heat as I listened to the details of the evidence that he had laid before me. When he had finished his report, I promised to bring a swift end to the problem. I immediately informed Dustin, and the two of us drove to that school which the caller had named. There, we spotted the culprit, driving slowly around the campus in his junky pickup truck – circling his prey like a hawk circles a den of mice.

"There he is!"

"Sure is, sure is," Dustin said. "Do you want me to chase him down?"

"No," I replied. "This is a very delicate situation. I need some time to think of how to handle it."

Later that evening, as dusk was falling, I hurriedly prepared supper. The flames heating the pots in which I was cooking were no match for the red hot flames of righteous anger that burned within me at the very thought of the evil that was working against the Lord in our midst.

---

[138] Mark 2:3–5 (KJV)

Suddenly, without warning, Dustin said, "Here he comes!" I passed the spoon that I had been holding to him, picked up a hatchet that we had been using to clear the brush from around the campsite, and walked outside to confront the culprit. As I approached his junky pickup truck, I spied a two-by-six-inch board that was about three feet in length lying on the ground, and I stooped to pick it up.

"Carry this!" I said and tossed it to Dustin, who had fallen in behind me along with several onlookers.

"Hey!" I hollered to the culprit as he was exiting his truck, "May I borrow your cell phone, please?"

"Sure," he replied and handed it to me. I motioned for Dustin to pass me the board, which he did; and I threw it on the ground at my feet. I then tossed the culprit's cell phone on top of the board and dealt it a crushing blow with the blunt end of the hatchet. As I raised the hatchet above my head, I whirled it around in my hand and brought the sharp end down on the phone once again in a decisive strike. After freeing the hatchet from the board, I gathered up the remains of the culprit's cell phone, handed them to him and said, "Get your stuff and get out of this camp! And, don't bother returning to the clinic because you've been discharged!"

His eyes oscillated back and forth between me and the shattered remains of his phone, and he proceeded to utter profanities the likes of which made my skin crawl.

"SILENCE!" I roared, shutting my ears to the hiss of evil. "I SAID GET OUT!"

The emissary of Satan whom I ejected from our camp shouted back at me as he drove away in his junky pickup truck, "My uncle is in law enforcement, and we'll get you for this!"

The storm that followed was almost incomprehensible in its fury; but Christ, demonstrating the blessed assurance and promises that we have in Him, arose and said unto that storm, "Peace, be still." And, when the winds had subsided, we discovered that we, being founded upon the Rock, had withstood the storm.

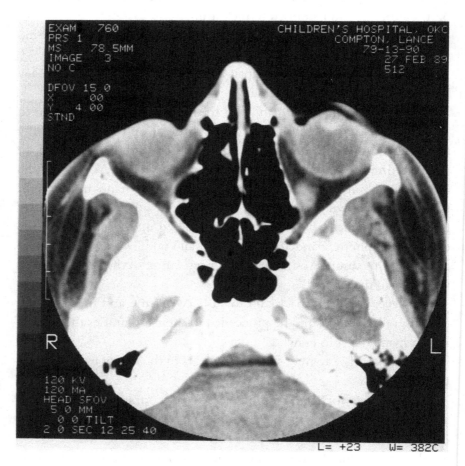

First CT scan view of the mass in the orbit of my left
eye, February 1989

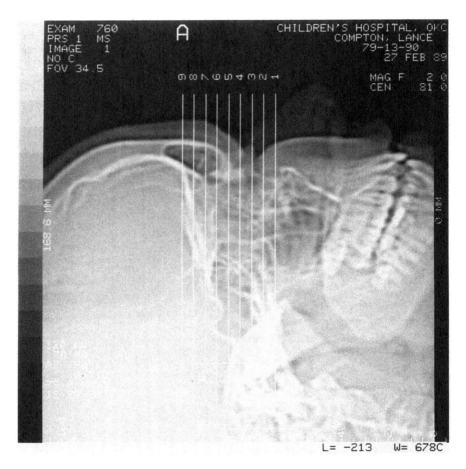

Second CT scan view of the mass in the orbit of my left eye, February 1989

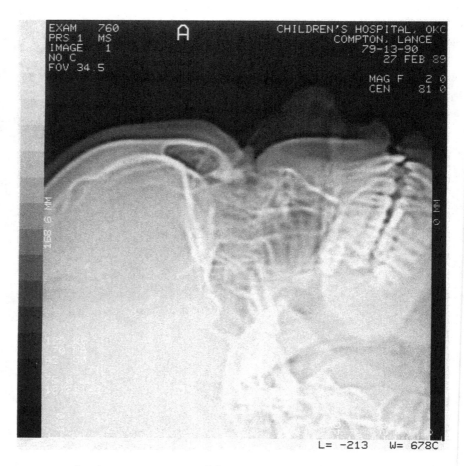

Third CT scan view of the mass in the orbit of my left
eye, February 1989

Me with Oklahoma State Senator Bruce Price in 1993, serving as his Page at the Oklahoma State Capitol

L to R: Bart Garbutt, me, and Kei; Oklahoma State University Inter-semester class at George Washington University; Washington, D.C., winter 1998

My cousin, Dalton Dorsey, and me at *Cattleman's Steakhouse* in Oklahoma City, OK after announcing my bid for United States Congress, 2002

Local Billy Graham Crusade Staff; Oklahoma City, OK; June 2003

Back Row, L to R: BGEA Employee, Ron Shea, Jeff Anderson, Lance Compton, Chris Mechsner, Ryan Free, Kent Withington, Sam Hardy, Scott Lenning, Rick Marshall

Middle Row, L to R: Wanda McCurdy, Jerrie Sue Pearson, Susan Allen, Vickie Chitty Parker, BGEA Employee

Front Row, L to R: Becky Evans, Jill Dean, Waynetta Thrailkill, Erin Helmuth, Brittany Lenning, Karen Woods, Scottie Lenning, Tami Lenning, M.J. Triplet, Kristi Hardy

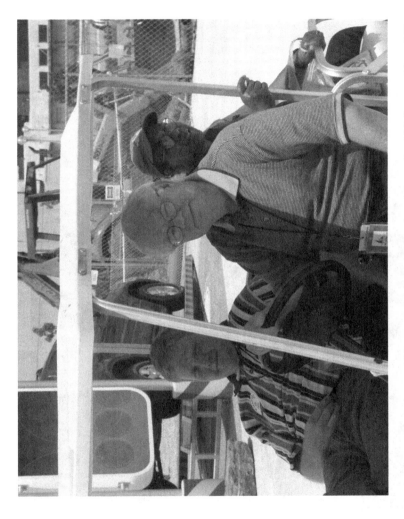

Working hard with Ron Shea and M.J. Triplet; *Billy Graham Crusade*; Oklahoma City, OK, June 2003

As it was fading, I took this picture of the Cross that suddenly appeared following a period of seclusion, prayer, and reflection in the Colorado Mountains, 2006

My white socks; *Valley of the Shadow of Death*; somewhere between Jerusalem and Jericho, December 2007

CHAPTER 12

Our Great Bereavement

As we walked through the narrow streets of Jerusalem's Old City, with George and Tony leading the way, they brought us to a knotty stone column and explained that it had stood in ancient Israel as a public bulletin board where notices of debt and discharge were posted for the entire city to see. According to George, whenever one of these debts was paid by a kinsman redeemer of the debtor, the corresponding notice was folded in half and signed by the kinsman. This practice was known as "possessing the double." The folded, signed notice was then left on the pillar so the public would know both that the debt had been paid in full and who had paid it. While contemplating the kinsman redeemer as a picture of the redemptive work of Jesus Christ, the Holy Spirit revealed to me the long-anticipated explanation as to why He had compelled me to publicly forgive a young man who had greatly bereaved my family. It was to the intent of publicly proclaiming that Christ has paid our sin debt in full.

With the warmth of the sun upon my neck on the lazy, spring day of Friday, April 7, 2006, I passed the hours waking the sleeping soil of my garden with my hands and nursing the seedlings that I had only recently planted. As the afternoon faded into evening, the sun slowly disappeared over the hills west of my house to the song of the whippoorwill, and I took my gardening tools to the garage before making my way up to the house. When I reached the front porch, the soft hum of crickets was suddenly silenced by the blood-chilling yelping of a pack of coyotes. The unusual pitch of their cries suggested that death had come to something, and I wondered whether another beloved dog had been lured to its death. Coyotes have not been judged wily without reason. One of a pack's common artifices is to use one of its in-heat females to cunningly entice a domesticated dog into leaving the safety of its master's home and following the female into the wilderness, where the rest of the pack is waiting to kill it.

Early the next morning, I arose and checked to see whether anyone had called while I was asleep. I was somewhat alarmed when I saw that I had received more than ten telephone calls from my cousin, Mike. His wife, Sue, had also left a message, saying that Dalton had been in an accident. At first, I was a little worried that Michelle and Jimmy had not called me themselves, but I figured it was probably because Michelle had gone to Dallas to celebrate a friend's birthday. Even so, a terrible sense of dread came over me as I sat down to dial Mike's number. Just a few months earlier, Dalton had broken his arm, femur, and collar bone in a dirt bike accident; and the Holy Spirit had convicted me at that time to have an important conversation with him. While he was recovering in the hospital, I accompanied Mom to deliver a basket of snacks and pop that she had put together for him. When we arrived, Michelle was entertaining some friends so I sat down on the left side of Dalton's bed and listened to their conversation. One of them was telling the rest of the group the intimate details of a recently-ended love affair between someone's son and his girlfriend. Though these friends of Michelle's were church-going ladies, it did not seem to bother them that their children were living in sin or that their conversation about it was unbecoming of professing Christians. Every one of them, with the exception of Michelle, was "upset" that the boy had broken up with his girlfriend on the eve of the high school prom after she had already purchased a dress for the occasion.

"These young people need to realize what's important!" one of them said.

"My sentiments exactly," I thought to myself, even though I had other priorities in mind.

"Mom," I said, with the deliberate intention of interrupting the conversation, "Why don't you take Michelle downstairs and get her something to eat while I stay here with Dalton?"

"That's a good idea!" Mom quickly replied as she and Michelle both sent me looks of gratitude, thankful that I had created a chance for them to get away from the frivolous chatter. After everyone had filed out of the room and I closed the door behind Mom and Michelle, I turned to Dalton and said, "You know, one of my favorite movies is *Misery* with Kathy Bates. Have you seen it?"

"Don't make me laugh!" he said with a grin, trying not to move his sore body.

"Oh, you won't laugh," I said slyly as I picked up the nurse's call button and moved it away from his reach.

Dalton was of the age where the temptation of sin was presenting itself in many forms. But, to me, he was still the innocent-looking little boy who had been at the center of my family's attention for as long as I could remember, who had made his way into every picture we had taken; the little helper on my political campaigns; and my crusade companion. Nevertheless, because I knew that he had been under a cloud of temptation for some time, his dirt bike accident was the impetus for me to inquire of him concerning his salvation.

"I want to ask you a very serious question," I said, returning the nurse's call button to him.

"What is it?"

"The accident that you had was pretty serious. The way you landed, you could've easily broken your neck. It only takes about sixty pounds of pressure to break a grown man's neck, you know. What would've happened if you had not survived?"

My question obviously caught him off guard because he just stared back at me with a frightened look.

"I guess what I'm asking is this: if you'd died, what would've happened to you?"

"I would've gone to Heaven," he replied.

"How do you know you would've gone to Heaven?" I asked.

I was blown away when, with child-like innocence and the wisdom of an adult rolled into one, he simply said, "Well, I have asked Jesus to come into my heart and forgive me of the bad things I've done."

He paused for a moment, and then with a big smile and playful giggle, sang a few strains of a song he had learned in *Kidz Gig* at the Billy Graham Crusade:

"Jesus put the song in my heart...
He gave me a treasure...
Jesus put the song in my heart...
He sang me His song..."[139]

I could still hear him singing those lines when Sue answered my telephone call and reported the horrific news that Dalton was dead. The tragedy that had befallen him was forever memorialized in the following affidavit of Caddo County Deputy Sheriff, Philip Paxton, which was filed on the following Tuesday, April 11, 2006 in the District Court of Caddo County, State of Oklahoma:

---

[139] "Jesus Put The Song In My Heart" (a song by Psalty)

IN THE DISTRICT COURT OF CADDO COUNTY
STATE OF OKLAHOMA

STATE OF OKLAHOMA

Vs.

Misael Galvan; a juvenile Hispanic male
DOB: 08-20-90
DEFENDANT

Case# CF-2006-92

CASE#: 2006040020

AFFIDAVIT FOR ARREST

I, PHILIP A. PAXTON, A CERTIFIED DEPUTY SHERIFF EMPLOYED BY THE CADDO COUNTY SHERIFF'S OFFICE, STATE OF OKLAHOMA, UPON OATH DEPOSES AND STATES AS FOLLOWS, TO WIT: On Friday, April 07, 2006 at approximately 22:49 hours the Hinton Police Department advised the Caddo County Sheriff's Office that there has been an accidental shooting out in the county and that the victim of the shooting is now at the Parkview Ambulance Service on East Main in Hinton. While in route to the Parkview Ambulance Office from the Carnegie area, I received a telephone call from Shannon Pack, the Hinton Chief of Police. Chief Pack told me that the victim was Dalton Dorsey and that Dalton had died of his wounds. Chief Pack said Dalton Dorsey had been brought to the ambulance service in the back of his father's pickup truck and this pickup was sitting in the driveway of the Hinton Police Department with Dalton's body still in the back. The Hinton Police Department and the Parkview Ambulance Service are located next door to each other with a breezeway/driveway separating them. I instructed Chief Pack to move the vehicle with the body to a secure location in the enclosed ambulance bay behind the Parkview Ambulance Offices to keep people away until I could arrive.

Deputy Traye Opitz and I arrived at the Hinton Police Department at approximately 23:21 hours this same date and met with Jim Dorsey, the victim's father. Jim Dorsey told me that his son Dalton and three of Dalton's friends had gone camping on one of the Dorsey pasture areas near the Dorsey home. Jim Dorsey said the camp site is located 3 miles north of Lookeba on U.S. 281 Highway then 8/10 of a mile west on CR 1110, then south through a gate into the Dorsey pasture. Mr. Dorsey went on to say the campsite is then approximately ½ mile south winding through the pasture to a wooded area. Mr. Dorsey said he allowed his 15-year-old son Dalton to drive his pickup truck, with his friends, over to the campsite for the night. Jim Dorsey said he was at his residence, located approximately 1 mile west of the pasture gate when two of Dalton's friends, Misael Galvan and Cory Bare, came driving up to the Dorsey home in the pickup truck and immediately ran toward the home. Jim Dorsey said he met them on the porch when they told him that Dalton had been shot and was lying in the back of the pickup truck. Jim Dorsey said he ran to the pickup and found his son with a head injury and bloody. Mr. Dorsey went on to say he could not feel a pulse on his son and feared he was dying. Jim Dorsey said he and the two boys got back in the pickup and headed toward Hinton all the time trying to call the Parkview Ambulance on their cell phones. Jim Dorsey said they were unsuccessful in contacting Parkview Ambulance because no one knew the ambulance phone number. Jim Dorsey said when they got to Hinton he went to the Parkview Ambulance Office for help. Mr. Dorsey said ambulance attendants went to check Dalton and found that he was dead. Jim Dorsey said while he was waiting for me to arrive at the police department he learned from Misael Galvan and Cory Bare that Dalton, Misael, Cory and another boy, Ryan Shelton, were sitting around a fire in a fire pit at the campsite talking. Jim Dorsey said the boys told him Dalton was holding his 22 rifle and some how the rifle discharged and struck Dalton in the head. Jim Dorsey said the boys told him they immediately loaded Dalton in the back of the pickup truck and headed to the Dorsey home for help. Jim Dorsey said the boys also said when they got to the pasture gate, Ryan Shelton became scared and got out of the pickup truck and told the other boys he would walk home or call his mother from his cell phone. According to Jim Dorsey the boys said they left Ryan Shelton on the county road near the pasture gate then Misael Galvan and Cory Bare continued on to the Dorsey home.

1

At that time Jim Dorsey gave me Dalton's vital information (DOB/Address).

At approximately 23:30 hours this same date, Deputy Opitz and I went to the Parkview Ambulance bay to view Dalton Dorsey's body and await the phone call from the medical examiner. At the ambulance bay we met with Parkview Paramedic Greg Black who told us he went out to the Dorsey pickup truck and checked Dalton Dorsey and found that he had died. Mr. Black said all that he disturbed in the pickup truck was that he rolled Dalton partially over to check for a pulse and breathing. Greg Black said he also covered Dalton with a sheet while the pickup truck was sitting outside between the buildings. Greg Black said he had stayed with the body and the vehicle after it was moved inside the ambulance bay until I could arrive. At that time Greg Black uncovered the face of Dalton Dorsey revealing that Dalton had a wound to the left eye. Dalton was lying on his back across the back of the pickup truck with his head toward the passenger side of the pickup truck. Blood covered his face from where it had been running from the mouth, ears, nose and left eye of Dalton Dorsey. Greg Black said when he first went out to the street to check Dalton Dorsey he found Dalton lying face down. When Mr. Black told us that we could see blood on the bed of the pickup truck where his face had initially laid. Without disturbing the body, photographs were taken of the wound to the left eye. A lever action rifle was noticed lying towards the front of the pickup bed. The gun was photographed without being moved. During this time, Jim Delbridge of the State Medical Examiners Office phoned me on my cell phone. Mr. Delbridge was given information about the incident and he stated he would be in Hinton soon. Mr. Delbridge reminded us not to disturb anything until he arrived.

With the pickup truck and the body secured in the ambulance bay, Deputy Opitz and I started interviewing the young boys that witnessed the incident. By that time Ryan Shelton had arrived at the ambulance office with his father, Randy Shelton. Parents of the other boys were contacted to come to the ambulance office.

At approximately 23:55 hours on 04-07-2006 Deputy Opitz and I met with 15-year-old Ryan Shelton and his father Randy Shelton in the dining area of the ambulance office to record his statement of the shooting incident. Ryan Shelton told us that he, Dalton, Cory, and Misael were camping on the Dorsey farm and were sitting around the campfire and that it had already gotten dark and the campfire was the only light they had. Ryan told us the pickup truck was backed up to the fire pit with the tailgate down and that he (Ryan) was sitting on the tailgate. Ryan went on to say that Dalton was sitting on the ground next to the fire pit, Cory was sitting on the ground in front of Ryan, and Ryan said he thought Misael was sitting on the ice chest just to the left of Dalton. Ryan said they were just sitting and talking about going to war. Ryan said he heard a noise to the front of the pickup and looked in that direction. Ryan said while he was looking away he heard a gun shot, and as he looked toward the shot he saw Dalton laying on the ground and the rifle was on the ground nearby. Ryan said he did not see the shot or who fired the shot, but when I asked who fired the shot Ryan said Misael because the gun appeared closer to Misael. Ryan said after Dalton was shot that Cory and Misael loaded Dalton in the back of the vehicle and they all headed toward the Dorsey home. Ryan said Misael drove the pickup, Cory was sitting on the passenger side and he (Ryan) was sitting in the middle. Ryan said as they got to the pasture gate at the road that he (Ryan) was so scared he got out of the pickup and walked up the road and used his cell phone to call his mother to come after him.

On 04-09-2006 at approximately 00:10 hours we interviewed 14-year-old Cory Bare along with his parents Clifford and Yvonne Bare in the dining area of the Parkview Ambulance office. Cory told us that he and his friends were sitting around the campfire talking about the war and if they could kill anyone in wartime. Cory said it was dark and that the fire was only light they had. Cory said Dalton was sitting on the ground beside him (Cory) watching the fire, Ryan was sitting on the tailgate of the pickup and Misael was sitting to the right of Ryan. Cory said that Dalton had the gun sitting with the gun between his legs sitting with his legs off in the fire pit. Cory said while they were watching the fire and talking, he heard a shot and Dalton fell over toward him (Cory). Cory said he was not looking toward him and did not see the shot. Cory said he thought Dalton was playing with them until he (Cory) lifted up Dalton's head and saw the blood. Cory said he and Misael loaded Dalton in the back of the vehicle and they headed toward the pasture gate. Cory said when he got out to open the pasture gate, that Ryan was so scared that Ryan got out of the pickup and refused to go any farther with them. Cory said he and Misael then went on to the Dorsey Home and got Jim Dorsey and headed to Hinton to find help for Dalton.

At that time we were waiting for the mother of Misael Galvan before interviewing him. Deputy Opitz and I used that time to go the scene of the shooting. Deputy Opitz and I found the campsite in a remote area well away from any road.

2

The campsite looked as the young men had described it and found where the vehicle had been sitting and found blood on the ground on the edge of the fire pit. It was extremely dark in the area and I felt photographing the area would be better in the daylight. I also decide that the scene would not be disturbed due to its remote location. While at the campsite we were notified by the Hinton Police Department that the medical examiner had arrived and that Misael Galvan's mother had also arrived.

On 04-09-2006 at approximately 02:04 hours Deputy Opitz and I interviewed 15-year-old Misael Galvan in the ambulance dining area. Irene Galvan, mother of Misael Galvan, was also present along with an English-speaking male relative of hers. Misael provided a similar story as Cory Bare. Misael said he and his friends were sitting around the campfire talking about war. Misael said Dalton and Cory were sitting on the ground around the fire and that Ryan was sitting on the tailgate of the pickup. Misael said he (Misael) got up to pick up wood to throw on the fire when he heard a shot. Misael said Dalton was holding the gun while sitting around the pit and did not see or know how the shot happened. Misael said after the shot occurred that he and Cory immediately loaded Dalton in the back of the pickup truck and headed to get help.

After the three young men were interviewed Deputy Opitz and I went back to the ambulance bay where, Jim Delbridge of the medical examiners office was examining Dalton Dorsey. Assistant District Attorney Tyler Lowe was called at that and informed of the shooting incident. It was discussed with Mr. Delbridge weather or not to contact the Oklahoma State Bureau of Investigation to handle the case. I then phoned the O.S.B.I. headquarters in Oklahoma City and requested to speak with an agent. The office took my number and said an agent would call shortly. Soon afterwards Agent Richard Goss called and was told of the shooting incident. At that time I felt the incident could have been an accidental self-inflicted injury. Agent Goss said he would come out to the scene but he would probably not do anything any differently. At that time I decided that the Caddo County Sheriff's Office would continue the investigation. At that time the rifle in the back of the Dorsey pickup truck was processed. When the rifle was inspected we found that the hammer was cocked and that there was an unfired bullet/ammunition in the chamber ready to fire. We could not explain how this could have happened. The three boys interviewed did not mention loading the rifle. Also Jim Dorsey was asked if he had handled the rifle after the shooting before the pickup truck was secured in the ambulance bay. Mr. Dorsey said he saw the rifle in the back of the pickup truck but did not handle the rifle. The rifle was photographed and taken as evidence in the incident.

On 04-08-2006 at approximately 09:30 hours I went to the campsite location to photograph the shooting incident scene. The campsite was untouched from the way it appeared the night before. While at the campsite I received a phone call from Jim Delbridge of the Medical Examiners Office. Mr. Delbridge want copies of photos that were taken at the scene and also said he would be coming to Hinton and pick up the photographs.

At approximately 11:30 hours this same date I met with Jim Delbridge at the Hinton Police Department. After reviewing the photos it was decided that I would take Mr. Delbridge to the campsite for a closer look.

At approximately 19:04 hours this same date I met with Ryan Shelton and his father at the Binger Police Department for a follow-up interview. Ryan basically said he did not see much and could not tell me any more than he did in the previous interview. Ryan Shelton could not tell me how the loaded round of ammunition became chambered in Dalton's rifle. Ryan Shelton was positive that he did not chamber the live round in the rifle nor did he see anyone chamber the round.

At approximately 20:05 hours this same date I met with Cory Bare and his parents at the Binger Police Department for a follow-up interview. Cory's story did not change from the first interview and he could not tell me why a live round was chambered in the rifle. Cory Bare was sure that he did not cock and load the rifle after the shooting nor did he see any one else load the rifle.

At approximately 22:11 hours this same date the Caddo County Sheriff's Office received a phone call from Clifford Bare stating that his son Cory wanted to talk with me, that he had information.

I met with Cory Bare along with his parents at the Binger Police Department at approximately 22:30 hours for another follow-up interview. Cory was crying and saying he could not continue lying about what happened to Dalton Dorsey at the campsite. Cory told me that he and his friends were sitting around the fire pit talking about the war in Iraq.

3

Cory said Dalton was on the far left sitting on the ground, and that he (Cory) was sitting on the ground next to him, and that Ryan was sitting on the tailgate of the pickup truck.
Cory said that Misael was standing next to the tailgate of the pickup truck on the far right of everyone else. Cory said they were talking about the war in Iraq and about the Army. Cory said Dalton was asking each one of them if they could kill some one. Dalton asked each one of them and Cory said every body answered, "No I could not kill anyone". Cory then said Misael was holding the rifle and Misael asked Dalton if he (Dalton) could kill anyone. Cory said Dalton replied he might be able to kill an Iraqi. Cory then said Misael moved the gun in his hand and the gun fired striking Dalton in the left eye. Cory said he did not know if the shot was intentional or not. Cory said after Misael fired the shot he threw the gun on the ground and screamed, "I just said I could not kill any one and I just killed my friend". Cory said Misael then went back to the gun, picked up the gun and chambered the live round in the rifle and put the rifle barrel in his (Misael's) mouth to kill himself. Cory said he (Cory) grabbed the gun away from Misael stopping him from killing himself. Cory said he and Misael then loaded Dalton in the back of the pickup truck and headed to the Dorsey home. Cory said the reason Ryan got out of the pickup at the pasture gate is because he was scared of Misael and that Misael might try to kill himself again or even one of the other two boys. Cory said Misael had a bad temper and that he (Cory) was extremely scared of Misael.

On 04-09-2006 at approximately 10:55 hours I met with Ryan Shelton and his father at the Binger Police Department for a third interview. I told Ryan that I had new information about what happened at the campsite. Ryan continued to tell me he did not know anything and did not see anything. After I finally told him that Cory had told the entire truth about the shooting did Ryan finally tell the truth of the shooting. I did not tell Ryan what Cory had told me, only that Cory had told me the truth of how Misael shot Dalton. Ryan then opened up and said that Misael had picked the gun up out of the pickup bed and was holding it when it fired hitting Dalton in the eye. Ryan did say that as Misael picked up the rifle he (Ryan) told Misael to be careful the rifle might be loaded.

At approximately 15:10 hours this same date Deputy Traye Opitz and I went to the Galvan residence located at 207 N. First Street in Lookeba, Oklahoma. At that time we interviewed Misael Galvan at the kitchen table. Misael was informed that we were conducting follow-up interviews and that he was not under arrest. At this interview it was asked if Misael was a U.S. citizen. Misael stated he was not a U.S. citizen and that he was born in Mexico. Misael did not change his story from his first interview. Misael stood by his statement that Dalton had shot himself. At the completion of the interview Misael was told that he was being taken into custody and that we would take him the Caddo County Sheriff's Office in Anadarko for a formal interview. Misael Galvan's mother, Irene, does not speak English, but her sister-in-law; Cynthia Galvan was present at the Galvan house. Cynthia speaks English and Spanish and told Irene Galvan what was happening. Irene Galvan was asked to come to the Caddo County Sheriff's Office in Anadarko for the interview. Mrs. Galvan said she would be there.

The Oklahoma State Bureau of Investigation was called and I spoke with Agent Richard Goss concerning he problem we have finding an interpreter for Irene Galvan. Agent Goss stated their department had a Spanish-speaking agent and would have him give me a call. Soon after, O.S.B.I. agent Daniel Flores called me to say he would help with the interview of Misael Galvan in explaining the Miranda Warning and parent's rights to Irene Galvan.

Once at the Caddo County Sheriff's Office and waiting for the arrival of Agent Flores, I spoke with Irene Galvan through her sister in law Cynthia Galvan. I told them that I had new information that Misael was the person that shot Dalton Dorsey and that the other boys had told that Misael had been the person holding the gun when it fired. I also told them that even though the shooting may have been accidental that Misael could be held accountable for his actions. After speaking with them Cynthia Galvan said Irene wanted to talk with Misael alone before the interview started. Misael was allowed to speak with his mother prior to the interview.

At approximately 17:50 hours on 04-09-2006 a video interview was conducted at the Caddo County Sheriff's Office. Present at the interview was Misael Galvan, his mother Irene Galvan, his aunt Cynthia Galvan, O.S.B.I. Agent Daniel Flores, Caddo County Deputies Traye Opitz and Philip Paxton. At the start of the interview Agent Flores explained the Miranda Warning to Irene Galvan and Mrs. Galvan agreed to let us speak with Misael. As the interview started Misael broke down and told us that he was the one that fired the shot that killed Dalton Dorsey. Misael said when he and the other three boys arrived at the campsite that Dalton pulled the rifle out of the pickup and pointed it at him (Misael). Misael said he told Dalton not to point the rifle at him and Misael said he went over to Dalton and took the rifle away from him.

4

Misael said it scared him when Dalton had the rifle pointed at him. Misael said a little while later as the boys sat around the campfire talking, Misael said he took the rifle out of the back of the pickup and held it. Misael did say that Ryan told him to be careful the rifle may be loaded. Misael said he thought he would point the rifle at Dalton just to show him how it feels to have the gun pointed at him. Misael said as he moved the rifle the rifle fired hitting Dalton in the eye. Misael said he did not intend to fire the rifle and that Dalton was his friend and he would never intentionally hurt him. Misael said he had never had a problem with Dalton, Ryan, or Cory before and considers them close friends. Misael said he told no one else about what really happened, he said when some one would ask him he told them that Dalton shot himself. I asked Misael if he tried to kill himself after he shot Dalton. Misael said right after the shot he felt so bad that he wanted to kill himself, but he said he has not had those kinds of thoughts since.

On conclusion of the interview Misael Galvan was taken into custody for the shooting of Dalton Dorsey. Coyetta Smith from the Juvenile Services Unit was called and started the process of finding a detention center to house Misael. Misael was transported to the Comanche County Detention Center in Lawton where he awaits a hearing.

Based on the statements of Ryan Shelton and Cory Bare that they saw Misael Galvan shoot the rifle killing Dalton Dorsey and by the admission of Misael Galvan that he did have in his hands the rifle as it fired striking Dalton Dorsey in the left eye, and the medical examiners initial findings that the gunshot wound to the left eye of Dalton Dorsey was not caused by a close contact shot; and that the discharging the firearm towards another is deemed reckless handling of a firearm; I request that Misael Galvan be charged with First Degree Manslaughter as outlined in Title 21, Section 711.1 of the Oklahoma Statutes.
BASED ON THE INFORMATION, THE UNDERSIGNED PRAYS THAT THE HONORABLE COURT ISSUE A FINDING OF FACT THAT PROBABLE CAUSE EXISTS TO BELIEVE THAT A CRIME HAS BEEN COMMITTED AND THAT THERE IS PROBABLE CAUSE TO BELIEVE THE DEFENDANT(S) ABOVE NAMED COMMITTED THAT CRIME.

Philip A. Payton
AFFIANT

SUBSCRIBED AND SWORN TO BEFORE ME THIS _10_ DAY OF _April_ 20 _06_
My Commission Expires:
_10-5-09_

Carol Nation
NOTARY PUBLIC

CAROL NATION
NOTARY
05009281
EXP. 10/05/09
PUBLIC
STATE OF OKLAHOMA

THE UNDERSIGNED JUDGE OF THIS COURT, UPON TESTIMONY AND/OR AFFIDAVIT, HEREBY DETERMINES THERE TO BE PROBABLE CAUSE TO DETAIN THE DEFENDANT.

DATED THIS _10th_ DAY OF _April_ 20 _06_

JUDGE OF THE DISTRICT COURT

5

140

---

[140] *State of Oklahoma v. Misael Galvan*, District Court of Caddo County, State of Oklahoma, Case No. CF-2006-92, filed April 11, 2006

On the day of Dalton's funeral, which was an unusually hot and humid day for April, only a slight southwesterly breeze stirred as we entered the high school gymnasium in Sickles, Oklahoma, which was filled to capacity. The first thing I noticed was that there was no air-conditioning, and the giant, industrial fans near the ceiling had been turned off so the service could be heard. The door in the far northwest corner of the building had been propped open, but the heat was still almost unbearable. From the front row on the gymnasium floor, I had an uninhibited view of the floral arrangements that cascaded down from the pulpit and covered the floor. In the midst of the flowers, there arose a sturdy, iron cross which had been endowed with a beautiful red ribbon. I stared motionless at the cross as the service began and the weight of Michelle's grief descended upon me. Approximately thirty minutes into the service, a sudden blast of cold air rushed through the open door in the northwest corner, cutting the sweltering heat like a knife and causing the ribbon on the iron cross to flutter. I instantly recognized the blast of air as the presence of the Holy Spirit, which strengthened me with the memory of my experience at the *Cedar Hills Youth Camp* tabernacle, the assurance of Dalton's salvation, and the words of Christ, "Marvel not that I said unto thee, Ye must be born again. The wind bloweth where it listeth, and thou hearest the sound thereof, but canst not tell whence it cometh, and whither it goeth: so is every one that is born of the Spirit."[141]

With a smile on my face, I nudged Mom and asked her, "What time is it?"

"2:35 P.M." she replied. "Why?"

"Just remember this moment, and I'll tell you later."

"The breeze?" she asked.

Nodding in the affirmative, I knew that she, too, remembered that a host of our brothers and sisters in Christ, including those at Southwestern Baptist Theological Seminary, K-LOVE Radio, the BGEA, and Samaritan's Purse, were all faithfully praying for the comfort and presence of the Holy Spirit at that very moment. Heartbreaking as the circumstances were, they were overshadowed, at least for me, by the Great Comforter's presence.

---

[141] John 3:7-8 (KJV)

When at last it was my turn to view Dalton's body, I stood over him, remembering that I was only sixteen years old – not much older than he was – when I drove him home from the hospital after he was born. As I leaned over to kiss his forehead and placed my hand upon his chest, I caught a glimpse of the disturbance above his left eye that had been inflicted by the gunshot. Though Andee had done a good job of concealing the wound, it was still noticeable enough for me to feel a slight twinge in my left eye as I realized that our enemy had stricken us in the same place.

At the cemetery, I stood at the edge of Dalton's grave alongside his younger brother, Dade. Though Jimmy, Michelle, and Dylan had been unable to stay behind for the burial, Dade dealt with his loss by studying its every detail and asking me a number of questions. Just as I finished explaining the Christian burial to him, the vault was sealed; and we each tossed a handful of red soil onto it as my gold tie flapped in the southwesterly wind.

Shortly after Dalton's funeral, disturbing facts began to surface which suggested that the shooting had been premeditated. First, the medical examiner ruled Dalton's death a homicide. Second, a witness to the shooting reported that Misael, the boy who shot Dalton, had invited himself to go camping with Dalton and his friends and enticed Dalton into bringing along the .22 caliber rifle that killed him even though Jimmy had forbidden them to take it. Third, we were warned by local law enforcement officials that certain of Misael's relatives could be connected to or associated with the Mexican drug cartel. Fourth, one of Misael's cousins, who was about the same age as Dalton, telephoned Michelle and described a dream she claimed to have had wherein she saw blood running out of Dalton's eyes, nose, and ears and filling the room. Fifth, Misael's mother and aunt made an unannounced visit to Jimmy and Michelle's home, whereupon they persistently implored Jimmy and Michelle to tell the district attorney not to file criminal charges against Misael. All the while, Misael's mother, who pretended to be incapable of understanding English, sat on the sofa, rocking back and forth and holding Misael's picture on her lap as his aunt shouted at Jimmy and Michelle, saying such things as, "We can't see or hold Misael because you've got him in jail!"

After Misael was charged with first degree manslaughter in the District Court of Caddo County in case number CF–2006-92, *State of Oklahoma v. Misael Galvan*, a pricey Oklahoma City attorney entered an appearance on his behalf. Thereafter, we learned that a plea agreement had been reached wherein he would plead guilty to first degree manslaughter in exchange for sentencing in accordance with Oklahoma's Youthful Offender Act. Due to his being sentenced under this law, my family was required to attend several court hearings, each of which forced us to relive Dalton's demise while coming face to face with the swarming mob of illegal aliens that descended upon the courthouse for each hearing to "support" him. This debacle caused some in my family to ask why the Sheriff could not just round up the illegals and see to it that they were deported, but the Holy Spirit alleviated my pain and discomfort with passages of scripture, reminding me that illegal immigration is strictly an earthly problem. Jesus declared in the Gospel according to John, "I am the way, the truth, and the life: no man cometh unto the Father, but by me."[142] In other words, nobody enters Heaven unless they enter by Christ. Jesus is the door: "Verily, verily, I say unto you, I am the door of the sheep. All that ever came before me are thieves and robbers: but the sheep did not hear them. I am the door: by me if any man enter in, he shall be saved, and shall go in and out, and find pasture."[143]

In the early stages of Misael's prosecution, my family and I met Karen Cunningham, the Caddo County Victim Rights Advocate, who went above and beyond the call of duty throughout the pendency of the case, shielding us from Misael's family and supporters, voicing our feelings to the district attorney, and offering kind, comforting words. Her compassion was very much appreciated by my family. As painful and difficult as the prosecution was for us, I realized that Misael needed to hear the Gospel of Jesus Christ and His message of salvation and forgiveness after I heard the testimony of a local woman who was brought in to testify to Misael's character. Notably, she testified that, "Misael has become a Christian this past summer. He – he was baptized into Christ, and he knows what that means, but he – he did mention

---

[142] John 14:6 (KJV)
[143] John 10:7-9 (KJV)

as good as it feels if he could go back in time and change things he would give it up to have his friend back." Her suggestion that Misael had become a Christian through water baptism concerned me, and my concerns were confirmed when a local pastor also testified that Misael had been "baptized for the forgiveness of his sins" at his church. This, in relevant part, was his testimony:

```
16                        JAMES CUDD
                   having been first duly sworn,
17                     testified as follows:

18          THE WITNESS:  I do.

19                    DIRECT EXAMINATION

20   MR. BROOKS-JIMENEZ:

21          Q.   Pastor Cudd, can you tell me how are you're

22   employed?

23          A.   I preach at the Church of Christ in Hinton.

24          Q.   Okay.  And can you tell me, did you know Dalton

25   Dorsey?


          DISTRICT COURT OF OKLAHOMA - OFFICIAL TRANSCRIPT
```

1   A.   I just knew -- knew of him. Didn't know him
2   personally.

3   Q.   You know his family?

4   A.   Yes.

5   Q.   How would you characterize these people?

6   A.   Good family, wonderful family.

7   Q.   Okay. How did you come to know Misael Galvan?

8   A.   Through the school activities at Lookeba-Sickles.
9   Of course, being at Hinton and Lookeba-Sickles we had
10   students in our church from both schools, so we would attend
11   the activities of both places and also our son coached a
12   couple of years at Lookeba-Sickles and coached Misael in
13   baseball and basketball.

14   Q.   Okay. So you had an opportunity to observe him
15   playing sports?

16   A.   That's right.

17   Q.   Okay. And what were your observations of him back
18   then?

19   A.   Back then as now he was a likable kid. He usually
20   had a smile on his face. Easy to talk to. Just really was
21   kind of attracted to him as far as a teenage young man that
22   you enjoyed being around.

23   Q.   Okay. Were there some circumstances that came --
24   that led you to get to know Misael better?

25   A.   Well, back then especially as our son was coaching

1 we would have the opportunity to be around the players a

2 little bit more than we had been previously.

3   Q.   Okay.

4   A.   So it was through -- through some of those ball

5 games that we attended that we were able to become more

6 acquainted with some of the players.

7   Q.   On the court, was he a sportsman or was he a bad

8 sport, did he pout, did he gloat any of those things?

9   A.   No. He was not only a good athlete, but also had

10 good sportsmanship and --

11   Q.   Okay. When this accident happened, what did you

12 do?

13   A.   Obviously, we were traumatized with the rest of the

14 Hinton and Lookeba-Sickles communities being a part of the

15 community. And attended the funeral at Lookeba-Sickles

16 gymnasium. And paid our respects and passed on our

17 condolences to the Dorsey family.

18   And then following that I -- I asked what good can

19 come from this tragedy?

20   Q.   Yes, sir.

21   A.   As a preacher, I firmly believe that God can work

22 good things out of bad situations and this was a terribly

23 bad situation.

24   And then knowing Misael, I thought perhaps I could

25 -- could have some influence on him to maybe bring some

1 good.

2   Q.   Okay.

3   A.   And being a minister I had access to him at Lawton

4 at the Comanche County Juvenile Detention Center so

5 arrangements were made to where I could visit with him while

6 he was down there. And I did so for -- once a week for

7 about six weeks while he was there.

8   Q.   Okay. What was the first thing he asked you when

9 he saw you, after talking to you catching up a little bit?

10   A.   First thing he asked was, when Dalton's funeral

11 would be? And I told him, "It was yesterday." And then he

12 asked if I attended? And I said, "Yes".

13   And as we talked further about some other things he

14 indicated to me that he had been praying for Jimmy and

15 Michelle, he wondered how they were doing. And so it struck

16 me, that here was a young man who was in trouble, he's in a

17 detention center and the first thing he wants to know about

18 is the family and how they're doing.

19   Q.   Okay. So where did it go from there. You said you

20 went to go visit him on a weekly basis, what did you guys

21 talk about?

22   A.   What I was mainly concerned about is -- is how a

23 young man who had because of his actions lead to the death

24 of his friend, how he was going to deal with the guilt and

25 the remorse and how he was going to be led to make better

1   decisions in the future and not repeat the mistakes of the
2   past?
3   So we talked about God's love, and God's grace.
4   That, yes, forgiveness is real. And I wanted him to
5   understand and this is basically what we dealt with from
6   that moment on. We read a lot of scriptures. We opened up
7   the bible and talked about spiritual matters, because I
8   wanted him to truly understand that he could receive
9   forgiveness for all of his wrongs.
10   Q.   Okay. Did he seem sincere?
11   A.   He did.
12   Q.   Did he seem like he was trying to do this to get
13   himself out of trouble?
14   A.   No.
15   Q.   When you guys read scriptures and then you would
16   come back a week later and discuss those scriptures, did it
17   seem like he was -- he had studied them or earnestly?
18   A.   Yes. I usually would advise him to read a
19   particular chapter such as -- or a particular book. For
20   example, the Gospel of John or the Book of Acts. And the
21   next time he would ask questions and refer to some of the
22   passages in those books, which let me know that he truly had
23   spent time reading his bible.
24   Q.   Did it seem like he was able to synthesize the
25   concepts and really kind of take those in and apply them?

DISTRICT COURT OF OKLAHOMA - OFFICIAL TRANSCRIPT

1   A.   Yes. I thought so.

2   Q.   And so you did that on a weekly basis for six

3   weeks.

4   A.   Did that on a weekly basis at Lawton until he was

5   released from there.

6   Q.   Then what happened after that?

7   A.   We continued our sessions together each week. And

8   studied the bible further and I took him through a series of

9   lessons that eventually led to his being back baptized for

10   the forgiveness of his sins.

11   Q.   And that was at your church?

12   A.   Yes, that was there at Hinton at the Church of

13   Christ.

14   Q.   Okay. And did you and your wife also graciously

15   offer to allow him to do some of his home-schooling there at

16   your house; is that right?

17   A.   We did the home-schooling there at the church

18   building. My wife would provide us lunch each day. So our

19   house served as the cafeteria I guess you'd say.

20   Q.   Okay. Was Misael ever a discipline problem or did

21   he ever act up or was there anything that kind of was out of

22   the ordinary about his conduct or behavior?

23   A.   No. Not -- not at all. He was always polite and

24   kind and did everything that we asked him or advised him to

25   do in trying to help him get through this time and to deal

DISTRICT COURT OF OKLAHOMA - OFFICIAL TRANSCRIPT

1 with this great tragedy.

2   Q.   When you first met -- have you gotten to know his

3 family any better as a result of this?

4   A.   We've been able to get acquainted with them a

5 little bit more because of our association with Misael.

6   Q.   Has Misael continued to go to church at your

7 church?

8   A.   Yes.   He would usually be there three times a week,

9 Sunday morning, Sunday night and Wednesday evening.   And

10 continued that until he went to Hollis.

11   Q.   Okay.   And so he went to Hollis; right?

12   A.   Right.

13   Q.   And what is -- where is he at Hollis -- in Hollis?

14   A.   He is at Westview Boys' Home.

15   Q.   Okay.   And how did he -- how did he find that

16 place?

17   A.   Well, it -- it was -- I guess was mentioned in the

18 course of conversations as far as a boys' home that would

19 provide him continued guidance and direction and spiritual

20 instruction that would really enhance and continue what we

21 were able to get started with him up to that time.

22   Q.   Okay.   Have you been able to maintain contact with

23 him while he's been in Hollis?

24   A.   Yes.

25   Q.   How is -- how is -- to the best of your knowledge

1   how has his conduct been since he's been in Hollis?

2   A.   All that -- all that I know about his conduct there

3   it's been -- been good.

4   Q.   Okay.

5   A.   And been exceptional.

6   MR. BROOKS-JIMENEZ: Let's see. Judge, if I could

7   have one moment, please?

8   THE COURT: Go right ahead.

9   MR. BROOKS-JIMENEZ: Thank you, sir.

10   THE COURT: Take all the time you need.

11 **BY MR. BROOKS-JIMENEZ:**

12   Q.   Sir, are you aware if Misael has brothers or

13 sisters?

14   A.   Yes.

15   Q.   Do you know how many brothers and sisters he has?

16   A.   I believe he has six siblings.

17   Q.   And where is he in the birth order?

18   A.   He's the oldest I believe.

19   Q.   And to the best of your knowledge have you -- were

20 you able to observe how -- did he take care of those

21 children or do anything to try and help with the care of

22 those children while his mother was at work?

23   A.   Yes. There were times in which taking him -- him

24 home from school that he needed to get home, you know,

25 because of some chores or things that he needed to do to

DISTRICT COURT OF OKLAHOMA - OFFICIAL TRANSCRIPT

1 take care of the smaller children until his mother does get
2 home from work.
3   Q.   Okay. And then helping to lead Misael on this
4 spiritual journey as well as being able to facilitate his
5 home-schooling while this case has been going on, did you
6 ever encounter any kind of, "intellectual deficits," I think
7 they put in the psychological profile?
8   A.   No, I've not -- I've not seen that.
9   Q.   Would you characterize Misael as a delinquent?
10   A.   No.
11   Q.   How would you -- how would you classify or
12 characterize this situation that we're in the right now?
13   A.   As far as the overall --
14   Q.   Just for the community and everybody here?
15   A.   It's tragic. It's a tragic situation for a small
16 community setting. And I don't suppose it's any worse than
17 if it's in the big city, but it effects a lot of people that
18 know each other that are friends with each other and it's
19 been very difficult for just about everyone who has had any
20 concern at all.
21   Q.   Yes, sir.
22   MR. BROOKS-JIMENEZ: No further questions.
23   THE COURT: Mr. Lowe, any questions?
24   MR. LOWE: No questions.
25   THE COURT: Thank you, Mr. Cudd, step down.

          DISTRICT COURT OF OKLAHOMA - OFFICIAL TRANSCRIPT

After the pastor was excused from the witness stand, another witness, who described himself as a full-time preacher and part-time police officer, had this to say:

```
                                                        50
1    A.    As a matter of fact in order for a boy to be
2    promoted from level three to level four, he must not only
3    conduct a -- he must not only be involved in a community
4    service project, but he himself has to plan, organize and
5    carry out that community service.
6        Q.    Okay.  So you'd also mentioned that you -- when
7    you're driving up here you had a chance to be able to talk
8    -- for driving up here from Hollis, you had a chance to be
9    able to talk to Misael at length about -- about the
10   circumstances and everything else that's going on.  Do you
11   think he understands what's happening?
12       A.    Very clearly he understands what's happening and he
13   understands the gravity of this situation and the heartache
14   involved and the tragedy of it.
15       Q.    Does he -- has he expressed any remorse to you?
16       A.    Every time that he discusses this situation tears
17   well up in his eyes beyond his control because of the great
18   remorse that he -- he feels inside.
19       Q.    Do you think that's sincere?
20       A.    Absolutely.
21       Q.    Okay.
22           MR. BROOKS-JIMENEZ:    Judge, I don't have any
23   further questions.
24           THE COURT:   Mr. Burns?
25                        CROSS-EXAMINATION


        DISTRICT COURT OF OKLAHOMA - OFFICIAL TRANSCRIPT
```

BY MR. BURNS:

Q.   Just briefly, sir. You know, you said he hasn't acted up in your school, hasn't acted out; right?

A.   Correct.

Q.   Would you expect him to?

A.   At this point -- in the time that I've been there in the 11 years, I have never seen a boy -- I've seen -- let me reflect back -- I've only seen two boys make it through the system to the point he's at, at the speed at which he has.

Q.   How many boys have you had in your system that's been charged with manslaughter fixing to go in front of a judge and be sentenced?

A.   None.

Q.   Okay. So if you're charged with manslaughter and you're fixing to go in front of the judge would you expect him to act out and do stupid things?

A.   I think it would be difficult to maintain that behavior were it not real in all settings for that long period of a time.

Q.   You said he made As, Bs and Cs in school?

A.   As, Bs and one C, yes, sir.

Q.   And one C. So he's an intelligent young man?

A.   He is showing the ability to -- he's exhibiting intelligence, yes.

DISTRICT COURT OF OKLAHOMA - OFFICIAL TRANSCRIPT

1   Q.   And you believe he knows right from wrong along

2   with that intelligence?

3   A.   Yes, I do.

4   Q.   You mentioned awhile ago, he was a man of extreme

5   integrity and honor?

6   A.   He is conducting himself currently with integrity I

7   believe. The young man that I've seen -- if he's asked to

8   do something he does it without any hesitation. If he says

9   he's going to do something, he does it without any --

10   without any resistance.

11   Q.   Well, integrity also means telling the truth

12   doesn't it?

13   A.   Yes, it does.

14   Q.   Are you aware Mr. Galvan when committed this crime

15   he lied to law enforcement officers and lied to people about

16   the way this happened?

17   A.   I was not aware of that.

18   Q.   Would you consider that to be a person of integrity

19   that lied about how they killed their friend?

20   A.   No, not at that point, no.

21   Q.   Are you aware of his doctor's report, his

22   psychological report where it said he was -- he has

23   resistant to assessment procedures?

24   A.   Yes, I am.

25   Q.   Okay. Explain to the Court what kind of resistance

1   he showed to his assessment?

2   A.   If I may look at that?

3   Q.   Sure.

4   A.   Which page is that?

5   MR. BURNS: May I approach, Your Honor?

6   THE COURT: Sure.

7   **BY MR. BURNS:**

8   Q.   Of Youthful Offender Report next to the last page?

9   I'll go -- actually the second page of yours.

10   A.   I'm not sure. Okay.

11   Q.   Here, use mine.

12   A.   Okay. This is one I -- okay.

13   Q.   "Considering his resistance to the assessment

14   procedures, it is unclear if he'd be willing to address his

15   problems, that places him in a moderate risk for

16   recidivism."

17   A.   Okay.

18   Q.   Explain that. You said he's willing to comply and

19   willing to do this or that, yet he's not willing to be

20   assessed?

21   A.   Well, at that point, based on the stress he was

22   under and the grief that he was experiencing, that can skew

23   the way a young man responds to testing situations.

24   Q.   Sir, you can't tell -- sit here and tell this Court

25   that Mr. Galvan won't re-offend and hurt another child can

1 | you?

2 | A.   I cannot. I can't predict what anybody will do.

3 | Q.   And you can't sit here and tell the Court he chose

4 | to take life of his friend can you?

5 | MR. BROOKS-JIMENEZ: Judge, I object. He's charged

6 | with manslaughter. It's reckless conduct with a firearm in

7 | that there was an accidental shooting that resulted as a

8 | result of that misdemeanor. There is nothing to indicate

9 | and he's not accused of choosing to take the life of anyone.

10 | THE COURT: I think that's how it's charged,

11 | Mr. Burns.

12 | **BY MR. BURNS:**

13 | Q. During your conversations with Mr. Galvan did he

14 | tell you why he pointed a gun at his friend and pulled the

15 | trigger?

16 | A.   He did not.

17 | Q.   Did you ask him?

18 | A.   I did not.

19 | Q.   Well, it seemed like you've gone pretty in depth

20 | with him on other things, his personality, his grades,

21 | everything. Why is it you wouldn't ask him that?

22 | A.   That was my own personal decision. I felt like

23 | he's been asked this time and time and time again by others

24 | and that through developing a relationship, in time, if

25 | wanted to discuss it with me that he would choose to do so.

1   Q.   Okay. Sir, tell me the name of your home again?

2   A.   Westview Boys' Home.

3   Q.   All right. And is it a secured facility?

4   A.   It is not.

5   Q.   So a parent can check their kid in, the next day

6   come them out?

7   A.   They can. There have been cases though where

8   Courts have ordered parents to place their children. And

9   the parents then cannot remove them without the Court's

10   permission.

11   Q.   Well, explain to me. If a parent can be ordered to

12   place your children in Westview Boys' Home, what's to keep

13   that 15, 16, 17, 18-year-old boy from just walking out the

14   door?

15   A.   Nothing.

16   MR. BURNS: No further questions, Your Honor.

17   **REDIRECT EXAMINATION**

18   MR. BROOKS-JIMENEZ:

19   Q.   Do you believe that if a 15, 16, 17, 18-year-old

20   was to walk out the door that there would consequences from

21   the Court if he had a pending case?

22   A.   Absolutely.

23   Q.   Do you think that might keep him from walking out

24   the door?

25   A.   I do.

     DISTRICT COURT OF OKLAHOMA - OFFICIAL TRANSCRIPT

As I listened to the testimony of these witnesses, the Holy Spirit revealed to me that they were actually hindering the message of Jesus Christ from reaching Misael by attempting to shield him from punishment. It was remarkable to me that two self-proclaimed ministers could, in good conscience, so nonchalantly overlook the paramount duty of their ministerial office – which was to make it clear to Misael that he was a sinner, incapable of self-rehabilitation, and offer him the only solution for his sin – the saving and liberating Truth of Jesus Christ. The zeal with which these witnesses endeavored to shelter Misael, even from this Truth, suggested to me that their "ministries" were nothing more than a public show and evidenced that Misael was not going to hear the message of Christ unless I delivered it to him myself. Therefore, when Jimmy and Michelle asked Dustin and me to deliver the victim impact statements in open court, I immediately recognized their request as an opportunity given to me by the Lord to deliver the message of Jesus Christ to Misael. Ironically, the law which paved the way for me to speak on this wise was authored by my friend, Senator Brooks Douglass, who, at sixteen years of age, was shot and left for dead after two intruders killed his parents and raped his sister. The day Dustin and I delivered the victim impact statements, the Holy Spirit reminded me that I was on trial and that my words and demeanor would be scrutinized against Christ's standard, regardless of whether those examining me believed in Him or not. Dustin, however, was the first to speak; and, these were some of his statements:

DIRECT EXAMINATION

BY MR. BURNS:

    Q.   Would you state your name, please.

    A.   Dustin Compton.

    Q.   Mr. Compton, what is your relationship in this case?

    A.   I'm Dalton's cousin.

    Q.   Okay. Have you been designated as one of the two representatives of the family to give a victim impact statement to the Court?

    A.   Yes, I have.

    Q.   And can you give the Court a brief glimpse of the emotional, financial, psychological effect of this crime on you and the other family members?

    A.   Yes, I can. I've got a -- some written things from the family, if I may?

    Q.   Would that be easier for you to read those in the report?

    A.   Yes, it would, thank you.

    MR. BURNS: With the Court's permission may he read his notes?

    THE COURT: Go right ahead.

    THE WITNESS: In Dalton's short 15 years he touched so many lives. His smile and excitement about life were contagious. Where ever he was, he always had people around

DISTRICT COURT OF OKLAHOMA - OFFICIAL TRANSCRIPT

1   I can't begin to tell you the impact this has had

2   on the community, but I can be sure of one thing, that

3   everyone is watching today to see what is decided today.

4   I plead with you, Your Honor, to take this into

5   consideration, these hundreds of innocent people that are

6   all having to serve their own sentence, a life sentence.

7   Dalton was so full of life and active, he loved to

8   ride his skateboard with his friends. Dalton's Aunt Lynda,

9   high school counselor, could describe to you the pain in the

10   school system even today. She describes how heartbreaking

11   it is to walk outside and see a young man on a skateboard

12   with tears in his eyes and ask, "Why did someone have to

13   kill Dalton?"

14   More than that, why after so many opportunities has

15   Mr. Galvan never told Dalton's family, Dalton's friends or

16   the community that he is sorry for shooting Dalton in the

17   face with a rifle and killing him or why he did?

18   If I may address Mr. Galvan. What was it that my

19   cousin said to you that made you shoot him in the face?

20   What really happened, Mr. Galvan? We all have waited for

21   nine months for some type of closure, some remorse or at

22   least a word, a note, something to Michelle, Jim or the two

23   young boys that you have taken someone away from --

24   MR. BROOKS-JIMENEZ: Judge, may I approach. I

25   apologize to interrupt, but this is something that -- may I

1 approach?

2   THE COURT: Sure.

3   MR. BROOKS-JIMENEZ: Thank you, sir.

4 (Whereupon, the following proceedings were held at the bench

5 outside the hearing of the spectators in the gallery.)

6   THE COURT: Make sure Malinda can hear you.

7   MR. BROOKS-JIMENEZ: Judge, did you read the

8 preliminary hearing? We're instructed not to contact the

9 victim's family at all. So as a result -- I understand this

10 is the testimony or what's coming from the family, but the

11 whole thing is, that we've only tried to comply with what

12 was asked of us. That apparently the parents as well as the

13 additional family, the extended family all said they didn't

14 want any contact whatsoever with him, and so as a result I

15 advised him as such.

16   MR. LOWE: I concur with what was just stated.

17   THE COURT: You know, it's getting away from the

18 victim -- he's talking directly to the --

19   MR. BURNS: I agree.

20   MR. BROOKS-JIMENEZ: For a 15-year-old I think

21 it's --

22   MR. BURNS: I agree. Can I have a minute with the

23 witness, Your Honor?

24   THE COURT: Sure, you can have a moment.

25 (Whereupon, the bench conference was concluded and after a

DISTRICT COURT OF OKLAHOMA - OFFICIAL TRANSCRIPT

brief moment for Mr. Burns to confer with the witness

Mr. Dustin Compton, the following proceedings were held in

open court.)

THE COURT: You may proceed.

THE WITNESS: Continuing on, I feel the most proud

I ever was of Dalton in 2003 when Lance spoke -- when Lance

worked on the Billy Graham mission in Oklahoma City. Dalton

was one of 12 chosen in Oklahoma to participate in the Kids'

Gig, which is an hour-long production at the Ford Center

viewed by thousands and produced by the Billy Graham staff.

Two days ago on the 16th, Dalton would have

celebrated his 16th birthday with his mother and father

planning -- had been planning this for several years. They

had an old Ford pickup truck that Dalton was so excited and

just couldn't wait to fix up.

Dylan -- Dalton's brothers Dylan and Dade live with

the loss everyday and their lives are destroyed because

they've lost their big brother. Dade and Dalton used to

ride scooters and skateboards together. Now Dade tells us

that he can't because Dalton is not there.

I can take the next year telling you about Dalton

and you would never tire. Sadly, Dalton's story ended on

April 7th, 2006 with a fatal gunshot wound to the head. My

mind was blank while often trying to draft this statement

for words cannot tell you the celebration that we all

1   enjoyed while Dalton was here, and it's even harder to

2   convey the utterly devastating blow of having him, Dalton, a

3   young living, loving boy yanked from our lives forever with

4   through one single act of stupidity or possibly rage, I'll

5   leave that up to God.

6   In my closing for the family, the family takes

7   peace in the fact that Mr. Galvan will be judged in the

8   afterlife and that many people will be brought a closer walk

9   to Christ through this event, but I set myself to pray for

10   more, Your Honor. You see, a few short years, my wife and I

11   will decide to have child of our own and the actions of this

12   Court will effect that child's safety when he or she is a

13   youth.

14   I pray for a message of deterrence, a message to

15   the community that it's not okay to take someone's life.

16   It's not okay to shoot someone in the face. And I know that

17   because of the long reaching impact of the decisions today

18   this is probably the most important case that has ever been

19   heard in this courtroom.

20   It is our request that Mr. Galvan be taken into

21   custody today and sentence reflects the maximum allowed by

22   law. Thank you.

23   I'd also like to present some pictures here.

24   Q.   Let me show you for the record, let's mark them

25   State's Exhibit 2 through 7. What are these pictures of,

Whether or not he knew it, the Holy Spirit had used Dustin to deliver the message of *Isaiah 1:4 (KJV)* with a persuasive, personal touch:

> "Ah sinful nation, a people laden with iniquity, a seed of evildoers, children that are corrupters: they have forsaken the LORD, they have provoked the Holy One of Israel unto anger, they are gone away backward."[144]

The charge that Misael had violated God's law was the perfect springboard from which I would offer the solution:

> "Come now, and let us reason together, saith the LORD: though your sins be as scarlet, they shall be as white as snow; though they be red like crimson, they shall be as wool. If ye be willing and obedient, ye shall eat the good of the land: But if ye refuse and rebel, ye shall be devoured with the sword: for the mouth of the LORD hath spoken it."[145]

Nothing but intermittent, quiet sobs could be heard from our side of the courtroom when the district attorney called me to the stand. Melinda Roy, the court reporter, followed my every move with her eyes as I stood up and walked toward the witness box. Her watchful gaze was somewhat of a gentle reminder that my words would be recorded – not only in an earthly transcript – but in an eternal book which will one day be opened in Heaven. When I reached the witness stand, the District Attorney, Bret Burns, held out a copy of God's Word, and I immediately thought to myself, "And be ye kind one to another, tenderhearted, forgiving one another, even as God for Christ's sake hath forgiven you."[146]

"Mr. Compton, raise your right hand please, sir," the Judge said.

"Do you swear to tell the truth, the whole truth, and nothing but the truth so help you God?" Bret asked as I laid my hand upon the Word of God.

---

[144] Isaiah 1:4 (KJV)
[145] Isaiah 1:18–20 (KJV)
[146] Ephesians 4:32 (KJV)

"Yes," I replied as I secretly asked the Holy Spirit to guide my words and let them be in accordance with His.

```
10           MR. BURNS:  State calls Lance Compton very briefly,
11  Your Honor.
12           THE COURT:  Mr. Compton, raise your right hand
13  please, sir.
14                    LANCE COMPTON
                  having been first duly sworn,
15                   testified as follows:
16           THE WITNESS:  Yes.
17                  DIRECT EXAMINATION
18  BY MR. BURNS:
19      Q.   Will you state your name, please.
20      A.   Lance Compton.
21      Q.   Okay.  Are you the brother of Dustin?
22      A.   Yes.
23      Q.   Do you have some remarks you'd like to tell the
24  court?
25      A.   Yes.


         DISTRICT COURT OF OKLAHOMA - OFFICIAL TRANSCRIPT
```

1   Q.   On how this murder has effected you and your

2 family?

3   MR. BROOKS-JIMENEZ: Judge?

4   THE WITNESS: It will be very brief.

5   MR. BROOKS-JIMENEZ: I think Prosecutor let it slip

6 -- did you say, manslaughter?

7   MR. BURNS: I said murder. I'm -- manslaughter.

8   THE COURT: Okay.

9 **BY MR. BURNS:**

10   Q.   How the death of this young man has effected you

11 and your family.

12   A.   Okay. Dustin got to represent some of the members

13 of the family. And I come to represent another member of

14 the family that has been a Savior to us and someone that

15 defines our very life, and that is Christ.

16   As an evangelist I've learned over the years that

17 there is always a cost to spreading the message of the

18 Gospel. And this perhaps is my most costly message that I

19 will give because it's cost me someone very dear to my

20 heart.

21   And I want everyone in the courtroom and, Your

22 Honor, and Misael to know that this message comes out of a

23 love that I hope someday you will realize. Out of heartache

24 and pain boils up the love of Christ and that is the message

25 that I'm giving you today.

1 When Dalton was born I remember being the one that

2 got to drive him home with his mother from the hospital.

3 And throughout his life I saw many good things.

4 When we end our life we come before the Judgment

5 Seat of Christ. In Romans 14:12 it tells us that every man

6 must give an account to God for his actions. In Second

7 Corinthians 5:10 it tells us, "For we must all appear before

8 the Judgement Seat of Christ to give an account and receive

9 what is due to each one of us."

10 And what I want to come from this courtroom today

11 is a respect for the law. The law it tells us in the Bible

12 was given to us to lead us to Christ. And everytime that

13 God's law is broken there is a blood sacrifice that is

14 required. When man's law is broken there is also a payment.

15 And that is why there is a penalty and that is so that there

16 is respect, because what happens in this courtroom today may

17 well define the choice that other people make.

18 True salvation comes when people by faith and by

19 sincerity admit who Christ is. He is God in the flesh, he

20 came to earth by virgin birth. He gave his self on the

21 cross and atoned for our sin with his blood.

22 When Christians come, and when we die, and we go to

23 heaven there is going to be a courtroom setting just like

24 this, and God will be seated where the Judge is, and Christ

25 will be seated at his right hand. And the devil tells us

DISTRICT COURT OF OKLAHOMA - OFFICIAL TRANSCRIPT

1   (sic) that Satan calls him the accuser -- will run back and

2   forth and tell everything what we've done. For Christians

3   that have put their faith in Christ, Christ will stand up

4   and say paid in full and they will enter the Kingdom of

5   Heaven forever.

6   For those who have not, they might believe there's

7   a Christ, they might believe in God, but they have not been

8   born again like it tells us in the Gospel of John. The

9   devil will accuse them before God, and Christ will say I

10   never knew you and they will be thrown into hell forever.

11   Even though the hurt that has come from us, it is

12   our wish and that is why we have requested the Court for

13   punishment is not because it's vengeful, but it's because of

14   a love that is a rare thing in this would. We love you

15   enough, Misael, to want you to have true salvation in Christ

16   and enter the Kingdom of Heaven.

17   And in closing, I was the one that got to ride with

18   Michelle and Jimmy and the boys in the family car as we took

19   Dalton to the cemetery. And it is my personal prayer that

20   you will know the salvation of Christ so when the

21   counterfeits of this world come to you and say, "take these

22   drugs, do this, join our club for protection, these are the

23   things you have to do to join," you will know and you will

24   flee from them because you know there is only one that

25   satisfies, and that is Christ.

DISTRICT COURT OF OKLAHOMA - OFFICIAL TRANSCRIPT

1   And I can tell you that the prayer of a mother --

2 of Dalton's mother -- is something that is very powerful and

3 her prayer is that even though she can't hold her child

4 anymore in this life and your mother can still hold you, she

5 prays that your mother will be able to hold you in Heaven.

6   Q.   Let me ask you, you brought one more picture up

7 here, State's Exhibit 8. What is that picture of?

8   A.   This is a picture of Dalton, I think it's one of

9 the favorites, it was one of the most recent ones.

10   Q.   How old was Dalton?

11   A.   He was 15, would have been 16 Monday.

12   MR. BURNS: No further questions. Thank you,

13 Judge.

14   MR. BROOKS-JIMENEZ: Judge, I don't have any

15 further questions.

16   THE COURT: Thank you, sir.

17   MR. BURNS: Judge, the State moves to admit

18 exhibits 2 through 8 at this time.

19   THE COURT: Any objection?

20   MR. BROOKS-JIMENEZ: No, Your Honor.

21   THE COURT: They'll be admitted.

22   MR. BURNS: Judge, the State moves to introduce

23 into the record State's Exhibit Number 1 which is a

24 restitution recovery form. This is for the funeral cost of

25 Dalton. The Hinton Turner Funeral Home, the total bill was

DISTRICT COURT OF OKLAHOMA - OFFICIAL TRANSCRIPT

1   A.   No, sir.

2   Q.   Is there anything you want to tell his family while

3   they're all together and they're here today?

4   THE COURT: Get the mich a little closer to him.

5   THE DEFENDANT: I want to say I'm sorry for

6   everything I've done and if I could, I would take this back.

7   And I'm so sorry, and I don't have the words to say.   So if

8   you could, please forgive me for everything I've done, poor

9   decisions that I took.

10 BY MR. BROOKS-JIMENEZ:

11 Q.   You're not ever going to forget Dalton are you?

12 A.   No, sir.

13 Q.   He was one of your best friends wasn't he?

14 A.   Yes, sir.

15 Q.   And you heard what the family had to say earlier?

16 A.   Yes, sir.

17 Q.   How did that -- how did that make you feel?

18 A.   Dirt.

19 Q.   You think they were right?

20 A.   No, sir.

21 Q.   What do you mean?

22 A.   Cause I never intended to take his life.

23 Q.   Okay.   But do you understand how they hurt?

24 A.   Yes, sir.

25 Q.   Okay.   When the second witness talked and he talked

1 about God and trying to find that -- that forgiveness and
2 being able to -- to pay a blood-debt, do you understand what
3 he was talking about?
4   A.   Yes, sir.
5   Q.   Is that something you intend to do?
6   A.   No, sir.
7   Q.   You don't intend to try and repent or to try to
8 make this right as much as you can?
9   A.   Yes, sir.
10   Q.   You do intend to do that? I'm sorry, I'm a lawyer
11 so I get people confused every time I ask people questions.
12   A.   Yes, sir.
13   Q.   But you intend to try and do the very best that you
14 can; is that right?
15   A.   Yes, sir.
16   MR. BROOKS-JIMENEZ: No questions.
17   MR. BURNS: Your Honor, I agreed not to ask
18 questions if he was going to apologize to the family.
19 That's what he's done, so I have no questions.
20   THE COURT: Thank you. You can step down.
21   MR. BROOKS-JIMENEZ: Judge, I have no further
22 witnesses to call. We would rest at this time.
23   THE COURT: Okay. Any rebuttal witnesses,
24 Mr. Burns?
25   MR. BURNS: No, Your Honor.

DISTRICT COURT OF OKLAHOMA - OFFICIAL TRANSCRIPT

Misael's sentence proved the Youthful Offender Act to be a veneer for sin and a shield against its consequences and reminded me of Jesus' words in *Luke 11:46 (KJV)*: "...Woe unto you also, ye lawyers! for ye lade men with burdens grievous to be borne, and ye yourselves touch not the burdens with one of your fingers." In addition to mandating Misael's release at the age of eighteen, it practically guaranteed him a tax-payer subsidized vacation in the interim. He was initially ordered to serve his sentence at the Foss Lake Adventure Program, an adventure-style camp not far from Clinton, Oklahoma. Among the objectives of his "rehabilitation" were completing the tenth grade with proper extracurricular activities, attending and participating in drug and alcohol awareness counseling, overcoming negative behavior, and developing skills to live as a self-supporting individual. What the system viewed as "punishment" was actually a slap to the faces of my family and Dalton's memory. Within a month of Misael's arrival at Foss Lake, which was less than an hour away from our homes, we learned that he habitually bragged about Dalton's murder and frequently ranted against my family, calling us "haters" as he threatened our demise. When we reported these things to the district attorney, Misael was moved to the Tenkiller Adventure Program in southeastern Oklahoma where he finished his sentence in an environment even more luxurious than Foss Lake.

Indeed, sin is a debt that does not immediately receive its due penalty and is often glossed over or ignored. This was evident in some of the "support letters" submitted to the court on Misael's behalf. In one of them, a church counselor wrote: "Misael is not aggressive toward others, not vindictive, not angry with those who believe that it was his fault."[147] In another, an employee of the Tenkiller Adventure Program wrote: "While working here at TAP, there is only 2 boys that I would consider taking home and being a father figure to and one of them is Misael."[148] In another, also written by an employee of the Tenkiller Adventure Program, the author stated, "When residents leave they usually thank me for all that I have done for them. In this case it is me

---

[147] *State of Oklahoma v. Misael Galvan*, District Court of Caddo County, State of Oklahoma, Case No. CF-2006-92, filed April 11, 2006
[148] Ibid.

who thanked the resident for all he has shown me. I would take him home with me in an instant if that would be best for Misael."[149] In a fourth, the author stated, "I also have grown to trust Misael...In my opinion Misael will do nothing but help society when he is released."[150] The apparent willingness and readiness of these people to affix their seal of approval to unrepentant sin and even invite it into their own homes painted a tragic picture of the world's spiritual condition, which is personified in the ninth chapter of *Proverbs*:

> "A foolish woman is clamorous: she is simple, and knoweth nothing. For she sitteth at the door of her house, on a seat in the high places of the city, To call passengers who go right on their ways: Whoso is simple, let him turn in hither: and as for him that wanteth understanding, she saith to him, Stolen waters are sweet, and bread eaten in secret is pleasant. But he knoweth not that the dead are there; and that her guests are in the depths of hell."[151]

As Misael's eighteenth birthday and the end of his sentence approached, and Dylan and Dade became more and more fearful that he would return to their school when he was released, my family made a collective decision. Mom explained our situation to a new friend of hers whose husband worked for U.S. Immigration and Customs Enforcement (ICE). And, Dustin contacted Senator Jim Inhofe, Congresswoman Mary Fallin, and Vice President Dick Cheney. Within two days of their decisive action, Misael was deported to Mexico. Afterward, we received a telephone call from an ICE agent, who reported that, when he had asked Misael why he killed Dalton, his cold-blooded reply was, "Does it matter? I was under eighteen and only had to lay low." We also received a follow-up telephone call from the Vice-President's private secretary, who left a voicemail message, stating, "Our information shows that Misael Galvan is no longer within the jurisdictional borders

---

[149] Ibid.
[150] Ibid.
[151] Proverbs 9:13-18 (KJV)

of the United States. We hope the proceedings were to your liking...
our condolences to you and your family."

Confirmation of Misael's deportation only brought me a fleeting
peace of mind. Nothing could stifle the overwhelming reality that
two young men were dead – one physically and the other, spiritually.
Hindsight has not yet granted me a thorough understanding of Dalton's
death, but I am comforted by the fact that Jesus Christ was publicly
proclaimed in the aftermath as well as the fact that the captive spectators,
from Misael to the attorneys and the Judge, the witnesses, and the
community supporters on both sides, had no choice but to hear the
message. I am also comforted by my obedience unto the deliverance
of Christ's message of salvation and forgiveness – not only because the
Holy Spirit asked me to do it – but so my family and I and everyone
else who heard it would be better equipped to hear, with spiritual ears,
the message of *Hebrews 12:14-15 (KJV)*:

> "Follow peace with all men, and holiness, without
> which no man shall see the Lord: Looking diligently
> lest any man fail of the grace of God; lest any root of
> bitterness springing up trouble you, and thereby many
> be defiled;"[152]

My principal comfort, however, continues to be the knowledge
that, insofar as someone may have come to Christ through this public
testimony, or may still yet come to Him, Dalton would have been
pleased that his death was not in vain.

---

[152] Hebrews 12:14–15 (KJV)

My Special Notes On This Chapter

During the editing of this book, it was discovered and brought to my attention that I misspoke during my Victim Impact Statement, which resulted in me witnessing to something not in accordance with sound, Biblical doctrine. Immediately, those around me viewed the discovery as a test of them from the Lord and in turn them testing me. Because I am a sincere minister, who wants to imitate and please my Master, I immediately accepted it as a blessing from the hand of Christ to right a wrong, and I view it as one more opportunity to exalt Jesus. Therefore, after much prayer, the Holy Spirit has shown me how to use this circumstance to please my Heavenly Father.

To begin with, I ask the forgiveness of those for whom I was speaking.

First, to my Lord and Savior, Jesus Christ, I want to publicly ask you to forgive me for speaking in testimony something that was contrary to your Word.

Second, to Jim and Michelle, who trusted me to speak for them when they could not, I faltered at the end; and for that, I am sorry.

Third, to those who were present in the courtroom on that awful, emotional day, I am sorry.

Fourth, to Misael Galvan, to whom the Lord asked me to bear witness of Christ, the message which I delivered to you was given under great stress, as many did not want it to be given. Some were unable to let go of their pain and see you publicly forgiven. Many of your supporters glared at me sternly, seemingly viewing me as the enemy. And, your behavior suggested to me that you would reject the words I spoke. These factors and others made the setting into which I spoke very difficult for me, yet I offer no excuse because I have a duty to Christ to rightly divide His Word as most ministry is conducted under such strenuous circumstances. Misael, even though are barred by law from ever becoming a citizen of this country, you still have the opportunity to become a citizen of the Kingdom of God by faith in Jesus Christ if you have not already done so. I urge you to find a minister who preaches and teaches the Truth, who can help you understand the mysteries of the Scriptures; and as I hope you learn from me here, always make the Word of God your primary source because men are fallible and will make mistakes, but God and His Word are infallible. Here are the corrections that I wish to make in regards to what I said:

1. On page 302, line 23, the concept of the "courtroom setting" as it pertains to the believer in Christ is illustrated in the *Book of Job, Zechariah 3*, and *Revelation 12:10*. As it pertains to the lost, the courtroom setting is illustrated in *Revelation 20:11-15*.

2. Beginning on page 302, line 25, I stated that, "And the devil tells us that Satan calls him the accuser," but I meant to say that the Bible tells us that Satan is the accuser of Christians. *See, Revelation 12:10*.

3. On page 303, line 8, I said, "the Gospel of John," but I should have said, "the Gospel *according to* John."

4. To clarify my statement from page 302, line 22, to page 303, line 5, Christians who die prior to the Rapture of the Church will immediately be with Christ after they die, and there will not be any period of time following death wherein the lost will have an opportunity to enter Heaven. *See, 2 Corinthians 5:6-8, 1 Thessalonians 4:15-16,* and *Luke 16:19-31.*

5. God judges us through His Son, Jesus Christ. All judgment is given to Christ. *See, Acts 17:31 and John 5:27*

6. As long as we are alive physically, God's mercy and grace is sufficient to forgive us of our sins if we will humble ourselves before Him. *See, 2 Corinthians 6:2*

CHAPTER 13

Anointed

In the *Valley of Elah*, southwest of Jerusalem, Tony took John, Christopher, and me to see the Elah brook, which is best known for contributing the stone with which David killed Goliath. While sharing the historical details of the familiar story, Tony proceeded to tie a sling to his finger and then retrieved, from the bed of the brook, a small stone so smooth that it could have passed as a marble.

"The Israelite army would've been camped on top of that ridge over there," he said pointing to the southeast. "And, the Philistines…" he said, pointing toward the northwest, "…would've been camped over there on that ridge."

> "And the Philistines stood on a mountain on the one side, and Israel stood on a mountain on the other side: and there was a valley between them."[153]

He stooped down again and chose another stone from the creek bed and said, "David chose the stones for his sling from this brook."

> "And he took his staff in his hand, and chose him five smooth stones out of the brook, and put them in a shepherd's bag which he had, even in a scrip; and his sling was in his hand: and he drew near to the Philistine."[154]

---

[153] 1 Samuel 17:3 (KJV)
[154] 1 Samuel 17:40 (KJV)

After demonstrating to us how the stones would have been placed in the sling, he launched one of them. Witnessing this demonstration was, to me, undeniable evidence that God had been with David in the battle. I was quite certain that he could not have killed Goliath without the Lord's help. After all, the adversary whom David dropped with nothing but a sling and rock as his tools is described in the Word of God as a champion:

> "And there went out a champion out of the camp of the Philistines, named Goliath, of Gath, whose height was six cubits and a span."[155]

The Hebrew word for champion in the original text is *benayim,* which is a substantive, meaning "man of the space between armies." This was a euphemism which essentially meant that Goliath was a hired solider. Naturally, as a professional fighter, he presented a physique worthy of his profession: he was six cubits and a span in height. In ancient times, a cubit was approximately eighteen to twenty inches; and a span, which was half the length of a cubit, would have been approximately nine to ten inches. Thus, if a cubit was eighteen inches, a span was nine inches, and Goliath was six cubits and a span in height, he would have been at least one hundred and seventeen inches tall, which is just over nine feet.

An imposing stature, however, was not Goliath's only qualification as a career soldier. He also had a penchant for intimidation:

> "And the Philistine drew near morning and evening, and presented himself forty days."[156]

This was clearly an intimidation tactic, and the scriptures reveal that he had others in his arsenal:

> "And he stood and cried unto the armies of Israel, and said unto them, Why are ye come out to set your battle

[155] 1 Samuel 17:4 (KJV)
[156] 1 Samuel 17:16 (KJV)

in array? am not I a Philistine, and ye servants to Saul? choose you a man for you, and let him come down to me. If he be able to fight with me, and to kill me, then will we be your servants: but if I prevail against him, and kill him, then shall ye be our servants, and serve us."[157]

It was because of these threats that David found the Israelite army intimidated and fearful when he arrived on the scene with food for his brothers from their father, Jesse. Unlike the Israelite army, David was capable of seeing past the grandstanding; and he realized, from the Lord's point of view, that the root of the problem was Goliath's defiance of the living God:

"And the men of Israel said, Have ye seen this man that is come up? surely to defy Israel is he come up: and it shall be, that the man who killeth him, the king will enrich him with great riches, and will give him his daughter, and make his father's house free in Israel. And David spake to the men that stood by him, saying, What shall be done to the man that killeth this Philistine, and taketh away the reproach from Israel? for who is this uncircumcised Philistine, that he should defy the armies of the living God?"[158]

Knowing that any battle he waged against Goliath would be the Lord's, David, who had accepted by faith that the consequences were in God's hands, was moved to action. However, not everyone believed that David's intentions in taking action were honorable:

"And Eliab his eldest brother heard when he spake unto the men; and Eliab's anger was kindled against David, and he said, Why camest thou down hither? and with whom hast thou left those few sheep in the wilderness? I know thy pride, and the naughtiness of

---

[157] 1 Samuel 17:8–9 (KJV)
[158] 1 Samuel 17:25–26 (KJV)

thine heart; for thou art come down that thou mightest
see the battle."[159]

By October 2005, a great storm, the cause of which I will always
believe began with the fact that I had thrown a criminal out of our
midst during the hurricane relief trip in Mississippi, had begun to rage
against *New Beginnings*. When it hit, I, like David, came face to face
with an imposing adversary as the Drug Enforcement Agency (DEA)
launched an investigation against *New Beginnings*, claiming to be in
receipt of a complaint regarding possible questionable practices during
the hurricane relief trip. Several reliable sources informed me that this
"complaint" had been made by the former patient who threatened to
sic his law enforcement family upon us; but, to this day, I have not been
able to confirm the information as fact.

Not surprisingly, the DEA's investigation led to collateral
investigations by our other regulators; and, in January 2006, the
ODMHSAS filed a petition to revoke *New Beginnings'* certification;
the U.S. Attorney's office sent us a civil contact letter in March, alleging
that they intended to initiate a civil penalty lawsuit; and the Oklahoma
Bureau of Narcotics (OBN) initiated a proceeding to revoke *New
Beginnings'* registration in July.

In the midst of the storm, however, I calmly responded to the call of
the Holy Spirit to be ordained into the ministry of the Gospel of Jesus
Christ on August 13, 2006.

The morning of my ordination found me in front of my antique
bedroom mirror, adjusting the gold tie that Granny had given me and
thinking of how long I had carried the burden to be ordained. It had
first begun to stir within me when Scott Lenning suggested, after the
Oklahoma City Billy Graham Crusade, that I join him on the staff of a
ministry in Dallas, Texas. Scott was a strong advocate of my ordination
and told me many times that he believed it was a necessary fulfillment
of God's purpose for my life. Another advocate of my ordination was
Chalkie Opitz, an elder in my church who had become one of my most
trusted friends and confidants since Brother Marty's death. Chalkie was
witness to the Lord being at work in my life, and our many discussions

---

[159] 1 Samuel 17:28 (KJV)

concerning the prospect of my ordination prompted him to inform the congregation of my calling. One of the longtime members of my church, Nelda Daughtry, moved that the church proceed to ordain me, saying, "This is what he wants, and I believe it's what the Lord wants." Her motion passed unanimously, but since the church was without a permanent pastor at the time and had never ordained a minister before, Chalkie suggested that I contact the Caddo County Baptist Association. Though I listened to his advice and made the telephone call, the man with whom I spoke did not express the same enthusiasm as was expressed by Scott, Chalkie, and my church. When I informed him why I was calling, there was a long pause; and judging from the sound of papers being shuffled and the whispering in the background, I gathered that I was on speaker phone. Finally, he very hurriedly said, "Tell me about your testimony!"

"Do you want to hear about my salvation experience or my call to the ministry?" I asked.

"Yes!"

Though I knew at this point that he was not listening, I proceeded to give an abbreviated version of my testimony anyway. Because the whispering and shuffling of papers was dominating my conversation, I asked him more than once whether I needed to call back at a more convenient time, but each time I asked, he told me to continue. When I finished my testimony, there was silence.

"Hello?"

"So what is it that you do now," he asked. "How do you make your money?"

Having answered that question in my testimony, it was now confirmed that he was not listening. I considered hanging up but remained courteous and answered the question again. I had not even finished my answer when he replied, "Well, you know this is going to affect you negatively on your taxes."

"I don't understand what you mean," I said, "But, I don't care if it does because I'm not doing this for money!"

"Well, you have to file differently; and, out of consideration for your best interests, I'm going to have to advise you against being ordained," he replied adamantly.

Unfortunately, because this man was held in such high regard by my church, I wondered whether I was somehow in the wrong, which led me to question my calling. He had made me feel like an outsider, but the fact that I was unable to discuss our conversation with anyone in my church for fear that my credibility as a person and minister would be ruined was much worse than how he had made me feel. I did, however, continue to pray over the prospect of being ordained, and the Holy Spirit gave me the confirmation I needed to see that my ordination was indeed the Lord's will for my life. Moreover, He showed me that only He and possibly those whom I was shepherding would care as much about my calling as I did. When my church finally called Joel Jackson to serve as pastor, I spoke with him about it. He reported that many within the church had testified to my calling, and so he agreed to preside over my ordination.

As I finished adjusting my tie, my thoughts turned to the sermon that the Holy Spirit had laid upon my heart for the ceremony, and I quietly asked the Lord to reveal himself through it. The message I was burdened to deliver was about faith in God – the kind of faith that sustained David in the face of Goliath and me in the face of *New Beginnings'* storm. I finished dressing, picked up my Bible, and drove to the church. A crowd was already gathering. Before the ceremony could begin, I had to appear before the ordination council, and so I made my way to the fellowship hall and waited to be summoned. A few of my seminary classmates had warned me that the council was akin to a formal inquisition so I attempted to prepare for it by studying a host of topics ranging from theology, post-millennialism, pre-millennialism, and the five points of Calvinism to pre- and post-tribulation thought and the rapture. But, somewhere in the process, the Holy Spirit gently spoke to me and reminded me that the Word of God was all I needed to know. As I waited to be brought before the council, I reached into my pocket and pulled out the silver, antique pocket watch that Grandma had given to Papa as a wedding gift. I had brought it with me because I believed it to be the appropriate timepiece for the day's ceremony. Just as I was nuzzling it back into my shirt pocket, the door opened, and I was called before the members of the council: Dr. Clyde Cain, my seminary professor and mentor; Phil Ratliff, the man who delivered the message on the evening I accepted Christ, baptized me, and mentored me for many years; Joel Jackson, my current pastor; Rev. Dennis King; and church deacons, Chalkie and Charlie Opitz, Keith DeVaughn, and Doyle Marlett. What I had feared might turn into an inquisition peppered with intellectual and theological fanfare turned out to be a pleasant conversation with brothers, all of whom pledged to walk with me on the journey of service to our Lord and Savior.

When Dr. Cain asked me, "How will you react if God changes your assignment?" I knew the Lord was planning to test my faith, but before I could reply, Brother Phil tailored the question to my own unique circumstances: "I think Clyde is asking what you will do if your ministry is taken away from you tomorrow? How will you respond?"

At first, I wanted to avoid telling them that the question had invoked a feeling eerily similar to the one I experienced when John sang *I Know Who Holds Tomorrow* at Papa's funeral; and I realized that poverty would find me, but the Holy Spirit convicted me to tell the story. When I finished, I committed myself to doing what I knew the Holy Spirit was prompting me to do, which was to publicly affirm that I would surrender all to Him in faith. Just then, Dustin knocked on the door and announced to us that the service was about to begin. Following prayer, the council adjourned, and we retired to an overflowing sanctuary, so packed that people were standing along the walls and outside. The sermon I delivered that afternoon turned out to be a prelude of what was to come for me – a setting of the stage, if you will, upon which I would demonstrate to the world that I truly had the faith I proclaimed.

The following day, while passing through Oklahoma City on the way home from my seminary classes, I stopped by the clinic to find John and Dustin discussing a letter in Dustin's office.

"You'd better sit down for this one!" Dustin said and handed me the letter he had received from the U.S. Attorney's office, wherein was cited the amount of the civil penalty they intended to seek in the United States District Court.

"How much are they after?" I asked.

"Oh, just a hundred and fifty million dollars!" Dustin replied. The only thing more unbelievable than the figure itself was how they had determined it.

Later that evening, after I had gone to bed, I lay in the dark, thinking. I knew full-well that only Christ could calm this storm so I turned to Him in prayer, and humbly petitioned Him, in the spirit of His Word as it is written in the 3*rd* *Psalm*, to guide, deliver, and show us exactly what to do:

> "Lord, how are they increased that trouble me! many are they that rise up against me. Many there be which say of my soul, There is no help for him in God. Selah. But thou, O LORD, art a shield for me; my glory, and the lifter up of mine head. I cried unto the LORD with my voice, and he heard me out of his holy hill. Selah. I laid me down and slept; I awaked; for the LORD sustained me. I will not be afraid of ten thousands of people, that have set themselves against me round about. Arise, O LORD; save me, O my God: for thou hast smitten all mine enemies upon the cheek bone; thou hast broken the teeth of the ungodly. Salvation belongeth unto the LORD: thy blessing is upon thy people. Selah."[160]

Sometime after I had fallen asleep – I do not know how long – I was suddenly awakened by the Holy Spirit, commanded to make our situation public, and directed to contact my old friend, Ryan Free, who was then a manager at *The Daily Oklahoman*. Later that same morning, I telephoned Ryan, informed him of our situation, and asked for his help. His reply to me was, "Give me two days."

Meanwhile, John said it was essential that we retain well-networked government relations counsel. Remembering that Rick Vernon had often spoken of former Oklahoma Attorney General, Larry Derryberry, a well-known attorney in the government relations area of practice, and longtime friend to Rick's family, I asked Rick if he could help us get an appointment with Mr. Derryberry. He agreed, and after making an introductory telephone call, advised John to contact his associate, Doug Rice, whom John and I met with the following day. It apparently did not take long for Doug to convince Larry to take our case because

---

[160] Psalm 3 (KJV)

he telephoned Dustin almost immediately to let us know they would represent us.

Ryan's promise to help us materialized around the same time when we were contacted by veteran newspaper reporter, Randy Ellis, who wanted to meet with us, tour the clinic, and write a newspaper article for *The Daily Oklahoman*. Mom, Dustin, John, and I met with him in the clinic's conference room late one afternoon and laid out the details. Following the interview, as he was touring the clinic, Randy said to Mom, "I was expecting something totally different from what I found here today."

"What do you mean?" she asked.

"Well, one of your regulators suggested that 'the family' is an organized crime family, operating out of this business, but now I've seen with my own eyes that you're just country folks trying to help others."

Curiously, before Mr. Ellis' newspaper article found its way into print, a local television network picked up the story on the wire and contacted us about doing live, on-camera interviews. John and Dustin said "absolutely not," but a brief statement was issued instead. This turned out to be a wise move because, when the television newscast aired, it was apparent that the story had been spun into practically nothing but inflammatory accusations as the camera zoomed in on a "stock photo" of some prescription Methadone bottles and a live shot of a section of our building's façade that was in minor disrepair. Also making an on-camera appearance was a live shot of the duct-taped, driver's side mirror of Mom's old Ford Taurus, which just happened to be parked outside when the camera men showed up, and a deck chair that had apparently been overturned by the wind earlier that afternoon. As all of these images played over and over again on the five-o'clock news, the six-o'clock news, the ten-o'clock news, and pretty much all day long on the news channel, I marveled. Sensationalism had triumphed in yet another of the media's trivial searches for the truth. Nevertheless, the pre-prepared statement that John issued, which was read at the end of the story and almost as an afterthought, together with Randy Ellis' article in *The Daily Oklahoman*, which was published shortly thereafter, made a meaningful impression.

Our media debut prompted Larry to ask if he could tour the clinic himself and interview some of our patients and the staff. He also said that he had analyzed the media blitz, spoken to our regulators and the U.S. Attorney's office, and wanted to have a "heart-to-heart" conversation with me alone. I could only imagine what he wanted to discuss and initially wondered whether it had something to do with accusations the OBN's general counsel had made to John, which was that they believed I was trading Methadone for sex with patients, "selling drugs out the back door of the clinic," and "running a theft ring." Though they were unable to articulate facts to support their accusations, they did offer a theory as to how I was able to carry out these nefarious activities with such stealth, and their theory was that I was using Methadone as a "carrot."

When I finally had that heart-to-heart with Larry and told him I believed *New Beginnings* to be in compliance with the law, he replied, "Well, I'm here to make sure you don't wake up tomorrow, thinking the Lord is telling you to ignore the law, and go out on your own accord." I understood and even appreciated Larry's concern. It was obvious that he wanted to know whether I was a genuine man of faith or just another imposter. His probing in this regard called to mind the responsibility of Sam Hardy's wife, Kristi, during the Crusade: it was her job to review the hundreds of counselor applications that poured in to the crusade office in the weeks before and determine which applicants were the true servants of Christ, qualified to counsel and lead to Christ those who came forward during the crusade, and which ones to discard. Larry was essentially doing the same thing, which impressed upon me a great need to expel any doubts or reservations he may have had. With the Word of God as my authority, I referred him to Paul's commandment that Christians subject themselves to the higher powers:

> "Let every soul be subject unto the higher powers. For there is no power but of God: the powers that be are ordained of God. Whosoever therefore resisteth the power, resisteth the ordinance of God: and they that resist shall receive to themselves damnation. For rulers are not a terror to good works, but to the evil. Wilt thou then not be afraid of the power? do that which is good, and thou shalt have praise of the same: For

he is the minister of God to thee for good. But if thou
do that which is evil, be afraid; for he beareth not the
sword in vain: for he is the minister of God, a revenger
to execute wrath upon him that doeth evil. Wherefore
ye must needs be subject, not only for wrath, but also
for conscience sake. For for this cause pay ye tribute
also: for they are God's ministers, attending continually
upon this very thing. Render therefore to all their
dues: tribute to whom tribute is due; custom to whom
custom; fear to whom fear; honour to whom honour."[161]

Paul commanded Christians to submit to the ordinances of man for
the Lord's sake and to silence the ignorance of foolish men:

"Dearly beloved, I beseech you as strangers and pilgrims,
abstain from fleshly lusts, which war against the soul;
Having your conversation honest among the Gentiles:
that, whereas they speak against you as evildoers, they
may by your good works, which they shall behold,
glorify God in the day of visitation. Submit yourselves
to every ordinance of man for the Lord's sake: whether
it be to the king, as supreme; Or unto governors, as
unto them that are sent by him for the punishment
of evildoers, and for the praise of them that do well.
For so is the will of God, that with well doing ye may
put to silence the ignorance of foolish men: As free,
and not using your liberty for a cloke of maliciousness,
but as the servants of God. Honour all men. Love the
brotherhood. Fear God. Honour the king. Servants,
be subject to your masters with all fear; not only to
the good and gentle, but also to the froward. For this
is thankworthy, if a man for conscience toward God
endure grief, suffering wrongfully. For what glory is it,
if, when ye be buffeted for your faults, ye shall take it

---

[161] Romans 13:1-7 (KJV)

patiently? but if, when ye do well, and suffer for it, ye take it patiently, this is acceptable with God."[162]

I also told him that rebellion is sin:

"For rebellion is as the sin of witchcraft, and stubbornness is as iniquity and idolatry..."[163]

Finally, I told him that believers in Christ, as dual citizens of this world and the Kingdom of Heaven, must submit to both the authority of this world and the Most High God and that disobedience to the authority of this world is justified only if necessary to obey God, a proposition that is clearly revealed in the responses of Peter and the other apostles when they were arrested for teaching the Gospel of Christ and brought before the priests and rulers:

"And when they had brought them, they set them before the council: and the high priest asked them, Saying, Did not we straitly command you that ye should not teach in this name? and, behold, ye have filled Jerusalem with your doctrine, and intend to bring this man's blood upon us. Then Peter and the other apostles answered and said, We ought to obey God rather than men. The God of our fathers raised up Jesus, whom ye slew and hanged on a tree. Him hath God exalted with his right hand to be a Prince and a Saviour, for to give repentance to Israel, and forgiveness of sins. And we are his witnesses of these things; and so is also the Holy Ghost, whom God hath given to them that obey him."[164]

Larry responded by telling me that some of the people involved in the investigations against *New Beginnings* were my brothers in Christ, that they were just as married to their faith, and that they were concerned about the allegations. Upon hearing this, I cited the criticism that David

---

[162] 1 Peter 2:11-20 (KJV)
[163] 1 Samuel 15:23 (KJV)
[164] Acts 5:27-32 (KJV)

had received from his eldest brother, Eliab, whose anger was kindled against David and who accused David of pride, naughtiness of heart, and of abandoning his sheep in the wilderness when David came down to the Israelites' battle against the Philistines and was moved to action for the Lord's sake. I also cited *Psalm 1*, wherein the Lord demonstrates that it is not expedient to take counsel from the ungodly:

> "Blessed is the man that walketh not in the counsel of the ungodly, nor standeth in the way of sinners, nor sitteth in the seat of the scornful. But his delight is in the law of the LORD; and in his law doth he meditate day and night. And he shall be like a tree planted by the rivers of water, that bringeth forth his fruit in his season; his leaf also shall not wither; and whatsoever he doeth shall prosper. The ungodly are not so: but are like the chaff which the wind driveth away. Therefore the ungodly shall not stand in the judgment, nor sinners in the congregation of the righteous. For the LORD knoweth the way of the righteous: but the way of the ungodly shall perish."[165]

Soon thereafter, the U.S. Attorney forwarded a draft complaint to Larry. The allegations in the complaint, which had previously been aimed mostly at me, were now aimed at Dustin; and being provoked to anger, I decided to pay a visit to my old friend, Senator Stipe. A few days after my visit with Gene, a box of copied files was delivered to me. The messenger who delivered them reported that I would find most of the information self-explanatory but advised me to follow the money trail if I had any difficulty piecing together the puzzle. Among the materials was a copy of a videotape of one of our regulators' employees and another man having sexual relations with an adolescent. Supplemental documentation identified the other man as the owner of a treatment center and the adolescent as a patient at his facility. Also among the materials was a copy of an audio tape on which was recorded a legislator being ordered to expedite the passage of a certain bill. There were also copies of several recorded communications between

---

[165] Psalm 1 (KJV)

high ranking government officials concerning the appointment, promotion, demotion, and relocation of various governmental and administrative officials and law enforcement agents. There were copies of bank statements that documented offshore money transfers. There were copies of pictures of secret meetings. And, there were copies of transcripts of private communications between various government officials and an out-of-state "businessman," all pertaining to regulating and limiting the sale and flow of certain drugs.

Among the more interesting items in the box was a copy of a brief pertaining to a known drug cartel in Oklahoma. Attached to this brief were copies of a profile and picture of a cartel lobbyist as well as detailed information revealing that almost every key player in the fight against *New Beginnings* had also been involved in a similar fight against a retail pharmacy wherein some of its stores were accused of violating regulations that limited the sale of certain over-the-counter medications commonly used in the manufacture of methamphetamine. While poring over the materials in the box, it was as if a blinding spotlight had suddenly illuminated the source of our many troubles; and I now realized that *New Beginnings* was a hindrance to the objectives of organized drug trafficking.

As I struggled to digest the information, a great spiritual battle ignited within my soul. The Holy Spirit responded by wooing me to that secluded, rocky mountain hideaway to which He had so oft summoned me during past times of trouble, saying, "Come hither." Upon my arrival there, the Spirit wrestled against my carnal desires for days. Knowing that the materials which I had been permitted to see had the potential to end careers and possibly even lives, my carnal mind enticed me to do a number of things with the information. But, the Holy Spirit gently resisted those desires with the Word of God, reminding me that:

> "To me belongeth vengeance and recompence; their foot shall slide in due time: for the day of their calamity is at hand, and the things that shall come upon them make haste."[166]

---

[166] Deuteronomy 32:35 (KJV)

The Holy Spirit also reminded me that David once had the opportunity to take Saul's life but, after cutting off the skirt of his robe instead, his heart was deeply convicted by what he had done:

"And it came to pass, when Saul was returned from following the Philistines, that it was told him, saying, Behold, David is in the wilderness of Engedi. Then Saul took three thousand chosen men out of all Israel, and went to seek David and his men upon the rocks of the wild goats. And he came to the sheepcotes by the way, where was a cave; and Saul went in to cover his feet: and David and his men remained in the sides of the cave. And the men of David said unto him, Behold the day of which the LORD said unto thee, Behold, I will deliver thine enemy into thine hand, that thou mayest do to him as it shall seem good unto thee. Then David arose, and cut off the skirt of Saul's robe privily. And it came to pass afterward, that David's heart smote him, because he had cut off Saul's skirt. And he said unto his men, The LORD forbid that I should do this thing unto my master, the LORD's anointed, to stretch forth mine hand against him, seeing he is the anointed of the LORD. So David stayed his servants with these words, and suffered them not to rise against Saul. But Saul rose up out of the cave, and went on his way. David also arose afterward, and went out of the cave, and cried after Saul, saying, My lord the king. And when Saul looked behind him, David stooped with his face to the earth, and bowed himself. And David said to Saul, Wherefore hearest thou men's words, saying, Behold, David seeketh thy hurt? Behold, this day thine eyes have seen how that the LORD had delivered thee to day into mine hand in the cave: and some bade me kill thee: but mine eye spared thee; and I said, I will not put forth mine hand against my lord; for he is the LORD's anointed. Moreover, my father, see, yea, see the skirt of thy robe in my hand:

for in that I cut off the skirt of thy robe, and killed thee not, know thou and see that there is neither evil nor transgression in mine hand, and I have not sinned against thee; yet thou huntest my soul to take it. The LORD judge between me and thee, and the LORD avenge me of thee: but mine hand shall not be upon thee."[167]

Resisting my carnal impulses with His Word, the Lord also called to my recollection the words of Frank Keating upon learning that I planned to be ordained, the prayer that Bruce had whispered into my ear at my ordination during the ceremonial laying on of hands, and Gene's advice during our last visit, whose collective message was that a servant of Christ must be a servant of servants. Additionally, the Lord forced me to consider the spouses and children of those who were named in the files, some of whom may have been my brothers and sisters in Christ, and how their lives would be affected if I took it upon myself to uproot the weeds:

"So the servants of the householder came and said unto him, Sir, didst not thou sow good seed in thy field? from whence then hath it tares? He said unto them, An enemy hath done this. The servants said unto him, Wilt thou then that we go and gather them up? But he said, Nay; lest while ye gather up the tares, ye root up also the wheat with them. Let both grow together until the harvest: and in the time of harvest I will say to the reapers, Gather ye together first the tares, and bind them in bundles to burn them: but gather the wheat into my barn."[168]

He even brought me to the point of contemplating the meaning of the word *decide*, which comes from the Latin word *decidre* and means to cut off all other possibilities. Knowing that my decision would carry eternal weight and that I could not reconcile destructive measures with

[167] 1 Samuel 24:1-12 (KJV)
[168] Matthew 13:27-30 (KJV)

my position as a servant of Christ, I came under great conviction, during which the Holy Spirit cast Jesus' arrest and betrayal before my eyes:

> "And, behold, one of them which were with Jesus stretched out his hand, and drew his sword, and struck a servant of the high priest's, and smote off his ear. Then said Jesus unto him, Put up again thy sword into his place: for all they that take the sword shall perish with the sword."[169]

In the original text, the Greek word for *perish* is *apollymi*, which is translated "shall perish" and means to render useless. After considering this scripture, I could not deny that revealing the identities of those named in the files would forever cut off any effective witness I could have of the love of Christ to anyone who learned of my actions, including my family and friends, and I truly believed the Lord was forcing me to decide between the sword of the flesh and the sword of the Spirit. In coming to a decision, I recalled the many wrestling matches in which I had harkened to my father's voice and the voice of my coach as they directed my moves from the sidelines. In a similar way, the Holy Spirit was directing my moves with Christ as my power and God my Heavenly Father asking me from the sidelines how badly I wanted to be His servant. I also remembered my father telling me once that, "With Jesus Christ, you will have more power than you can possibly imagine!" With that, I placed my complete trust in God, just as David had done; and just as I had encouraged those listening to my ordination sermon to do, I began tossing the worldly weapons, one by one, into the consuming campfire, knowing that only my faith in the Lord Jesus Christ could deliver a kill shot to the enemy's head and calm the raging storm. As the hot embers carried my offering toward Heaven and the fire illuminated me against the darkness, as those in Christ are illuminated against the darkness of this world, I thought of those whose sins were summarized on the burning pages and was saddened by the possibility of the lake of fire being their eternal destiny.

---

[169] Matthew 26:51-52 (KJV)

The following day, before descending the mountain, I stopped along the path for a breath of fresh air and to absorb the beauty of the alpine landscape. Amidst the peaceful calm, as the birds chirped around me and the chipmunks chattered in the distance, I retrieved my camera and started taking pictures. Suddenly, without warning, the wind began to stir, swirling foliage around in the atmosphere and increasing in volume until the sound was as it were rushing water in the tops of the spruce trees. A few moments later, after the wind subsided, I turned around and saw in the distance a majestic, white cross – perfectly framed by the trees on either side of it. Once again, I was transfixed by the overwhelming presence of the Lord; and, feeling like a piece of iron that was being drawn toward a powerful magnet, yet held in place, I confessed all my sins to God and asked Him to forgive me. I also asked Him to continue to teach and mold me into the servant He wanted me to become, to anoint me as He has anointed few in history, and allow me to minister to all who will listen. Then, thinking of all who are hindered from coming to the cross of Jesus Christ by workers of iniquity and deceived believers, I boldly requested that He delay His wrath upon this world and allow me and the remainder of His servants a little more time to plant and water the seed of His Truth. I also requested that He protect and provide for my ministry and subordinate it to Him alone. The cross remained visible for a long time; and, just as it was fading and I was preparing to descend the mountain's old logging road, the Holy Spirit reminded me of King Jehoshaphat, who, like David, trusted in the Lord, knowing that the battle belonged to Him.

CHAPTER 14

The Counselor

In the Negev wilderness, Tony showed us the site believed to be the actual place where Jesus' was tempted by Satan:

> "Then was Jesus led up of the Spirit into the wilderness to be tempted of the devil. And when he had fasted forty days and forty nights, he was afterward an hungred. And when the tempter came to him, he said, If thou be the Son of God, command that these stones be made bread. But he answered and said, It is written, Man shall not live by bread alone, but by every word that proceedeth out of the mouth of God. Then the devil taketh him up into the holy city, and setteth him on a pinnacle of the temple, And saith unto him, If thou be the Son of God, cast thyself down: for it is written, He shall give his angels charge concerning thee: and in their hands they shall bear thee up, lest at any time thou dash thy foot against a stone. Jesus said unto him, It is written again, Thou shalt not tempt the Lord thy God. Again, the devil taketh him up into an exceeding high mountain, and sheweth him all the kingdoms of the world, and the glory of them; And saith unto him, All these things will I give thee, if thou wilt fall down and worship me. Then saith Jesus unto him, Get thee hence, Satan: for it is written, Thou shalt worship the Lord thy God, and him only shalt thou serve. Then

the devil leaveth him, and, behold, angels came and ministered unto him."[170]

This scripture reveals Satan's method of tempting every man, but it also shows us the key to overcoming the tempter. Each time the devil tempted Christ in the Negev wilderness, it was a solicitation to be disobedient and insubordinate to the will and purpose of God, but Jesus overcame Satan and his temptations by using the Word of God as His offensive weapon. If we are to overcome the temptations of Satan, we must first understand that the objective of the temptations is our disobedience to God. Second, we must respond to the devil's temptations by using God's Word as our offensive weapon. Seeing the Negev wilderness and the place believed to be the site of Jesus' temptation reminded me of the time I had helped a young Christian apply the Word of God to offensively attack the temptation that Satan had placed before her to have an abortion.

A few months after accepting Jesus Christ as her Lord and Savior, a young patient whom I will call Tiffany came to my office looking for help. Unwed and pregnant, she was being tempted by Satan to commit one of society's most divisive sins. Though I was disappointed to learn that she had been living in sin, I saw that she was very different from most of the patients who came to me looking for help. The difference could only be attributed to her being a child of God. It was no coincidence that she stopped by my office when she did because she desperately needed a strong Christian brother, knowledgeable in God's Word, to help raise her shield of faith and sword of the spirit against the tempter.

"Well, don't just stand there," I said, looking up from my work and seeing a pair of big, brown eyes peering through the crack in my partially opened office door. "Come on in and show yourself."

Tiffany entered with a big smile on her face, and I invited her to have a seat across from my desk. We passed several minutes in idle chit-chat before she finally found the courage to tell me that she was pregnant. Upon hearing the news, I immediately asked the Holy Spirit for guidance and wisdom before inquiring further. She confirmed

---

[170] Matthew 4:1-11 (KJV)

to me that the father was her longtime boyfriend, another patient whom I will refer to as Josh. Although Josh had been attending my Bible studies, I suspected he was hoping to gain my favor rather than being on a meaningful quest to learn about God – a suspicion that was later confirmed when I challenged him to take responsibility for his unborn child.

"What can we do to help you?" I asked.

Tiffany hesitated for a moment, as if she were gathering the nerve to disclose something even more momentous.

"I'm thinking of having an abortion," she replied. "My mother is pushing me to do it, but I'm scared and having trouble deciding. What do you think I should do?"

Her revelation, coupled with the fact that she wanted to know what I thought she should do, hit me like a baseball to the chest, but I instantly recognized that she had come to me because she wanted Godly counsel and knew I had a duty to advise her:

> "If thou forbear to deliver them that are drawn unto death, and those that are ready to be slain; If thou sayest, Behold, we knew it not; doth not he that pondereth the heart consider it? and he that keepeth thy soul, doth not he know it? and shall not he render to every man according to his works?"[171]

"Well," I began. "Let me ask you, what does your boyfriend think? And...what about your father...what does he think?"

"My boyfriend won't talk to me about it. The only thing he will say is 'whatever decision you make will be fine with me.' But, he's not excited about raising a baby. As for my father, I haven't known his whereabouts since my parents divorced."

"Where are all the real men?" I mumbled audibly.

"What?" Tiffany asked.

"Oh, nothing," I replied. "I was just thinking out loud...I'll tell you what...Let me talk to your boyfriend. I'm pretty sure that's all it'll take for him to accept responsibility. He'll need a better paying job, and

---

[171] Proverbs 24:11–12 (KJV)

it'd be a good idea for him to consider technical training or college. I'll discuss that with him. However, let's get back to the question you asked earlier. It's not a matter of what I think you should do. It's a matter of what God has said concerning abortion. There is obviously a conflict within you or you wouldn't be having trouble deciding what to do. That conflict is a manifestation of two competing voices. One of those voices is the voice of shame and death – your old sin nature. The other is the voice of life and conviction – the Holy Spirit. The only reason you hear the Holy Spirit's voice is because you've been born again, and your spirit is alive in Christ. If you were not a Christian, you would not hear that voice. From the very moment that you were born again, your senses became cognizant of His Truth and sensitive to the things of God, one of which is life itself; and, in this case, you're sensitive to the life of your unborn child. Because you are born of the Spirit of God as a believer in Christ, you are able to hear the Holy Spirit compassing your conscience."

I retrieved a Bible from the table next to my desk and opened it to *Hebrews*.

"If it's alright with you," I said, "I'd like to read you a few passages of scripture that illustrate what I'm talking about."

"Please do," she replied.

"In his letter to the Hebrews, Paul wrote:

'How much more shall the blood of Christ, who through the eternal Spirit offered himself without spot to God, purge your conscience from dead works to serve the living God?'[172]

How does this apply to you?" I asked. Then, answering my own question, I said, "The blood of Christ is purging your conscience at this very moment and drawing you away from choosing death. That's why you're here."

I then turned in my Bible to *Romans* and read the first verse of the ninth chapter:

---

[172] Hebrews 9:14 (KJV)

"I say the truth in Christ, I lie not, my conscience also bearing me witness in the Holy Ghost..."[173]

Next, I read two passages from *2 Corinthians*:

"For our rejoicing is this, the testimony of our conscience, that in simplicity and godly sincerity, not with fleshly wisdom, but by the grace of God, we have had our conversation in the world, and more abundantly to you-ward."[174]

"Therefore seeing we have this ministry, as we have received mercy, we faint not; But have renounced the hidden things of dishonesty, not walking in craftiness, nor handling the word of God deceitfully; but by manifestation of the truth commending ourselves to every man's conscience in the sight of God."[175]

I stopped for a moment and asked if she had questions. When she told me to continue reading, I read a passage from each of *Acts, Hebrews,* and *Romans*:

"And herein do I exercise myself, to have always a conscience void to offence toward God, and toward men."[176]

"Let us draw near with a true heart in full assurance of faith, having our hearts sprinkled from an evil conscience, and our bodies washed with pure water."[177]

"Which shew the work of the law written in their hearts, their conscience also bearing witness, and their

---

[173] Romans 9:1 (KJV)
[174] 2 Corinthians 1:12 (KJV)
[175] 2 Corinthians 4:1-2 (KJV)
[176] Acts 24:16 (KJV)
[177] Hebrews 10:22 (KJV)

thoughts the mean while accusing or else excusing one another;)"[178]

"When you're obedient to God," I said, "You have a clear conscience, but you must know His Word in order to be obedient to Him. That is the meaning of *Hebrews 10:22 (KJV)* when it mentions having our bodies washed with pure water; water represents the Word. My job is to help you understand the Word so you can know the will of God, submit to His will, and learn how to use His Word as an offensive weapon in your fight against the tempter. It's not my place to tell you what you should do or even give you my opinion. Even though you may know what my opinion is, it's not important. What's important is that you yield to Christ, study and meditate on His Word, and allow the Holy Spirit to lead you."

I then prayed with Tiffany, gave her several passages of Scripture to study, told her to ask God to make His voice clear to her through prayer, and scheduled our next appointment. Afterward, my spirit ached for Tiffany because of the temptation she was under. I knew several women who had made the choice to have an abortion, and every one of them had suffered greatly because of that choice. Although a few proclaimed they had been forgiven by the Lord for choosing sin, they continued to live in the realm of "what ifs" and constantly wrestled with the consuming void created by their choice. I did not want Tiffany to live with those consequences so I prayed diligently for guidance in teaching the Word to her and asked the Holy Spirit to make the lessons real for her.

When Tiffany came to the clinic for our next appointment, the staff was waiting to surprise her with a baby shower. Afterward, when she came to my office, she proudly showed me the gifts they had given her.

"Do you have a few minutes to spare," I asked.

"Yes," she replied.

"Okay then, let's take a short ride. I have a gift for you too!"

"Where are we going?" she wanted to know as we drove toward downtown Oklahoma City.

---

[178] Romans 2:15 (KJV)

"Well, I've got to make a quick delivery first," I replied, cradling a box of candy on the console. "And then there is something I want you to see. I promise it won't take long."

Within a few minutes, I turned into the driveway of a small daycare center, parked the pickup truck, put the box of candy under my arm, and said, "Let's go!"

We made our way to the entrance of the daycare center, whereupon we entered the foyer and at least two dozen children began to chant, "Brother Lance, Brother Lance!"

Sandy, the center's manager, came out of her office, greeted us with a smile, and said, "I see you came bearing gifts."

"A little something for the kids — and just before naptime, too," I replied, handing the box to her, unsure of whether the children were glad to see me or just thankful to be getting some candy.

"You must be Tiffany!" Sandy said and proceeded to compliment her appearance. "Lance has told me that you may need some practice with children."

"Yes, maybe so," she replied. "How do you know Lance?"

"We've been friends for a long time," Sandy replied. "He helps us out a lot by donating toys and clothing for the kids."

Not wanting to take credit for the Lord's work, I interrupted her and asked, "Can you give us a tour?"

Sandy complied, and we ended up spending more than an hour with the children, entertaining and listening to them tell us about their friends, pets, and toys. We finally departed, whereupon I drove Tiffany to an old cemetery that had a rusty gate at its entrance. We passed through the gate, and I followed a narrow, gravel road that led to a solitary tombstone. We exited my truck and walked over to it. As I looked down at the white, marble marker with an engraved lamb sitting on top of it, Tiffany came up behind me and said in a quiet voice, "Is this what you wanted me to see?"

"Yes," I replied. "It's a sight that doesn't need explanation."

"Who is it? Someone from your family?" she asked.

"I don't know who he was, but he was someone's child; someone mourned for him. I want to read you something," I said, removing a piece of crumbled, yellow notebook paper from my shirt pocket on which I had written a few notes.

"The hormones of pregnancy... Hormones are chemical substances that are released into the bloodstream due to some type of stimulus and command cell function according to their purpose..."[179]

Tiffany began to chuckle, and we both broke into laughter.

"This is the kind of talk you should be having with your father," I said, straightening the paper with my shaking hands. "Since he's not in the picture, you're stuck with me – so you'll just have to humor me:

- hCG stands for Human Chorionic Gonadotropin. It is produced immediately following conception and early in a pregnancy and causes the ovaries to produce Estrogen and Progesterone.
- Estrogen prepares the womb to house the baby, the breasts for feeding, and assists in regulating progesterone.
- Progesterone calms and builds up the lining of the womb so it can support the baby.
- Prolactin causes an increase in milk-producing cells, and
- Relaxin prepares the womb and cervix for delivery.
- Prostaglandins initiate labor at the appointed time."[180]

I stopped, hoping Tiffany would ask me why I was telling her these things, but she was silent.

"The moment you conceived," I said, folding the piece of paper and handing it to her, "Your body became a vessel of life, and all the changes

[179] John W. Santrock, *Life-Span Development* (New York: McGraw-Hill, 2006), 103–105.
[180] Ibid.

271

your body is undergoing are evidence that your body's purpose during pregnancy is to be that vessel for your unborn child. You're already a mother, Tiffany. You've been one since the moment you conceived. God and your body are both witnesses to that fact. If you have an abortion, there may not be a physical grave, but there will be a spiritual grave because you will have ended a life. You have the power to choose. You can choose to be a vessel of life like the Lord Jesus Christ or an instrument of death like Satan. I hope you will pray earnestly about this choice and make the right decision."

I did not see or hear from Tiffany for several days following our visit to the daycare center and cemetery and was beginning to fear the worst when she telephoned and told me that her mother had reacted violently to the things I had told her and wanted to know if I would be willing to talk to her mother.

"Somebody has got to talk to her..." she said, "...because I just don't think I can have an abortion."

Per Tiffany's request, I agreed to meet and talk with her mother. Tall and professionally dressed, Tiffany's mother wasted no time in making me aware that she had taken off work to accommodate her "nagging daughter." She was also very vocal in her opinions concerning her nagging daughter's pregnancy. The all-important consideration, she believed, would be whatever lost career opportunities the pregnancy might cause. Nevertheless, I politely listened to her point of view until she mentioned Planned Parenthood and said she had consulted with an abortion clinic in Kansas. At that point, I stood up from my desk and proceeded to arrange three chairs around the same table at which Papa and I had witnessed to his friend, Tom. Hoping Tiffany and her mother would see that I was not attempting to come between them, I placed the chairs in such a way that they would be seated together at one side of the table and I at the other.

"I think we'd all be more comfortable at this table," I said as I motioned them to have a seat. They each took a seat, and I said, "Let's begin with a quick prayer."

I bowed my head and prayed aloud that the Holy Spirit would surround us, and I asked Him to guide our discussion. When I finished, I looked up to see Tiffany's mother staring at me with an expression of hate on her face.

"I don't know why we must have this little chat," she said condescendingly. "I'm for women's rights! Women have the right to choose! The Bible doesn't say anything about abortion; and quite frankly, I find it offensive that you've taken it upon yourself to explain to my daughter the changes a woman goes through during pregnancy."

"It is Christ who is the champion of women's rights," I thought to myself as the Holy Spirit led me to retrieve a Bible and a textbook from the bookcase. While opening the Bible to *Deuteronomy*, I said, "I totally agree with you that a woman has the right to choose because the Bible says, 'See, I have set before thee this day life and good, and death and evil;'"[181] You certainly have the right to choose, but it's a choice between good and evil. I want to help your daughter make the right decision for her—the decision that God has commanded her to make. I am an ordained minister of the Gospel of Jesus Christ, and I believe the fact that Tiffany has come to me for guidance in seeking the Lord's will is going to overshadow whatever advice she may receive which is contrary to the Word of God. Moreover, with all due respect, you are wrong in your claim that the Bible doesn't say anything about abortion. The Bible addresses abortion in many ways, but you must have spiritual eyes and ears and a submissive heart to see, hear, and understand. If there is anything offensive about Tiffany's situation, it is that you have sought the advice of the wicked and advised your daughter to place her health and future in their hands. Believe me, this conversation is more than a little chat to your daughter and to God, and it's for her sake that I am asking you to hear me out because she will be the one to answer for her choice when she stands before Christ."

Tiffany's mother, offended by my words, stared hard at her daughter, her lips compressed tightly; but then, to my surprise, she looked back at me and nodded.

I opened the Word of God to the *Book of Psalms* and the textbook, *Life-Span Development*, to the chapter entitled Prenatal Development and Birth.[182] From the textbook, I relayed the following information: that all cells in the human body, with the exception of sperm and egg cells, have forty-six chromosomes, which are arranged in twenty-three

[181] Deuteronomy 30:15 (KJV)
[182] John W. Santrock, *Life-Span Development* (New York: McGraw-Hill, 2006), 106.

pairs; that these cells reproduce through mitosis, during which the cell's nucleus—including its chromosomes—duplicates itself and the cell divides; that each of the new cells contain the same DNA as the original and twenty-three paired chromosomes; that egg and sperm cells, however, divide through a process known as meiosis, during which the cells duplicate their chromosomes then divide twice, forming four cells, each of which has half the genetic material of the parent cell; that meiosis results in an egg or sperm cell having twenty-three unpaired chromosomes; that during fertilization, an egg and sperm cell fuse, creating a single cell called a zygote; and that, in the zygote, the twenty-three unpaired chromosomes from the egg combine with the twenty-three unpaired chromosomes from the sperm to form one set of twenty-three paired chromosomes.[183]

I pushed the textbook across the table so Tiffany and her mother could see the corresponding pictures. While they examined them, I proceeded to read several passages of scripture and explain the meanings of the words that were used in the original text. First, I read this passage from *Psalms*:

> "O lord, thou hast searched me, and known me. Thou knowest my downsitting and mine uprising, thou understandest my thought afar off. Thou compassest my path and my lying down, and art acquainted with all my ways. For there is not a word in my tongue, but, lo, O Lord, thou knowest it altogether. Thou hast beset me behind and before, and laid thine hand upon me. Such knowledge is too wonderful for me; it is high, I cannot attain unto it. Whither shall I go from thy spirit? or whither shall I flee from thy presence? If I ascend up into heaven, thou art there: if I make my bed in hell, behold, thou art there. If I take the wings of the morning, and dwell in the uttermost parts of the sea; Even there shall thy hand lead me, and thy right hand shall hold me. If I say, Surely the darkness shall cover me; even the night shall be light about me. Yea, the darkness

---

[183] Ibid.

hideth not from thee; but the night shineth as the day: the darkness and the light are both alike to thee. For thou hast possessed my reins: thou hast covered me in my mother's womb. I will praise thee; for I am fearfully and wonderfully made: marvellous are thy works; and that my soul knoweth right well. My substance was not hid from thee, when I was made in secret, and curiously wrought in the lowest parts of the earth. Thine eyes did see my substance, yet being unperfect; and in thy book all my members were written, which in continuance were fashioned, when as yet there was none of them. How precious also are thy thoughts unto me, O God! how great is the sum of them! If I should count them, they are more in number than the sand: when I awake, I am still with thee. Surely thou wilt slay the wicked, O God: depart from me therefore, ye bloody men. For they speak against thee wickedly, and thine enemies take thy name in vain. Do not I hate them, O LORD, that hate thee? and am not I grieved with those that rise up against thee? I hate them with perfect hatred: I count them mine enemies. Search me, O God, and know my heart: try me, and know my thoughts: And see if there be any wicked way in me, and lead me in the way everlasting."[184]

Here, in verse thirteen, "For thou hast possessed my reins: thou hast covered me in my mother's womb," the word *covered* is translated from the Hebrew word *cakak*, which literally means "to weave together." This is an interesting choice of words because weaving is actually a very apt, descriptive explanation of what occurs during fertilization, mitosis, and meiosis.

Second, I read this passage from *Isaiah*:

"Thus saith the LORD that made thee, and formed thee from the womb, which will help thee; Fear not, O

---

[184] Psalm 139 (KJV)

Jacob, my servant; and thou, Jesurun, whom I have chosen."[185]

Here, in the original text, the Hebrew word for *made* is *asah*, which literally means to fashion, attend to, or put in order; and the word for *formed* is *yatsar*, which speaks of conception and means to form, fashion, or frame. *Yatsar* also means to pre-ordain, create of divine purpose, and to be predetermined.

Third, I read another passage from *Psalms*:

"Thy hands have made me and fashioned me: give me understanding, that I may learn thy commandments."[186]

Here, in the original text, the Hebrew word for *fashioned* is *kawn*, which means to constitute, make, arrange, order, and prepare.

Fourth, I read *Jeremiah 1:5 (KJV)*, which states, "Before I formed thee in the belly I knew thee; and before thou camest forth out of the womb I sanctified thee, and I ordained thee a prophet unto the nations."[187] Here, once again, is the Hebrew word, *yatsar*, for *formed*, evidencing that we are known by God even before our conception.

Fifth, I read *Zechariah 12:1 (KJV)*, which declares that man's spirit is present at his conception:

"The burden of the word of the LORD for Israel, saith the LORD, which stretcheth forth the heavens, and layeth the foundation of the earth, and formeth the spirit of man within him."[188]

In *Psalms*, King David wrote that the spirit of man is not only present when he is conceived but is in correspondence with God:

"But thou art he that took me out of the womb: thou didst make me hope when I was upon my mother's

---

[185] Isaiah 44:2 (KJV)
[186] Psalm 119:73 (KJV)
[187] Jeremiah 1:5 (KJV)
[188] Zechariah 12:1 (KJV)

breasts. I was cast upon thee from the womb: thou art
my God from my mother's belly."[189]

Evidence of this fact is recorded in the first chapter of the Gospel
according to Luke, wherein it is written that the unborn John the
Baptist, who was in his mother's womb, leapt for joy when his mother
came into the presence of Mary, who was carrying the unborn Lord
Jesus Christ:

> "For, lo, as soon as the voice of thy salutation sounded
> in mine ears, the babe leaped in my womb for joy."[190]

"All of these scriptures..." I said when I had finished reading and
explaining them, "...prove that life begins at conception but also that
science and scripture are in agreement!"

What is more, *Psalm 139:16 (KJV)* declares, "Thine eyes did see
my substance, yet being unperfect; and in thy book all my members
were written, which in continuance were fashioned, when as yet there
was none of them." Here, the Hebrew word for *book* in the original
text is *cepher,* which means a legal document. The word for *written* is
kathab, which means to register, enroll, or record. Together, these words
illuminate a great Truth: just as legal effect is given to the registering or
recording of legal documents at the courthouse, God registers us and
we are given legal effect from the moment of conception, not at birth.

"Let me show you something else," I said, retrieving a chart from
my desk and spreading it out on the table for them to see.

"Day 1...Fertilization...all human chromosomes are present, unique
human life begins. Day 22...the heart begins to beat with the child's
own blood. We know that a child and its mother do not have the same
blood because their blood types are often different. We also know that
Moses wrote in the seventeenth chapter of *Leviticus,* 'For the life of the
flesh is in the blood...'[191] Therefore, it logically follows that an unborn
child, because it has its own blood, also has life. This is a proposition

---

[189] Psalm 22:9-10 (KJV)
[190] Luke 1:44 (KJV)
[191] Leviticus 17:11 (KJV)

that is confirmed in God's Word by the Lord's conversation with Cain after he had slain his brother, Abel:

> 'And the LORD said unto Cain, Where is Abel thy brother? And he said, I know not: Am I my brother's keeper? And he said, What hast thou done? the voice of thy brother's blood crieth unto me from the ground. And now art thou cursed from the earth, which hath opened her mouth to receive thy brother's blood from thy hand...'"[192]

I explained that the cry of Abel's blood had come from his spirit, emphasizing that one of the reasons Tiffany was in such turmoil was because she was attuned to her baby's spiritual cries. I also explained that, since she was a believer in Christ, the Holy Spirit was communicating with her spirit, telling her that God has said the hands which shed innocent blood are an abomination unto Him:

> "These six things doth the LORD hate: yea, seven are an abomination unto him: A proud look, a lying tongue, and hands that shed innocent blood, An heart that deviseth wicked imaginations, feet that be swift in running to mischief, A false witness that speaketh lies, and he that soweth discord among brethren."[193]

"By the end of third week," I said, returning to the chart on the table, "The child's backbone, spinal column, and nervous system are forming. The liver, kidneys, and intestines also begin to take shape; and within the next three weeks, the eyes, legs, and hands begin to develop, and brain waves can be detected. By the next week, every organ is in place, and the baby can hear. By the twentieth week, it recognizes its mother's voice."

At that point, I stopped reading, looked at Tiffany's mother and said, "You mentioned earlier that you have contacted Planned Parenthood

---

[192] Genesis 4:9–11 (KJV)
[193] Proverbs 6:16–19 (KJV)

and an abortion clinic in Kansas so I want to read a few passages of scripture that address the kind of people you're dealing with. First,

> 'Holding faith, and a good conscience; which some having put away concerning faith have made shipwreck:'[194]

Second, in the fourth chapter of the same book:

> 'Now the Spirit speaketh expressly, that in the latter times some shall depart from the faith, giving heed to seducing spirits, and doctrines of devils; Speaking lies in hypocrisy; having their conscience seared with a hot iron;'[195]

Finally, in *Titus*:

> 'Unto the pure all things are pure: but unto them that are defiled and unbelieving is nothing pure; but even their mind and conscience is defiled. They profess that they know God; but in works they deny him, being abominable, and disobedient, and unto every good work reprobate.'[196]

Each of these scriptures mentions conscience. In the original text, the Greek word for conscience is *syneidesis,* and it refers to the spirit distinguishing between what is morally right and wrong – commending that which is good while condemning that which is bad. The people referenced in these scriptures are incapable of distinguishing between what is morally right and wrong, and I'll be the first to suggest that even an affiliation with an abortion clinic or Planned Parenthood reveals the affiliate's incapacity to discern between what is morally right and wrong. Such people have rejected the counsel of God and faith in Jesus Christ, they have chosen disobedience, and they have harkened to the counsel of this world. Therefore, they have been blinded to the Truth."

---

[194] 1 Timothy 1:19 (KJV)
[195] 1 Timothy 4:1-2 (KJV)
[196] Titus 1:15-16 (KJV)

Making eye contact with Tiffany, I said, "I believe God has made it very clear what He thinks of abortion. And, it's not just a decision you'll have to live with – you'll also have to die with it. You cannot avoid the personal responsibility that will attach to your choice. If you have an abortion, you'll deny what you know to be the Truth and you'll tread on grace. Moreover, you won't be able to silence the spiritual cries of your unborn child. That sound will bleed into your mind, body, and soul. Before you make a decision, I challenge you to answer these questions for yourself: First, do you want to become a hardened, callused abortionist? Second, do you want to shipwreck yourself in sin? Third, are you prepared to give an accounting for your decision? Finally, if you choose to follow the world's advice, what will you say to the Lord when He asks, 'Where is your child?'"

I then turned to Tiffany's mother and asked, "What say you?"

This meeting with Tiffany and her mother was a very challenging assignment for me, but the Lord used it to teach me three cardinal duties of a minister. The first, exemplified by *Joshua 1:8*, was to elevate the Word of God to its rightful place in the life of another believer in Christ: "This book of the law shall not depart out of thy mouth; but thou shalt meditate therein day and night, that thou mayest observe to do according to all that is written therein: for then thou shalt make thy way prosperous, and then thou shalt have good success." The second was this: "Defend the poor and fatherless: do justice to the afflicted and needy. Deliver the poor and needy: rid them out of the hand of the wicked."[197] Third, a true under-shepherd of Jesus Christ must never execute his duties through the voicing of personal opinions, the citing of religious or political beliefs, or by consulting psychology or offering worldly advice. This exercise showed me that a minister's duties must always be executed through use and application of God's Word.

Several months after meeting with Tiffany and her mother, Josh and Tiffany, who were now no longer patients at the clinic, came by the clinic to visit and tell us they had gotten married.

"There is someone we want you to meet!" Tiffany said when she saw me. Josh, who was holding a newborn baby girl, walked over to me and carefully placed her in my arms. When she looked up at me, her big,

[197] Psalm 82:3-4 (KJV)

beautiful eyes widened; and, making immediate eye contact with me, she studied me with great interest. Trying to hold back tears, I made an attempt at humor and said, "She has never seen anything so ugly."

"You're the first hillbilly she has ever seen," Tiffany replied with a laugh, but Josh quickly responded, "I want you to know that you were right. The first time I held her in my arms, everything changed for me."

Though he thanked me for helping him find a better paying job, I was too focused on baby Natalie to pay much attention. She grasped my forefinger and continued to look me in the eyes as Tiffany quietly whispered into my ear, "This is not the first time that you've held her. The first was when you convinced me with the Word of God not to have an abortion."

I looked into baby Natalie's eyes, hoping nobody would see the tears in mine, and thought to myself, "Yes, it is Christ who is the true champion of women's rights."

CHAPTER 15

The Messenger

The ghastly remains of Sodom and Gomorrah along the coast of the Dead Sea serve as a reminder to this day that God turned those cities into ashes as an example to all who would, thereafter, live ungodly. The sins of Sodom and Gomorrah, as declared by the Lord through the prophet *Ezekiel*, were pride, fullness of bread, abundance of idleness, refusal to strengthen the hand of the poor and needy, haughtiness, and the abominations of their inhabitants.[198] Despite God's recitation of these sins, homosexuality has been singled out by secular society and the church as the impetus for God's wrath upon those cities. Next to abortion, homosexuality is considered the most abhorrent of sins by each, yet *all* of Sodom and Gomorrah's sins, as enumerated by Almighty God, are widely practiced and accepted by contemporary society and many in the church. Though man has always endeavored to categorize sin by degree of severity, the Truth is that all sin will be judged equally by God. The greedy businessman and drug-peddling church deacon will be in the same boat with the homosexual if they die without accepting Christ. The lesson of Sodom and Gomorrah is one that should be heeded, especially by those who limit their condemnation of sin to certain ones. The ashen ruins of those once great cities are a sobering reminder of the fate awaiting all sinners who do not turn to Christ and a sight that would convict any believer to focus on delivering the Word of God to a lost world rather than casting stones, singling out certain sins, and turning sinners away from Christ with remarks like, "I can't believe God would create someone to be destined for Hell."

---

[198] Ezekiel 16:49-50 (KJV)

While thinking on these things, I recalled ministering to two homosexuals, both of whom were patients at *New Beginnings*. The first, whom I will call Shane, had accepted Christ but struggled daily to overcome the temptations of his old sin nature. The second one, whom I will refer to as Mattie, spent most of his life believing that God hated him because of the misrepresentations of others concerning his sin, but he finally accepted Christ on his deathbed.

My ministry to Shane concerning his struggle with homosexuality began one afternoon as *New Beginnings* was preparing to close for the day when one of our counselors told me Shane had been sitting in his car for a long time and suggested that I check on him. I immediately went outside, took a seat on the wooden deck beneath the shady pine trees, and motioned to Shane to join me. He got out of his car, came over to where I was sitting and without even saying hello, sat down, and commenced to staring at the ground.

"What seems to be your troubles?" I asked.

He began to cry.

"My dad kicked me out of the house, and I don't know where to go."

"Now what did he go and do a thing like that for?" I asked as I considered the potential reasons.

Shane did not answer, but after several minutes had gone by, he finally blurted out, "He found out about me being gay after I broke up with my girl. I tried to talk to him about it, but he blew up and went crazy. He said I was going to Hell and that God hates me. He said God destroyed Sodom and Gomorrah because of people like me and that we're responsible for God's judgment being on us today. Then he said he couldn't stand to look at me and told me to get out."

Without so much as a pause, he then asked, "What makes a person gay?"

I silently prayed, and after the Holy Spirit answered, I said, "Based on my ministry experience, I believe there are three possible answers to your question. First, when man disobeyed God in the Garden of Eden and ate of the forbidden fruit, the entire DNA structure was corrupted with sin. This is known as Adamic Sin. Same-sex attraction is one of the ways in which this corruption of the sin nature manifests itself. Second, in some instances, same-sex attraction may be the result of sexual abuse which was perpetrated during the formative years of a victim's life. Third, some people choose to be homosexual. Whatever the reason, however, homosexuality is a sin which most people would rather analyze and explain than confess to Jesus Christ."

Objecting, Shane answered, "Well, I have put my faith in Jesus Christ and prayed about this problem more times than I can count, but it seems to just get worse. I'm afraid that I'm not really saved and that I'm going to Hell because of it."

"I believe you're saved," I replied. "I witnessed your prayer of salvation, but only you know the sincerity of your belief in Christ and submission to Him. The fact that your attraction to men bothers you and the fact that you've prayed about that suggests to me that the Holy Spirit is living within and convicting you. Conviction of sin is a basic characteristic of a born again believer."

"I know two things for sure," Shane replied in earnest. "First, I have placed all of my faith in Jesus Christ, and I believe He has forgiven me. Second, I have no doubt that I was born gay because I've had these feelings for as long as I can remember; and I've been with a lot of women trying to change, but it still plagues me."

"Do you remember what the Lord said to Paul after he asked the Lord three times to remove the thorn from his flesh?" I asked. "He said, 'My grace is sufficient for thee: for my strength is made perfect in weakness.'[199] And, do you remember Paul's response? He said, 'Most gladly therefore will I rather glory in my infirmities, that the power of Christ may rest upon me.'[200] Now, I'm not suggesting that Paul had a sexual sin; what I'm saying is that you've got to do what he did... glory in your infirmities that the power of Christ may rest upon you. It has pleased the Lord not to separate us from our sin nature because living with a sin nature is one of the ways in which our trust and reliance upon the Lord is fostered. We have the power to overcome our temptations, whatever they may be, through the power of Christ. And, we grow closer to Him and learn to trust Him completely by having to depend upon Him to help us restrain sin in our lives."

---

[199] 2 Corinthians 12:9 (KJV)
[200] 2 Corinthians 12:9 (KJV)

When Shane expressed interest in learning what the Word of God had to say on the matter, I assigned some Scriptures for him to study and instructed him to pray for the presence, guidance, and understanding of the Holy Spirit. I also gave him some money for a motel room and told him to return to the clinic the following week. Afterward, I prayed daily that Shane would diligently seek the Lord's counsel and that I would be granted the ability to speak the Truth in love. I also prayed for the Lord to help Shane overcome his temptations before he became another statistic like Mattie.

Mattie came to *New Beginnings* for help with the alcoholism that had cost him everything, including his job and friends. I spoke with him for the first time over the telephone, and it was during that conversation that he told me he was curious about *Operation Paul,* which he had read about on our website. He also opened up to me concerning the details of his addiction, most of which were so tragic that I found it difficult to listen. Following our first telephone conversation, he cancelled so many appointments that none of us expected him to ever come in. A few months later, however, he did show up, insisting upon talking to me.

"There is something I need ya'll to know before I have any blood tests," he said anxiously. "I have AIDS."

Trying not to express any shock or surprise, I replied, "I appreciate your honesty, but the nurses always take precautions so there is nothing for you to fret about."

"Dude, you really are from the country, aren't you!" he said, making fun of my thick accent.

"Well, that's the rumor!" I said as I walked out of my office to find a nurse.

After telling the nurses about his condition and experiencing their caring, nurturing response, Mattie seemed reassured of our acceptance of him despite a disease that separated him from the world. Since he did not have a car and the nearest bus stop was over a mile away, I volunteered to drive him to the clinic each week, knowing the thirty-minute drive would give me a chance to share Christ with him. Without fail, Mattie invited me into his apartment each week when I arrived to pick him up, and like an excited child during show and tell, showed me all of his collectibles and introduced me to his Siamese cat. He did not have much in the way of possessions but was so proud of what he did have. Before long, he confided that he had contracted AIDS from gay sex and reported having battled homosexuality all of his life, without any help from his family. He did not know his father and was the only child of a Godless, Christ-rejecting mother, who was ashamed of him and maintained that she regretted his birth. When Mattie was eight years old, one of his mother's boyfriends beat him up and another one of her boyfriends raped him at the age of twelve. Not long after he was raped, he moved in with a much older man, who gave him a home in exchange for sex, and was soon exposed to HIV.

I often felt, because of the circumstances and overwhelming sense that time was limited, that my ministry to Mattie was more of a death ministry than anything else. Indeed, it was not long before I received a telephone call from a nurse at a local hospital. Having no family to speak of, Mattie had listed me as his emergency contact, and the nurse was calling to report that he was gravely ill. Once again, the sobering reality of life and death choices was palpable, and I wondered what awaited me as I drove to the hospital. I remember thinking I would rather have my teeth pulled than walk into his room. When I got there, I stopped at the double doors of the intensive care unit and searched for the strength to walk inside. At last, I took a deep breath, opened the doors, and there was Mattie, stretched lifelessly upon a bed, connected to a few small, life-sustaining machines. The clicking of the ventilator sounded just like the clanking of a gravedigger's tools, and the tangible presence of death infected the very pores of my skin. Terrorized by the thought that Mattie could die without Christ, I picked up his limp hand and begged the Lord to give him another chance to come to Christ.

Within a few moments, a nurse came into the room and said, "You must be Lance, his pastor...I'm Kim, the charge nurse."

Encouraged that Mattie had named me as his pastor and considered me a representative of the Lord, I asked Kim about his prognosis as we stepped into the hallway.

"Well, on the record, I can't talk to you about his condition, but off the record is a different story," she said with a smile. "He was able to talk before we intubated him, and I know he would not mind me talking to you. At this point in time, your job is much more important than ours. Mattie has double pneumonia but also has full blown AIDS. We are hopeful that he will pull through, but this cycle will continue to repeat itself until his body finally succumbs to something. Even if he recovers this time, he probably won't live for more than six months to a year."

As I braced myself against the counter of the nurse's station, she asked, "Is there anything we can do to help you?"

"Yes, there is," I replied. "Pray that he will wake up and that I can convince him of his desperate need for Christ's forgiveness."

For the next several days and sometimes for hours at a time, I sat at Mattie's bedside, reading and talking to him — and praying for him to wake up. I read several books of the Bible and other books, including *The Pilgrim's Progress* by John Bunyan, the newspaper, and the assigned readings for my seminary classes. I even read articles about the latest advancements in addiction treatment. I do not know if he could hear me, but the medical staff assured me that he probably could. A week later, Nurse Kim met me in the hallway as I was walking to Mattie's room and said, "He began to stir during the night and started breathing on his own again. We have totally weaned him off the ventilator. He has been awake most of the morning and has been asking for you."

"That is great news!" I said.

"I knew you would be pleased. Oh, and we've all been praying about what we talked about the other day."

"Thank you," I replied and hurried into the ICU cubicle and over to Mattie's bed. I placed my hand upon his chest. Feeling his heartbeat against my palm reminded me of the gears of a clock winding down with each tick.

"Mattie?"

He opened his eyes and looked up at me.

"That nurse is pretty smitten with you," he said, trying to smile.

"She likes the way I talk," I replied.

"She said you've been here most of the time, reading to me?"

"Well, just at meal times. You were playing opossum, and I couldn't bear to let good hospital food go to waste."

"Did the doctor tell you how bad it is?" he asked and started to cry when I nodded my head. I reached for the box of tissue on the counter and prayed earnestly for the Holy Spirit to give me the strength to say what needed to be said.

"Thank you for being here," he sobbed.

"That's my job," I reassured him.

"No, Lance it's not. My family should be here. My own mother won't even touch me, and who knows who my father is."

He looked up at me with an expression I shall never forget.

"This isn't your job, but you're the only father I've ever known. You're doing this out of love, not labor, and I can tell the difference."

Recognizing the opening I had been praying for, tears welled up in my eyes as I pulled up a chair, took his hand, and extended the invitation of the Lord Jesus Christ to become a child of God. There, in a hospital bed and just a few breaths away from death, Mattie accepted Christ as his Savior, and a young man who had known nothing but death in this world finally discovered that he had a Father. Mattie went home to be with the Lord less than four months later. His was an untimely death, hastened by the many sins he had committed against his own body:

> "Flee fornication. Every sin that a man doeth is without the body; but he that committeth fornication sinneth against his own body."[201]

Wishing I could have ministered to Mattie in time to save his physical life, I knew it was imperative to minister the Truth to Shane before he found himself in the same situation because, although AIDS cannot be called a venereal disease in the strictest sense of the word, sex is the primary vehicle by which it is transmitted. The following week, when Shane showed up at the clinic for our scheduled visit, I asked if he would prefer to drive out to my farm in Binger where our conversation would be free from interruptions, and he said, "Yes."

"I love this place," he remarked as we turned into the driveway of my house. The mid-morning breeze rustled through the sturdy,

---

[201] 1 Corinthians 6:18 (KJV)

century-old pecan tree branches, and we walked up the sidewalk to the front porch. "It's so peaceful here."

"The peace and security that permeates this land is not geographical," I replied. "It comes from the people who live here and the God in whom we believe. Never forget that."

I opened the front door so Badges, my dachshund, could join us on the porch, and Shane took a seat on the stoop and opened his Bible.

"How about I read and you explain?" he asked.

"Okay," I replied, taking Badges in my lap and sitting down in Papa's antique, aluminum chair, "We're ready..."

Shane laughed and then began reading verse after verse in rapid succession, plucking from several books in the Old Testament and from Revelation.

"No, No, No, No, No, Noooooo!" I replied upon recognizing what he was attempting to do.

"What you're trying to do isn't going to work. You're not going to find justification for your sins in the Scriptures. The Bible is a Holy book, and it's a manual for Holy living. You're at the point in your sanctification where the Holy Spirit is wrestling with you over the pride of your sin. As a result, you are feeling the conviction and have questions. The same thing happened to Jacob, and it happens to every believer so let's turn to the thirty-second chapter of *Genesis* and see what God says about it."

After reading the entire chapter aloud, Shane then yielded to me for a commentary.

"Jacob," I explained, "did not want to wrestle. He just wanted to rest. He had just come out of a deceptive environment with his uncle Laban and was facing uncertainty and possible death at the hand of his brother, Esau, but the Lord wanted something from Jacob and had to wrestle him to get it. The Lord wanted his complete surrender and obedience, but Jacob's past had been filled with running from the truth so the Lord touched him in a weak spot, from which he could not flee. So, what did he do? He held onto the Lord and begged Him for the same blessing he had stolen some twenty years earlier. Why? Because he understood the Lord was the only answer. The subsequent change of Jacob's name to Israel is the evidentiary mark that he allowed the Lord to transform him into an obedient man. The Lord is wrestling with you in a very similar way. You want to be left alone to cleave to your old sin nature, but the Lord is attempting to get you to surrender completely and be fully obedient to Him. He has touched you in a weak spot in the flesh and crippled you. You are not going to find peace or grow in your faith until you admit your weakness in your iniquity; and before God can use you and execute His plan for your life, it is essential that you stop struggling against His Word, cling to Jesus, and be obedient to Him. You profess salvation in and knowledge of the Lord Jesus Christ. Well, He wants you to know Him as Lord and Master, too, so you can experience the abundance of His blessings."

"Okay. So what do I need to do?" he asked.

"Come, let me show you something," I said, getting up from my chair and motioning him to follow me. We walked through the pasture toward my parents' house, which was just over the hill east of my house. When we got to their front yard, I stopped in front of a small pecan tree.

"I want you to describe this tree for me," I said. Shane examined it for a minute and wrapped one of his fingers around its trunk.

"It's puny, pitiful, and really useless!"

"Okay," I said, and led him into the back yard to the foot of the largest tree on the place. "Now, describe this one."

He studied it for a moment, attempted to embrace it, and replied, "It's massive! It must be at least sixty or seventy feet tall, and the branches are just as wide! It's bearing pecans because I see hulls on the ground, and judging from the chairs underneath it, I would say you've used it as a shade tree."

"Both trees are the same age," I explained. "Dad and I planted them at the same time, about twenty-five years ago. The difference between them is the amount of light they get. The puny one doesn't get any light, but this one gets plenty. You and I are just like these trees – just as they need the sunlight, we need the light of God's Word, and we can't grow or produce fruit without it. In *Galatians*, Paul wrote:

'But the fruit of the Spirit is love, joy, peace, longsuffering, gentleness, goodness, faith, Meekness, temperance: against such there is no law. And they that are Christ's have crucified the flesh with the affections and lusts. If we live in the Spirit, let us also walk in the Spirit.'[202]

Walking in the Spirit is something you must learn to do just like you learned how to walk physically. You must learn to put one foot in front of the other, spiritually speaking. You will fall and stumble, but the important thing is to begin and then keep trying until you've got it down. When you're walking in the Spirit, one of the fruits of the Spirit you can expect to see is temperance, as Paul wrote. In the original text, the Greek word for temperance is *egkrateia* which literally means self-control or the virtue of one who masters his desires and passions – especially those which are sensual. But, this is not self-control that comes from your own efforts – it is self-control that comes from yielding your will to the will of Christ."

"But…how can I know the mind of God?" Shane asked.

"One of the greatest characters in the Bible asked essentially the same question in the midst of his greatest trial:

'But he is in one mind, and who can turn him? and what his soul desireth, even that he doeth.'"[203]

"What does that mean?" Shane asked as we walked through the pasture back to my house and reclaimed our seats on the front porch.

"Open your Bible and read the twenty-third chapter of Job," I replied. The sound of rustling pages filled the stillness as Shane found *Job* and began to read:

"Then Job answered and said, Even to day is my complaint bitter: my stroke is heavier than my groaning. Oh that I knew where I might find him! that I might come even to his seat! I would order my cause before him, and fill my mouth with arguments. I would know the words which he would answer me, and understand

---

[202] Galatians 5:22–25 (KJV)
[203] Job 23:13 (KJV)

what he would say unto me. Will he plead against me with his great power? No; but he would put strength in me. There the righteous might dispute with him; so should I be delivered for ever from my judge. Behold, I go forward, but he is not there; and backward, but I cannot perceive him: On the left hand, where he doth work, but I cannot behold him: he hideth himself on the right hand, that I cannot see him: But he knoweth the way that I take: when he hath tried me, I shall come forth as gold. My foot hath held his steps, his way have I kept, and not declined. Neither have I gone back from the commandment of his lips; I have esteemed the words of his mouth more than my necessary food. But he is in one mind, and who can turn him? and what his soul desireth, even that he doeth. For he performeth the thing that is appointed for me: and many such things are with him. Therefore am I troubled at his presence: when I consider, I am afraid of him. For God maketh my heart soft, and the Almighty troubleth me: Because I was not cut off before the darkness, neither hath he covered the darkness from my face."[204]

It is the Holy Spirit who reveals the mind of God to believers in Christ. Paul wrote to the *Romans*, "For who hath known the mind of the Lord?"[205] and answered the question in *2 Corinthians*:

"For what man knoweth the things of a man, save the spirit of man which is in him? even so the things of God knoweth no man, but the Spirit of God. Now we have received, not the spirit of the world, but the spirit which is of God; that we might know the things that are freely given to us of God. Which things also we speak, not in the words which man's wisdom teacheth, but which

---

[204] Job 23 (KJV)
[205] Romans 11:34 (KJV)

the Holy Ghost teacheth; comparing spiritual things with spiritual."[206]

It is the Holy Spirit by which we know the things which are freely given to us of God, and those things are in His Word:

> "And they said one to another, Did not our heart burn within us, while he talked with us by the way, and while he opened to us the scriptures?"[207]

"Therefore," I said, "Let's look at what His Word says about homosexuality in *Leviticus*:

> 'Thou shalt not lie with mankind, as with womankind: it is abomination.'[208]

God called homosexuality an abomination, and since *Leviticus* was written by Moses, it is obvious that homosexuality is not a sin that is unique to this generation. The Truth is that homosexuality has plagued men and women since the fall of man, and there is evidence of this in the Scriptures:

> 'There hath no temptation taken you but such as is common to man: but God is faithful, who will not suffer you to be tempted above that ye are able; but will with the temptation also make a way to escape, that ye may be able to bear it.'"[209]

"But Lance..." Shane interrupted, "...this isn't like stealing, cussing, or drinking — it's constant torment! I've begged God to remove this problem so I can be normal, but it hasn't gone away. Sometimes I want to just embrace who I am and live how I want to live; but other times, I want to kill myself. And, I don't have anyone to talk to about it. I

---

[206] 2 Corinthians 2:11-13 (KJV)
[207] Luke 24:32 (KJV)
[208] Leviticus 18:22 (KJV)
[209] 1 Corinthians 10:13 (KJV)

can't tell anyone at my church because they'll just broadcast it or treat me like a pedophile."

As Shane stood in the red sand of the hilltop vegetable garden to which we had retreated, I turned on my tomato plant irrigation system and began working my way in and out of the perfectly aligned rows, tending to each plant. The more I listened to Shane make excuses for his sin, the more I realized he needed a spiritual slap in the face so I said, "Anyone contemplating suicide is listening to the voice of Satan. Furthermore, if anyone in church gossips about your sin, uses it against you, or turns their back on you because you're a sinner, they may not even be a Christian. Remember the scribes and Pharisees who brought an adulterous woman to Jesus while He was teaching in the Temple, hoping to entrap Him? What do you think it was that Jesus wrote on the ground after they accused her? I believe it may have been a list of their own sins or maybe even the names of those with whom they had committed sin. Whatever it was, it was strong enough to convict all of them to walk away."

I then picked up a stick and wrote in the loose soil some of the sins I knew his mother and father to be guilty of as well as some of which I had committed and said, "There are people around today who still want to cast stones at other sinners, and a lot of them are in the church. The difference between them and your brothers and sisters in Christ is that they, your true family, will tell you the Truth. A church that is led by Christ and steeped in the Word of God will care deeply about your soul. Moreover, if your brothers and sisters in Christ talk to you about your sins, remember that they're only doing what they've been commanded to do by God's Word. Jesus' washing of His disciples' feet in the upper room the night before His crucifixion symbolized the forgiving of their sins through the cleansing water of His Word. Jesus told Peter he would have no part with Him if Peter did not allow Him to wash his feet. This meant that Peter would have been out of fellowship with Jesus. After washing their feet, Jesus told them to wash each other's feet, a commandment referred to by Paul when he said, 'Brethren, if a man be overtaken in a fault, ye which are spiritual, restore such an one in the spirit of meekness; considering thyself, lest thou also be tempted.'[210] We

---

[210] Galatians 6:1 (KJV)

need Jesus to wash our feet because we've been walking in this world. And, if we see a brother with dirty feet, we need to wash his so he can return to fellowship with Christ. However, if you just go on and frolic in habitual sin, you have no right to complain about your brothers and sisters in Christ."

I pointed to the old chicken house at the edge of the garden and told Shane to go inside and fetch the bucket with the twine and pegs in it. A few seconds later, I heard a loud noise coming from inside the chicken house and, chuckling to myself, hollered, "Did ya trip?"

Darting out with the bucket in hand, he replied, "That place is full of spiders!"

"Of course it is!" I exclaimed. "Why do you think the chickens moved out? Better yet, why do you think I sent you in there to fetch that bucket?"

He dropped the bucket at my side, frantically brushing the spider webs from his shirt, unsuspecting of the reason I had for sending him inside that old hen house.

"You city slickers turn timid over a harmless little spider."

"Harmless? They're venomous! You should see some of the pictures of spider bites on the internet!"

"Satan's workers," I replied, "Are just like spiders. They watch the undiscerning like a spider watches a fly. They may appear harmless but multitudes have been entangled in their web of lies and deceit and fallen prey to their poisonous bite. Don't believe the Godless people of this world who say homosexuality is not a sin. The Word of God says, 'If we say that we have no sin, we deceive ourselves, and the truth is not in us. If we confess our sins, he is faithful and just to forgive us our sins, and to cleanse us from all unrighteousness.'[211] Follow the Holy Spirit and let Him be your guide. Learn and commit God's Word to memory so the Holy Spirit can lead and direct you. Remember the lesson of Jesus' temptation in the wilderness. Christ was proven through His temptations. The power of God was with Him to overcome His temptations, and He overcame by the sword of the Spirit – the Word of God – which was His offensive weapon. We, too, must be proven through our temptations and rely on His Word to overcome them. The

---

[211] 1 John 1:8-9 (KJV)

Lord will not abandon you in your time of need because God said, 'And the LORD, he it is that doth go before thee; he will be with thee, he will not fail thee, neither forsake thee: fear not, neither be dismayed.'[212] I understand the temptation you're living with is difficult, but as I said earlier, the Bible declares, 'There hath no temptation taken you but such as is common to man.' Don't give in to sin but rest in the full power of God and His Word and please Him by abstaining from the life you lust after. Jesus told His disciples: 'He that loveth his life shall lose it; and he that hateth his life in this world shall keep it unto life eternal.'[213] Remember, too, that Paul said to take pleasure in our infirmities for Christ's sake because we overcome them through His strength:

> 'And lest I should be exalted above measure through the abundance of the revelations, there was given to me a thorn in the flesh, the messenger of Satan to buffet me, lest I should be exalted above measure. For this thing I besought the Lord thrice, that it might depart from me. And he said unto me, My grace is sufficient for thee: for my strength is made perfect in weakness. Most gladly therefore will I rather glory in my infirmities, that the power of Christ may rest upon me. Therefore I take pleasure in infirmities, in reproaches, in necessities, in persecutions, in distresses for Christ's sake: for when I am weak, then am I strong.'"[214]

"Why do some Christians like me have severe temptations while others seem like their temptations are petty?" Shane asked.

"Well, it's not petty to them," I replied, "But to answer your question, take this crop of tomato plants, for instance. Which plants are getting the bulk of my attention?"

Shane thought for a moment then asked, "Which ones?"

"The sick and needy ones," I replied. "I believe the Lord gives special attention to those with the severest temptations. I once had

---

[212] Deuteronomy 31:8 (KJV)
[213] John 12:25 (KJV)
[214] 2 Corinthians 12:7-10 (KJV)

the same question, and the Holy Spirit used Mom's career in special education, of all things, to teach me this answer. Some people just need more spiritual attention than others. By way of analogy, some people are born with good physical health or a capacity for intelligence but others have disabilities. Those with disabilities have greater needs than those who do not. Similarly, because the sin nature manifests itself differently from one person to another physically, it also manifests itself differently from one person to another spiritually, and this means some people will have greater spiritual needs than others. The temptation of sexual sin is one of the most grievous manifestations of the sin nature because sex is so closely tied to love; and we all want love, but the only satisfying love is God's love."

"You say we all want love," Shane interrupted, "But, what about the love between gay people – are you saying it's not real?"

"Feelings and emotions are very real," I replied. "And, so is the sin they often lead us into. Remember what I told you about the fruit of the Spirit."

"Well, what about gay marriage?" he continued.

"What about it!" I exclaimed, throwing the question back at him as I pushed myself up from the soft soil and limped to the water hydrant to wash my hands. "Marriage is an institution that was created and ordained by God, and both the Old and New Testaments make it very clear that marriage is between one man and one woman AND that no man can change what God has ordained. Marriage is a portrait of the True love Christ has for His Church and since Christ's love is not perverted, neither is the representation of His love."

"So, what happens if I get involved in the gay lifestyle or a relationship? Is Dad right? Will God destroy me like He did Sodom and Gomorrah?"

"Once you're saved," I replied, "Your identity is in Christ, and all of your sins – past, present, and future – have been atoned for by His blood. The Apostle John wrote, 'And if any man sin, we have an advocate with the Father, Jesus Christ the righteous: And he is the propitiation for our sins: and not for ours only, but also for the sins of the whole world.'[215] Furthermore, Isaiah declared, 'All we like sheep

---

[215] 1 John 2:1-2 (KJV)

have gone astray; we have turned every one to his own way; and the LORD hath laid on him the iniquity of us all.'[216] If you fall into sin, confess your sins in prayer to the Lord and ask Him to forgive you. He will wash your feet, and you will return to fellowship with Him. But, don't forget what Jesus told the impotent man whom He healed at the Bethesda pool in the fifth chapter of *John*. Upon seeing him in the Temple, the Lord said, 'Sin no more, lest a worse thing come unto thee.' If you're a child of God, you can't get away with sin. He will chasten and discipline you. If you ever find yourself in a relationship contrary to the Word of God, ask yourself who you would rather hurt, someone living in sin or the God who died so you could live. The more distance that you place between yourself and sin, the easier it will be to obey God. I recommend that you find a Christ-led church which is preaching and teaching the Word of God and become a faithful member, avoid pornography, do not associate with those congregating in darkness, study the scriptures and pray daily, and heed this scripture:

> 'But he giveth more grace. Wherefore he saith, God resisteth the proud, but giveth grace unto the humble. Submit yourselves therefore to God. Resist the devil, and he will flee from you. Draw nigh to God, and he will draw nigh to you. Cleanse your hands, ye sinners; and purify your hearts, ye double minded.'"[217]

Well it is gettin' hot out here," I finally said. "We better get you back to the big city before another venomous insect takes interest in you."

We began descending down the long-sloping, wooded hill that forms my backyard. Rays of sunlight cascaded through the sparse hollows in the gnarled, blackjack oak tree branches, forming guideposts along the worn pathways that lead back to the barn and house.

"I have such a peace now," Shane said. "Thanks for letting me talk to you about things and shedding light on the Scriptures. How do you

---

[216] Isaiah 53:6 (KJV)
[217] James 4:6–8 (KJV)

know all of this stuff? Who taught you – your parents or grandparents?" he inquired in a calm but subdued voice, from which I perceived a hint of envy.

I smiled as scenes of yesteryear unfolded in my mind and humbly answered, "Family, true friends, teachers, mentors – the Lord has used them all to teach me, but I have most of my knowledge simply because I asked God as I have walked with Him, and He has told me through His Word."

Shane's eyes lit up like an amazed child as I continued, "You can have the same wisdom if you just ask. 'If any of you lack wisdom, let him ask of God, that giveth to all men liberally, and upbraideth not; and it shall be given him.'"[218]

Nearing the old barn at the end of our path, I summed up our conversation: "You know, whatever decision you make, I will still love you and so will Christ. I may tell you the harsh message of Truth, but the message must be given, and I am motivated by the same love with which that Truth was written in delivering it. We live in an ever changing and decaying world, but just because the times have changed, the Word of God has not. Remember this, 'Jesus Christ the same yesterday, and to day, and for ever. Be not carried about with divers and strange doctrines. For it is a good thing that the heart be established with grace; not with meats, which have not profited them that have been occupied therein.'[219] Some sins that once lurked in the alley ways or hid behind the shed now parade down Main Street like a prideful rooster strutting across the barn yard. But, don't you carry on with that crowd – it just ain't fittin' for a child of God. He said: 'My son, walk not thou in the way with them; refrain thy foot from their path: For their feet run to evil, and make haste to shed blood.'[220] I guess what I am trying to say is this: live not as a peasant orphan of the world, but as a royal child of God, and find True love and peace in His commands."

---

[218] James 1:5 (KJV)
[219] Hebrews 13:8-9 (KJV)
[220] Proverbs 1:15-16 (KJV)

CHAPTER 16

The Seed

The first sight I beheld as we approached Bethlehem, the city of David, was Israel's political answer to the threat of Arab-Palestinian terror – the Bethlehem wall. Some twenty-five feet in height and accessorized with guard towers, razor wire, and trenches, it was undeniably reminiscent of the Berlin Wall. While we waited to pass through the security checkpoint, Tony reported that, since the wall's erection, Israel's confinement of Arabs within Bethlehem has allowed Muslims to seize control of the city. This has had devastating humanitarian consequences, especially for Christians. Many have been killed or forced to abandon their homes and flee the city. Sadly, Christians who have chosen to remain in the city have endured violence and are continually threatened with it for refusing to renounce Christ and turn to Allah.

After we were cleared to pass through the security checkpoint, Tony drove us to a small curio shop, the proprietors of which have found it increasingly difficult to survive in the city, being Christians themselves. We were heartily and warmly greeted by these Christian brothers just inside the door of their shop and made ourselves at home as they eagerly marketed their collection of Bibles, iconography, and wood works. While John and Christopher browsed for something worthy of their loved ones back home, I watched and listened to the eldest proprietor show and explain to me how to determine the grade and authenticity of olive wood. At the conclusion of the lesson, I spied a magnificent representation of Jesus' flight from Bethlehem to Egypt and decided to buy it for Mom. Examining the wooden storybook's fine artistry with nerve-sensitive fingertips, I contemplated how interesting it was that, more than two millennia after Christ's flight from Bethlehem, His followers were fleeing the city too. Suddenly, a voice behind me interrupted my thoughts.

"It is very beautiful, yes? When I asked the owner what it looked like before they started carving it, he said 'just one big block of wood!'"

"Kinda like us before the Lord started working on us," I replied and turned around to see a young, professional-looking Arab man holding out his hand to greet me.

"Yes," he said. "I am Misho or Michel, from Jerusalem. You are from the States? I listen to you talk. Texas?"

"States yes, Texas no," I said and shook his hand.

Just then, there arose a great commotion from the street outside with the sound of voices, music, and drums. Michel extended his hand in a gesture for me to follow him.

"Come, see!" he said and led me outside and up a crowded sidewalk to a side street where a military parade was passing by. I watched as young Palestinian soldiers marched with their arms and legs in perfect precision through the long, canal-like street of lifeless, abandoned buildings. Like a dry sponge, I absorbed every detail of the unfolding scene, being deeply moved that these soldiers had bound themselves to a cause of deception. Nationality had dealt them the hand of discrimination, but they had allowed themselves to be lured so deep into hate and violence that it had reduced them to mindless sacrifices, marching to the beat of death. As they marched by, I made eye contact with them, looked directly into their souls, and saw their eternal destination. Grieved, I wanted to be more than just a spectator in a foreign land. I wanted to turn each one aside from his path and lead him to Jesus Christ; but I knew the Lord had brought me to Bethlehem to observe. When the tail of the parade was at last at hand, I watched a group of adolescent boys fall in behind the troops and follow them down the street, imitating their cadence as they marched along. Behind them, onlookers from the crowd emptied the sidewalks and cascaded down the street, cheering and heralding the train of lost souls. The remnant Christians in the crowd were all too recognizable, the sorrow on their faces being plainly visible.

Michel placed his hand on my shoulder.

"We must go now. It is not safe for you any longer."

"What a great dishonor to Abraham!" I thought, realizing this seed-bed of terror was the consequence of two peoples trusting in physical, ancestral ties to Abraham for hundreds of years, in opposition to that great principle declared by Jesus Christ when He told the non-believing Pharisees, "If ye were Abraham's children, ye would do the works of Abraham."[221]

The Word of God introduces Abraham in the eleventh chapter of *Genesis* where we are told that he lived in Ur[222] – a sprawling city that covered approximately four square miles of the Tigris and Euphrates River Delta and boasted a population of almost three-hundred thousand. By worldly standards, Ur was a center of greatness. It was a birthplace of mathematics and the showcase of some of history's finest secular universities and libraries. Nevertheless, by God's standards, Ur was a place of great iniquity. Its polytheistic, pagan inhabitants worshipped a different god every day of the week but honored one above all the rest – the Sumerian moon god, Nanna, whose symbol was the crescent. Interestingly, the crescent is associated with Islam today. In the *Book of Judges,* we find it was also a prominent pagan symbol during Gideon's time:

> "Then Zebah and Zalmunna said, Rise thou, and fall upon us: for as the man is, so is his strength. And Gideon arose, and slew Zebah and Zalmunna, and took away the ornaments that were on their camels' necks."[223]

Here, the Hebrew word for ornaments in the original text is *saharon,* meaning moon or crescent. The spiritual force that was behind Nanna is the same force behind all religions that do not proclaim Jesus Christ as the Son of God. This spiritual force, which is comprised of Satan and his legions, has assumed many aliases other than Nanna throughout history, including Baal, Beelzebub, and Allah and is worshiped today just as it was worshiped in Abraham's and Gideon's day.

---

[221] John 8:39 (KJV)
[222] Genesis 11:31 (KJV)
[223] Judges 8:21 (KJV)

Joshua actually reveals that Abraham's father was in the priesthood of this spiritual force:

> "And Joshua said unto all the people, Thus saith the LORD God of Israel, Your fathers dwelt on the other side of the flood in old time, even Terah, the father of Abraham, and the father of Nachor: and they served other gods."[224]

Abraham was commanded to flee this religious system by the LORD, who is the Most High God, the God of the Bible, the God of Israel, and the possessor of all Heaven and Earth:

> "Now the LORD had said unto Abram, Get thee out of thy country, and from thy kindred, and from thy father's house, unto a land that I will shew thee: And I will make of thee a great nation, and I will bless thee, and make thy name great; and thou shalt be a blessing: And I will bless them that bless thee, and curse him that curseth thee: and in thee shall all families of the earth be blessed. So Abram departed, as the LORD had spoken unto him; and Lot went with him: and Abram was seventy and five years old when he departed out of Haran."[225]

Abraham chose to believe the One and only Living God and obeyed Him:

> "And he believed in the LORD; and he counted it to him for righteousness."[226]

Today, the true children of Abraham are those who, like Jesus said, do the works of Abraham – that is to believe the One and only Living God and obey Him, as the Scripture says:

---

[224] Joshua 24:2 (KJV)
[225] Genesis 12:1-4 (KJV)
[226] Genesis 15:6 (KJV)

"Even as Abraham believed God, and it was accounted to him for righteousness. Know ye therefore that they which are of faith, the same are the children of Abraham. And the scripture, foreseeing that God would justify the heathen through faith, preached before the gospel unto Abraham, saying, In thee shall all nations be blessed. So then they which be of faith are blessed with faithful Abraham."[227]

And, this gospel which was preached unto Abraham was the Gospel of Jesus Christ:

"Be it known unto you all, and to all the people of Israel, that by the name of Jesus Christ of Nazareth, whom ye crucified, whom God raised from the dead, even by him doth this man stand here before you whole. This is the stone which was set at nought of you builders, which is become the head of the corner. Neither is there salvation in any other: for there is none other name under heaven given among men, whereby we must be saved."[228]

It is not the physical descendants of Abraham but those who accept Jesus Christ who are entitled to the inheritance of God's promise:

"Now to Abraham and his seed were the promises made. He saith not, And to seeds, as of many; but as of one, And to thy seed, which is Christ."[229]

Abraham's seed are those who are in Christ, that is, all who believe in Him:

"For ye are all the children of God by faith in Christ Jesus. For as many of you as have been baptized into

[227] Galatians 3:6-9 (KJV)
[228] Acts 4:10-12 (KJV)
[229] Galatians 3:16 (KJV)

Christ have put on Christ. There is neither Jew nor
Greek, there is neither bond nor free, there is neither
male nor female: for ye are all one in Christ Jesus. And
if ye be Christ's, then are ye Abraham's seed, and heirs
according to the promise."[230]

These great Truths reveal the triviality of unbelievers' efforts to alter
God's plan as they have been endeavoring to do in the Middle East since
the birth of Christ. Try as they might to foil God's will, unbelievers
will actually end up fulfilling it. As the Psalmist wrote:

"Why do the heathen rage, and the people imagine a
vain thing? The kings of the earth set themselves, and
the rulers take counsel together, against the LORD, and
against his anointed, saying, Let us break their bands
asunder, and cast away their cords from us. He that
sitteth in the heavens shall laugh: the LORD shall have
them in derision."[231]

I witnessed this principle at work when I was forced to leave *New
Beginnings*. The fundamental objective behind my departure from the
clinic was to silence God's Word in the ears of a sub-population whose
sins were being exploited for profit and power, yet God's Word cannot
be silenced nor can its transforming power be prevented. Jesus Himself
declared:

"And he said, So is the kingdom of God, as if a man
should cast seed into the ground; And should sleep, and
rise night and day, and the seed should spring and grow
up, he knoweth not how."[232]

One way or another, the seed will spring up. Following my physical
departure from *New Beginnings*, I took refuge on my farm where I
was utterly divorced from a host of Satan's distractions and totally

---

[230] Galatians 3:26-29 (KJV)
[231] Psalm 2:1-4 (KJV)
[232] Mark 4:26-27 (KJV)

uninhibited from teaching God's Word. The environment was more favorable for ministry and being there quickly affirmed the Lord's declaration that, "For where two or three are gathered together in my name, there am I in the midst of them."[233]

By way of example, Blake, who was saved at the Billy Graham Crusade in Kansas City, had been locked in a struggle with his old sin nature since the night he accepted Christ. Having come from a family of non-believers, he had no support system at home. He also lacked understanding of God's Word. Because the Truth of the Scriptures and conviction of the Holy Spirit conflicted with his lifestyle and the behavior of his family and he did not know how to confront these issues with the Word, he just continued to live as he had lived before he accepted Christ. When in my presence and the presence of other Christians, he praised Christ and boasted about his progress, quoted some passages of scripture, and exhorted those around him, but as the seeds of his secret, sinful lifestyle sprouted and grew, they furiously produced more sin. Eventually, Blake withdrew from treatment, claiming he was cured, but he actually slid deeper into drug use and all other conceivable sin. After several months of being convicted by the Holy Spirit, he returned to *New Beginnings,* begging for help. His former counselor and the medical staff convinced me of his sincerity so I decided to hear his plea. The day he telephoned, I was at the farm. From a chair on my front porch, I listened as he relayed the awful sins he had indulged in since ending his treatment. Suddenly, as I was looking toward my garden, my eyes were drawn to the long row of carrots that had been overtaken by weeds and were on the brink of ruin.

"Be out here no later than eight o'clock in the morning," I replied. "You're not going to get free treatment any longer so we'll have to talk about how you're going to pay your bill."

After hanging up the phone, I looked once again at the row of carrots and laughed. Remembering an accusation made against me by the OBN's general counsel, I said to God, "Lord, you have a great sense of humor!"

Blake arrived just shy of noon the next day. I was waiting for him on the porch.

---

[233] Matthew 18:20 (KJV)

"Are you ready to get started," I asked when he got out of his old car. "I guess," he mumbled.

I led him down the hill to the garden and over to the row of carrots and surrounding weeds that had become an eye sore.

"Growing these here in this type of soil is tedious business," I said. "You've gotta plant the seed just beneath the surface and water them each morning and evening so they'll have the right environment to sprout. Unfortunately, this also creates a good environment for weeds. The tricky part is discerning the carrot seedlings from the counterfeit weeds. The seedlings need to grow for a few weeks before you can distinguish them from the weeds, but by that time, it's quite a task to clear out the weeds. If you don't get the weeds out though, the carrots will be choked, and there won't be a harvest. It's alot like the parable of the sower you learned at the clinic."

I bent over and brushed some of the weeds aside, exposing the fern-like carrot plants.

"Are we going to weed this entire row?" he asked.

"Yes, we are! But, there's more. While you're weeding, I want you to think about this Scripture:

'Let him that is taught in the word communicate unto him that teacheth in all good things. Be not deceived; God is not mocked: for whatsoever a man soweth, that shall he also reap. For he that soweth to his flesh shall of the flesh reap corruption; but he that soweth to the Spirit shall of the Spirit reap life everlasting. And let us not be weary in well doing: for in due season we shall reap, if we faint not. As we have therefore opportunity, let us do good unto all men, especially unto them who are of the household of faith.'[234]

It was on this very plot of soil that Papa taught me that we always reap what we sow. Perhaps he was prompted by the Holy Spirit to teach me as I've been prompted to teach you because I was at a crossroads then just like you are now. Papa said, 'Each time we sin, it's like planting a

---

[234] Galatians 6:6-10 (KJV)

seed. Eventually, that seed will sprout, grow, and the whole world will see it. The seed of sin is like the seed of a bull nettle: it can lie dormant for seven years before sprouting, but if it's allowed to grow, it'll become a perpetual nuisance.'"

I got down on my knees and began plucking weeds away from the carrots. Blake knelt down opposite me and followed suit.

"For every weed you pull," I continued, holding up an uprooted weed, "I want you to think of the many sins you've indulged in. The secret life you think you've been living is not really a secret. It's just as noticeable as these weeds. You haven't deceived anyone by pretending to be righteous and cured. You say you want to please God but live a life that only pleases Satan and deceives you! You hold yourself out as loyal and faithful but steal from everyone and are nothing but an alley-way drug dealer."

The wind rustled through the treetops as I tossed the weeds aside.

"Now don't that look nice," I said after clearing several weeds from the row of carrots. "These ought to yield a good crop now. If you want your life to look this pleasing to the Lord, heed the Word of God and get the weeds of sin out of your life. Walk with Christ, and you'll have respect and blessing. You're too smart and talented to be an ole drugged up sot who falls asleep in the middle of a conversation. Listen and learn. Sin must be dealt with! God demands it."

Just then, my neighbor Allen drove up in his old green pickup.

"You keep working," I said. "I'll be right back."

It was midday, and the sun was uncomfortably hot when I returned to check on Blake. He was on his hands and knees, meticulously pulling weeds from amongst the carrots. I said to him, "I'm gonna leave it with ya! If ya need a drink, the water hose is over there."

"You mean you're not going to help?"

"Nosir!" I snapped.

"But, this is your garden. You planted these seeds—not me!" he exclaimed.

"No, you planted the seeds. You're expecting me to clean up your mess, but I didn't do the sinnin'. Well, I can't clean it up for you. We all have to do things we don't want to do. There are just some things a man has to do on his own. This row of carrots is yours," I replied, hoping he would grasp the spiritual lesson I was trying to teach him.

"If you'd been on time this morning, those old pecan trees would have yielded you a bit of shade!" I said, pointing to the orchard.

"So this is my punishment?" he angrily asked in disbelief sprinkled with a bit of pity.

"No, this is your gift!" I said and walked away.

Upon reaching the front porch, I looked back and saw him all alone in the garden below and knew the Holy Spirit would remind him of this lesson for many years to come.

This was not the only spiritual lesson I taught in my garden. On another day, when Dale was visiting, he said to me, "I know I'm saved, but there seems to be an area of my life that is still a mess."

His concern was the result of the Holy Spirit convicting him of the sin he was continuing to practice, and I felt led of the Holy Spirit to demonstrate the walk with Christ, using the spring plant as an analogy. We retreated to the garden, where we measured and marked each row with twigs I had taken from a nearby elm tree. Then, I drove Papa's antique tractor alongside the marks while Dale rode the planter, making sure the sprockets deposited the seeds in their proper locations. Afterward, while we were admiring our work from the garden's edge, I likened gardening to Godly living and brought Dale's attention to a certain passage in Paul's epistle to the *Galatians*:

> "This I say then, Walk in the Spirit, and ye shall not fulfil the lust of the flesh. For the flesh lusteth against the Spirit, and the Spirit against the flesh: and these are contrary the one to the other: so that ye cannot do the things that ye would. But if ye be led of the Spirit, ye are not under the law. Now the works of the flesh are manifest, which are these; Adultery, fornication, uncleanness, lasciviousness, Idolatry, witchcraft, hatred, variance, emulations, wrath, strife, seditions, heresies, Envyings, murders, drunkenness, revellings, and such like: of the which I tell you before, as I have also told you in time past, that they which do such things shall not inherit the kingdom of God."[235]

---

[235] Galatians 5:16-21 (KJV)

The complete definition of each of these enumerated works of the flesh is clearly revealed by the meanings of the Greek words that Paul used to identify them in the original text. They are as follows:

- **Adultery** comes from *moicheia,* which means sexual relations of any kind outside of a Godly-defined marriage;
- **Fornication** comes from *porneia,* which means any and all illicit sexual intercourse, whether it be adultery, homosexuality, bestiality, oral or anal sex, prostitution, or incest;
- **Uncleanness** comes from *akatharsia,* which means physical or moral uncleanness that is manifested through impure thoughts and motives or unclean lifestyles that are contradictory to the Word of God. This word also refers to the impurity of lustful, luxurious, profligate, vulgar, or blasphemous living;
- **Lasciviousness** comes from *aselgeia,* which means unbridled lust, excess, licentiousness, wantonness, outrageousness, shamelessness, or insolence;
- **Idolatry** comes from *eidoloatria,* which means the worship of false gods, including praying to saints and worshipping mammon;
- **Witchcraft** comes from *pharmakeia,* which means use or administration of drugs, poisoning, sorcery, and magical arts. *Pharmakeia* often appears together with idolatry because it can be fostered by it and also refers to its deceptions and seductions;
- **Hatred** comes from *echthra,* which means enmity or the cause of it;
- **Variance** comes from *eris,* which means contention, wrangling, and strife;
- **Emulations** comes from *zelos,* which means jealously, the fierceness of indignation, punitive zeal, or an envious and contentious rivalry;
- **Wrath** comes from *thumos,* which means passion, quick anger, heat, and ardour, or the wine of passion which either drives the drinker mad or kills him with its strength;
- **Strife** comes from *eritheia.* This word was found prior to the New Testament period only in Aristotle's writings and denotes

a self-seeking pursuit of political office by unfair means. It also means electioneering, the desire to put one's self forward, partisanship, or fractiousness;

- **Seditions** comes from *dichostasia*, which means dissension or division;
- **Heresies** comes from *hairsis*, which means dissensions arising from diversity of opinions or goals;
- **Envying** comes from *phthonos*, which means prompted by envy or coveting;
- **Murder** comes from *phonos*, which means slaughter, killing, abortion, or unwarranted anger;
- **Drunkenness** comes from *methe*, which means intoxication; and
- **Reveling** comes from *komos*, which means a revel or carousal and generally refers to parties of feasting and/or drinking that are protracted till late at night.

After discussing the complete meanings of these works of the flesh with Dale, I said, "You recently told me that you couldn't find something in your room so you cleaned the entire room in an effort to find it. In the process, you found what you were looking for, but you also found a lot of trash. When you mentioned the trash that was under your bed, I said 'cleanliness is next to Godliness.'"

"Yes, yes I remember that, hillbilly," he said with a laugh.

"Well, think of your life in the same way," I told him. "After you accepted Christ, you continued to allow your heart to be filled with the things of this world. Although you've repented of some of those sins and begun to clean up your ways, God demands a total cleaning. You can't get away with a partial cleaning. Your world view and pride are keeping you from confessing all of your sin and convincing you that some of the things you're doing don't constitute sin, and that is why the Holy Spirit is convicting you. What does the Word of God have to say about a young man who stops abusing prescription drugs but won't stop smoking marijuana? Based on what Paul wrote to the *Galatians*, that young man would be guilty of practicing witchcraft. What about this... what does God's Word say about an unmarried man who is sexually active? He's guilty of adultery and fornication. And how about this... what if that same young man was getting intoxicated? Well, God's Word says he's guilty of drunkenness."

Attempting to justify his actions, Dale suddenly became defensive, but I interrupted him and said, "Let me just tell you this...the beliefs of others or society's acceptance of certain behaviors does not change God's opinion. And, a true child of God is going to submit to the Holy Spirit's conviction, clean up his whole life, and get rid of *all* the trash."

On another day, Dale brought his brother, Lane, out to the farm, giving me the opportunity to teach yet another spiritual lesson. While they helped me clear out an old pig pen so I could plant a pumpkin patch, I listened to them talking about "some guys from their neighborhood" who had been "enjoying a new batch of shrooms." As they talked, Lane boasted about his sins, describing them as if they were a badge of honor.

"Tell me something," I interrupted. "What are shrooms? Are you referring to garden variety mushrooms?"

I was curious as to whether someone had found a way of getting high off food.

"No," Dale replied somewhat hesitantly, "These mushrooms are different. You cook them and either breathe the vapors or drink the juice."

"You said they hunt them – where do they grow?" I asked.

Sheepishly, Dale said, "The best place to find them is on the underside of fresh cow patties – early in the morning when the sun first comes up and begins to heat up the ground. The cool ground and heat from the sun is what makes them grow."

"Beelzebub!"

"What?" Lane asked and both of them stared at me blankly.

"They're worshipping Beelzebub!" I said. "Beelzebub was known as the lord of the flies; and flies, as you know, are attracted to dung. The New Testament identifies Beelzebub as the prince of demons or Satan."[236]

It took a minute for me to grasp the deep-seeded depravity of young men searching for mind-altering filth under cow manure in the early morning hours; and as I endeavored to understand it, the Holy Spirit

---

[236] Mark 3:22-23 (KJV)

showed me the distinction between such lifestyles and the one I had chosen: "I love them that love me; and those that seek me early shall find me."[237] Gathering my thoughts, I leaned against an old creosote post and said, "As a dog returneth to his vomit, so a fool returneth to his folly."[238]

"That has to be your favorite verse!" Lane retorted.

Knowing I was about to rebuke his brother, Dale hurried off.

"Yes," I replied, "And, it must have been a favorite of the Apostle Peter, too, because he quoted it:

> 'But it is happened unto them according to the true proverb, The dog is turned to his own vomit again; and the sow that was washed to her wallowing in the mire.'[239]

Have you ever seen an ole dog come back and eat its vomit?" I asked.

"Yes it's disgusting!" Lane replied.

"What about a pig wallowing in its own excrement? Spiritually, that is exactly what you're doing! And you're right; it's disgusting! Peter's reference to the sow returning to its mire was a reference to the parable of the prodigal son, wherein the son went out and sinned against his father's rules and ended up in a manure-filled pig pen. Once he realized that even his father's servants were living better, he abandoned his sinful ways and returned to his father. If he had not been a son, he never would've returned but would've continued to live a vile life. If you return to God and your walk with Christ, you're truly a son; but if you keep living like you have been and boasting about the filthy sins you've committed, you should probably question whether you've been saved. Your experiences in the drug world are not a badge of honor. They're the mark of an unbeliever. The question you need to ask yourself is whether you're a son or a pig?"

Before we parted, I gave him this Scripture to think on:

---

[237] Proverbs 8:17 (KJV)
[238] Proverbs 26:11 (KJV)
[239] 2 Peter 2:22 (KJV)

"They went out from us, but they were not of us;
for if they had been of us, they would no doubt have
continued with us: but they went out, that they might
be made manifest that they were not all of us."[240]

On another day, James and Christopher came out to the farm to help me restore Papa's old fishing boat. The gnawing tooth of decay had taken its toll on the boat's wood and wires. The three of us spent days repairing the old boat and preparing it for the water again, and when our work was completed, we set sail. After several hours passed without even a snag, we reached the western edge of the lake where Papa, Dustin, and I happened upon our large catch so I told James and Christopher the tale as we glided across the water, hoping for a repeat of the experience. A few hours later, we headed for the dock without any fish. Christopher manned the boat with James sitting beside him. From my perch near the front of the vessel, I wondered why we had not caught anything.

"Why couldn't we have caught something?" I thought.

"They are in the boat with you!" a still, small voice replied.

When James first came to *New Beginnings*, his addiction to drugs was so bad that his loved ones were afraid he would not live much longer. Having been completely devastated by the loss of his mother in the Oklahoma City bombing in 1995, he was almost beyond reach, and his struggle did not seem to improve with treatment. Compounding his pain was the fact that some of his family wanted to cut him off. Some thought "tough love" was the answer and suggested that he be expelled from his grandparents' home for a time. Others did not care what happened to him, perhaps because they were content for the spotlight to remain on his sin rather than on theirs. In time, James' grandparents and I decided that he needed inpatient treatment.

He quietly seethed the day his grandmother and I accompanied him to the inpatient treatment center. He had reluctantly agreed to enter the program but made it very clear that he was doing it for his son, not for his grandmother or me. Within hours of being admitted, Satan's fiery darts began to pummel James as his emissaries seduced James with sinful

---

[240] 1 John 2:19 (KJV)

314

suggestions. He was so hoodwinked by these wicked influences that his relationship with his family and our friendship deteriorated to the point that he refused to take our telephone calls or visit with us when we went to see him. I knew James was locked in a deadly spiritual battle and that I had a responsibility to deliver the Word of Truth to him. So, after consulting the Holy Spirit in prayer, I drafted a letter to him, honestly believing that, since people generally hate the messenger of Truth, it would be the last word to pass between us. In the letter, I plainly stated that he had been seduced by and turned to that same evil which conspired to take the physical life of his mother in 1995. I questioned why he would serve and allow it to wreck his life and the lives of his grandparents and son. Though I wanted to reveal the prayer I had prayed at the bombing memorial during the Billy Graham Crusade and its connection to his grandparents' prayer for a Godly, father-like mentor who could minister to him according to God's will, I submitted to the Lord's admonition that the time for that revelation had not yet come.

Not long after I sent the letter, James finished treatment but took up with the wicked influences that had befriended him, and we did not know his whereabouts for several months thereafter. Whether he read my letter, I do not know, but I believe he did. He eventually grew tired of the influences he had surrounded himself with and returned home. It was then that we learned he had been living out of a car. The day he returned to *New Beginnings*, I was talking to a counselor and our receptionist in the private waiting room when he suddenly walked in and, without saying a word, embraced me as if I was the only person in the room. In that moment, I knew somewhat of how the Lord must have felt when I returned to Him and how He feels when every prodigal son has safely returned to His father's house.

The transformation I observed in the lives of all these young men can only be attributed to Christ, and the fact that the Lord allowed me to continue teaching and ministering to them and others even after I no longer maintained a physical presence at the clinic was a great blessing. Through these ministries, the Lord has revealed to me that varied needs are at least one reason why He has given four separate accounts of the Gospel of Jesus Christ in His Word. As Paul declared:

> "All scripture is given by inspiration of God, and is profitable for doctrine, for reproof, for correction, for instruction in righteousness: That the man of God may be perfect, thoroughly furnished unto all good works."[241]

Dale was one who needed instruction in righteousness. Lane had a need for correction. James needed reproof. But, all of them needed doctrine and needed it ministered unto their spirit personally. This is one of the purposes of the four separate Gospel accounts. Each one allows the Holy Spirit to minister the Truths and person of Christ to every individual according to their unique needs and in a very personal way.

I believe support for this proposition is found in what we know about the spiritual and physical authorship of the Gospels. For instance, Matthew, the first synoptic gospel, was written by a converted publican – a tax collector who became a disciple of Jesus Christ. Originally written in Hebrew, the text reveals many intricacies of Jewish law. This gospel account was directed to the Jews, particularly those who were looking for the Messiah, and presents Jesus Christ as King, Messiah, Redeemer, and emphasizes His miracles. Matthew makes reference to more Old Testament prophecies and speaks further into the New Testament than any of the other gospel accounts.

Mark, the second synoptic gospel, though written down by Mark, was actually Simon Peter's account. It was directed to the Roman man of action in simple, concise terms. The Romans had strong convictions to serve their country, which they believed was capable of conquering and ruling the world through law and government. Therefore, this account strongly emphasizes Christ as the servant of God, the Mighty Conqueror, and ultimate Ruler of the World. It also highlights His service, focuses on His miracles, and describes the peace of His Kingdom.

Luke, the third synoptic gospel, was written by a physician to the Greek intelligentsia of the day and the thinker of all ages. Accordingly, particular attention is given to Jesus' parables, and the book emphasizes Christ as our High Priest by showing Him as the perfect man, touched by the feeling of our infirmities. Luke, a close friend to Paul and the

---

[241] 2 Timothy 3:16-17 (KJV)

nephew of Barnabas, was a Gentile doctor; and although he penned the text, this gospel account is considered by many to be the account of Jesus' mother, Mary.

The Gospel according to John was directed to the spiritual man in general and to the mystics of Asia and the Orient in particular. John's account, in which the deity and humanity of Jesus Christ are paramount, was written in simple language; but though the words are simple, the meaning behind them is profound.

Desiring to reward these young men for submitting to the transforming power of Christ, I invited them to spend a few days rafting through the Colorado Rockies in the late summer of 2007, but only Christopher accepted my invitation. Prior to the trip, I spent many hours in prayer, asking God to choose the roads we would travel, the rivers we would raft, and the trails we would walk. As always, the Lord was faithful, and because we had sought His guidance, He was in our midst. On the last day of our journey, as we were hiking high in one of Colorado's National Forests, Christopher spotted a large bear through the lens of his binoculars. We watched it for a while before deciding to track him. A mile or so into the pursuit, we happened upon a small ice glacier measuring about thirty feet thick, one hundred feet long, and one hundred feet wide. Just above the ice was a small cave in the cleft of the rock. Giving in to exhaustion and my many physical ailments, I decided to rest upon a boulder in the nearby creek bed at the base of the ice while Christopher made his way up to the cave.

"You go on up!" I hollered. "I'm gonna stay here and rest my old bones."

I sat down, shifting around on the hard stone, trying to find a comfortable position.

"Oh, and be careful not to fall!" I added. "I don't wanna have to climb up there for some tedious rescue!"

As Christopher scaled the rocky cliff, I took in the view and silent peace of the high mountains. After a few minutes, I just happened to glance at the ground. I did not know whether to laugh or cry. All my life I had dreamed of finding it. Throughout my childhood, each family trip to the Rockies had included time set aside for me to search for gold and now there it was at my feet. Squinting, hoping I was not hallucinating, I bent over and retrieved a rock the size of the palm of my hand, examined it, and saw that it was indeed gold. I laughed out loud and looked around for the source. Within a few moments, I had discovered a large, distinctive vein of gold, exposed in the side of the mountain by a trickling waterfall of melting snow, and instinctively knew the rare find was the result of my prayers before the trip.

"Hey!" I hollered to Christopher at the top of my lungs. "Get down here!"

"What is it?" he yelled from the mouth of the cave.

"Just get down here!"

He descended the cliff and hurried over toward me.

"Come here and tell me what this is," I said, touching the side of the rocky wall.

"Is that...?" he gasped.

"Yes it is!"

We scoured the rock bed underneath our feet for more as I explained how to distinguish between fool's and genuine gold. Christopher attempted to break some off the exposed vein with a hatchet. Suddenly, I was burdened by the Holy Spirit.

"Stop for a minute," I said. "Come over here and look at something."

We walked to the brow of the mountain and looked out over the vast valley below us.

"What do you see, hear, and feel?" I asked.

He looked at me as if I had lost my mind so I asked him again, "What do you feel from the stillness of this place? This is why I brought you here!"

"Oh, cus you knew there was gold here?" he inquired sarcastically.

"You smartaleck! I'm tryin' to have a moment here. Peace...Joy... the presence of the Lord!" I exclaimed. "That's the real treasure. The gold find is great, and I'm lovin' it just as much as you are, but a joyous time with the Lord, free from the influences, cares, and substances of the world is far more precious than gold. Always remember that. You'll never forget this trip, will you?"

"No," he replied.

Upon returning to Oklahoma, I learned that tropical storm Erin had left her calling card by completely destroying my home. The waters of that unprecedented storm flooded parts of Oklahoma that had never anticipated such a storm. Termed a mysterious meteorological phenomenon, Erin never strengthened beyond a tropical depression while over water but changed dramatically after making landfall. On August 16, the weak and disorganized storm hit the Texas coastline and circled up over Oklahoma where it reorganized and developed a powerful eye over Caddo and Blaine counties. The maximum sustained winds topped fifty knots with gusts up to seventy. Yes, a hurricane had formed over Oklahoma! The storm claimed several lives and wiped out ninety percent of the roads and bridges in Caddo County. President Bush declared most of Oklahoma a natural disaster area as a result of the storm.

While salvaging possessions from my devastated home, I found and opened the old trunk that housed my coin collection. Remarkably, the gold and silver proof coins were unharmed. As I held them in my hands, examining them ever so carefully, my spirit returned to Colorado, whereupon the Holy Spirit used mine and Christopher's Rocky Mountain gold find to illustrate a great Truth.

The mining of raw gold is a picture of salvation in Jesus Christ. Believers are mined out of the world, forgiven of their sins, and set apart as joint heirs with Christ. After raw gold is mined, the ore is then crushed and separated from the rock adhering to it. This is a picture of the sanctification that follows salvation, a process wherein believers in Christ are separated from their old carnal lifestyles and the impurities of the world and given power over their old sin nature through the Word of God by the Holy Spirit. By studying the Word of God, believers are empowered by the Holy Spirit and become conscious of their deepest sins; and the Holy Spirit, by the Word, washes and cleanses their fleshly lusts and desires, making it possible for the refinement process to continue. After the ore is crushed and separated from the rock, it is placed into a cauldron and melted through the application of great heat. A goldsmith or refiner sits near the melting pot and periodically scrapes the dross and scum that bubbles to the surface. The goldsmith continually monitors the changing, developing ore as its impurities are released and the purity and value increase. This pictures the great trials which the believer in Christ faces in this world and includes, but is not limited to, overcoming temptation and dealing with its consequences, the testing of difficult circumstances, and the removal of anything that retards the spiritual development of a child of God. Referred to by many Christians as "the valley", such times of testing actually produce great and prosperous changes in the believer's heart, life, and relationship with Christ, as attested by the Word of Truth:

> "And not only so, but we glory in tribulations also: knowing that tribulation worketh patience; And patience, experience; and experience, hope: And hope maketh not ashamed; because the love of God is shed abroad in our hearts by the Holy Ghost which is given unto us."[242]

Perhaps the greatest change is that faith and trust in the Lord are increased as we realize that it is the Lord who has remained by our side throughout the process, carefully monitoring and attending to our refinement.

After the ore has been heated to the point that most of the dross can be removed, it is strained, which removes even more impurities. The ore is then poured into molds that shape the liquid into varying forms according to the refiner's desired use. Once the ore solidifies in its mold, it is polished extensively so that any remaining blemishes or impurities are buffed out. This process pictures the believer's spiritual gifts and service to God and fruit-bearing period, respectively.

The final stage of the gold's journey is the presentation of the purified, refined, and finished product, which is a picture of both the believer's final presentation to God the Father and his being held up in the world before men as God's chosen and sanctified. Before the world, like a pure and beautiful gold vessel, a refined believer in Jesus Christ emanates the Lord's holy and pure characteristics, which shine as light into a dark, perishing world and attest to His righteousness:

> "Whosoever shall confess that Jesus is the Son of God, God dwelleth in him, and he in God. And we have known and believed the love that God hath to us. God

---

[242] Romans 5:3–5 (KJV)

is love; and he that dwelleth in love dwelleth in God, and God in him. Herein is our love made perfect, that we may have boldness in the day of judgment: because as he is, so are we in this world."[243]

The process of sanctification is similarly presented by the Word of God in *Malachi 3:2-3 (KJV)*:

"But who may abide the day of his coming? and who shall stand when he appeareth? for he is like a refiner's fire, and like fullers' soap: And he shall sit as a refiner and purifier of silver: and he shall purify the sons of Levi, and purge them as gold and silver, that they may offer unto the LORD an offering in righteousness."[244]

In this passage of scripture, *Tsaraph* is the Hebrew word for refiner and *taher* is the Hebrew word for purifier. *Tsaraph* is both a verb and a participle. As a verb, it means to smelt, refine, test, or test and prove true; but as a participle, it refers to a goldsmith, refiner, or smelter – in other words, *tsaraph* embodies both the one who smelts, refines, and tests and the refinement itself. Similarly, *Taher*, a verb, means to cleanse or purify physically, ceremonially, and morally. The Hebrew word for fullers' soap is *kabac*. It, too, is both a verb and a participle. As a verb, it means to wash. As a participle, it is the washer, the fuller, or the treader who performs the act of washing. The Hebrew words for soap and purge are *boriyth* and *zaqaq,* respectively. *Boriyth* means lye, potash, soap, or alkali, all of which are cleaning agents; and *zaqaq* means to purify, distil, strain – as if to squeeze through a strainer.

Admiring the flawless, mirror-like surfaces of the refined coins in my hands, I tilted one of them slightly and saw my reflection, remembering that something like four tons of raw gold ore must be refined just to extract a single, pure ounce. Standing amid the ruins of my home, the devastation of which the Lord had apparently thought necessary to move me closer to the ends of my own refinement, I

---

[243] 1 John 4:15-17 (KJV)
[244] Malachi 3:2-3 (KJV)

shivered at the thought of what events He may use in the future as I realized there was dross yet to be scraped. Nevertheless, peace flooded my soul when the Holy Spirit directed my thoughts to *Philippians 1:6 (KJV)*:

> "Being confident of this very thing that he which hath begun a good work in you will perform it until the day of Jesus Christ..."[245]

Since tropical storm Erin had struck at a time when my home was uninsured, thanks to exorbitant fines and attorney fees, traceable to our regulatory woes, and *New Beginnings'* continuing subpar financial condition, John suggested that I apply to FEMA for emergency assistance. Initially, I doubted the potential of his suggestion, but when he continued to persist, asking me daily whether I had completed the paperwork, I finally agreed to apply and was later approved for a federal grant. My outlook heightened in mid-September when the check arrived, but as I was sitting at home in my recliner, contemplating using it as a down-payment on a home reconstruction loan, the telephone rang. It was John, calling to inform me that *New Beginnings* had just been served with a forcible entry and detainer lawsuit for unpaid rent – another secret which Dustin had attempted to shoulder himself. Accordingly, we had five days to fork over approximately twenty thousand dollars. The alternative, eviction, would have assured our ruin. Unaware that I had received my check from FEMA, John said, "We have fifteen hundred dollars in the bank, and we've only brought in about eight hundred today. What do you want me to do?"

"I'll be right over," I replied. After hanging up the telephone, I immediately fell prostrate upon the floor before the Lord and thanked Him for His divine intervention. The FEMA check was just a few dollars short of covering the past-due rent; thus, the Lord had saved us once again, demonstrating His absolute control, not just over our situation, but over all of nature. He had used a rare hurricane, *Katrina*, to expose evil and an even rarer one, *Erin*, to save us in a way that revealed His majesty.

---

[245] Philippians 1:6 (KJV)

Prior to September 2007, the only government agency that had not bothered *New Beginnings* was the IRS so it did not come as much of a surprise when they audited us for delinquent payroll taxes. Hoping to resolve the matter with a check for the full amount, I once again visited a bank, but this time it was with Dustin. Our loan application was denied rather quickly, but the loan officer did attempt to console us with the statement that, "If you were Native American, I could process the loan today." Though we could have postured ourselves as victims of discrimination and marched in the streets, we chose instead to accept responsibility and worked even harder to pay the debt, but the IRS was dissatisfied with the amount of time it was taking. Consequently, Mom, Dustin, and I each took our turn in the interrogation booth and endured with patience the bitterest scrutiny. Ironically, the agent who questioned us suffered from a severe vision disorder. Through coke bottle glasses, he pored over our financial and bank statements, which he held less than two inches from his nose, while periodically glaring at me over the rims of those glasses as if I were some kind of leper; but he failed to see the bigger picture. None of us had disagreed that we owed the money. Moreover, he was aware that we were under contract to sell *New Beginnings* for a significant amount of money and that we had committed to paying the debt immediately after the sale. It was upsetting to see that time and resources which could have been better utilized had instead been carelessly invested in threats to seize my old fishing boat and tractor and lecturing Dustin for having three old automobiles, two of which were worn out. Ultimately, all of our bank accounts were swept clean, liens were placed on our property, and the rogue agent with the coke bottle glasses became a permanent fixture in our lives, periodically coming to *New Beginnings* to "take inventory." Like the hitchhiker in *The Twilight Zone*, he seemed to be everywhere. We even spotted him watching the building a few times. I did not know who or what had prompted the intrusion, but since we were on the eve of our final accreditation survey and the sale of the clinic hinged on the outcome, I had strong suspicions that the sudden intrusion was not coincidental.

This experience with the tax man certainly coddled my empathy with the collective, Biblical-era disdain of tax collectors; but more importantly, the Holy Spirit used the experience to impart to me a greater appreciation for Christ's transforming power. By providing a small potatoes point of reference, the Lord showed me just how profound had been His transformation of Zacchaeus, a man described in the Scriptures as *chief* among the tax collectors of that day:

> "And Jesus entered and passed through Jericho. And, behold, there was a man named Zacchaeus, which was the chief among the publicans, and he was rich. And he sought to see Jesus who he was; and could not for the press, because he was little of stature. And he ran before, and climbed up into a sycomore tree to see him: for he was to pass that way. And when Jesus came to the place, he looked up, and saw him, and said unto him, Zacchaeus, make haste, and come down; for to day I must abide at thy house. And he made haste, and came down, and received him joyfully. And when they saw it, they all murmured, saying, That he was gone to be guest with a man that is a sinner. And Zacchaeus stood, and said unto the Lord: Behold, Lord, the half of my goods I give to the poor; and if I have taken any thing from any man by false accusation, I restore him fourfold. And Jesus said unto him, This day is salvation come to this house, forsomuch as he also is a son of Abraham."[246]

Meanwhile, *New Beginnings'* final accreditation survey arrived, and it was radically different from prior surveys in that Dustin, Mom, and I were no longer at the center of the process. Having made a family decision to bring an end to the many, senseless regulatory woes, Dustin and I decided to relinquish our positions at the clinic and sell it, making it possible for our attorneys to negotiate an agreement that brought an end to all of our legal battles. While we patiently awaited an update on the outcome of the survey that followed this decision, John telephoned and said the auditors wanted to meet with me. Surprised to say the least, I agreed to meet with them the next day.

---

[246] Luke 19:1-9 (KJV)

The following morning, while sitting in the private waiting room adjacent to my former office, I found it mildly serendipitous that I, like so many patients before me, was now in a position not unlike the one in which they had once been – patiently waiting to be seen by someone who could possibly make a difference. Within a few minutes, the door to my former office swung open, and I was invited to come inside. I took a seat at the conference table, which was now at the center of the room, as the auditors perused their file folders and attempted to ignore me for as long as possible.

Finally, the lead auditor asked me, "So what is your role here?"

Gracing both of the auditors with a smile that only I could understand, I replied, "I'm just the janitor."

"That's not what we've been told," the other one said with a mild laugh, unaware that I had provided a spiritual answer to the question. When they perceived that I had no intention of responding further, the lead auditor said, "There are a few items we need to get cleared up. The first one is the issue of the payroll taxes…"

"That problem…" I interrupted, "…has been resolved. My brother has already provided you with the documentation."

Hoping to convince me that he had not yet seen the documentation to which I was referring, the lead auditor proceeded to take his time going through the portable file containers on the floor before changing the subject.

"We had a nice lunch with the state methadone authority yesterday," he began. "He educated us on *New Beginnings'* standing with the Department of Mental Health and Substance Abuse Services and voiced a few concerns."

I showed no emotion as they glared at me intensely.

"We also visited with some of your patients and all of your staff," the other one replied. "And, there is great disparity between the perceptions of the two groups – one being the regulatory officials and the other being your staff and patients."

Again, I showed no emotion.

"From your patients, we learned some very interesting things about your family," the lead auditor continued. "A woman who described herself as a 'former prostitute' told us that your brother made her get a real job to pay her bill. She reported that it was the first legal job she'd ever had. She practically glowed as she told us about how much she'd improved. Additionally, a young couple told us they've only paid one dollar for their treatment in the whole time they've been coming to your clinic and said that you bought them a baby mattress so their newborn would have a clean place to sleep. Besides these things, someone on your staff told us that you allowed one young man to teach you his Native American language as payment for his treatment and that you agreed to accept handmade fishing lures from another as payment for her treatment. Another painted you a picture, but our favorite is the family from whom you agreed to accept homemade brownies every month in exchange for their treatment."

While the lead auditor expressed a few of our good deeds, the other wrote notes in a folder. Presently, his pen ran out of ink, and my eyes followed his hand as he selected another one from the handmade pencil holder sitting in the center of the conference table. My eyes locked onto the pencil holder, and my mind wandered as the chatter inside the room faded to distant, background noise. The pencil holder had been given to me by Betsey Wright. It was made by a young man on death row in Arkansas whom she had befriended during her prison ministry. Simple in appearance and signed with a child-like signature, it had become a cherished possession for the simple reason that the Holy Spirit had, on the eve of my departure from *New Beginnings*, used it to inspire me with the proper words to lead a lost soul to Christ.

That lost soul was a young man whom I will refer to as Jack, one of the most hopeless of all the patients I counseled concerning Christ. Though Jack was faithful to the routine of treatment, his heart was far from it. He reaped minimal, if any, benefits and rarely had a good reason for being delinquent on his bill. Moreover, despite many invitations, he never attended a single Bible study.

As I got to know Jack, I saw that his life was built on the foundation of sin. And, like a house constructed on sand, it finally came crashing down around him when the storm began to rage. One day, he showed up at the clinic, wanting to visit with me immediately about yet another of many gut-wrenching predicaments into which he had gotten himself since I first laid eyes on him. While I waited for him to pull himself together long enough to translate his latest problem into words, I secretly wondered whether listening to his crisis would be yet another pointless endeavor.

"I'm responsible for a death!" he said with slurred speech. Detecting the presence of barbiturates, I leaned forward in my chair to observe him more closely.

"What are you talking about?" I asked. "Have you been in an accident?"

"My cousin just died of a drug overdose!" he said, sobbing. I searched for comforting words, but "I'm sorry" was all I could come up with. After crying himself almost to the point of unconsciousness, he explained that he had given his cousin the drugs which took his life.

"Nobody knows, and I can't tell anyone!" he exclaimed. "I'm in agony! If I tell, I'll go to jail!"

I tried to calm him down, but his unbridled emotion and drug-induced haze had rendered his mind practically impenetrable.

"Jack, you're in a fog," I said. "You need to focus if you want my help. I cannot help you if you're not going to help yourself."

I fell hard into the cushion on the back of my chair when he just stared back at me with a glazed look in his eyes. Having spent the better part of four years begging and pleading with him to accept Christ, warning him that his destruction was nigh, and advocating for him, I was just plumb tired. And, receiving news of this caliber after all I had done, knowing he had ignored every warning, filled me with a disgust that even I could not comprehend. Just as I was about to tell him to leave, a still, small voice said, "Continue, Lance…I can work through a fog."

I immediately recognized the Holy Spirit's voice so I quietly asked Him for the proper words to woo Jack to Christ. As I prayed, the handmade pencil holder on the conference table at which we sat suddenly stood out, and the words came to me like lightning.

"You're harboring this secret because you have a fear of being charged with a crime, perhaps even murder. But, Jack, I want you to know that you're already a condemned man! The Lord already knows about your sin, and the indictment has been drafted."

Jack immediately sobered up and appeared to be consumed with paralyzing fear, but I calmly reached into my messenger's satchel, retrieved my Bible, turned to the third chapter of *John,* and proceeded to read aloud:

> "For God so loved the world, that he gave his only begotten Son, that whosoever believeth in him should not perish, but have everlasting life. For God sent not his Son into the world to condemn the world; but that the world through him might be saved. He that believeth on him is not condemned: but he that believeth not is condemned already, because he hath not believed in the name of the only begotten Son of God. And this is the condemnation, that light is come into the world, and men loved darkness rather than light, because their deeds were evil. For every one that doeth evil hateth the light, neither cometh to the light, lest his deeds should be reproved. But he that doeth truth cometh to the light, that his deeds may be made manifest, that they are wrought in God."[247]

I then turned to the eighth chapter of *Romans* and continued:

> "There is therefore now no condemnation to them which are in Christ Jesus, who walk not after the flesh, but after the Spirit. For the law of the Spirit of life in Christ Jesus hath made me free from the law of sin and death."[248]

Hoping to cement these scriptures in his mind, I repeated and explained them to him while exposing all of his sins to which I was privy.

"Jack," I said when he hung his head in shame, "Look at me! Why have you confided in me concerning this matter? I believe it's because you're under conviction to know what God thinks."

---

[247] John 3:16-21 (KJV)
[248] Romans 8:1-2 (KJV)

I paused for a moment to read another verse of scripture:

"For to be carnally minded is death; but to be spiritually minded is life and peace."[249]

Then, I slid the crude-looking pencil holder directly in front of him and said, "I want you to take a good look at this pencil holder. It was made by a young man around your age who is on death row. The wrath of the State of Arkansas is fast approaching him. Now, you may not be on death row physically, but you're on a death row that is much worse. You're on spiritual death row, and the wrath of God is fast approaching you."

"What can I do?" he asked.

It was then that I suddenly remembered the stick people Betsey had sketched on a piece of notebook paper to show me how to personally convey my campaign message when I was running for Congress. Like the message I wanted to convey when fishing for votes, this one also had to be short and personal. I pushed the pencil holder aside, explained the passages of scripture I had just read one more time, and testified as to how it came about that I realized my need to be born again. I even shared my own personal prayer of salvation and testified of the love between me and the Lord.

"I want you to have that same love," I said. "But, I also want you to have the same comfort, peace, and joy I have continuously experienced in my relationship with Christ. All of this is within your reach! You can have peace with God, but you must admit that you're a sinner, believe that Jesus Christ is the Son of God and ask Him to forgive your sins, turn to Him and away from your sins, and trust Him."

Afterward, Jack struggled through a very emotional prayer of salvation as I held his hand.

Without warning, the peaceful stroll through that particular archive of my memory was shattered by the lead auditor, who was saying, "Mr. Compton? Mr. Compton?"

"Oh, I'm sorry," I replied. "I was thinking of something else."

---

[249] Romans 8:6 (KJV)

"Well," he continued, exhibiting facial expressions which I believe were aimed at trying to convey understanding, "Let's just get to the point. It doesn't actually matter what anyone says. What matters is what the regulators say; and off the record, we are here to make sure you have no presence here."

And with that, the interview ended. I politely bid the auditors farewell and departed. As I drove away, I knew that, although I may have been driven away physically, my spiritual work was founded upon Jesus Christ and could never be removed from that foundation.

Surprisingly, *New Beginnings* passed its final accreditation survey with flying colors – not one single recommendation was made, and we were awarded a three-year accreditation. Additionally, our patient care and staff qualifications and performance placed us in the top three percent of opioid treatment providers in the nation. Despite these achievements, however, certain DEA and OBN agents continued to harass us. Three from the DEA even attempted to inhibit the clinic's sale, spending more than two hours onsite, speaking with the new owners, trying to dissuade and discourage them from proceeding with the acquisition. I believe at least one of their objectives was to separate us from any means whereby we might relieve ourselves of the massive debt we had incurred defending against their attacks. Additionally, had we been unable to sell *New Beginnings*, I believe our regulators would have eventually bankrupted or forced us to close, at which point many patients would likely have returned to the street. The DEA did manage to delay the sale for two months by refusing to issue a registration number to the new owners. We reported this to the U.S. Attorney's office, but they did nothing. Consequently, we had no choice but to report the incident to Senator Inhofe and Congresswoman Fallin who, once again, intervened on our behalf. Time after time, Senator Inhofe and Congresswoman Fallin, together with their staffs, had protected and helped us with no expectation of receiving anything in return. Their only response to our thank you was, "We believe in what you're doing. Never let us down." Within two days of informing them of the DEA's latest action, the new owners of *New Beginnings* received their registration number.

On Friday, November 16, 2007, *New Beginnings'* final day, we commemorated the end of an era with a banquet-sized, family-style barbeque, to which Dustin and I invited all of our patients. It was a great day of fellowship, wherein we thanked the patients who attended and expressed our heartfelt gratitude and belief that God had sent each and every one of them to us for a reason – some for salvation and ministry, some for edification, and some for protection. Later, after the crowd had dispersed, I walked the hallway between my former office and the front lobby, looking at the pictures of Christ that hung outside the counselors' offices, and contemplating *New Beginnings'* legacy, which I believe was cemented in stone from the moment we chose to abide by the Golden Rule and follow this commandment of Christ: "And whosoever shall compel thee to go a mile, go with him twain."[250]

To understand why our faithful deference to this commandment had molded our legacy, one must understand why Jesus said it. In the ancient Persian Empire, there was a law whereby Persian soldiers had the authority to command citizens of conquered lands to carry their armor for one mile. Rome also adopted this law, but imposed it harshly upon the Jews after gaining control of ancient Israel. The Jews' pride was so wounded that they erected mile markers along roadways so they would not have to carry the burden any further than necessary. Antithetical to this stance is the great gem of Truth which Jesus wanted us to observe and benefit from, to-wit: when one carries another's burden further than required, his character is revealed, fellowship and relationships are fostered and flourish, and blessings travel beyond the boundaries of mile markers and upon a two-way street. Since delegating my first significant assignment at *New Beginnings* – a young man whose burdens I was willing to and did carry further than necessary – the Lord has taught me much about the blessings of that extra mile. Going the extra mile really was *New Beginnings'* theme of ministry and, I believe, a necessary component to its success. By carrying the physical and spiritual burdens of our patients a second mile, we heaped to ourselves eternal treasure and testified of the God we serve.

Before leaving for the very last time, the Lord again asked me to go an extra mile. It took less than five minutes but was a poetic summary of my service to Christ in the previous four years. Two young brothers, who had only recently been admitted to the clinic, arrived

---

[250] Matthew 5:41 (KJV)

for their appointments just before the close of business. Approximately twenty years old, they had both fallen into Satan's snare at a young age, becoming dependent upon Oxycontin. After they were seen by the medical staff, I gave each one of them a leather-bound Bible, the front covers of which had been engraved with their names. As I secured their grip on the Word of Truth, I told them that the best thing I could ever do for them was to give them a copy of the Word of God. After praying with and for them, I accompanied them to the front door where they shook my hand and departed.

As our receptionist, Tara, and I watched them drive away from behind the glass door, she looked at me and said, "They'll be ok."

"I pray they will," I replied and turned the key, locking the front door for the last time. "I pray they will."

With that, our time at *New Beginnings* came to an end. Dustin held the side door open as some of the lingering staff, Mom, Carrie, and I walked through it. The clanking of the deadbolt resonated loudly in my ears; but as I made my way to the car, I could hear the sound of the wind, sighing through the tops of the swaying pines above me, and I knew that the Holy Spirit had blown through and around the lives of all who had converged on this site, leaving the visible, physical effects for all to see:

> "The wind bloweth where it listeth, and thou hearest the sound thereof, but canst not tell whence it cometh, and whither it goeth: so is every one that is born of the Spirit."[251]

---

[251] John 3:8 (KJV)

CHAPTER 17

A Watercolor Portrait

One of my greatest experiences in the Holy Land was baptizing my friend, Christopher, in the Jordan River. For me, this event was yet another God-given opportunity to partake in fulfilling the Great Commission. Having witnessed Christopher's transformation from the pitiful slave of sin which he was when I first laid eyes on him to the trustworthy brother in Jesus Christ he had become, I counted it a privilege to be the one lowering him beneath Jordan's waters, encasing him in a liquid tomb that not only symbolized the burial of his sins with Christ but publicly proclaimed that he was identified with Christ. Since identification with Christ is the purpose of water baptism, the method by which it is effectuated must mirror His death, burial, and resurrection. Baptism by immersion is the only method which accurately portrays these events. Moreover, it is the only method recorded in the Word of God. Therefore, it is the proper method, despite the fact that tradition and denominational doctrine have given rise to others.

Two passages in the first chapter of Mark's account of the Gospel reveal that Jesus was baptized by immersion. In verse nine:

> "And it came to pass in those days, that Jesus came from Nazareth of Galilee, and was baptized of John in Jordan."[252] *(emphasis added)*

In verses ten and eleven:

---

[252] Mark 1:9 (KJV)

"And straightway <u>coming up out of the water</u>, he saw the heavens opened, and the Spirit like a dove descending upon him: And there came a voice from heaven, saying, Thou art my beloved Son, in whom I am well pleased."[253] *(emphasis added)*

Additionally, the third chapter of *John* reveals that John the Baptist baptized by immersion:

"After these things came Jesus and his disciples into the land of Judaea; and there he tarried with them, and baptized. And John also was baptizing in Aenon near to Salim, <u>because there was much water there</u>: and they came, and were baptized."[254] *(emphasis added)*

There is no doubt that immersion requires "much water," which is why Aenon was chosen as a baptismal site. It would have been entirely unnecessary to baptize there had sprinkling, pouring, or some other method not requiring a large amount of water been acceptable. Immersion was not disputed as the proper method of water baptism until the Church at Rome decided that water baptism was necessary for church membership and one's entrance into Heaven. When, subsequent to adopting these requirements, questions arose concerning the eternities of those who could not be immersed, including infants, the handicapped, and those who made deathbed confessions, the Church at Rome responded by implementing sprinkling, a method of baptism that completely denies the death, burial, and resurrection of the Lord Jesus Christ. As is always the case when men depart from the Truth of the Word of God, false, perverted teachings are substituted for Truth.

Sprinkling, which comes from the Greek word *rhantizo*, meaning to sprinkle or scatter in drops, does not portray Christ's death, burial, or resurrection. Neither does pouring, which comes from the Greek word *cheo*, meaning to turn out in a stream. In fact, no method of water baptism other than immersion accurately portrays Christ's death, burial,

---

[253] Mark 1:10-11 (KJV)
[254] John 3:22-23 (KJV)

and resurrection. The translators of the King James Bible understood this and properly dismissed sprinkling and pouring in the early 1600s when they refused to translate the Greek work *baptizo,* which means to immerse or submerge like a sunken vessel, to *rhantizo* or *cheo.* Though King James I was a proponent of sprinkling and the translators did not wish to anger him, they knew translating *baptizo* to *rhantizo* or *cheo* would be a deliberate alteration of the Word of God. They also knew that anyone familiar with the Greek language would know such a translation was an error. Their solution was to substitute *baptizo* with the transliterated word, *baptize,* which cites to the meaning of *baptizo.*

Just as important as the method of water baptism, however, is its meaning. Paul wrote in his first epistle to the Corinthians, "Moreover, brethren, I would not that ye should be ignorant, how that all our fathers were under the cloud, and all passed through the sea; And were all baptized unto Moses in the cloud and in the sea; And did all eat the same spiritual meat; And did all drink the same spiritual drink: for they drank of that spiritual Rock that followed them: and that Rock was Christ."[255] I believe this Scripture is the definitive scripture on water baptism's meaning. The Israelites to whom Paul was referring were not baptized with water. Moses never baptized anyone with water. The phrase "baptized unto Moses" refers to their identification with Moses, and ultimately, with Christ.

Water baptism is not a requirement for membership in the True Church of God as some have supposed, nor is it necessary for salvation or forgiveness. It is simply a proclamation of one's identification with Jesus Christ – an identification summarized by Paul in his epistle to the *Romans*:

> "What shall we say then? Shall we continue in sin, that grace may abound? God forbid. How shall we, that are dead to sin, live any longer therein? Know ye not, that so many of us as were baptized into Jesus Christ were baptized into his death? Therefore we are buried with him by baptism into death: that like as Christ was raised up from the dead by the glory of the Father, even so we

---

[255] 1 Corinthians 10:1-4 (KJV)

also should walk in newness of life. For if we have been planted together in the likeness of his death, we shall be also in the likeness of his resurrection: Knowing this, that our old man is crucified with him, that the body of sin might be destroyed, that henceforth we should not serve sin. For he that is dead is freed from sin. Now if we be dead with Christ, we believe that we shall also live with him: Knowing that Christ being raised from the dead dieth no more; death hath no more dominion over him. For in that he died, he died unto sin once: but in that he liveth, he liveth unto God. Likewise reckon ye also yourselves to be dead indeed unto sin, but alive unto God through Jesus Christ our Lord. Let not sin therefore reign in your mortal body, that ye should obey it in the lusts thereof. Neither yield ye your members as instruments of unrighteousness unto sin: but yield yourselves unto God, as those that are alive from the dead, and your members as instruments of righteousness unto God. For sin shall not have dominion over you: for ye are not under the law, but under grace."[256]

Because water baptism is meant to portray the believer's inward change which results from accepting Christ, it is essential that the baptism follow the believer's acceptance of Christ, as it does in the Scriptures, rather than preceding or supplanting it. Luke recorded two instances of this chronological progression in *Acts*:

"But when they believed Philip preaching the things concerning the kingdom of God, and the name of Jesus Christ, they were baptized, both men and women. Then Simon himself believed also: and when he was baptized, he continued with Philip, and wondered, beholding the miracles and signs which were done."[257]

---

[256] Romans 6: 1-14 (KJV)
[257] Acts 8:12-13 (KJV)

Again, he wrote:

> "And as they went on their way, they came unto a
> certain water: and the eunuch said, See, here is water;
> what doth hinder me to be baptized? And Philip said, If
> thou believest with all thine heart, thou mayest. And he
> answered and said, I believe that Jesus Christ is the Son
> of God. And he commanded the chariot to stand still:
> and they went down both into the water, both Philip
> and the eunuch; and he baptized him."[258]

Being privy to the inward change which led to Christopher's
baptism, mindful of the role I had played in his transformation, and
privileged to perform my first baptism in the Jordan River, I found
myself being lifted up with pride. But, the Holy Spirit quickly responded
to my pride by reminding me of something I had seen a few days earlier
when Tony had taken the three of us to a hilltop overlooking the Valley
of the Shadow of Death. This valley, in ancient times, was the main
thoroughfare between Jerusalem and Jericho and was, because of its
geography, the perfect hunting ground for predators and criminals. Its
history is a spiritual picture of the world's hostility toward Christians
and a poignant reminder of our need for Christ. Because He is our
Shepherd, we know the Truth of His words in the twenty-third Psalm:

> "The LORD is my shepherd; I shall not want. He maketh
> me to lie down in green pastures: he leadeth me beside
> the still waters. He restoreth my soul: he leadeth me
> in the paths of righteousness for his name's sake. Yea,
> though I walk through the valley of the shadow of
> death, I will fear no evil: for thou art with me; thy rod
> and thy staff they comfort me."[259]

On a hilltop above that valley, all of us took turns riding a camel
and posing for the camera. In one picture taken of me on the camel's

---

[258] Acts 8:36–38 (KJV)
[259] Psalm 23:1–4 (KJV)

back, my white socks were prominently exposed. Upon seeing the digital photograph in my camera, I recalled the day I had been publicly ridiculed and made fun of for wearing white socks. Remembering how the culprit and her associates had sought my destruction as I passed through the valley of this world, I began to take comfort in the thought of their coming punishment and the fact that the Lord had so richly blessed me – even making it possible for me to visit the Holy Land – while they remained in spiritual squalor. But, no sooner had these thoughts crept into my mind than, as we were boarding the van to continue our journey to Jericho, Christopher pointed to some young shepherds corralling a herd of goats, the largest of which was subdued and herded into a shallow pit, where the shepherds shouted and threw rocks at it.

"What are they doing?" Christopher asked.

"They are punishing the lead goat," replied Tony as we all watched the scene with great interest.

"They're doing what?" I asked.

"Certain goats are trained to be leaders. If the leader ignores his master, the whole herd is vulnerable and could be lost," he replied. "It's just like with people...when the leader doesn't listen to God's voice – people die."

With those words, the Holy Spirit immediately convicted me of my sinful thoughts, which I knew were displeasing to the Lord, and revealed to me that my sinful thoughts and desires are just as dangerous to my witness as my enemies. Having pierced my heart with His Truth, the Lord then flooded the wound with His Word: "My brethren, be not many masters, knowing that we shall receive the greater condemnation."[260] In other words, God will judge those He has chosen to lead and teach more strictly than He will judge others, just as He did Moses:

> "And Moses went and returned to Jethro his father in law, and said unto him, Let me go, I pray thee, and return unto my brethren which are in Egypt, and see whether they be yet alive. And Jethro said to Moses,

[260] James 3:1 (KJV)

Go in peace. And the LORD said unto Moses in Midian, Go, return into Egypt: for all the men are dead which sought thy life. And Moses took his wife and his sons, and set them upon an ass, and he returned to the land of Egypt: and Moses took the rod of God in his hand. And the LORD said unto Moses, When thou goest to return into Egypt, see that thou do all those wonders before Pharaoh, which I have put in thine hand: but I will harden his heart, that he shall not let the people go. And thou shalt say unto Pharaoh, Thus saith the LORD, Israel is my son, even my firstborn: And I say unto thee, Let my son go, that he may serve me: and if thou refuse to let him go, behold, I will slay thy son, even thy firstborn. And it came to pass by the way in the inn, that the LORD met him, and sought to kill him. Then Zipporah took a sharp stone, and cut off the foreskin of her son, and cast it at his feet, and said, Surely a bloody husband art thou to me. So he let him go: then she said, A bloody husband thou art, because of the circumcision."[261]

God called Moses to represent His covenant to the Israelites yet Moses was disobedient to God by refusing to circumcise his own children. For this disobedience, God determined to kill Moses for his disobedience. God is sovereign and does not need the help of men in accomplishing His work, but He chooses and allows certain men to teach and lead as a blessing to them. He holds these leaders to an elevated standard and deals harshly with them when they misrepresent His character. My heart fluttered in terror as I considered what God might do to me if I made the same mistake Moses made so I humbled myself and begged Him to forgive me of my sinful thoughts and desires.

Afterward, I realized my involvement in Christopher's transformation and baptism was certainly not because it was necessary but because the Lord had allowed it for the purpose of being a blessing to me. The Holy Spirit then revealed that the Lord may have other such blessings reserved

---

[261] Exodus 4:18-26 (KJV)

for my future, but whether they will be realized is contingent upon my continued pursuit of His Truth and conformance to the character and image of Christ. A true servant of Christ must be, as my old friends, Frank Keating, Bruce Price, and Gene Stipe reiterated to me, a servant of servants, meaning he must conduct himself uprightly amongst the flock so the flock will know who anointed him. Some people, when they see the picture of me sitting on the camel with my white socks so prominently featured, will laugh; but that picture will always remind me to walk in that newness of life I have received from the Lord and Savior with whom I am identified.

CHAPTER 18

The Greatest Olympian

Fresh off my Holy Land pilgrimage, I was on a spiritual high and eager to share my experience with anyone who would listen. Through a chain of events, the Lord gave me the opportunity to teach the Wednesday night *Royal Ambassadors* at my home church in Binger, an assignment which called to mind the prayer I lifted up to Him back on the mountaintop in Colorado. From the outset of this new assignment, I was anxious to say the least. Heretofore, my service to Christ had consisted of ministering to and teaching shipwrecked sinners, but now I was assuming a new and exciting responsibility – instilling in the hearts and minds of fifth and sixth graders, who were still encased in innocence yet standing at the edge of the great precipice of choice, a hunger for the Truth of God's Word.

After perusing the teaching materials being peddled by the denominational association, the Holy Spirit reminded me that, to successfully teach these youngsters how to position their rudders against worldly currents and cast their sails to catch the breath of God, I only needed the Word of God. I did realize, however, that I must adopt an age-appropriate teaching method conducive to allowing the Holy Spirit to capture these young souls in the net of the Gospel of Jesus Christ. So, I began the first class as it were a great treasure hunt, the first trove of which I arranged to be the leather-bound study Bibles I had purchased for each student. Each Bible was personalized, having the students' names embossed in gold on the front covers. To intensify the students' anticipation of the first find, I secretly placed the Bibles inside a large brass treasure chest and asked them to decipher its contents as we discussed the great gift of God's Word. I was greatly overjoyed when the chest was opened and small hands eagerly retrieved their very own copy of the Word. Then, with the Word of Truth as our treasure map, we embarked upon a great path of discovery, meeting each week for the next year to open the Bible together in faith and expectation of great finds.

On this treasure hunt, we witnessed the genesis of creation, hovering over the deep as God created the Heavens and the Earth and measured them with the span of His mighty hand.

We peered through the microscope's lens and pondered in amazement the volumes of information contained in our DNA.

We watched as the waters of the great deep were opened up, splitting the Earth into seven continents, and continued to behold as the moistures of the atmosphere were wrenched and flooded the entire Earth. Contemplating Noah's three-story ark as a foreshadowing of Jesus Christ, we felt the waves of judgment crash against its wooden bow and swayed to and fro as God tilted the Earth on its axis and spun the seasons into existence in a foretelling of the Gospel of His One and Only Son.

We allowed the warmth of the burning bush to warm our skin as we heard the voice of God call to Moses. Then, hiding behind the cloaks of Moses and Aaron, we watched as they confronted the Pharaoh of Egypt. Later, we stretched our arms toward the heavens as the mighty rushing wind of God parted the Red Sea.

Our hands touched the ancient tile floor of Herod's palace, inspiring a vision of the tearful scene of Herod's step-daughter dancing for and receiving John the Baptist's head on a platter.

Chills of guilt surged through our bodies when we held a similitude of the cat of nine tails and other instruments of torture that pierced the innocent flesh of our Lord Jesus Christ, allowing His blood to drip upon our very souls.

Our lungs burned as we sprinted with John and Peter to behold Jesus' empty tomb.

We read from Paul's letter to the *Colossians*:

> "Who is the image of the invisible God, the firstborn
> of every creature: For by him were all things created,

that are in heaven, and that are in earth, visible and invisible, whether they be thrones, or dominions, or principalities, or powers: all things were created by him, and for him: And he is before all things, and by him all things consist."[262]

Afterward, pondering the meaning of "consist," which comes from the Greek word *synistempi,* and literally means "to draw or bind together by way of composition or combination or unite parts into one entity," we stood hand-in-hand with the Apostle John at the end of time, beholding that mysterious electromagnetic force, atomic glue, or 'God particle' vanish as Jesus Christ loosened His grip on the world. In that moment, we saw that science and faith are tied together by the scarlet thread of Truth as electrons, protons and neutrons flew apart, bringing a cataclysmic end to time itself.

Knowing the limits of my teaching, I counted it critical to execute, by my teaching, the essential task of shifting their dependence for learning and guidance from me to the Holy Spirit. The first step in that process was to position them in front of God's Law. With the law as their mirror, it would serve its proper function, which is to reveal deep-seated iniquity, the sin nature, and the individual's need for the atoning sacrifice of the blood of Jesus Christ. In his letter to the *Galatians*, the Apostle Paul wrote:

> "Wherefore the law was our schoolmaster to bring us unto Christ, that we might be justified by faith. But after that faith is come, we are no longer under a schoolmaster. For ye are all the children of God by faith in Christ Jesus."[263]

The word "schoolmaster" in this passage of Scripture comes from the Greek word, *paidagogos.* By using this word, Paul was referencing Greek and Roman culture to illustrate the law's role and function. In those cultures, a *paidagogos* was a particular type of tutor or guide to

---

[262] Colossians 1:15-17 (KJV)
[263] Galatians 3:24-26 (KJV)

the young boys of an affluent, upper class father. Often a trusted slave, the *paidagogos'* responsibility was to instruct the children. Boys under the tutelage of a *paidagogos* were forbidden, until reaching adulthood, to leave their homes without this stern enforcer of the highest moral standards present with them at all times.

The next step in shifting their dependence to the Holy Spirit was to prevent them from acquiring an apathetic attitude toward the Word of Truth, and following much prayer and thought on how to do this, the Holy Spirit laid it upon my heart to teach them what a Christian can expect when he arrives in Heaven and stands before Jesus Christ. To help me convey, in age-appropriate terms, the deep meaning of this Truth, the Holy Spirit used a tall, lanky Olympic swimmer from the state of Maryland to provide me with an illustration.

When it comes to sports, I am not an enthusiast who can name all the teams, players, conferences, or the current status of each. However, when it comes to the Olympics, I am enthralled with nearly every competition and intrigued with the individual athletes. Michael Phelps captured my attention as well as the attention of every other person on the planet when he swam his way into the history books in the summer of 2008. With each of his triumphs, we all got to know a little more about him; and, through win after win, we all fell in love with him and his family. Some of us even prayed for him. From in front of televisions throughout the world, we all strained and heaved with his every stroke and kick. We rejoiced with him when he won and teared up with him when he was decorated in Gold and crowned with glory. We showed allegiance with him to the country he represented before the world. Through him, we experienced the warmth of victory under the glow of the Olympic torch. As a participant in this phenomenon from my farm in western Oklahoma, I thought about how wonderful it would be if more people fell in love with and gave their hearts to Jesus Christ, and like victorious Olympians, opened their hearts to the glow of eternal victory under the torch of the Gospel of Jesus Christ, showing a lost world, as newly-minted representatives of Christ, what it means to pledge allegiance to Him and His Kingdom.

The Holy Spirit, using the unforgettable image of Michael Phelps crowned with a green laurel wreath, basking in triumph on the victory stand, inspired me to teach the *Royal Ambassadors* about the five crowns that can be earned by all Christians during this life. I began by first distinguishing the two separate judgments that will occur in Heaven: first is the Judgment Seat of Christ; second is the Great White Throne Judgment. The Judgment Seat of Christ is also known as the Bema Seat Judgment. While the Greek word *bema* is used in the Gospels and the *Book of Acts* to depict a raised platform where a Roman magistrate or ruler sat to make decisions and pass sentence,[264] Paul used *bema* in his epistles for the purpose of alluding to the Grecian Olympics, wherein contestants competed for prizes under the careful scrutiny of a judge who ensured that every rule of the competition was strictly obeyed.[265] In these ancient games, the victor of any given competition who competed in and finished the competition in accordance with the rules was led by the judge to the winner's platform, called the *Bema*. There, a laurel wreath was placed on his head as a symbol of ultimate victory.[266] This allusion conveys what happens to a believer in Jesus Christ after he is born again and places his exclusive faith in Christ. Like an Olympian, the believer has the opportunity to win rewards, or crowns. These will be bestowed at Christ's Bema immediately after the Rapture of the Church.[267] The Judge of the competition and presenter of these crowns is the Lord Jesus Christ. The Word of God reveals five different crowns which a child of God can earn. They are: the Incorruptible Crown, the Crown of Rejoicing, the Crown of Righteousness, the Crown of Life, and the Crown of Glory.

As a class, we discussed Michael Phelps and the other Olympians, their training, coaches, determination, the sacrifices they had to make, the mastery they had to gain over their bodies, and all the other rewards they received from their victories in addition to gold medals. We also discussed the ancient Grecian Olympics and compared its athletes and rewards to those of the present hour. Rather than receiving medals to hang around their necks, victorious Grecian athletes received crowns, called *stephanos* in Greek, to place upon their heads. Being led of the

---

[264] Matthew 27:19 (KJV) and John 19:13 (KJV)
[265] 2 Timothy 2:5 (KJV)
[266] 1 Corinthians 9:24-25 (KJV)
[267] 1 Corinthians 4:5 (KJV)

Holy Spirit to create an atmosphere of interest, I enlisted the assistance of Mom and her fellow teachers, Lee Ellen Heldermon, Cindi Dorsey, and Billie Elliot, to construct laurel wreaths so each youngster would have his own personal *stephanos* for the lesson.

The Lord was very careful in His selection of the word to describe the crowns to be awarded at the Bema Seat Judgment, a point demonstrated by the fact that, in the New Testament, two of the original Greek words used for "crown" depict two types of crowns. One of these, the *diadema,* is symbolic of the authority to rule, much like that of a king or queen. The *diadema* is a badge of royalty. A *stephanos,* on the other hand, is a victory crown, used specifically in ceremonial settings. The Word of God uses the Greek word *diadema* in reference to Jesus' rule over His Kingdom while using the Greek word *stephanos* in reference to His victory. Satisfied that each student had learned the distinction, I then moved to ensure that they understood, beyond the shadow of a doubt, that the crowns to be bestowed by Christ will have nothing whatsoever to do with salvation. Here, I once again paused to discuss the plan of salvation, telling them Jesus has declared that we must be born again.

I then explained that the crowns are not rewarded as part of any competition between fellow brothers and sisters in Christ. Rather, they are given as rewards for the deeds we do individually in service to Christ following salvation, as His co-laborers in the Great Commission. I explained, too, that the crowns, unlike our eternal salvation, can be stolen. Compelled to reiterate this warning, I read Christ's words in *Revelation*:

> "Behold, I come quickly; hold that fast which thou hast,
> that no man take thy crown."[268]

The word "take" as used in this Scripture comes from the Greek word *lambano,* which is a verb meaning to take by craft or to circumvent one by fraud. I then read this excerpt from Paul's letter to the *Colossians,* which reveals what is meant by craft and circumvention by fraud:

> "Let no man therefore judge you in meat, or in drink,
> or in respect of an holyday, or of the new moon, or

---

[268] Revelation 3:11 (KJV)

346

of the Sabbath days: Which are a shadow of things to come; but the body is of Christ. Let no man beguile you of your reward in a voluntary humility and worshipping of angels, intruding into those things which he hath not seen, vainly puffed up by his fleshly mind, And not holding the Head, from which all the body by joints and bands having nourishment ministered, and knit together, increased with the increase of God."[269]

Paul warned the Colossians not to allow the false teachings of the time to beguile them of their reward. This warning is still pertinent today. The false teachings of the present hour, including the New Age movement, Mormonism, Islam, Scientology, teachings of the Jehovah's Witnesses, and all others that oppose the doctrine of Jesus Christ, can still beguile the Christian of his reward, just as they did in Paul's day, if the believer does not hold fast to the Word of Truth.

In keeping with our treasure hunt theme, I then discussed the crowns as a portion of the treasure Jesus spoke of in His Sermon on the Mount:

"Lay not up for yourselves treasures upon earth, where moth and rust doth corrupt, and where thieves break through and steal: But lay up for yourselves treasures in heaven, where neither moth nor rust doth corrupt, and where thieves do not break through nor steal: For where your treasure is, there will your heart be also. The light of the body is the eye: if therefore thine eye be single, thy whole body shall be full of light. But if thine eye be evil, thy whole body shall be full of darkness. If therefore the light that is in thee be darkness, how great [is] that darkness! No man can serve two masters: for either he will hate the one, and love the other; or else he will hold to the one, and despise the other. Ye cannot serve God and mammon."[270]

---

[269] Colossians 2:16–19 (KJV)
[270] Matthew 6:19–24 (KJV)

We then considered the Bema Seat Judgment itself by accompanying the Apostle John to the Throne Room of Heaven in the fourth chapter of *Revelation*:

> "After this I looked, and, behold, a door [was] opened in heaven: and the first voice which I heard [was] as it were of a trumpet talking with me; which said, Come up hither, and I will shew thee things which must be hereafter. And immediately I was in the spirit: and, behold, a throne was set in heaven, and [one] sat on the throne. And he that sat was to look upon like a jasper and a sardine stone: and [there was] a rainbow round about the throne, in sight like unto an emerald. And round about the throne [were] four and twenty seats: and upon the seats I saw four and twenty elders sitting, clothed in white raiment; and they had on their heads crowns of gold. And out of the throne proceeded lightnings and thunderings and voices: and [there were] seven lamps of fire burning before the throne, which are the seven Spirits of God. And before the throne [there was] a sea of glass like unto crystal: and in the midst of the throne, and round about the throne, [were] four beasts full of eyes before and behind. And the first beast [was] like a lion, and the second beast like a calf, and the third beast had a face as a man, and the fourth beast [was] like a flying eagle. And the four beasts had each of them six wings about [him]; and [they were] full of eyes within: and they rest not day and night, saying, Holy, holy, holy, Lord God Almighty, which was, and is, and is to come. And when those beasts give glory and honour and thanks to him that sat on the throne, who liveth for ever and ever, The four and twenty elders fall down before him that sat on the throne, and worship him that liveth for ever and ever, and cast their crowns before the throne, saying, Thou art worthy, O Lord, to receive glory and honour and power: for thou hast

created all things, and for thy pleasure they are and were created."[271]

This is the setting in which Christians will find themselves following the Rapture of the True Church. There, in the Throne Room of Heaven, after being crowned by Jesus Christ Himself, we will fully understand that our crowns were made possible solely by Him, and we will follow the lead of the elders in showing our appreciation to Him by casting our crowns at His feet, saying:

"Thou are worthy, O Lord, to receive glory and honour and power: for thou hast created all things, and for thy pleasure they are and were created."[272]

Following this, I reiterated that, with great opportunity comes great responsibility. In the race to win these crowns, there are tremendous consequences for not running as great Olympians; and, they are eternal.

"Imagine!" I said. "The great sorrow of standing before our Savior with nothing to give Him, nothing to cast at His feet to show your great love for what He did for you." At that point, one of the sharper students in the class spoke up and asked in a somewhat puzzled manner, "But I thought there would be no sorrow or crying in Heaven?"

"Well," I answered, "The Apostle John laid out a sequence of events in the writing of *Revelation*; the Bema Seat Judgment occurs in chapter four, but the verse you're thinking about occurs in chapter twenty-one following the Great White Throne Judgment."

We then turned to *Revelation* and read the Scripture:

"And I saw a great white throne, and him that sat on it, from whose face the earth and the heaven fled away; and there was found no place for them. And I saw the dead, small and great, stand before God; and the books were opened: and another book was opened, which is [the book] of life: and the dead were judged

---

[271] Revelation 4 (KJV)
[272] Revelation 4:10 (KJV)

out of those things which were written in the books, according to their works. And the sea gave up the dead which were in it; and death and hell delivered up the dead which were in them: and they were judged every man according to their works. And death and hell were cast into the lake of fire. This is the second death. And whosoever was not found written in the book of life was cast into the lake of fire. And I saw a new heaven and a new earth: for the first heaven and the first earth were passed away; and there was no more sea. And I John saw the holy city, new Jerusalem, coming down from God out of heaven, prepared as a bride adorned for her husband. And I heard a great voice out of heaven saying, Behold, the tabernacle of God [is] with men, and he will dwell with them, and they shall be his people, and God himself shall be with them, [and be] their God. And God shall wipe away all tears from their eyes; and there shall be no more death, neither sorrow, nor crying, neither shall there be any more pain: for the former things are passed away."[273]

I asked the boys to consider their family, friends, and all the people they loved and cared for and told them to imagine, if they could, the grief of not telling those loved ones about Jesus Christ and what He could do for them. Afterward, I posed a solemn question: "What will you think of yourself when you stand before Christ, or better yet, when you watch those to whom you could have witnessed cast into the fires of Hell?"

Judging from the wide-eyed looks throughout the classroom, I knew I had their undivided attention, which ushered in the right moment to detail the five crowns. To do this, I asked one of the high school students assisting me to help me recreate, in the backyard of the church, the forum of the scene we had previously read about – the Throne Room of Heaven. Once the model was set up, I asked each student to step forward, one at a time, and give an account concerning

[273] Revelation 20:11-21:4 (KJV)

questions I had tailored to each of them. Once they had given their answers or lack thereof, we all retired to the shade of a cottonwood tree behind the church, where I proceeded to tell them about the crowns.

The first is the *Incorruptible Crown*. This crown is detailed in Paul's first recorded letter to the church at Corinth, a letter that portrays the many difficulties of maintaining a Christian way of life in a cosmopolitan society. Corinth was the capitol of southern Greece and, being located on the Mediterranean Sea, was a giant commercial and economic hub. With nearly a million inhabitants, it easily set the standard for immorality. Paul lived there for over a year and established a church there, but following a period of his absence, several evils infiltrated the congregation and brought the church to a pivotal condition. Throughout his letter, Paul uses several analogies and, in the ninth chapter, compares Christian living to running a race for a prize:

> "Know ye not that they which run in a race run all, but one receiveth the prize? So run, that ye may obtain. And every man that striveth for the mastery is temperate in all things. Now they [do it] to obtain a corruptible crown; but we an incorruptible. I therefore so run, not as uncertainly; so fight I, not as one that beateth the air: But I keep under my body, and bring [it] into subjection: lest that by any means, when I have preached to others, I myself should be a castaway."[274]

Examining the letter verse by verse, we find that Paul's comparison accurately echoes the teaching of Christ, who said:

> "... Whosoever will come after me, let him deny himself, and take up his cross, and follow me."[275]

This self-denial and taking up of one's own cross by the follower of Christ is well-portrayed in Paul's letter, at verse twenty-four, as an allusion to a race:

---

[274] 1 Corinthians 9:24-27 (KJV)
[275] Mark 8:34 (KJV)

"Know ye not that they which run in a race run all, but one receiveth the prize? So run, that ye may obtain."[276]

Here, the word "race" comes from the Greek word *stadion,* meaning a place where running contests were held. In these contests, which were typically six-hundred-feet dashes, the fastest runner received a prize, which was a *stephanos.*

Paul continues his portrayal by referencing this allusion in other letters. To a group of Hebrew believers in Rome, whose faith he was attempting to strengthen, he wrote:

"Wherefore seeing we also are compassed about with so great a cloud of witnesses, let us lay aside every weight, and the sin which doth so easily beset [us], and let us run with patience the race that is set before us, Looking unto Jesus the author and finisher of [our] faith; who for the joy that was set before him endured the cross, despising the shame, and is set down at the right hand of the throne of God. For consider him that endured such contradiction of sinners against himself, lest ye be wearied and faint in your minds. Ye have not yet resisted unto blood, striving against sin."[277]

Again, in the *Book of Acts,* when giving a farewell message to the elders of the church at Ephesus, he wrote:

"But none of these things move me, neither count I my life dear unto myself, so that I might finish my course with joy, and the ministry, which I have received of the Lord Jesus, to testify the gospel of the grace of God."[278]

In his second letter to Timothy, he penned:

---

[276] 1 Corinthians 9:24 (KJV)
[277] Hebrews 12:1-4 (KJV)
[278] Acts 20:24 (KJV)

"I have fought a good fight, I have finished my course,
I have kept the faith:"[279]

Returning to Paul's first recorded letter to the *Corinthians*, we find that verse twenty-five signifies the preparation under which we must run:

"And every man that striveth for the mastery is temperate
in all things. Now they do it to obtain a corruptible
crown; but we an incorruptible."[280]

Here, the word "mastery" comes from the Greek word *agonizomai,* which means to contend in the gymnastic games, to struggle with difficulties and dangers, or to fight with strenuous zeal. The word "temperate" comes from the Greek word *egkrateuomai,* which refers to athletes who are preparing for the games by abstaining from unwholesome food, wine, and sexual indulgence. These words portray how a Christian is to approach the race: with preparation. This same idea is echoed in verse twenty-six: "I therefore so run, not as uncertainly; so fight I, not as one that beateth the air..." Here, the phrase "fight I" comes from the Greek word *pykteuo,* which is a verb meaning to box or to be a boxer. Use of this word demonstrates the importance of training – the same kind of training exhibited by Jesus when He defended against Satan's temptations in the wilderness with precise, relevant Truths from the Word of God, which He had committed to memory and which He knew in his heart, mind, and soul. Also portrayed in verse twenty-six is the resolve with which the race is to be run: with absolute certainty. To run with preparation and absolute certainty reveals the believer's awareness and acceptance of the absolute Truth for which the race is run.

Finally, in verse twenty-seven, we read:

"But I keep under my body, and bring it into subjection:
lest that by any means, when I have preached to others,
I myself should be a castaway."[281]

[279] 2 Timothy 4:7 (KJV)
[280] 1 Corinthians 9:25 (KJV)
[281] 1 Corinthians 9:27 (KJV)

Here, the phrase "I keep under" comes from the Greek word *hypopiazo*, which is a verb meaning to buffet the body like a boxer buffets his body, to handle it roughly, or discipline it by hardships. Furthermore, the phrase "bring it into subjection" comes from the Greek word *doulagogeo,* which means to make a slave and to treat as a slave, with severity and subjection to stern and rigid discipline. To illustrate the idea presented by these words, I used as an example the self-control and tremendous self-imposed conditioning of ice skater, Evan Lysacek, in his preparation for attaining the Olympic gold medal. Then, looking to the word "church," which comes from the Greek word *ekklesia,* meaning a group of believers who are called out from their homes into some public place, I explained that the Christian, like an Olympian, publicly sets himself apart from the masses, but the Christian does it to the intent that he set himself apart from the carnal world and deny himself the indulgences thereof so he can be a witness to others and find himself worthy of praise and honor at the Bema Seat.

The second crown is the *Crown of Righteousness.* This crown is detailed in Paul's final recorded letter to Timothy, one of three letters he wrote to pastors Timothy and Titus, warning, encouraging, and urging them to hold true to sound doctrine. The historical backdrop of this letter finds Paul having been sentenced to death by Roman Emperor Nero for preaching the Gospel of Jesus Christ. From inside the dark cell of a Roman prison, he writes out of concern, warning believers to guard and protect the Word of God, telling us that, in the last days there will be a devastating departure from God as men glorify sin:

> "I charge [thee] therefore before God, and the Lord Jesus Christ, who shall judge the quick and the dead at his appearing and his kingdom; Preach the word; be instant in season, out of season; reprove, rebuke, exhort with all longsuffering and doctrine. For the time will come when they will not endure sound doctrine; but after their own lusts shall they heap to themselves teachers, having itching ears; And they shall turn away [their] ears from the truth, and shall be turned unto fables. But watch thou in all things, endure afflictions,

do the work of an evangelist, make full proof of thy ministry. For I am now ready to be offered, and the time of my departure is at hand. I have fought a good fight, I have finished [my] course, I have kept the faith: Henceforth there is laid up for me a crown of righteousness, which the Lord, the righteous judge, shall give me at that day: and not to me only, but unto all them also that love his appearing."[282]

At the time Paul wrote this letter, just as today, there were more false teachers than true shepherds of God's people, and they preached crowd pleasing, friend and money making messages rather than the true Word of God. The waters of Truth were being muddied by false teaching in that day just as they are being muddied today, and Paul and his band were some of the only true representatives of the Lord. Knowing that his death is imminent, Paul sweats his emotion in the final verses of the letter as he sets his eyes upon Jesus and anticipates the crown he will receive for holding fast to the Truth. In verse six, he wrote:

"For I am now ready to be offered, and the time of my departure is at hand."[283]

The word "offered" comes from the Greek *spendo,* which means to pour out as a drink offering and is used in reference to one whose blood is poured out in a violent death for the cause of God. Additionally, the word "departure" comes from the Greek word *analysis,* meaning "an unloosing like unharnessing an animal after years of labor setting it free or discharging a soldier from military duty or unloosing from moorings preparatory to setting sail." These words were Paul's prediction of what would become historical fact: he was brought before Nero, laid his head upon the chopping block, and, for the Truth of Christ, submitted to the axe that beheaded him; but as his head fell to the ground and his blood poured from his body, his soul was immediately present with the Lord.

---

[282] 2 Timothy 4:1-8 (KJV)
[283] 2 Timothy 4:6 (KJV)

In verse seven, he wrote:

> "I have fought a good fight, I have finished my course,
> I have kept the faith:"[284]

Paul testifies in this trifecta to overcoming all obstacles and completing the race set before him in submission to the Truth of God's Word. The words he used paint the picture of the circumstances under which he did it. "Fought" comes from the Greek word *agonizomai,* which means to contend with adversaries or to struggle with strenuous zeal against difficulties and dangers. This was certainly characteristic of how he fought. "Course" comes from the Greek word *dromos,* which refers to the course of life, of office, or assignment. Indeed, from that day on the road to Damascus, Paul's course for Christ was his life, his office was that of apostle, and his assignment was to spread the Gospel. "Kept" comes from the Greek word *tereo,* which means to attend to carefully, to take care of, or guard. We know from Paul's writings and contribution to the Church that he tended to his assignment carefully and accomplished it well.

Finally, in verse eight, Paul looked past his physical death to his eternal future:

> "Henceforth there is laid up for me a crown of righteousness, which the Lord, the righteous judge, shall give me at that day: and not to me only, but unto all them also that love his appearing."[285]

Here, "righteousness" comes from the Greek word *dikaiosyne,* meaning "integrity, virtue, correctness of thinking, feeling, and acting." Thus, Paul's use of this word reveals that the *Crown of Righteousness* is awarded for the things done according to Truth. Notice also that Paul looks forward to standing before the Righteous Judge, Jesus Christ, meaning he is looking forward to being fairly judged for the things He did according to Truth. Juxtapose Paul's anticipation of appearing

---

[284] 2 Timothy 4:7 (KJV)
[285] 2 Timothy 4:8 (KJV)

before Christ to the circumstances that led him to write this letter: he had been sentenced to death by a wicked and unjust judge, Nero, for preaching and teaching the Truth of Christ. At this point in the lesson, I paused to discuss the great Olympian speed skater, Apolo Ohno, who received unjust rulings from the judges who judged his races and reminded the students that, Christ's followers will face unjust judges on this earth; but we must hold fast to the Truth just as Paul did, no matter what the consequences are.

At the end of verse eight, Paul wrote that all who love Christ's appearing will receive this crown. I personally believe that, in order to love His appearing, one must read and study the entirety of God's Word, spend time with Him in daily prayer, and yearn to see His coming as we live our lives.

The third crown is the *Crown of Life,* which will be awarded to those who, in the name of Christ, endure suffering through temptation and testing. This crown has nothing to do with salvation and eternal life. Eternal life is a free gift, offered by God through His one and only Son, Jesus Christ, and freely given to all who, by exclusive faith, put their trust in Him. The *Crown of Life,* like the other crowns, is a reward; it is detailed in the imbedded letter to the church of Smyrna in the *Book of Revelation*:

> "He that hath an ear, let him hear what the Spirit saith unto the churches; To him that overcometh will I give to eat of the tree of life, which is in the midst of the paradise of God. And unto the angel of the church in Smyrna write; These things saith the first and the last, which was dead, and is alive; I know thy works, and tribulation, and poverty, (but thou art rich) and [I know] the blasphemy of them which say they are Jews, and are not, but [are] the synagogue of Satan. Fear none of those things which thou shalt suffer: behold, the devil shall cast [some] of you into prison, that ye may be tried; and ye shall have tribulation ten days: be thou faithful unto death, and I will give thee a crown of life. He that hath an ear, let him hear what the Spirit

saith unto the churches; He that overcometh shall not
be hurt of the second death."[286]

Though many people believe that, once they have been saved
everything is smooth sailing, the Word of God and this crown in
particular teach the very opposite. In his letter to the church at Rome,
Paul wrote:

> "Therefore being justified by faith, we have peace with
> God through our Lord Jesus Christ: By whom also
> we have access by faith into this grace wherein we
> stand, and rejoice in hope of the glory of God. And not
> only [so], but we glory in tribulations also: knowing
> that tribulation worketh patience; And patience,
> experience; and experience, hope: And hope maketh
> not ashamed..."[287]

Here, Paul is telling us that salvation brings peace with God but
great suffering from the world. Suffering was a subject of which Paul
had first-hand knowledge for, as a believer in and teacher of the Truth,
he was a chosen vessel of God to suffer greatly for the name of Christ.
This fact is clearly conveyed in the *Book of Acts*:

> "But the Lord said unto him, Go thy way: for he is a
> chosen vessel unto me, to bear my name before the
> Gentiles, and kings, and the children of Israel: For I
> will shew him how great things he must suffer for my
> name's sake."[288]

Peter, too, was very familiar with suffering for the name of Christ,
for he wrote:

> "Beloved, think it not strange concerning the fiery
> trial which is to try you, as though some strange thing

---

[286] Revelation 2:8-11 (KJV)
[287] Romans 5:1-5 (KJV)
[288] Acts 9:15-16 (KJV)

happened unto you: But rejoice, inasmuch as ye are partakers of Christ's sufferings; that, when his glory shall be revealed, ye may be glad also with exceeding joy. If ye be reproached for the name of Christ, happy [are ye]; for the spirit of glory and of God resteth upon you: on their part he is evil spoken of, but on your part he is glorified. But let none of you suffer as a murderer, or [as] a thief, or [as] an evildoer, or as a busybody in other men's matters. Yet if [any man suffer] as a Christian, let him not be ashamed; but let him glorify God on this behalf. For the time [is come] that judgment must begin at the house of God: and if [it] first [begin] at us, what shall the end [be] of them that obey not the gospel of God? And if the righteous scarcely be saved, where shall the ungodly and the sinner appear? Wherefore let them that suffer according to the will of God commit the keeping of their souls [to him] in well doing, as unto a faithful Creator."[289]

Moreover, the fifth chapter of *Romans* mandates that a believer in Jesus Christ will endure great trials and testing, and although God has authority over the same, there are many sources. Some trials and testing comes from God as He tests and strengthens our faith. Others come from Satan as he attempts to ensnare and destroy us. Many come from the world as it endeavors to mold us into its image:

"I beseech you therefore, brethren, by the mercies of God, that ye present your bodies a living sacrifice, holy, acceptable unto God, [which is] your reasonable service. And be not conformed to this world: but be ye transformed by the renewing of your mind, that ye may prove what [is] that good, and acceptable, and perfect, will of God."[290]

---

[289] 1 Peter 4:12-19 (KJV)
[290] Romans 12:1-2 (KJV)

Even more come from within, from our old sin nature, the flesh:

> "[This] I say then, Walk in the Spirit, and ye shall not
> fulfill the lust of the flesh. For the flesh lusteth against
> the Spirit, and the Spirit against the flesh: and these are
> contrary the one to the other: so that ye cannot do the
> things that ye would."[291]

Nevertheless, in verse three of the fifth chapter of *Romans*, we read:

> "And not only so, but we glory in tribulations also:
> knowing that tribulation worketh patience;"[292]

The word "tribulation" comes from the Greek word *thlipsis,* which means "a pressing, pressing together, or pressure also used to denote oppression, affliction, or distress." This word is the very same word that was used when referring to the crushing and pressing of grapes into wine or olives into oil. Therefore, use of this word reveals that, through tribulation, God presses our belief into trust in the same way that grapes are pressed into wine and olives into oil. The word "patience" comes from the Greek word *hypomone,* which means "steadfastness, constancy, or endurance." This word literally speaks of the man who, through even the greatest trials and suffering, is not swerved from his deliberate purpose or his loyalty to faith and piety. At this point in the lesson, we paused to discuss how this characteristic was exhibited in Olympic skier, Lindsey Vonn, who fought through devastating injuries to win the Olympic gold medal. For Christians on the slopes of life, when bones are broken by the pressures of affliction and calamity, some dump their wine and oil onto the rocky ground and turn to food, drugs, the bottle, the cold, dull needle, or the gun rather than persevering. Others become angry with God, themselves, loved ones, or the entire world, and, in so doing, allow their wine to turn bitter with resentment. Some just sit down and give up, allowing their wine and oil to become stale and stagnant. But, the greatest Olympian – the great man of God – by

---

[291] Galatians 5:16-17 (KJV)
[292] Romans 5:3 (KJV)

his faith in Jesus Christ, allows his trials and testing to press his raw belief into the fine wine and oil of trust.

Continuing to verse four, we discover the end to which we encounter tribulation:

"And patience, experience; and experience, hope:"[293]

The word "experience" comes from the Greek word *dokime,* which means "proving or approved." This word speaks of a tried character. A believer's tried character should reflect the character of Christ, much like a specimen of gold or silver that has been tried in the fire reflects the refiner. The idea here is that experience which has been refined to this extent begets hope – a hope that is tantamount to assurance. The word "hope" comes from the Greek word *elpis* which speaks of a joyful and confident expectation of eternal salvation. Here, we paused to consider the great confidence of Olympian snowboarder, Shaun White, who performed the Double McTwist 1260. One of only two people to ever perform this maneuver, he was able to do it because his talent, endless practice, and endurance begat the kind of assurance he needed to follow through. Similarly, the Christian who endures great trials, while holding onto Christ as his anchor, is capable of enduring any storm, giving him the assurance he needs to face any tribulation. Those who receive the *Crown of Life* will, upon casting it at the feet of Christ, surely be able to say, "Jesus, you defined my life as I totally submitted to your perfect will."

The fourth crown is the *Crown of Rejoicing* and is perhaps, in my opinion, the greatest of all the crowns and will likely be the least rewarded. Paul first refers to this crown in his letter to the church at Philippi:

"Therefore, my brethren dearly beloved and longed for, my joy and crown, so stand fast in the Lord, [my] dearly beloved. I beseech Euodias, and beseech Syntyche, that they be of the same mind in the Lord. And I intreat thee also, true yokefellow, help those women which

---

[293] Romans 5:4 (KJV)

361

laboured with me in the gospel, with Clement also, and [with] other my fellowlabourers, whose names [are] in the book of life."[294]

Then, in his first letter to the church at Thessalonica, he wrote:

"For this cause also thank we God without ceasing, because, when ye received the word of God which ye heard of us, ye received [it] not [as] the word of men, but as it is in truth, the word of God, which effectually worketh also in you that believe. For ye, brethren, became followers of the churches of God which in Judaea are in Christ Jesus: for ye also have suffered like things of your own countrymen, even as they [have] of the Jews: Who both killed the Lord Jesus, and their own prophets, and have persecuted us; and they please not God, and are contrary to all men: Forbidding us to speak to the Gentiles that they might be saved, to fill up their sins alway: for the wrath is come upon them to the uttermost. But we, brethren, being taken from you for a short time in presence, not in heart, endeavoured the more abundantly to see your face with great desire. Wherefore we would have come unto you, even I Paul, once and again; but Satan hindered us. For what [is] our hope, or joy, or crown of rejoicing? [Are] not even ye in the presence of our Lord Jesus Christ at his coming? For ye are our glory and joy."[295]

In his letter to the *Philippians*, Paul made an impassioned plea to two women in the Philippian church to end their feud. Each time I read this Scripture, I remember my professor and mentor, Dr. Clyde Cain, commenting on the subject: "How would you like to have your name in the Holy Writ only because you could not get along with your brethren?" Indeed, that is something to ponder. In *1 Thessalonians*

---

[294] Philippians 4:1-3 (KJV)
[295] 1 Thessalonians 2:13-20 (KJV)

12:19-20 (KJV), Paul declares that those to whom God gave him the opportunity to share and teach the Gospel will make up his *Crown of Rejoicing*:

> "For what is our hope, or joy, or crown of rejoicing?
> Are not even ye in the presence of our Lord Jesus Christ
> at his coming? For ye are our glory and joy."[296]

Therefore, the rationale behind his concern for the feuding women in the Philippian church was on this wise: they are to be his *Crown of Rejoicing*. In this Scripture, Paul used the word "hope," which is confidence. That hope, or confidence, was the multitude whom Paul had brought to Christ though his ministry. Those believers are Paul's confidence of pleasing the Lord at the Bema Seat Judgment.

Describing the characteristics of this crown, Paul called it joy, bringing to remembrance the words of Christ:

> "Likewise, I say unto you, there is joy in the presence
> of the angels of God over one sinner that repenteth."[297]

We often experienced this kind of joy at *New Beginnings* whenever a patient accepted Christ. We expressed that joy by ceasing work, joining hands in a prayer circle, and rejoicing and boasting with the new believer over the saving power of our Lord Jesus Christ. Speaking of boasting, that is the precise meaning of the *Crown of Rejoicing*. The word "rejoicing" comes from the Greek word *kauchesis,* a noun defined as "an act of glorying or boasting." At the clinic, we boasted not for anything we had done, but for the work of the Holy Spirit in bringing the new believer to Christ. This is the same kind of boasting to which Paul was referring.

Another characteristic to this crown, as Paul declared in *1 Thessalonians*, is worship. The word "glory" translates to "worship." Therefore, when we stand before Christ, each individual who has received Christ through our witness will be our *Crown of Rejoicing* and our joy and worship to the King.

---

[296] 1 Thessalonians 2:19-20 (KJV)
[297] Luke 15:10 (KJV)

The fifth and final crown is the *Crown of Glory*. The Apostle Peter wrote of this crown in his first epistle:

> "The elders which are among you I exhort, who am also an elder, and a witness of the sufferings of Christ, and also a partaker of the glory that shall be revealed: Feed the flock of God which is among you, taking the oversight [thereof], not by constraint, but willingly; not for filthy lucre, but of a ready mind; Neither as being lords over [God's] heritage, but being ensamples to the flock. And when the chief Shepherd shall appear, ye shall receive a crown of glory that fadeth not away."[298]

Many people falsely believe this crown will only be given to pastors or elected leaders and officials of the church, but Scripture does not limit this crown to certain individuals. The entire flock of Christ is eligible. Examination of the above passage of Scripture reveals that every follower of Christ has the opportunity to receive this crown by using his or her gifts of the Spirit to shepherd the flock of Christ. And, the entirety of Scripture reveals that this crown will be given to all Christians who are mature in Christ and His Word and, by their lives, impress upon others the extreme importance of obedience to God. I believe this crown will be awarded to individuals like my grandparents, who used everyday farm life to exemplify and teach me about God's Word, and my parents and some former teachers, who live in obedience to and taught me to stand for the Word of God no matter what the consequences. I also believe there could be a lot of surprised ministers, deacons, Sunday school teachers, and other congregational and denominational leaders at the Bema Seat Judgment when they are passed over for this wonderful crown because they have lived their lives according to the very same principles of exclusion by which they have believed this crown is reserved only for the select few.

I believe those who receive this crown will not receive it because working for Christ was their "career" or because they were forced to do something for Him or because they showed up to every single church

---

[298] 1 Peter 5:1-5 (KJV)

business meeting and taught Sunday school for sixty years but because, as spiritually mature Christians, it was in their very natures to teach, obey, and imitate Christ. According to the entirety of Scripture, and *Revelation 1:6 (KJV)* in particular, all born again believers in Christ are His priests. Therefore, we all have the same responsibility to be ministers and under-shepherds to each other, especially to younger generations and the spiritually immature. In my walk with Christ, I have learned that the most effective ministry comes, not from the pulpit, but by extended one-on-one interaction. Mature Christians understand that the Word of God is not just words but living actions of God's obedient children:

> "Trust in the LORD with all thine heart; and lean not unto thine own understanding. In all thy ways acknowledge him, and he shall direct thy paths."[299]

Concluding my lesson on the crowns, I instructed each of the *Royal Ambassadors* to take his *stephanos* home with him, tell his parents about the lesson on the Bema Seat Judgment and the crowns, and place the *stephanos* in a prominent position in the home where all of them could watch it die. It was my sincere hope in giving this instruction that my students would, even as the world clamored to mesmerize them with sporting events and the worthless trappings of the same after memories of their ole Bible teacher had long since faded, allow the Holy Spirit of the Living God to call to their memories the sight of their withering laurel wreaths and, having reminded them of our treasure hunt, renew their thirst for the eternal treasures and crowns they shall one day cast at the feet of their Savior, Jesus Christ.

---

[299] Proverbs 3:5-6 (KJV)

CHAPTER 19

Pharisaical Rust

"The elder unto the wellbeloved Gaius, whom I love in the truth. Beloved, I wish above all things that thou mayest prosper and be in health, even as thy soul prospereth. For I rejoiced greatly, when the brethren came and testified of the truth that is in thee, even as thou walkest in the truth. I have no greater joy than to hear that my children walk in truth. Beloved, thou doest faithfully whatsoever thou doest to the brethren, and to strangers; Which have borne witness of thy charity before the church: whom if thou bring forward on their journey after a godly sort, thou shalt do well: Because that for his name's sake they went forth, taking nothing of the Gentiles. We therefore ought to receive such, that we might be fellowhelpers to the truth. I wrote unto the church: but Diotrephes, who loveth to have the preeminence among them, receiveth us not. Wherefore, if I come, I will remember his deeds which he doeth, prating against us with malicious words: and not content therewith, neither doth he himself receive the brethren, and forbiddeth them that would, and casteth them out of the church. Beloved, follow not that which is evil, but that which is good. He that doeth good is of God: but he that doeth evil hath not seen God. Demetrius hath good report of all men, and of the truth itself: yea, and we also bear record; and ye know that our record is true. I had many things to write, but I will not with ink and pen write unto thee: But I trust I shall shortly see thee, and we shall speak face to face. Peace be to thee. Our friends salute thee. Greet the friends by name."[300]

The Apostle John's third epistle contrasts the fruit of the True and false Christian. Of Gaius, one of the true, John said the brethren testified that he walked in the Truth and had the Truth in him. Of the other true, Demetrius, John said he had a good report among the brethren and of the Truth itself. Of the false, Diotrephes, John said that he loved to have preeminence among the True Church; that he spoke malicious words against John and other believers; and that he refused to receive John and the brethren, forbad those who would, and cast them out of the church.

Men like Diotrephes are still active among the congregation of the True Church. Jesus warned of them in the *Gospel of Matthew:*

> "Beware of false prophets, which come to you in sheep's clothing, but inwardly they are ravening wolves. Ye shall know them by their fruits. Do men gather grapes of thorns, or figs of thistles? Even so every good tree bringeth forth good fruit; but a corrupt tree bringeth forth evil fruit. A good tree cannot bring forth evil fruit, neither can a corrupt tree bring forth good fruit. Every tree that bringeth not forth good fruit is hewn down, and cast into the fire. Wherefore by their fruits ye shall know them. Not every one that saith unto me, Lord, Lord, shall enter into the kingdom of heaven; but he that doeth the will of my Father which is in heaven. Many will say to me in that day, Lord, Lord, have we not prophesied in thy name? and in thy name have cast out devils? and in thy name done many wonderful works? And then will I profess unto them, I never knew you: depart from me, ye that work iniquity."[301]

---

[300] 3 John 1 (KJV)
[301] Matthew 7:15-23 (KJV)

The Apostle Paul also warned of them in the *Book of Acts:*

> "Take heed therefore unto yourselves, and to all the
> flock, over the which the Holy Ghost hath made you
> overseers, to feed the church of God, which he hath
> purchased with his own blood. For I know this, that
> after my departing shall grievous wolves enter in among
> you, not sparing the flock. Also of your own selves
> shall men arise, speaking perverse things, to draw away
> disciples after them. Therefore watch, and remember,
> that by the space of three years I ceased not to warn
> every one night and day with tears."[302]

These men are easily identified, just as Diotrephes was identified, by examining their fruit. From John's testimony, we find that one of these fruits is loving preeminence among the True Church. The word "preeminence" comes from the Greek word *philoproteuo*, which means to desire to be first, to be fond of being first, or to be ambitious of distinction. Accordingly, these men are often found in positions of leadership or authority inside local churches and Christian organizations. There, they endeavor to run the cause of Christ like a business or social club, competing with each other for positions of authority, and either casting out True Christians or hindering them from obtaining any position of influence. Because they are not true followers of Christ but rather slaves to fleshly appetites, they use local churches and Christian organizations as a means to satisfy their fleshly desires at the expense of True Christians; and whether or not they are aware of it, they are ministers of Satan, as Paul declared in his second epistle to the *Corinthians:*

> "For such are false apostles, deceitful workers,
> transforming themselves into the apostles of Christ. And
> no marvel; for Satan himself is transformed into an angel
> of light. Therefore it is no great thing if his ministers

---

[302] Acts 20:28–31 (KJV)

also be transformed as the ministers of righteousness; whose end shall be according to their works."[303]

As touching the characteristic of loving preeminence, I have encountered several men who exhibited it. One was that self-appointed gate-keeper to the ministry who cared not that I had been called into the ministry by Christ Himself but tried instead to dissuade me from being ordained, citing the potential tax consequences of being a minister. Another was the man in charge of the Baptist General Convention's interim pastor training program. This individual refused to allow me to enroll in the program, presuming to conclude that I was not a "real pastor."

During my first and only meeting with this man, when he had inquired about my ministerial background, and I had told him that my family owned and operated a drug and alcohol treatment center, that many of our patients had recently accepted Christ, and that I was responsible for ministering to and teaching them the Word of God, he replied in a rather derogatory tone, "Oh...how nice...I wonder why I haven't heard of you?"

After this, he reached into the top, left-hand side drawer of his desk, retrieved a small notebook and asked, "What's the name of your clinic?"

"New Beginnings Medical Center," I replied as he flipped through the pages.

"Nope! I don't see it," he said and tossed the notebook back into the drawer and slammed it shut.

"You should advertise in our newsletter. If you advertised with us, our churches would know where you're located and that they can trust you."

With that, he concluded our meeting by telling me, "I don't understand why you want to participate in this program. I don't know that anyone would take you seriously. You're not a real pastor, and I don't think this is for you."

On another occasion, while attempting to organize a crusade in western Oklahoma, I was contacted by the director of the ministerial alliance in the town where I planned to hold the event after securing

---

[303] 2 Corinthians 11:13-15 (KJV)

a prominent venue there. To my surprise, this individual was very upset because I had not obtained his "permission" to hold a crusade in "his town." He proceeded to dress me down, saying that no Christian ministry would be allowed to come to that town without his approval. Thereafter, I was promptly contacted by the managers of the venue and told to forget about holding a crusade there. Meanwhile, when the pastor of a certain church, to which I had been invited by some of its members to speak about the crusade and solicit volunteers, learned that I would be preaching at the crusade rather than some "celebrity preacher," he cancelled my appearance and then refused to take my telephone calls to discuss it.

Perhaps my most memorable encounter with one of these men, however, transpired on this wise: I had organized a non-profit organization to encourage students to plant extracurricular Bible clubs in schools across the country. Inspired by the Lord's calling of the Prophet Samuel when he was a child, who needed help recognizing the Lord's voice and responding to it, my "vision" for this ministerial idea, which I had dubbed *Vision Bible Clubs*, was to utilize the clubs as a vehicle to teach young people how to recognize and respond to God's calling. Admittedly, it was a bold venture, and I knew I needed the expertise of a professional fundraiser if it was to succeed. A casual conversation with a friend about the idea yielded the name and contact information of a certain individual at the Baptist General Convention, but because of my prior dealings with the man in charge of the interim pastor training program, I was reluctant to call. When I finally did, the individual to whom I spoke replied, "I tried to help you people out there, but you didn't want my help!"

"I'm not sure I know what you mean," I said, a little bewildered.

"There is nothing more I can do for you!" he barked and hung up on me.

Later, I learned that before my home church had built its new sanctuary, the finance committee had considered but ultimately decided against financing the project through the Convention. The man who hung up on me was some kind of liaison between the Convention and our church and had apparently taken the church's decision personally. I reported the incident to my friend, whereupon he gave me the name and telephone number of another individual at the Convention, whom I will call Mr. Moore.

I spoke to Mr. Moore at least four or five times on the telephone before we actually met in person. During those conversations, he greatly encouraged me concerning *Vision Bible Clubs'* objective and convinced me that he wanted to help me find a professional fundraiser. However, the last time we spoke on the telephone, which was for the purpose of setting up a meeting, he dashed my hopes and aroused my suspicions by asking me to bring copies of *Vision Bible Clubs'* tax returns to the meeting, saying when I hesitated that he *did* have the right to request them in triplicate. At that point, I pretty much knew the meeting would be a waste of time but decided to go anyway, mostly because his odd request had piqued my curiosity, and so I asked John to go with me.

After arriving at the Convention's headquarters, we were given a visitor's badge and admitted by the security detail. Once inside the elevator, we were whisked, in the twinkling of an eye, into the sky and promptly deposited into plush surroundings on one of the top floors where I noted the large suite of offices, framed with rich wood paneling and accessorized with luxurious furniture.

"Reminds me of one of those tall-building law firms," John remarked as a receptionist greeted and escorted us to a large conference room. Waiting there was Mr. Moore. John and I shook his hand and took a seat at the table with our backs to the floor-to-ceiling glass entrance. After a bout of pleasantries, Mr. Moore launched into an intriguing presentation of his resume, in which he outlined a number of accomplishments and emphasized the fact that he had funneled millions into the Convention's treasury.

"I tell all of my friends that I deal in filthy lucre!" he said leaning back in his swivel chair and laughing like Santa Claus.

Then, as if he had forgotten himself, he sprang forward in the chair, carefully placed his elbows on the conference table, and asked if I had remembered to bring the tax returns. When I replied in the negative, he was visibly upset. However, to my surprise, he abandoned the tax return issue rather quickly and launched instead into a rant against the IRS, wherein he claimed to be always on the lookout for pastors or ministers who were willing to go up against them, saying that, "Whenever there's a fight with the IRS, I'm there!"

When he had finished his rant, he then proceeded to regale us with decorated but offensive tales of how he had cunningly extracted a multi-million dollar donation from one of the late founders of a retail outlet chain; manipulated a southern Oklahoma banker into becoming a reliable source of cash; and secured all or most of the funding for a Biblical artifact museum on the campus of some seminary, which claimed feat was the jewel in his crown of achievements.

"We were lucky enough to get to bring back some artifacts from our trip to Israel last year," I replied.

"What did you bring back?" he asked.

"Some shards of Solomonic pottery," I said. "They're small but well-preserved, and I've been using them as a teaching tool."

"Oh," he snorted and began another tale of how he had secured "big money" to purchase "intact" pieces of pottery.

While the prospect of cutting the meeting short danced in my head, the conversation abruptly turned to the underlying reason for the meeting – to discuss whether Mr. Moore could help me find a professional fundraiser. Couched within a critique of my website was the carefully phrased question, "Do you have any evidence of the number of people who have been saved as a result of your ministry?" When I replied that the work of the Holy Spirit was not quantifiable, he said, "Well, people want to see numbers. If you can't give 'em numbers, you'll have a slow go of it…"

True is the proposition that, when it comes to the Great Commission, many Christians do want to see statistics. But, the practice of contributing to the Great Commission based on statistics is a great sin. King David sinned in like manner when Satan provoked him to number Israel:

> "And Satan stood up against Israel, and provoked David to number Israel. And David said to Joab and to the rulers of the people, Go, number Israel from Beersheba even to Dan; and bring the number of them to me, that I may know it. And Joab answered, The LORD make his people an hundred times so many more as they be: but,

my lord the king, are they not all my lord's servants? why then doth my lord require this thing? why will he be a cause of trespass to Israel? Nevertheless the king's word prevailed against Joab. Wherefore Joab departed, and went throughout all Israel, and came to Jerusalem. And Joab gave the sum of the number of the people unto David. And all they of Israel were a thousand thousand and an hundred thousand men that drew sword: and Judah was four hundred threescore and ten thousand men that drew sword. But Levi and Benjamin counted he not among them: for the king's word was abominable to Joab. And God was displeased with this thing; therefore he smote Israel. And David said unto God, I have sinned greatly, because I have done this thing: but now, I beseech thee, do away the iniquity of thy servant; for I have done very foolishly."[304]

It is impossible to account for the work of the Holy Spirit. Moreover, correlating decisions for Christ to financial contributions credits the work of the Holy Spirit to money rather than to Him, and the Word of God specifically states that the power of the Holy Spirit cannot be bought:

"And when Simon saw that through laying on of the apostles' hands the Holy Ghost was given, he offered them money, Saying, Give me also this power, that on whomsoever I lay hands, he may receive the Holy Ghost. But Peter said unto him, Thy money perish with thee, because thou hast thought that the gift of God may be purchased with money. Thou hast neither part nor lot in this matter: for thy heart is not right in the sight of God."[305]

---

[304] 1 Chronicles 21:1-8 (KJV)
[305] Acts 8:18-21 (KJV)

Misinterpreting my position as an inability to provide evidence of the Holy Spirit's work, Mr. Moore proceeded to belittle my vision with statements to the effect that *Vision Bible Clubs* would probably not get off the ground and suggestions that my vision was unattainable. Interestingly though, he disclaimed his statements and suggestions by stating, "But, anything is possible with the Lord..." When I mentioned that I had asked Karen and Wanda, two black ladies with whom I had worked on the Billy Graham Crusade in Oklahoma City, to help me lead *Vision Bible Clubs*, he remarked, "Oh, I think that would be a big mistake!"

Springing forward in his chair again, he brought his hands together in a tightly clasped fist and rested them upon the table.

"You have to remember this is Oklahoma. This is the south! Nobody in this state is going to take any ministry seriously if it's headed by a black woman!"

Angered by his words, I informed him that Karen and Wanda were both true Christians with years of ministry experience to their credit and that, since they had also been my mentors and prayer partners, I knew they were dedicated to Christ and capable of leading a ministry.

"Now Lance," he interrupted, "Just think about this for a minute... Do you think the people back in Caddo County will listen to a black woman about Jesus? I'm thinking of the success of your ministry in saying this. I just want to protect all of you!"

While he spoke, someone came and stood outside the glass doors behind me. Distracted by whoever it was, Mr. Moore continued to carry on a full conversation with us in speech but conversed with the intruder through body language as a slight grin formed at one corner of his mouth. So distracting was the commotion outside that I finally asked, "Do we need to leave?"

"Oh, not at all..." he replied, tilting his head to one side. "Our fearless leader is out there making faces and gestures, trying to mess me up."

He then stretched both arms out to his side and fluttered his hands wildly while pivoting around in his chair.

"If your two black friends worked on the Billy Graham Crusade, that man knows them. He's a great man!"

As soon as the man disappeared, John spoke up, attempting to explain the roles I wanted Karen and Wanda to assume, but Mr. Moore interrupted him, exclaiming, "You need to hire a Baptist! If you hire someone who isn't a Baptist, they should be willing to convert. I mean, that's who we are, isn't it?"

"Well, actually, I consider myself a Christian, first and foremost," John replied.

"Oh...well, yes...of course..." he said, rolling his eyes and tugging at his necktie. "We're all that..."

"Why don't you take this fundraising job," I said with all the sarcasm I could muster. "You seem overly-qualified."

"Oh no, I couldn't do that! Being here at the Convention is a God thing."

His hands fumbled aimlessly about the table until he had found and picked up my proposed budget. He examined it closely.

"Well," he said, tossing it back down on the table, "I just don't know anyone with pockets deep enough for a project like this. I don't know of anyone who'd be willing to donate."

For a moment, I was speechless, and then it suddenly dawned on me that his intent in meeting with me had been to try to uncover the identities of anyone who might have donated to *Vision Bible Clubs* so he could fleece them. He must have sensed from my expression that I had figured out his angle because he quickly began to bring the meeting to a close, saying as we stood to leave, "I'm sure this is the first of many meetings that we'll have..."

But, I thought to myself, "I never plan on laying eyes on you again!"

As John and I were leaving, I just could not shake how utterly gaulded my spirit felt and said, "I feel like I need a bath," to which he replied, "It sure was an eye-opener, wasn't it?"

As touching the characteristics of prating against the brethren with malicious words, refusing to receive the brethren, and forbidding those who would, I have encountered several men who produced this fruit as well. Though it is difficult to imagine Diotrephes slandering and refusing and forbidding others to receive the Apostle John, a man whom Jesus Christ gave authority to raise the dead, heal the sick, cleanse lepers, and cast out demons;[306] one of the two men whom Jesus surnamed "The Sons of Thunder;"[307] the man who reclined on Jesus' chest the night before His crucifixion;[308] and the man to whom Jesus entrusted His mother's care following His crucifixion and resurrection,[309] I have learned from my own encounters with men like him that they simply do not care about a Christian's relationship with Christ. In fact, they count it as a thing of naught.

After the pastor who presided over my ordination left my home church, I volunteered to teach the *Royal Ambassadors*, leading me to spend more time at the church building. Because the members were without a full-time shepherd and because of my increased presence, several of them came to me to discuss their problems. Consequently, I learned that being without a pastor was very difficult for them. Among those who needed someone to talk to was an elderly couple who wanted Godly advice concerning a grandson whose poor choices were affecting their entire family. The first time I visited their home as a minister, the wife said to me, "Not having a pastor is awful!"

"I mean to tell ya!" her husband replied. "When we've got problems, we don't want to talk to the church secretary. We don't want a deacon telling us what he thinks, either. We want a minister of Christ to show us from the Scriptures what God wants us to do!"

As the wife served me a piece of homemade apple pie and a tall glass of cold water with shaky hands, she said, "We've been without a pastor for a long time, and we can't just wait for a search committee to find a candidate who has enough kids to fill the school's baseball team."

While listening to the plight of my brethren, the Lord placed a burden upon my heart which became a test of obedience. Until then, I had never wanted to be a pastor nor did I find the prospect all too appealing, but after a great deal of prayer and advice from my family concerning my burden, I surrendered to the Lord and submitted an application to pastor my home church. At the time, the search

---

[306] Matthew 10:8 (KJV)
[307] Mark 3:17 (KJV)
[308] John 13:23 (KJV)
[309] John 19:25-27 (KJV)

committee had not found a new pastor. A local minister was preaching the Sunday and Wednesday services, but he was unable to serve full-time. At first, I believed I was best suited to be the interim pastor and was a little concerned about making a long-term commitment to my home church; but the Holy Spirit made it clear to me that, if I truly loved and trusted God, I would allow Him to assign my duties – anything less would be disobedience.

I decided not to make my application public because I wanted to avoid any appearance of campaigning for the position; and since I knew several members would insist that the position be offered to me, I did not want to create a stir or cause dissension. For these reasons, I submitted my application for the pastorate to three leading families in the church. The moment I submitted it, a massive burden lifted from my soul. I knew I had passed the Father's test of obedience. I could feel His pleasure and basked in the warmth of knowing my obedience pleased Him.

My faithful friend, Chalkie Opitz, asked me to preach the following Sunday, and I was obedient to preach the message which the Holy Spirit had laid upon my heart. My sermon, however, was not well-received by the church's leadership. Moreover, their reaction to my application for the pastorate was not a pleasurable one. After my sermon, what I once believed were healthy and respectful relationships suddenly became awkward as their attitudes toward me disintegrated. Some pretended they had never even known me while others took to leaving the room whenever I entered. So strange was their behavior that I confided in Mom and Dustin. Mom attempted to encourage me by saying, "Maybe they are trying to protect you from being hurt or maybe they're afraid you'll be angry if they hire someone else."

But, this was not the case. After several months passed without an answer, Chalkie took me aside one Wednesday night following the weekly *Royal Ambassadors* meeting and said the church had chosen a young, youth minister to fill the position. I was relieved, excited to meet and serve the Lord alongside our new pastor, and overjoyed for our little church because it desperately needed a shepherd. Sadly, however, I soon learned that a small group from among the church's leadership, having designated themselves as the official welcome wagon, had usurped my budding relationship with our new pastor by telling him that I disliked him and was angry because I was not offered the pastorate. To my horror, they even divulged my personal failures to him, including my bankruptcy and political defeats.

"We never seriously considered him," one said.

"He's not the image we want!" said another.

Despite my hurt, I said nothing and kept everything inside, even when one of the boys in the *Royal Ambassadors* quizzed me specifically about my failures after overhearing some of the things his mother was saying about me and after a deacon snidely, and publicly, referred to *Vision Bible Clubs* as my "little backyard ministry."

In the weeks after our new pastor assumed his duties, calamity struck my personal life, and I spiraled into yet another deep and painful depression. Heart and lung problems landed me in the hospital, and I required medical attention for several months to come. Meanwhile, the failure of another business venture left me penniless once again, and my weight skyrocketed to the point where I was almost ashamed to be in public. When I was finally able to work again, I pursued a business opportunity that required me to travel all over Oklahoma and outside the state so I resigned from teaching the *Royal Ambassadors*. It was upon entering this dark and dreadful valley that all of my past encounters with these modern-day versions of the Diotrephes whom the Apostle John wrote about slowly began to suffocate the quiet whisper of the Holy Spirit, and I again questioned whether I had truly been called into the ministry. Compounding my doubt was the fact that even my own family did not seem to take my ministry seriously. I wondered whether I was just making a fool of myself, and I seriously considered the prospect that I had just allowed my love for Christ and His sacrifice to turn me into an overly-excited zealot. Ultimately, I allowed myself to be cast out of the ministry by my own sorrowful and painful decision to leave.

I have often wondered how many God-called ministers and ministries have failed because of the negative influences and destructive deeds of these men and the fact that some Christians remain complacent, turn a deaf ear, and do not take a public stand against them as the Apostle John did. My encounters with these individuals have taught me that just because someone holds a position among the congregation of the True Church or in a Christian organization or professes to be a Christian does not mean he is a child of God. His fruit will give him away every time. As Jesus said, "Do men gather grapes of thorns, or figs of thistles?"[310]

---

[310] Matthew 7:16 (KJV)

CHAPTER 20

The Shepherd

"And in those days Peter stood up in the midst of the disciples, and said, (the number of names together were about an hundred and twenty,) Men and brethren, this scripture must needs have been fulfilled, which the Holy Ghost by the mouth of David spake before concerning Judas, which was guide to them that took Jesus. For he was numbered with us, and had obtained part of this ministry. Now this man purchased a field with the reward of iniquity; and falling headlong, he burst asunder in the midst, and all his bowels gushed out. And it was known unto all the dwellers at Jerusalem; insomuch as that field is called in their proper tongue, Aceldama, that is to say, The field of blood. For it is written in the book of Psalms, Let his habitation be desolate, and let no man dwell therein: and his bishoprick let another take. Wherefore of these men which have companied with us all the time that the Lord Jesus went in and out among us, Beginning from the baptism of John, unto that same day that he was taken up from us, must one be ordained to be a witness with us of his resurrection. And they appointed two, Joseph called Barsabas, who was surnamed Justus, and Matthias. And they prayed, and said, Thou, Lord, which knowest the hearts of all men, shew whether of these two thou hast chosen, That he may take part of this ministry and apostleship, from which Judas by transgression fell, that he might go to his own place. And they gave forth their lots; and the lot fell upon Matthias; and he was numbered with the eleven apostles."[311]

True under-shepherds of Jesus Christ are chosen by Him. There are many examples of this Truth in the Scriptures but perhaps the best is the Apostle Paul. Following Judas Iscariot's suicide, the apostles gathered to determine who would replace him. They chose Matthias by the casting of lots, but Matthias was not the Lord's choice. God's replacement for Judas Iscariot was the Apostle Paul. At the very beginning of his epistle to the *Galatians*, Paul revealed that his position had been given to him by Jesus Christ and not by men or by one man alone:

"Paul, an apostle, (not of men, neither by man, but by Jesus Christ, and God the Father, who raised him from the dead;)"[312]

Moreover, since Paul exhibited the apostolic gift of resurrection in the twentieth chapter of the *Book of Acts*, his apostleship cannot be questioned or debated:

"And upon the first day of the week, when the disciples came together to break bread, Paul preached unto them, ready to depart on the morrow; and continued his speech until midnight. And there were many lights in the upper chamber, where they were gathered together. And there sat in a window a certain young man named Eutychus, being fallen into a deep sleep: and as Paul was long preaching, he sunk down with sleep, and fell down from the third loft, and was taken up dead. And Paul went down, and fell on him, and embracing him said, Trouble not yourselves; for his life is in him. When he therefore was come up again, and had broken bread, and eaten, and talked a long while, even till break of

[311] Acts 1:15-26 (KJV)
[312] Galatians 1:1 (KJV)

day, so he departed. And they brought the young man
alive, and were not a little comforted."[313]

The lesson of the Lord's selection of Paul over Matthias is one
which the Church has either forgotten or never learned. Since the lot
was cast to insert Matthias into Judas' seat nearly two thousand years
ago, Church members have continued to choose ministers, pastors,
deacons, and other leaders in the same way that the apostles chose
Matthias – by worldly methods, at the wrong time, and for the wrong
reasons. Unfortunately, when the wrong people are chosen, they are
propelled into influential positions where they often interfere with,
discourage, and hinder the true ministers of Christ from doing the work
to which they have been called. Nevertheless, a True under-shepherd
of Jesus Christ should never allow those whom the Lord has not called
to interfere with the work He has assigned because the cause of Christ
is too great and a multitude of eternities are at stake. This is the lesson
which the Lord began teaching me soon after I departed from the
ministry, beginning with the awful news that yet another young patient
to whom I had ministered at the clinic had met with a tragic end.

While I was sitting at home one evening, the telephone rang.

"Hello?"

"What's up hillbilly?" replied a familiar voice at the other end of
the line.

It was Dale.

"Oh, not much," I said. "How are you?"

Dale and I had recently fallen out of fellowship because he refused
to abandon his sinful ways or heed my admonition that we could walk
together only in obedience to Christ. The pain caused by our lost
fellowship, coupled with the sudden concern that he might ask me for
something, hit me hard when I heard his voice.

"I just wanted to call and let you know that Greg overdosed and
died last night," he said.

Greg, of course, was not his real name, but that is how I will refer to
the young man who, like so many other patients, came to *New Beginnings*
hoping to find peace from his travesty of a life and freedom from

---

[313] Acts 20:7-12 (KJV)

something more than just drug addiction. Greg had failed at treatment and started over more times than I could remember, but it was his final attempt that Dale's devastating news ushered to the forefront of my mind.

When our medical director had declined to give Greg one last chance, he came to me, pleading with such desperation that it roused two Scriptures within my heart:

"Blessed are the merciful: for they shall obtain mercy."[314]

And,

"With the merciful thou wilt shew thyself merciful; with an upright man thou wilt shew thyself upright..."[315]

I rang for the file clerk, asked her to bring Greg's file to my office, and reviewed the recent notes as he looked on.

"Do you realize I'll be going against the recommendation of almost everyone in this office if I talk to the medical director about whether he can readmit you?" I asked him.

"Yessir," he replied. "But, I promise..."

"That's not good enough," I interrupted. "That's a promise you have no idea whether you can keep, and I need something more than that."

I motioned him to take a seat at the old domino table against the wall.

"What's going on in your life?" I inquired as the wooden chairs creaked and popped under our weight. "What's causing you so much turmoil? What are you running from?"

As he opened up, I learned that he had spent most of his nineteen years searching for the approval of worldly, ungodly people. Because of his feminine demeanor and besetting sin, he was accustomed to being verbally abused by his father and brothers. He lived with his grandparents, but that was by no means a blessing. Each morning, he awoke to find his grandmother impaired on Xanax and grandfather

---

[314] Matthew 5:7 (KJV)
[315] Psalm 18:25 (KJV)

passed out at the kitchen table with a rig in his arm. The portrait of his sad, wasted existence made me all the more thankful for the wonderful relationships I had with my grandparents and the joy of finding them waiting to spend the day with me each morning. I wanted desperately to impart some of God's blessings to Greg, but I knew it had to begin with pointing him to Christ.

"All I want is for someone to love me for who and what I am!" he muttered as the tears cascaded down his face.

"Let me introduce you to someone who does and always has loved you for who you are," I responded and began sharing Scriptures and testifying of what Jesus Christ had done for me.

When I finished, he replied, "You're the only person who has ever really tried to help me."

Because Greg had almost reached the end of his rope, I knew readmission was crucial for him because it could present one last opportunity for him to accept Christ, but I also knew it could possibly stir up contention amongst the staff. Weighing the probable fallout brought the Lord's words through the prophet Hosea into my ears:

> "Hear the word of the LORD, ye children of Israel:
> for the LORD hath a controversy with the inhabitants
> of the land, because there is no truth, nor mercy, nor
> knowledge of God in the land."[316]

I doubted Greg would hear the Truth or receive the knowledge of God anywhere else. Moreover, I did not want the Lord to have a controversy with me for showing no mercy so I discussed Greg's situation with one of our best counselors. After reviewing his file, she conceded that he needed to be readmitted and took up the issue with our medical director. Following our discussion, I returned to my office, got down on my knees, and prayed for the Lord to intervene. I did not have to wait long. The next morning, as John and I were leaving a meeting in downtown, I received word that the medical director's decision to re-admit Greg had stirred up a

---

[316] Hosea 4:1 (KJV)

hornet's nest. I decided immediately to silence the opposition and, upon returning to the clinic, terminated two of the troublemakers for cause. Greg had no idea, but I was fighting the world to bring him to Christ.

At the funeral, I was reunited with many of Greg's friends who had also been patients at the clinic and was saddened to learn that some were still living in sin but overjoyed when others testified to having left their sinful lifestyles behind. At the cemetery, I stood afar off from the grave in the shade of a locust tree with Dale by my side.

"I begged and pleaded with Greg to come to Christ. I really hope that somewhere along the way he did," I said.

"You did all you could do," Dale replied, his eyes focused on the ground. "Whatever decision he made was his own."

"Dale, you need to be in church and studying the Bible," I said, but he continued to look at the ground and replied somberly, "You're the only one I listen to about God."

Later, after I had taken him home, I returned to the cemetery and waited patiently for everyone to leave. When the last mourner had retreated, I climbed out of my car and walked over to the funeral director and grave workers who were preparing to close Greg's grave.

"Do you mind if I stay for the final closing?"

"You're more than welcome to," the funeral director replied. Offering his hand, he said, "I'm John Ireland, owner of the funeral home. Are you family?"

"No..." I said, shaking his hand. I stopped briefly as sadness welled up within my chest, but continued, "I was once his friend, counselor, and minister..."

"Why did you not preach the funeral?"

"Greg's family does not know about me. He came to me for help with his drug addiction and was one of my boys. I once promised him that I would walk with him as far as I could – and this is it."

I eased my shiny black shoes to the very edge of the pit.

"I see," he replied softly. "Stand anywhere you like."

He spoke briefly to the grave workers then stood back as they lowered the casket into the ground and spread the turf grass so neatly upon the pile of dirt that it no longer looked like a grave. I could not help but notice how different it was from the graves of my grandparents. There was no perpetual care to be performed here. Metaphorically speaking, the opportunity for work had ceased.

"This is a hard lesson," one of the workers said to the other. "Maybe some of the people who were here will change their ways."

Sadly, I knew his sentiment was wishful thinking. Most people love their sin more than they love God, and judging from the looks of the motley crew that had attended Greg's funeral and graveside service, I knew they would continue in the broad way, forget about Greg, and eventually die in their own sins.

"Oh, what I would give to trade places with him so he could have one more chance to accept Christ and make peace with God," I thought as I drove home from the cemetery. The shadows of the trees raced across the hood of the black Cadillac as I remembered him telling me that I was the only one who had ever really tried to help him, but I wondered whether I had truly done enough in my efforts to bring him to Christ. Greg's words, coupled with Dale's confession that I was the only one he listened to about God, gave me much to contemplate and answer for in light of my recent decision to leave the ministry.

Greg's untimely and tragic death came at a time when I was endeavoring to replace the ministry I had left behind with something else – an exercise which the Lord transformed into an illustration that my effort to find purpose and achieve success and contentment in the world irrespective of God's plan would be futile. For instance, Dustin and I had just invested in a bio-diesel company and wanted to acquire an oil concern, but our credit scores were standing in the way of transforming that desire into a reality. While trying to find an alternative to our undesirable credit predicament, it suddenly dawned on me that the credit score, a good one of which is a condition precedent to so many worldly endeavors, is actually a forerunner to the mark of the beast, spoken of in the *Book of Revelation*:

> "And he causeth all, both small and great, rich and poor,
> free and bond, to receive a mark in their right hand, or
> in their foreheads: And that no man might buy or sell,

save he that had the mark, or the name of the beast, or the number of his name. Here is wisdom. Let him that hath understanding count the number of the beast: for it is the number of a man; and his number is Six hundred threescore and six."[317]

Then, without warning, financial catastrophe struck the United States and the rest of the world in 2009. The depression that followed caused Dustin and me to lose our entire investment in the bio-diesel endeavor and left us practically penniless. During that time, watching the news on television and reading the newspaper became an exercise in sitting idly by while greedy politicians secured their own wealth. The helplessness birthed by that exercise, together with the nausea that accompanied the talking heads' continuous rattle concerning gold's security, reminded me of this Scripture:

"Go to now, ye rich men, weep and howl for your miseries that shall come upon you. Your riches are corrupted, and your garments are motheaten. Your gold and silver is cankered; and the rust of them shall be a witness against you, and shall eat your flesh as it were fire. Ye have heaped treasure together for the last days. Behold, the hire of the labourers who have reaped down your fields, which is of you kept back by fraud, crieth: and the cries of them which have reaped are entered into the ears of the Lord of sabaoth. Ye have lived in pleasure on the earth, and been wanton; ye have nourished your hearts, as in a day of slaughter. Ye have condemned and killed the just; and he doth not resist you. Be patient therefore, brethren, unto the coming of the Lord. Behold, the husbandman waiteth for the precious fruit of the earth, and hath long patience for it, until he receive the early and latter rain. Be ye also patient; stablish your hearts: for the coming of the Lord draweth nigh."[318]

---

[317] Revelation 13:11-18 (KJV)
[318] James 5:1-8 (KJV)

Because we had no money, I was forced to face the reality of having to suspend the rebuilding of my home. Vacant and seemingly abandoned, it presented an attractive opportunity to a group of drug-addicted thieves who stole all the building materials and custom supplies that were not nailed down and thousands of dollars' worth of tools which had belonged to my grandfather and great-grandfather. My first reaction to the thought of thieves pawning my family's heirlooms in the name of a cheap, fleeting high and for pennies on the dollar was anger, but it quickly morphed into an obsession with bringing the perpetrators to justice. Hoping the thieves would return so I could catch them in the act, I took to sitting in my pickup truck near the house practically every night. For several nights in a row, I sat there, armed and waiting. But, as I waited in the darkness, I thought of this Scripture:

> "Watch therefore: for ye know not what hour your Lord doth come, But know this, that if the good-man of the house had known in what watch the thief would come, he would have watched, and would not have suffered his house to be broken up. Therefore be ye also ready: for in such an hour as ye think not the Son of man cometh. Who then is a faithful and wise servant, whom his lord hath made ruler over his household, to give them meat in due season?"[319]

With these words, the Holy Spirit implored me to consider the spiritual state of those who had robbed me and to evaluate their ill-gotten, transitory gain against my eternal security. For the first time, my anger subsided as I realized there was much more at stake than material possessions. The uncertainty of the perpetrators' eternities burdened me so greatly that I immediately forgave them and began to pray for their salvation. Because I suspected who they were, I later purchased Bibles for all of them and saw that they got them.

Meanwhile, in California, my cousins had organized a property preservation business and were making good money from the residential mortgage crisis that sprang to life in the wake of the financial catastrophe

---

[319] Matthew 24:42-45 (KJV)

and ridiculous legislation that followed it. Before long, Dustin and I were expanding our cousins' business into Oklahoma, and I soon found myself delivering certified foreclosure notices – a responsibility not unlike what I had been doing as a minister – delivering spiritual notices, warning sinners of the Lord's coming judgment upon their unpaid sin debt. Within a few months, a temporary opportunity arose to expand my cousins' business to Memphis, Tennessee. Since I needed an assistant and had been praying that mine and Dale's friendship could be renewed, I offered the job to him, and he accepted. For several weeks, we secured, inspected, and reported on foreclosed properties from the ghettos to the country clubs around Memphis. The homes, many of which were on the banks of the Mississippi River and bordering cotton fields, were nothing but deserted shells with dark secrets, giving me a glimpse into the souls of the residents who had once dwelt in them. Within five minutes of entering an abandoned home, I knew the occupation, manner of life, and lusts of the former resident as well as their personal view of Christ. It was apparent that some had fallen on hard times, but others were trapped in great sins. I mourned and prayed for all of them because they all needed Christ.

The homes also testified to the greed of business and industry. The moral reconciliation of high interest loans upon those properties was inconceivable. Most were in such deplorable condition that they were unfit to be used as chicken houses and should have been burned to the ground as a matter of public safety. Even the river rats kept their distance. As I labored amidst the consequences of greed and sin, the Holy Spirit gently reminded me that I had departed the ministry only to join the machine that was restoring and making these heaps suitable to enslave others. Suddenly, I was burdened to the bones by my pitiful attempt to achieve purpose apart from the Lord's calling. The Holy Spirit was reminding me how desperately Christ's ministers are needed to shine His light into the world's darkness and forcing me to admit that I had abandoned that responsibility. I could not deny that turning my back on my calling would bring accountability at the Bema Seat Judgment:

> "My brethren, be not many masters, knowing that we
> shall receive the greater condemnation."[320]

---

[320] James 3:1 (KJV)

With Greg's and Dale's words and the visions of what I had seen while preserving properties perpetually weighing on my soul, and the Holy Spirit convicting me every day, I turned back toward the ministry, but deciding to return was not exactly easy. Besides the memories of rejection and ridicule, my family was encouraging me to seek a career and expressing the collective opinion that ministry could only be a hobby. Diverted briefly by a desire to please them, I submitted resumes to various churches but just wound up seeing more of the same old behavior that I wanted to escape. Of the two churches that interviewed me, one concluded that I was not right for the position on the basis that I had worn cufflinks to the interview. The other rejected me on the basis of a report they had received from one of the bad seeds at my home church who told them I did not have "the right image." Doubt, confusion, and insecurity lunged at me as Satan attempted to prevent me from reuniting with my calling. Despite his interference, however, I could not escape the persistent voice of the Holy Spirit, who reminded me daily that time is short. In those days, John shared a scripture with me that his cousin had recently preached upon:

> "After these things Jesus shewed himself again to the disciples at the sea of Tiberias; and on this wise shewed he himself. There were together Simon Peter, and Thomas called Didymus, and Nathanael of Cana in Galilee, and the sons of Zebedee, and two other of his disciples. Simon Peter saith unto them, I go a fishing. They say unto him, We also go with thee. They went forth, and entered into a ship immediately; and that night they caught nothing. But when the morning was now come, Jesus stood on the shore: but the disciples knew not that it was Jesus. Then Jesus saith unto them, Children, have ye any meat? They answered him, No. And he said unto them, Cast the net on the right side of the ship, and ye shall find. They cast therefore, and now they were not able to draw it for the multitude of fishes. Therefore that disciple whom Jesus loved saith unto Peter, It is the Lord. Now when Simon Peter heard

that it was the Lord, he girt his fisher's coat unto him, (for he was naked,) and did cast himself into the sea. And the other disciples came in a little ship; (for they were not far from land, but as it were two hundred cubits,) dragging the net with fishes. As soon then as they were come to land, they saw a fire of coals there, and fish laid thereon, and bread. Jesus saith unto them, Bring of the fish which ye have now caught. Simon Peter went up, and drew the net to land full of great fishes, an hundred and fifty and three: and for all there were so many, yet was not the net broken. Jesus saith unto them, Come and dine. And none of the disciples durst ask him, Who art thou? knowing that it was the Lord. Jesus then cometh, and taketh bread, and giveth them, and fish likewise. This is now the third time that Jesus shewed himself to his disciples, after that he was risen from the dead."[321]

This Scripture was the Lord's answer to my diffidence and hesitation; it affirmed to me that I can do nothing apart from Christ. Moreover, if Christ's apostles were unable to return to their pre-ministry positions, neither could I go back to mine. When the Lord calls a man into ministry for Him as He did all of His apostles, including Paul, He equips that man and expects him to accomplish the purpose for which he was created. Man's approval is immaterial. And, as for my lingering concerns regarding how I had been treated by so many who claimed to be Christ's servants, Lona Canada, Granny's cousin, whose wisdom mirrored Granny's such that they could have been twins, put them into perspective. After telling her my reasons for leaving the ministry and pouring out my conviction to return, she looked at me and sternly replied, "Lance, a man on a mission cannot stop and listen to every barking dog."

---

[321] John 21:1-14 (KJV)

CHAPTER 21

The Witness, A Broken Vessel

It was the end of autumn, and Dale and I had just returned from an extended, out-of-state property preservation trip. Burdened in thought, I decided to take a walk and inspect my farm because seeing the grounds over which the Lord has given me stewardship has always given me joy. Standing atop the great bluff at the center of my farm, I breathed in the crisp, north wind that was rustling the tall brown grass and ushering in grayish-white clouds that resembled dry bones and noticed that the outflows of the shifting jet stream had lent a helpful tailwind to the skein of honking Canadian geese that were passing overhead on their southward migration. Many end-of-season changes were in the air. I looked down upon my home and the home of my parents and reminisced about the events of my life that had brought me to this moment, knowing that the Lord has allowed me to physically live many Truths I have studied in His Word. He has greatly blessed me with unique circumstances, through which His Truth, presence, and love have allowed me to live a wonderful adventure. From the realization that my Creator and I have shared an intimate relationship since I was very young sprang security and warmth. But, a quivering chill – spawned by the staggering reality that the Lord has chosen me to be His pupil and servant – accompanied that warmth.

I then lifted my eyes toward the horizon and was suddenly pierced in the spirit by a great, crushing weight: the plight of the addict, the blindness of the deceived, the loneliness of the outcast, the unheard cries of the oppressed, the bloodcurdling, misdirected screams by the youth of modern-day Persia for deliverance from a false God, and even the untapped potential of my own community and home church all rent me sore; but with this burden, came the Holy Spirit's solution:

> "For whosoever shall call upon the name of the Lord shall be saved. How then shall they call on him in whom they have not believed? and how shall they believe in him of whom they have not heard? and how shall they hear without a preacher? And how shall they preach, except they be sent? as it is written, How beautiful are the feet of them that preach the gospel of peace, and bring glad tidings of good things!"[322]

I once again looked down upon my unfinished home, troubled by the great difficulties preventing me from resuming its reconstruction, but the Holy Spirit again turned my thoughts to my unfinished service for Him and let me know that the situation with my unfinished home, though bothersome, had come upon me to the intent that God could fulfill my long-standing request for His knowledge, wisdom, and skills and the ability to use them to serve Him. Accepting the Lord's revelation, I added a fourth element to my ongoing prayer – that the Lord would grant me the ability to handle the great burdens that accompany the gifts of His wisdom and knowledge. While I prayed, the Holy Spirit called to my remembrance the answer Zerubbabel gave to King Darius' riddle:

> "1. (31) AFTER the slaughter of the Magi, who, upon the death of Cambyses, attained the government of the Persians for a year, those families which were called the seven families of the Persians appointed Darius, the son of Hystaspes, to be their king. Now he, while he was a private man, had made a vow to God, that if he came to be king, he would send all the vessels of God that were in Babylon to the temple at Jerusalem. (32) Now it so fell out, that about this time Zorobabel [or Zerubbabel], who had been made governor of the Jews that had

---

[322] Romans 10:13-15 (KJV)

been in captivity, came to Darius, from Jerusalem; for there had been an old friendship between him and the king. He was also, with two others, thought worthy to be guard of the king's body; and obtained that honor which he hoped for.

2. (33) Now, in the first year of the king's reign, Darius feasted those that were about him, and those born in his house, with the rulers of the Medes, and princes of the Persians, and the toparchs of India and Ethiopia, and the generals of the armies of his hundred and twenty-seven provinces. (34) But when they had eaten and drunk to satiety, and abundantly, they everyone departed to go to bed at their own houses, and Darius the king went to bed; but after he had rested a little part of the night, he awakened, and not being able to sleep any more, he fell into conversation with the three guards of his body, (35) and promised, that to him who should make an oration about points that he should inquire of, such as should be most agreeable to truth, and to the dictates of wisdom, he would grant it as a reward of his victory, to put on a purple garment, and to drink in cups of gold, and to sleep upon gold, and to have a chariot with bridles of gold, and a headdress of fine linen, and a chain of gold about his neck, and sit next to himself, on account of his wisdom; "and," says he, "he shall be called my cousin." (36) Now when he had promised to give them these gifts, he asked the first of them, "Whether wine was not the strongest?"—the second, "Whether kings were not such?"—and the third, "Whether women were not such or whether truth was not the strongest of all?" When he had proposed that they should make their inquiries about these problems, he went to rest; (37) but in the morning he sent for his great men, his princes, and toparchs of Persia and Media, and set himself down in the place where he used to give audience, and directed

each of the guards of his body to declare what they thought proper concerning the proposed questions, in the hearing of them all.

3. (38) Accordingly, the first of them began to speak of the strength of wine, and demonstrated it thus: "When," said he, "I am to give my opinion of wine, O you men, I find that it exceeds everything, by the following indications: (39) It deceives the mind of those that drink it, and reduces that of the king to the same state with that of the orphan, and he who stands in need of a tutor; and erects that of the slave to the boldness of him that is free; and that of the needy becomes like that of the rich man, (40) for it changes and renews the souls of men when it gets into them; and it quenches the sorrow of those that are under calamities, and makes men forget the debts they owe to others, and makes them think themselves to be of all men the richest; it makes them talk of no small things, but of talents, and such other subjects as become wealthy men only; (41) no more, it makes them insensible of their commanders, and of their kings, and takes away the remembrance of their friends and companions, for it arms men even against those that are dearest to them, and makes them appear the greatest strangers to them; (42) and when they are become sober, and they have slept out their wine in the night, they arise without knowing anything they have done in their cups. I take these for signs of power, and by them discover that wine is the strongest and most insuperable of all things"

4. (43) As soon as the first had given the beforementioned demonstrations of the strength of wine, he left off; and the next to him began to speak about the strength of a king, and demonstrated that it was the strongest of all, and more powerful than anything else that

appears to have any force or wisdom. He began his demonstration after the following manner; and said, (44) "They are men who govern all things; they force the earth and the sea to become profitable to them in what they desire, and over men do kings rule, and over them they have authority. Now those who rule over that animal which is of all the strongest and most powerful, must needs deserve to be esteemed insuperable in power and force. (45) For example, when these kings command their subjects to make wars, and undergo dangers, they are hearkened to; and when they send them against their enemies, their power is so great that they are obeyed. They command men to level mountains, and to pull down walls and towers; nay, when they are commanded to be killed and to kill, they submit to it, that they may not appear to transgress the king's commands; and when they have conquered, they bring what they have gained in the war to the king. (46) Those also who are not soldiers, but cultivate the ground, and plough it, and when, after they have endured the labor and all the inconveniences of such works of husbandry, they have reaped and gathered in their fruits, they bring tributes to the king; (47) and whatever it is which the king says or commands, it is done of necessity, and that without any delay, while he in the meantime is satiated with all sorts of food and pleasures, and sleeps in quiet. He is guarded by such as watch, and such as are, as it were, fixed down to the place through fear; (48) for no one dares leave him, even when he is asleep, nor does anyone go away and take care of his own affairs; but he esteems this one thing the only work of necessity, to guard the king, and accordingly to this he wholly addicts himself. How then can it be otherwise, but that it must appear that the king exceeds all in strength, while so great a multitude obeys his injunctions?"

5. (49) Now when this man had held his peace, the third of them, who was Zorobabel, began to instruct them about women, and about truth, who said thus: "Wine is strong, as it the king also, whom all men obey, but women are superior to them in power; (50) for it was a woman that brought the king into the world; and for those that plant vines and make the wine, they are women who bear them, and bring them up: nor indeed is there anything which we do not receive from them; for these women weave garments for us, and our household affairs are by their means taken care of, and preserved in safety; (51) nor can we live separate from women. And when we have gotten a great deal of gold and silver, and any other thing that is of great value, and deserving regard, and see a beautiful woman, we leave all these things, and with open mouth fix our eyes upon her countenance, and are willing to forsake what we have, that we may enjoy her beauty, and procure it to ourselves. (52) We also leave father, and mother, and the earth that nourishes us, and frequently forget our dearest friends, for the sake of women; nay, we are so hardy as to lay down our lives for them. But what will chiefly make you take notice of the strength of women is this that follows: (53) Do not we take pains, and endure great deal of trouble, and that both by land and sea, and when we have procured something as the fruit of our labors, do not we bring them to the women, as to our mistresses, and bestow upon them? (54) Nay, I once saw the king, who is lord of so many people, stricken on the face by Apame, the daughter of Rabsases Themasius, his concubine, and his diadem taken from him, and put upon her own head, while he bore it patiently; and when she smiled he smiled, and when she was angry he was sad; and according to the change of her passions, he flattered his wife, and drew her reconciliation by

the great humiliation of himself to her, if at any time he saw her displeased at him."

"6. (55) And when the princes and rulers looked one upon another, he began to speak about truth; and he said, "I have already demonstrated how powerful women are; but both these women themselves, and the king himself, are weaker than truth; for although the earth be large, and the heaven high, and the course of the sun swift, yet are all these moved according to the will of God, who is true and righteous, for which cause we also ought to esteem truth to be the strongest of all things, and that what is unrighteous is of no force against it. (56) Moreover, all things else that have any strength are mortal and short-lived, but truth is a thing that is immortal and eternal. It affords us not indeed such a beauty as will wither away by time, nor such riches as may be taken away by fortune, but righteous rules and laws. It distinguishes them from injustice, and puts what is unrighteous to rebuke."

7. (57) So when Zorobabel had left off his discourse about truth, and the multitude had cried out aloud that he had spoken the most wisely, and that it was truth alone that had immutable strength, and such as never would wax old, the king commanded that he should ask for something over and above what he had promised, for that he would give it him because of his wisdom, and that wisdom wherein he exceeded the rest; "and you shall sit with me," said the king, (58) "and shall be called my cousin." When he had said this, Zorobabel put him in mind of the vow he had made in case he should ever have the kingdom. Now this vow was, "to rebuild Jerusalem, and to build therein the temple of God; as also to restore the vessels which Nebuchadnezzar had pillaged, and carried to Babylon. And this, "said he,

"is that request which you now permit me to make, on account that I have been judged to be wise and understanding."

8. (59) So the king was pleased with what he had said, and arose and kissed him; and wrote to the toparchs and governors, and directed them to conduct Zorobabel and those that were going with him to build the temple. (60) He also sent letters rulers that were in Syria and Phoenicia to cut down and carry cedar trees from Lebanon to Jerusalem, and to assist him in building the city. He also wrote to them, that all the captives who should go to Judea should be free; (61) and he prohibited his deputies and governors to lay any king's taxes upon the Jews; he also permitted that they should have all that land which they could possess themselves of without tributes. He also directed the Idumeans and Samaritans, and the inhabitants of Coele-Syria, to restore those villages which they had taken from the Jews; and that besides all this, fifty talents should be given them for the building of the temple. (62) He also permitted them to offer their appointed sacrifices, and that whatever the high priest and the priest wanted, and those sacred garments wherein they used to worship god, should be made at his own charges; and that the musical instruments which the Levites used in singing hymns to God should be given them. (63) Moreover, he charged them, that portions of land should be given to those that guarded the city and the temple, as also a determinate sum of money every year for their maintenance; and in addition he sent the vessels. And all that Cyrus intended to do before him relating to the restoration of Jerusalem, Darius also ordained should be done accordingly.

9. (64) Now when Zorobabel had obtained these grants from the king, he went out of the palace, and looking

up to heaven, he began to return thanks to God for the wisdom he had given him, and the victory he had gained thereby, even in the presence of Darius himself; for, said he, "I had not been thought worthy of these advantages, O Lord. Unless you had been favorable to me." (65) When therefore he had returned these thanks to God for the present circumstances he was in, and had prayed to him to afford him the like favor for the time to come, he came to Babylon, and brought the good news to his countrymen…"[323]

Pondering Zerubbabel's words as I walked back down the hill toward my home, I began to think about the young man we had seen sitting at that stone wall in Israel, diligently engaged in creating a mosaic from shattered ruins, and wondered what his final masterpiece looked like. While contemplating this and the events of the past year, I questioned how I fit into Christ's masterpiece.

The previous spring, sometime in March, I found myself with Mom in the emergency room of an Oklahoma City hospital after she had experienced a bout of excruciating pain in her right side. Fearing our family history of colon cancer might be manifesting itself again, she sought medical attention, but routine blood work and a CT scan showed nothing according to the ER physician who examined her so he prescribed pain medication and hurried us out the door as it was the end of his shift. Later, our family physician, Dr. Jennifer Garner, discovered irregularities in Mom's blood work; specifically, her platelets were dangerously low, which suggested cancer. Dr. Garner sent Mom to an oncologist, Dr. Vikki Canfield, but she was unable to find any cancer. The source of the abnormal blood was a mystery. When the oncologist learned of Mom's prior CT scan, she promised to review the records as a precautionary measure. Days later, she telephoned Mom in the late evening hours and informed her that the CT scan results indicated a serious problem with her liver. Mom was then referred

---

[323] Flavius Josephus, *The New Complete Works of Josephus*, trans. William Whiston, comment. Paul L. Maier (Grand Rapids, Michigan: Kregel Publications, 1999), 361–364.

to gastroenterologist, Dr. Randy Kakish, who diagnosed Mom with severe cirrhosis of the liver and sent her to the Nazih Zuhdi Transplant Institute at Integris Baptist Medical Center in Oklahoma City.

Sitting alone with Mom in the exam room at the transplant institute gave me a strange sense of déjà vu. Approximately two years earlier, a patient at *New Beginnings*, whose love for the Lord had blessed us with a great friendship, was suffering from end stage emphysema and awaiting a lung transplant; and in the process of taking her to medical appointments, I learned a great deal about organ transplantation from her physicians. Additionally, Bart Garbutt's wife, Kim, who worked at the Nazih Zuhdi Transplant Institute and is a transplant recipient herself, has been an invaluable resource for us. Throughout my journey, God has placed His people in key positions to help me carry the great burdens of life, and these are just two of those people.

Mom was seen at the transplant institute by Dr. Hany Elbeshbeshy. Following his confirmation that she had stage-four cirrhosis, we informed our church congregation and local communities of her illness so the believers among them could join us in petitioning the Lord for healing. Mom's condition was very delicate. Her physicians concluded that, since she had never consumed alcohol or abused drugs, the disease must have been caused by long-term thyroid problems, and further complicated by Type 2 Diabetes. Her liver was still functioning to the surprise of all her doctors, but she was told that, to maintain its function, her glucose levels and thyroid function had to be monitored constantly because further damage could cause her liver to fail at any time. Even worse, its compromised cells could mutate into cancer without warning.

Mom's illness and its unthinkable, potential effects have been difficult enough to bear in their own right, but the fact that her diagnosis coincided with what appears to be the beginning stages of socialized medicine in the United States have made the burden even more difficult to shoulder. All serious illnesses are accompanied by financial strain, but such strain is only exacerbated by oppressive health care reforms and the governmental tyranny that drives them. As I contemplated the financial mountain that we would all have to climb if Mom's condition required a transplant and we were forced to bear the cost ourselves, I wondered what assets we could sell but pitifully concluded that, even if we sold everything down to the clothes on our backs, we would not even make a dent in the cost. Mom's diagnosis has forced me to face one of my greatest fears; and at times, the uncertainty of healthcare's future in this country has been maddening.

Though Mom is a Christian and I am confident that, whatever the outcome, it will be well with our souls, I, like anyone else, want my mother around for as long as possible – not only for myself, but for my family and community as well. The Lord has, on many occasions, used her as an instrument to guide and teach me and not only me but a host of others, too. Because I want that guidance and teaching to continue, I began to beg and plead with God to cure her of this dreadful disease and grant her a longer, happier, and healthier life. During one of these emotional pleas, I was alone in the back yard, filling up the bird feeders before a winter storm. Then and there, the Holy Spirit reminded me of one of the greatest Scriptures to which a believer in Christ can cling:

> "Therefore I say unto you, Take no thought for your life, what ye shall eat, or what ye shall drink; nor yet for your body, what ye shall put on. Is not the life more than meat, and the body than raiment? Behold the fowls of the air: for they sow not, neither do they reap, nor gather into barns; yet your heavenly Father feedeth them. Are ye not much better than they? Which of you by taking thought can add one cubit unto his stature? And why take ye thought for raiment: Consider the lilies of the field, how they grow; they toil not, neither do they spin: And yet I say unto you, That even Solomon in all his glory was not arrayed like one of these. Wherefore, if God so clothe the grass of the field, which to day is, and to morrow is cast into the oven, shall he not much more clothe you, O ye of little faith? Therefore take no thought, saying, What shall we eat? or, What shall we drink? Wherewithal shall we be clothed? (For after all these things do the Gentiles seek:) for your heavenly Father knoweth that ye have need of all these things. But seek ye first the kingdom of God,

and his righteousness; and all these things shall be added unto you. Take therefore no thought for the morrow: for the morrow shall take thought for the things of itself. Sufficient unto the day is the evil thereof."[324]

Here, Jesus reveals how wasteful it is to spend time and energy worrying. The word "thought" comes from the Greek word, *merimnao*, which means to be anxious, troubled with cares, or ripped or torn into pieces. There are two great reasons why Christians should not surrender to worry or anxiety. First, as believers in Christ, we are servants of God, and because we are His property, He is bound to care for our needs. Second, and perhaps most important of all, we are His children. Therefore, He will care for us with His great fatherly love, and those things which burden us will also burden Him.

When I had finished filling the bird feeders, the Holy Spirit called me to prayer. I went inside and lay prostrate on the floor, clutching my opened Bible with an aching soul, and trusting with all my being in this Scripture:

> "Likewise the Spirit also helpeth our infirmities: for we know not what we should pray for as we ought: but the Spirit itself maketh intercession for us with groanings which cannot be uttered."[325]

Physically, I was upon the floor; but spiritually, through prayer, I had entered God's presence like never before. As my spirit approached His glory in Heaven and rushed into the throne room, the accuser attempted to block my approach, shouting out my iniquities, but I continued to run and saw Jesus silence him as I recalled His word:

> "Believe me that I am in the Father, and the Father in me: or else believe me for the very works' sake. Verily, verily, I say unto you, He that believeth on me, the works that I do shall he do also; and greater works than

---

[324] Matthew 6:25-34 (KJV)
[325] Romans 8:26 (KJV)

these shall he do; because I go unto my Father. And whatsoever ye shall ask in my name, that will I do, that the Father may be glorified in the Son. If ye shall ask any thing in my name, I will do it."[326]

As I lowered my head, unable to look upon God, the Holy Spirit prepared me with a Scripture:

"...for your Father knoweth what things ye have need of, before ye ask him."[327]

I fell, in spirit, before the throne of the Most High God and began to petition Him for the desire of my heart – Mom's healing. Amazingly, after I had poured that desire out to Him, He turned my attention away from her illness altogether and focused my thoughts on the lost. Suddenly, I was struck with the awe-inspiring magnitude of the privilege I held as a believer in His Son, Jesus Christ; and He reminded me that not everyone could come boldly before Him, make their requests known, and have them considered and granted. In that instant, I believe I must have felt somewhat of the sorrow and longing He possesses for those who do not know Him, albeit a mere fraction, and began to weep with joy over what I possess in Christ and with sorrow over what millions are missing. Then, the Holy Spirit reminded me of my meeting with Dr. Paige Patterson, president of Southwestern Baptist Theological Seminary, to whom I had gone for assistance with *Vision Bible Clubs*. Dr. Patterson was one of few who offered helpful advice, but what I remember most about meeting him was that he prayed with me in his office, asking God to grant me the desires of my heart. With that, I came under conviction. Knowing Mom had been blessed and that the Lord would take care of her, I admitted to God that the true desire of my heart was to share Jesus Christ and the treasures to be had in His Truth with the lost and petitioned of Him that any future ministerial work to which He assigned me would bear more fruit than I could possibly imagine. Following my petition to the

[326] John 14:11-14 (KJV)
[327] Matthew 6:8 (KJV)

Most High God, I picked my physical body off the floor, and made my way to the sink where I washed away the residue of my emotion. In the mirror, I caught the reflection of the scar above my left eye and remembered the vow I made if I were healed and given more time. At that moment, I knew my seal had been broken and God told me to walk with you—not as a salesman of religion, motivational speaker, or social crusader—but as a redeemed sinner, a believer in Him and brother in the royal priesthood to other believers, and a vessel by which His message of Truth is conveyed. It is our walk together that is a culmination of a fulfillment of promises. God has permitted me to fulfill my long-ago promise to Him to tell you about His Love; He has permitted me to fulfill a promise to Mom and my family to tend to her medical and financial needs; and He is fulfilling many promises in His word as you and I intimately walk together.

Now, having read about a relationship which allows me to come boldly before the throne of grace and make my petitions known to the Most High God, you may wonder whether He has "favorites," but *Deuteronomy 10:17 (KJV)* declares: "For the LORD your God is God of gods, and Lord of lords, a great God, a mighty, and a terrible, which regardeth not persons, nor taketh reward..." Moreover, Luke dispelled this notion in *Acts 10:34-36 (KJV)*: "Then Peter opened his mouth, and said, Of a truth I perceive that God is no respecter of persons: But in every nation he that feareth him, and worketh righteousness, is accepted with him. The word which God sent unto the children of Israel, preaching peace by Jesus Christ: (he is Lord of all:)" Paul also dispelled it in *Galatians 2:6 (KJV)*: "...God accepteth no man's person...," and Peter dispelled it in the first chapter and seventeenth verse of his first epistle: "And if ye call on the Father, who without respect of persons judgeth according to every man's work, pass the time of your sojourning here in fear..."

Though God does not have "favorites," He does have intimates, for the Word of Truth plainly reveals in *James* that He does:

"Draw nigh to God, and he will draw nigh to you. Cleanse your hands, ye sinners; and purify your hearts, ye double minded. Be afflicted, and mourn, and weep:

let your laughter be turned to mourning, and your joy to heaviness. Humble yourselves in the sight of the Lord, and he shall lift you up."[328]

And again, in *1 Samuel*:

"Wherefore the LORD God of Israel saith, I said indeed that thy house, and the house of thy father, should walk before me for ever: but now the LORD saith, Be it far from me; for them that honour me I will honour, and they that despise me shall be lightly esteemed."[329]

Don't you want to be lifted up and honored by the one and only living God? Don't you want to be spiritually alive as only you can be by faith in Jesus Christ? Don't you want to, by comprehending spiritual Truth, be shielded from deception and your own pride? Don't you want to live out the following scripture?

"Howbeit we speak wisdom among them that are perfect: yet not the wisdom of this world, nor of the princes of this world, that come to nought: But we speak the wisdom of God in a mystery, even the hidden wisdom, which God ordained before the world unto our glory: Which none of the princes of this world knew: for had they known it, they would not have crucified the Lord of glory. But as it is written, Eye hath not seen, nor ear heard, neither have entered into the heart of man, the things which God hath prepared for them that love him. But God hath revealed them unto us by his Spirit: for the Spirit searcheth all things, yea, the deep things of God. For what man knoweth the things of a man, save the spirit of man which is in him? even so the things of God knoweth no man, but the Spirit of God.Now we have received, not the spirit of

---

[328] James 4:8–10 (KJV)
[329] 1 Samuel 2:30 (KJV)

the world, but the spirit which is of God; that we might know the things that are freely given to us of God. Which things also we speak, not in the words which man's wisdom teacheth, but which the Holy Ghost teacheth; comparing spiritual things with spiritual. But the natural man receiveth not the things of the Spirit of God: for they are foolishness unto him: neither can he know them, because they are spiritually discerned. But he that is spiritual judgeth all things, yet he himself is judged of no man. For who hath known the mind of the Lord, that he may instruct him? but we have the mind of Christ."[330]

And if you are spiritually alive in Christ, don't you want to be more than mediocre? Don't you want to be one of God's intimates and experience all of the Love that God has to offer? As I have walked with the Lord over the years, He has revealed four characteristics of His love.

God's love is **unconditional.** Perhaps you have heard someone say they love or are loved "unconditionally." This is not possible without Christ. Human nature prevents us from true, pure, unconditional love. By our very natures, we see others' differences and divide. There is always some event or circumstance that is able to alter our love at some level. All we have to do to see this is to look at our families, communities, nation, world, and yes, even to our churches. We allow the most trivial things such as actions, sins, looks, place of origin, and financial well-being to influence or totally change our love or feelings toward one another. It is only in the love of Christ that we can have unconditional love.

The fourth chapter of the Gospel according to John presents the beautiful Truth that the unconditional love of God, through His Son, Jesus Christ, is freely offered to all who will believe and call upon His name in faith. While traveling from Judaea to Galilee, Jesus was appointed to go through Samaria, a land occupied by a race of people whom the Jews despised. There, Jesus, being wearied from His journey, stopped and sat down on a well, to which came a woman of Samaria

---

[330] 1 Corinthians 2:6-16 (KJV)

to draw water. She was an outcast in her own community and family, a woman with a past. One of the purposes of Jesus' appointed visit to Samaria at that particular time was to demonstrate that His love is freely offered to all peoples, transcending all barriers. Jesus' discourse with the Samaritan woman reveals that there is nothing you can do that will cause Christ to reject you if you will call on Him. His love is unconditional and pure, and His arms are open to receive you.

God's love is **unchanging.** In the Old Testament, through Malachi, God said: "For I am the LORD, I change not..."[331] In the New Testament, through Paul, He said: "Jesus Christ the same yesterday, and to day, and for ever."[332] And, through John, He said: "...for God is Love."[333]

God's love is **everlasting.** In the Old Testament, the prophet Jeremiah wrote, "The LORD hath appeared of old unto me, saying, Yea, I have loved thee with an everlasting love: therefore with lovingkindness have I drawn thee."[334]

God's love is **unfailing.** King David cried out to the Lord, "Let, I pray thee, thy merciful kindness be for my comfort, according to thy word unto thy servant. Let thy tender mercies come unto me, that I may live: for thy law is my delight."[335] He also prayed, "Cause me to hear thy lovingkindness in the morning; for in thee do I trust: cause me to know the way wherein I should walk; for I lift up my soul unto thee."[336]

Wouldn't you rather be like King Solomon, an intimate of the Lord who, by the Holy Spirit, knew the deep things of God and will receive crowns in Heaven rather than Roman Emperor Hadrian who, on his death bed, muttered words similar to these: "No more crown for this head, no more beauty for these eyes, no more music for these ears, and no more food for this stomach of mine. But my soul, oh, my soul, what is to become of you?"[337] Don't you want to be more than mediocre?

---

[331] Malachi 3:6 (KJV)
[332] Hebrews 13:8 (KJV)
[333] 1 John 4:8 (KJV)
[334] Jeremiah 31:3 (KJV)
[335] Psalm 119:76-77 (KJV)
[336] Psalm 143:8 (KJV)
[337] J. Vernon McGee, *Thru the Bible with J. Vernon McGee: Proverbs through Malachi* (Nashville, Tennessee: Thomas Nelson, Inc. 1982), 100.

Don't you want to be a great servant of the Lord? Don't you want to live the adventure of Truth? Don't you want to possess the greatest treasure of all, the Truth?

You see, Truth is not an ideology. It is not relative. It is not of an individual or private interpretation. It is not defined by philosophers, great thinkers, political leaders, or media pundits. Truth is absolute. It is a person. It is Jesus Christ:

> "Jesus saith unto him, I am the way, the truth, and the life: no man cometh unto the Father, but by me. If ye had known me, ye should have known my Father also: and from henceforth ye know him, and have seen him."[338]

And, like Abraham, I believe God—do you? As for my own future, it will be according to *Romans 8:28 (KJV)*: "And we know that all things work together for good to them that love God, to them who are the called according to his purpose."

---

[338] John 14:6-7 (KJV)

The Extra Mile

"And whosoever shall compel thee to go a mile, go with him twain."
– Matthew 5:41 (KJV) –

A portion of the proceeds from the sale of this book will be tithed, in obedience to the Lord, to the Great Commission and the furtherance of the Kingdom of God through The Extra Mile. As a minister, the Lord has taught me much about carrying the burdens of others and the blessings of the extra mile. When Christians carry the burdens of others further than necessary, their character in Christ is revealed, fellowship and relationships are fostered and flourish, and blessings travel beyond the boundaries of mile markers and upon a two-way street. I believe the Lord has called me to sow the seed of the Word of God in fulfillment of my duty to the first mile and to nurture its growth and seek other ways wherein it can be sown in fulfillment of The Extra Mile. If you have a suggestion for a unique way in which we can walk the extra mile and the Lord is leading you to share your idea with us, I invite you to do so. We will consider all suggestions and if yours is chosen, you will have the opportunity to participate, together with us, in supporting the same. Please submit your suggestions through our website at www. thecountrypreacher.net or by mail to P.O. Box 156, Binger, Oklahoma 73009. I look forward to walking The Extra Mile with you.

About the Author

Lance Compton is an ordained minister of the Gospel of Jesus Christ. Miraculously healed of cancer in the seventh grade, he has since devoted his life to spreading the seed of God's Word. Lance has a bachelor's degree in political science from Oklahoma State University and lives in Binger, Oklahoma.

Bibliography

Abanes, Richard. *One Nation Under Gods: A History of the Mormon Church*. New York, New York: Basic Books, 2003.

Bryant, T. Alton. *Zondervan's Compact Bible Dictionary*. Grand Rapids, Michigan: Zondervan, 1999.

Davies, Douglas J. *An Introduction to Mormonism*. Cambridge, United Kingdom: Cambridge University Press, 2003.

Josephus, Flavius. *The New Complete Works of Josephus*. Translated by William Whiston. Commentary by Paul L. Maier. Grand Rapids, Michigan: Kregel Publications, 1999.

McGee, J. Vernon. *Thru the Bible with J. Vernon McGee: Proverbs through Malachi*. Nashville, Tennessee: Thomas Nelson, Inc., 1982.

Otfinoski, Steven. *Roman Catholicism*. Tarrytown, New York: Marshall Cavendish Benchmark, 2007.

Santrock, John W. *Life-Span Development*. New York: McGraw-Hill, 2006.

Smith, Joseph. *Book of Mormon*. Salt Lake City, Utah: Church of Jesus Christ of Latter-day Saints, 1981.

Tillotson, John. *A Discourse Against Transubstantiation* (New Edition). London: Gilbert & Rivington, 1833.

Tusser, Thomas (1573, 1577, 1580). *Five Hundred Pointes of Good Husbandrie*. Edited by W. Payne and Sydney J. Herrtage. London: Trübner & Co., 1878.